DONACIANO VIGIL

MAURILIO E. VIGIL &
HELENE BOUDREAU

Donaciano Vigil

The Life of a
Nuevomexicano Soldier,
Statesman, and
Territorial Governor

University *of New Mexico Press* ✦ *Albuquerque*

© 2022 by the University of New Mexico Press
All rights reserved. Published 2022
Printed in the United States of America

First paperback printing 2024

ISBN 978-0-8263-6341-1 (cloth)
ISBN 978-0-8263-6638-2 (paper)
ISBN 978-0-8263-6342-8 (electronic)

Library of Congress Cataloging-in-Publication Data
is on file with the Library of Congress.

Founded in 1889, the University of New Mexico sits on the traditional homelands of the Pueblo of Sandia. The original peoples of New Mexico— Pueblo, Navajo, and Apache—since time immemorial have had deep connections to the land and have made significant contributions to the broader community statewide. We honor the land itself and those who have remained stewards of this land throughout the generations and also acknowledge our committed relationship to Indigenous peoples. We gratefully recognize our history.

Cover illustrations: Donaciano Vigil, governor of New Mexico, 1847–1848. Photograph ca. 1850 by Albright's Art Parlors, Santa Fe, NM. Courtesy of Palace of the Governors Photo Archives, NMHM/DCA, negative no. 011405; and Palace of the Governors, Santa Fe, ca. 1860–1900. Source: ZIM, UNM, CSWR, PICT COLLS 000-742-0649.
Designed by Mindy Basinger Hill
Composed in Adobe Jenson Pro and Remsen Script Regular

Dedicated to Alberta

———

OUR CHILDREN:

David Michael Vigil
Teresa Anita Vigil
Daniel Donaciano Vigil

Tristan Jesse Campbell
Jamia Al Khan Salvarezza
Elisha Santiago Wofford
Naomi Rebekah Salvarezza
Layla Sophia Salvarezza
Elena Nicola Salvarezza

A complete history of Governor Vigil for the past century would be an almost complete history of the territory for the same period.

EDITOR OF THE *Santa Fe Weekly New Mexican*, 28 AUGUST 1877

CONTENTS

List of Illustrations *xi*

Preface *xiii*

Introduction *1*

CHAPTER 1. Spanish Origins: Donaciano Vigil as a Link in the Chain of New Mexico History *7*

CHAPTER 2. New Mexico Beckons: Restoring the Colony *24*

CHAPTER 3. Conditions in Santa Fe During Donaciano's Youth *39*

CHAPTER 4. The Soldier *46*

CHAPTER 5. A Political Leader in the Department of New Mexico under the Mexican Regime *76*

CHAPTER 6. The Winds of War in North America *102*

CHAPTER 7. An American Political Leader: Preserving a Civil Government amid an Insurrection *119*

CHAPTER 8. The Formalization of the American Territorial Civil Government of New Mexico *132*

CHAPTER 9. At Last, the Territory of New Mexico: The Legal, Political, and Cultural Transformation *155*

CHAPTER 10. Assault on a Giant, Part I: Donaciano Vigil and Spanish/Mexican/Pueblo Land Grants *176*

CHAPTER 11. Assault on a Giant, Part II:
The Los Trigos Land Grant 195

12. Assault on a Giant, Part III:
The Cruzate Land Grants 207

Conclusion 236

Notes 253

Bibliography 281

Index 289

ILLUSTRATIONS

FIGURE 1. Governor Donaciano Vigil 3

FIGURE 2. Donaciano Vigil residence in Santa Fe 52

FIGURE 3. Governor Manuel Armijo 65

FIGURE 4. General Stephen Watts Kearny 104

FIGURE 5. Kearny expedition postcard 114

FIGURE 6. Palace of the Governors, Santa Fe 114

FIGURE 7. Governor Charles Bent 120

FIGURE 8. Colonel Sterling Price 126

FIGURE 9. Arrival of a caravan at Santa Fe 162

FIGURE 10. Donaciano Vigil affidavit 211

FIGURE 11. Donaciano Vigil bronze bust 251

MAP 1. Historic trails and roads of New Mexico 28

MAP 2. Texas land claim 70

TABLE 1. Donaciano Vigil's *Cuaderno* 248

PREFACE

The Search for Donaciano Vigil, My Great-Great-Grandfather
Maurilio E. Vigil

This book has been a long time coming for me personally and professionally, truly a lifelong project. A milestone occurred in 1966 when I was working at the Library of Congress while simultaneously writing my master's thesis. I discovered Father Stanley Crocchiola's book, *Giant in Lilliput: The Story of Donaciano Vigil*. This book provided an incentive, which structured my research on Donaciano. My serious academic study of the life and career of Donaciano Vigil began in earnest during my career as a college professor at New Mexico Highlands University in 1972. My first essay on Donaciano was incorporated in my book *Los Patrones: Profiles of Hispanic Political Leaders in New Mexico History* (1980). I now look at that piece and see it as a brief and superficial account of a profound, complicated, sometimes controversial but important historical and political figure, who by his words and deeds shaped the course of New Mexico history. The connection between the two disciplines of political science and history in my primary area of research, Hispanic politics, intrigued me. The political-historical events leading to the American occupation of New Mexico and their consequences drew my focus.

The dearth of historical or political analyses of Hispano involvement in New Mexico at the time only made my concentration on Donaciano Vigil more compelling as he was a central figure in the New Mexico of that era. Two themes are the focus here, as the book's title suggests. First, Donaciano Vigil was the Hispano most directly involved in the political incorporation of the New Mexico Territory into the American political system. Second, he foreshadowed how the circumstances of that integration would lead to the socialization of

Hispanos into a unique political culture of direct involvement and activism in New Mexico politics.

It is appropriate from an epistemological perspective to address concerns regarding the fact that the lead author of this biography is the great-great-grandson of the subject. While it is true that my interest in Donaciano is partially due to the familial connection, the goal of producing an objective history has always been paramount. In this book, our purpose as historians and scholars has been to produce an objective, balanced, and unvarnished history of Donaciano Vigil.

Diverse sources, including archives, interviews, collections, and libraries, have provided the bits and pieces of information, facts, stories, and genealogical research for this project. This endeavor has taken me beyond the Donnelly Library at New Mexico Highlands University to the Zimmerman Library and the Center for Southwest Research and Special Collections at the University of New Mexico; the New Mexico State Library; the New Mexico State Records Center and Archives and the Fray Angélico Chávez Library in Santa Fe; the Albuquerque Main Public Library and Special Collections; and the National Hispanic Cultural Center in Albuquerque. I have gleaned information from the Archivo General de Indias in Seville, Spain; the Biblioteca Nacional de España in Madrid, Spain; the Huntington Library in San Marino, California; and the National Archives and the Library of Congress in Washington, DC.

Over time, I collected so much research material in dozens of notebooks, cards, and journals that I feared that all my work would be lost. I began writing the manuscript several times, and as new information emerged, there was constant revision. During my career as a political science professor at New Mexico Highlands University, I placed the project on the back burner as I tended to my primary duties of teaching, research, and writing about New Mexico's government and Hispanic politics.

I was sidetracked when it was necessary to research land grant issues in order to evaluate the validity of arguments by historians who targeted Donaciano Vigil for his alleged negative role, particularly in relation to Pueblo land grants and issues. At stake was not only Donaciano's reputation, but his legacy as a preeminent political leader in New Mexico history.

THE PROJECT BECOMES A COLLABORATIVE EFFORT

In 2016, I enlisted the help of a former graduate student, my friend and colleague Helene Boudreau, to assist with the manuscript. Together we have fashioned a book that we feel provides an accurate, readable, and interesting narrative of the life, career, and contributions of Donaciano Vigil. Ultimately, the success of our efforts will not be measured by our publication of this biography, but by generating a serious discussion about his ultimate legacy and the role he played in guiding New Mexico through one of its most critical historical eras.

As often happens, new developments occurred that related to the topic at hand. On 11 July 2019, a public announcement was made that the Order of the Crown of Charlemagne in the United States, a prestigious lineage society, had recently recognized the lineage from Charlemagne to Juan Montes Vigil, a common ancestor for many people with deep Hispanic roots in New Mexico. The announcement recognized Juan Montes Vigil as the colonist in 1611 who established the Vigil surname in North America and New Spain (Mexico). That Juan Montes Vigil is the same person identified in our biography as Juan Montes Vigil II and as the fourth-tier great-grandfather of Donaciano Vigil. In our narrative, we write that Juan Montes Vigil II and his wife, Catalina Herrera de Cantillana (married in 1619), were the parents of Juan Montes Vigil III (born circa 1621) and María (born circa 1623), who became the first Spaniards born in New Spain with the Vigil surname. We also mention that Juan II and Catalina were the grandparents of Francisco Montes Vigil, who with his wife, María Jiménez de Ancizo, introduced the Vigil surname in New Mexico as colonists in 1695. Francisco Montes Vigil was Donaciano Vigil's great-great-grandfather.

The significance of the Charlemagne connection is that by recounting the largely unknown story of Donaciano Vigil, we are revealing his linkage to an obscure but intrepid figure, Juan Montes Vigil II, an orphan who risked everything to seek fame and fortune in what was still an exotic and unfamiliar land. One result of that risk was to forever forge a direct relationship between the Montes Vigil clan in the Americas and one of the most iconic and legendary figures—Charlemagne—in the history of Western civilization. That is a remarkable story to be told in any era. It is an honor to be shared with all people with Spanish surnames.

Recognition is accorded to the European, American, and southwestern genealogists whose work contributed to the Vigil family research. We are indebted to many administrators and librarians for their individual and cumulative professional assistance. We especially acknowledge Phillip B. Gonzales and A. Gabriel Meléndez, distinguished professors at the University of New Mexico, for valuable suggestions that improved the manuscript. We would like to acknowledge Thomas Jaehn, Cindy D. Abel Morris, Nancy Brown-Martínez, and Samuel Sisneros of the UNM Center for Southwest Research and Special Collections; Marcus Flores, Alvin Regensburg, Melissa Salazar, Felicia Lujan, and Gail Packard of the New Mexico State Records Center and Archives in Santa Fe; Lisa Kindrick and Brandon Padilla of the Genealogy Center at the Albuquerque Main Public Library; Ruben Aragón, Kathleen J. Gray, April Kent, Leslie Broughton, Raymond Chávez, Paul Tenorio, Irisha Corral, Kevin Corcoran, and the late Joe Odermatt of the Donnelly Library at New Mexico Highlands University; Catie Carl of the Palace of the Governors Photo Archives; and Mark Montoya for technical assistance with maps. We especially express our appreciation to our editor at UNM Press, Michael Millman, for his patient guidance and his excellent editorial and logistical counsel throughout the publication process.

INTRODUCTION

In 1967, Bill Tate, a local history writer in New Mexico, authored a small booklet titled *Guadalupe Hidalgo Treaty of Peace, 1848, and the Gadsden Treaty with New Mexico, 1853*.[1] Tate's message was reflected on page 1, which quoted volume 1, article 2, section 5, of the New Mexico Statutes as follows: "The rights, privileges and immunities, civil, political and religious, guaranteed to the people of New Mexico by the Treaty of Guadalupe Hidalgo shall be preserved inviolate."[2] Tate wrote, "The Treaty of Guadalupe Hidalgo is still binding... and may rightly be called a 'bonus freedom paper,' extended by the United States government to the Spanish speaking population, and should take its rightful place along with the Constitution and the Bill of Rights."[3] Tate correctly attributed the guarantee of basic civil rights and freedoms to New Mexicans to the above provision in the Treaty of Guadalupe Hidalgo, and for that alone, the treaty should be forever celebrated in New Mexico.

The year 2023 will mark the 175th anniversary of the signing of the Treaty of Guadalupe Hidalgo, and we feel it is a good time to commemorate this treaty. Our contribution to that commemoration is to offer a biography of one New Mexican who played a significant role ensuring the peaceful transition of New Mexico and enabling New Mexico to take its place as a territory of the United States. Donaciano Vigil played a central role in the first American civil government of the territory and in succeeding efforts to secure official status as a full-fledged territory of the American nation.

New Mexico has been unique among American states because its Hispanic residents constitute the highest proportion (48 percent) of its total population, and the political participation of Hispanics has been exceptional. This is reflected in the high proportion of Hispanics in the state's congressional delegations, in the state's elected officials (including seven governors), and in county, municipal, and school board governments. It has also been reflected in the state's constitution, laws, and public policies. New Mexico's constitution provides original safeguards for Hispanics, such as the rights to vote and to a trial by jury, and the nonsegregation of schools. Its laws provide for bilingual (English and Spanish) education, bilingual ballots, and unofficial bilingual discourse. Public policies are endowed with concern for health, welfare, and economic and social justice. However, this importance has not always been reflected in New Mexico's history books where the topic of Hispanic politics and history remains sadly neglected.

This began to change in 2016 with the publication of Phillip B. Gonzales's *Política: Nuevomexicanos and American Political Incorporation, 1821–1910*. This book was a significant breakthrough on the topic of New Mexico because of its depth of coverage of Hispanic *herencia* (heritage) and *querencia* (culture), and how they have permeated the essence of Hispanic political life from the period of Spanish colonization through Mexican independence and then to New Mexico's status as an American territory and state. Our book is indelibly anchored to Gonzales's book as we expand on the theme of the incorporation of Hispanics into American politics as manifested in the life and career of one of the first key actors in the New Mexico stage of the new American politics. Also neglected have been dozens of other Hispanic *nuevomexicanos*, who have had personal and public agency in the region's history, but whose roles and contributions have been ignored.

The purpose of this book is to tell the story of Donaciano Vigil, the life he lived, the struggles he encountered, the challenges he faced, the momentous choices he made, and the impact they had on New Mexico. His history is the history of New Mexico in perhaps its most momentous transitional period. Our chronicle of the life of Donaciano Vigil reveals the nature and circumstances of politics, society, culture, and life in New Mexico during the first half of the nineteenth century when in the span of thirty years, New Mexico changed allegiance from Spain to Mexico and then to the United States. The editor of the *Santa Fe Weekly New Mexican* wrote in his introduction to the 28 August 1877 front-page obituary commemorating the recent death of Donaciano Vigil, "The following biographical sketch has been prepared in compliance with a resolution of the meeting of the Senate Chamber of the 11th instant. . . . A complete history of Governor Vigil for the past century would be an almost complete history of the territory for the same period."[4]

Donaciano Vigil has been an enigma, generally ignored in New Mexico history. He was born in Santa Fe, New Mexico, in 1802, and as a child was tutored

FIGURE 1. Donaciano Vigil (ca. 1850), soldier and officer of militia; secretary and assemblyman for the Department of New Mexico in the Mexican regime; territorial governor, secretary, and legislator in the New Mexico Territory under the United States. This is the only known photograph of Vigil and was taken at Albright's Art Parlors, Santa Fe. Source: Palace of the Governors Photo Archives, NMHM/DCA, negative no. 011405.

at home by his father. At the age of twenty-one in 1823, he enlisted in the local Santa Fe presidio of the New Mexico militia and embarked on a long military career. In the twenty-five years of his enlistment, he participated in numerous Navajo campaigns, a major internal rebellion, and an invasion by armed forces from Texas. In the Rio Arriba rebellion of 1837, Donaciano fought against New Mexican rebels as a Mexican soldier supporting Mexican authority. Defeated in the first major battle, he was captured and forcibly assigned as secretary to the governor of the rebellion forces. At the end of this rebellion, he was restored in status as a sergeant of the militia. In 1841, he advanced to the rank of captain of the San Miguel del Vado company and was awarded an Escudo de Honor (Medal of Honor) by President Antonio López de Santa Anna for his role in the capture of the Texas forces in the notorious Texan–Santa Fe expedition.

In 1838, he embarked on a public career as a *vocal* (representative) in the New Mexico *diputación* (assembly). In June 1846, he emerged as the leading dissident against Mexico's centralization of power when he presented a momentous speech urging the assembly to issue a formal protest against Mexican authority, which historian David Weber memorialized in his book *Arms, Indians, and the Mismanagement of New Mexico*.

On the eve of the American invasion of New Mexico, Donaciano reverted to his role as an officer in the New Mexico militia where he served on the general staff of Governor and Commander Manuel Armijo, planning for the defense of the territory against the American army at Cañoncito/Apache Canyon. But Armijo arrived at the site, declared that there would be no resistance, disbanded the army, and ordered the troops to return to their homes. Consequently, General Stephen Watts Kearny proceeded without resistance to Santa Fe where the military occupation of New Mexico was completed.

Once General Kearny performed the formal ceremonies of his army's occupation of New Mexico, he began to lay plans for governing the new territory under the Kearny Code. He sought able and qualified officials to participate in a new "civil government." Kearny offered Donaciano the position of secretary of the territorial civil government, second in the chain of command to the newly appointed governor, Charles Bent. In January 1847, an insurrection against the new government erupted in Taos. Governor Bent, a Taos resident, went there to quell the rebellion, but he was murdered. Colonel Sterling Price, who had replaced Kearny as military commander, called on Donaciano Vigil to assume the governorship. Together, Colonel Price and Donaciano were able to calm the population and suppress the insurrection.

In the fall of 1847, Governor Vigil, with the support of Price, issued a proclamation to convene the first territorial legislature under the new civil government. He then issued a call for the first elections under the American government. He urged New Mexicans to honor the privilege of voting in the first direct popular election held in the territory of New Mexico. In his first message to the legislature as governor, noting that there was only one school in the territory, he declared the importance of education and called for the establishment of a public school system. He urged, "If our government here is to be republican . . .

if it is to be based upon democratic republican principles, the people must be enlightened and instructed.... Every man should be able to read, to inform himself ... of matters important to his country and government."[5]

Governor Vigil also endorsed the territorial legislature's call for a territorial convention to convene in 1848 to consider the formal annexation of New Mexico by the United States and the form of government—territorial or state—to be sought. Donaciano chose to lead New Mexico toward membership in the American community because he knew that New Mexico and its people's fortunes would not improve under Mexico.

Colonel John M. Washington replaced Donaciano as governor in October 1848. Donaciano then reverted to the office of territorial secretary and served there until April 1851 when the new territorial officials took office. However, he was not done with public life and was elected to the territorial House of Representatives. During the next decade (1854–1865), he served several terms in both houses of the legislature.

In 1854, Donaciano bought some land in Pecos, New Mexico, and moved with his family the next year to pursue the leisurely life of a farmer-rancher in the small rural village. Still, the pull of public service was strong, and he became involved as a frequent witness and expert advisor to the surveyor general, who had been appointed to review, investigate, and report on land grant matters to the General Land Office in Washington. In most respects, the surveyor general was not ideally prepared for the task because he did not speak, read, or write Spanish and was not familiar with Spanish/Mexican land law. He needed help, and Donaciano was familiar with Spanish laws, land grant procedures, and land records because he had served as the territorial secretary of New Mexico under both Mexico and the United States. Donaciano provided valuable assistance to the surveyor general, but the advice and testimony he provided involved him in a quagmire of land grant issues, which have become very controversial in modern times. Because of his involvement, he became a scapegoat for some writers, who cast him in a negative light. As biographers, we have necessarily had to wade into those murky land grant waters to assess the validity of the criticisms Donaciano has faced at the hands of modern land grant historians. Chapters 10, 11, and 12, all labeled with the title "Assault on a Giant," are our contribution to land grant history in New Mexico, specifically in relation to the Pecos Pueblo land grant, the Los Trigos land grant, and the notorious Cruzate land grant documents.

Ralph Emerson Twitchell, an eminent New Mexico historian, best characterized and summed up the role and legacy of Donaciano when he wrote in his book *The Leading Facts of New Mexican History*, "The history of the career of Donaciano Vigil, the firm friend of liberty and humanity, belongs to the people of New Mexico. His is a record, which all lovers of free government will more delight to honor as time elapses and his distinguished merits are best understood.... It is a record which the native son[s] of New Mexico should ever try to emulate."[6] Such lofty praise might seem exaggerated, but we feel that our research confirms Twitchell's assessment of Donaciano Vigil.

1

SPANISH ORIGINS

Donaciano Vigil as a Link in the Chain of New Mexico History

Donaciano Vigil was born in Santa Fe in the northern province of New Mexico in 1802. At the time, Santa Fe and New Mexico were part of the Virreinato de Nueva España (Viceroyalty of New Spain), which had been created in 1502. New Mexico remained under Spanish rule until 1821 when New Spain (also known as Mexico) gained its independence and retained the name of Mexico. Thus, for the first two decades of his life, Donaciano was a Spanish subject. This background had a profound impact on his life and identity, even as he embraced his Mexican citizenship over the next twenty-five years. Donaciano had a distinguished career as a Mexican soldier and statesman until 1846 when New Mexico became a territory of the United States. That year, he declared pridefully, "The Spanish race... has not degenerated in New Mexico as is well attested to by some recent... deeds... and we, by our own virtues, are worthy... of the inheritance of our forefathers."[1] Between 1846 and 1866, Donaciano continued as an American statesman for New Mexico under the US government. Given his study of the Spanish/Mexican Archives and his active participation in the transitional events of New Mexico—from Spain to Mexico to the United States—Donaciano's life can be considered as a nexus or virtual link between New Mexico's Spanish colonial heritage and the modern era of New Mexico.

The Vigil family history reflects the evolution of many typical Hispanic families dating to the earliest Spanish colonization of New Mexico. Today there are thousands of families in New Mexico and the Southwest with the surname Vigil who attribute their presence in the United States to a single individual, Juan Montes Vigil II, a young Spaniard who arrived in the New World in 1611, searching for fame and fortune. A study of the Vigil family, first in Spain, then in New Spain/Mexico, and then in New Mexico, up to and beyond the life of Donaciano provides an opportunity to recount a continuous linkage that many New Mexican Hispanos have sought between their own lives and their ancestors in Spain.

The patrilineal genealogy of Donaciano provides an example of one family's historical origins in Spain and the family's evolution in New Spain and New Mexico over a period of four centuries. This book is not intended to be a complete genealogical study of the Vigil family, but rather is a historical study of the male line of descent of the Vigil family surname as it manifests in the history of New Mexico from the colonial to the modern period.

The choice of Donaciano Vigil as the subject of this genealogy is purposeful as well as incidental. Donaciano is a good choice because he lived in the midst of New Mexico's transition between three different nationalities and cultures—the Spanish, the Mexican, and the American. Moreover, he studied and observed the history of the three different civilizations as they existed in the world of his day. Our study of the Spanish patrilineal genealogical origins of one Hispanic family in New Mexico, apart from the simple revelation of those origins, helps to explain the motivations of the middle- and lower-class Spaniards who ventured to the New World. By examining the culture and motivations of the lesser nobility and commoners, we are better able to understand and explain the social, economic, and political factors that both drove them from Spain and attracted them to the "Indias" (the Indies or America). Securing property, wealth, title, and success became increasingly difficult in Spain, but could be attained in the New World. Our goal is to consider not only the initial motivation of the Spaniards to come to the New World, but also their continued motivation to extend the search into the farthest frontiers of New Spain.

SPAIN AND THE AMERICAN COLONIES

When Spain began its colonization of the New World in the latter part of the fifteenth century following the discoveries by Christopher Columbus, it was in a relative infancy as an independent European nation. Spain had been formed, in fact, by the tenuous coalition in 1469 of three separate Iberian provinces—Castile, Aragon, and Navarre—brought together by the marriage of Ferdinand II of Aragon and Isabella II of Castile, *los reyes católicos*. Following this unification, in the span of one year, 1492, Spain achieved its greatest glory with the expulsion of the Moors from the Iberian Peninsula and the "discovery" of the New World by Columbus.

Both before and after the unification, Spanish sovereigns sought the support of the nobility, the great lords, and military leaders, who provided their personal armies.[2] Originally landless, the nobility had created small mercenary armies that fought Muslims and other enemies on behalf of the sovereigns. The monarchs, poor in capital, but rich in land, made vast concessions of land to reward the nobles and their mercenary armies.[3] The nobles then used their increased power and influence to exact titles and even larger concessions of land from the monarchs. In time, the nobility established numerous *mayorazgos* (entailed estates) governed by the well-established social institution of primogeniture, in which an estate is passed down through each generation from a nobleman to his firstborn son, which created an upper nobility that controlled vast amounts of land. María Angeles Faya Díaz, a modern Spanish scholar, noted, "In the Asturias of the end of the [sixteenth] century, the principal means of wealth of the nobility was from land rentals ... which enabled its consolidation of the economic patrimonies which [gave the nobles] the privilege to create mayorazgo[s]."[4]

The next natural progression of upward mobility for the nobles who controlled entailed mayorazgos was to acquire through marriage, inheritance, purchase, or some combination thereof further titles of nobility, of which the *marquesado* (*marquisate*) was the most common. This honorific was accorded to a Spanish marquis, and he exercised jurisdiction over a sizable region. Given that these official positions were acquired by primogeniture, they were held in relatively few hands and created not only an elite nobility, but also elites within families. Those not part of the entitled elite were relegated, along with all of the common people, to an inferior social status with no hope of acquiring land or titles to achieve any measure of social mobility. They would thus occupy this subordinate status in perpetuity.[5]

It is a common generalization among historians that the primary motivation for Spain's interest in a New World empire was a thirst for the three Gs (gold, glory, and God).[6] Less known is the motivation of the thousands of Spanish subjects who voluntarily sought to migrate to the New World. These brazen adventurers embraced the challenge of seeking a new life and opportunities based on sketchy assurances of opportunities that might exist in the newly discovered territories of the Indies. According to a number of Spanish scholars who have revisited the subject and offered revisionist theories on the matter, the primary motivation for commoners to journey to the New World was the desire for landownership, public offices, and the titles of nobility, which were not easy to come by in Spain. However, even members of the lesser nobility, who were not the firstborn and were therefore locked out of potential family honors, ventured to the Indies to seek rewards there.[7]

The Austrian Habsburg monarchs, who succeeded to the Spanish throne in the sixteenth century, instituted a policy of selling public offices and titles to noblemen. The concentration of vast amounts of land in the hands of the elite, due partly to this practice by Spanish monarchs, prompted the noted Spanish philosopher, statesman, and scholar Gáspar Melchor Jovellanos to observe in his *Cartas* that the "*mayorazgos, monasteries e iglesia* [entailed estates, monasteries, and the church] are about the only property owners in Asturias."[8]

Faya Díaz's central argument is that the Austrian monarchs used the sale of offices as a means not only to support their ostentatious lifestyle, but to finance efforts to expand their vast realm by further exploration, colonization, and war. The oligarchy in Spain readily invested in purchasing these offices because of the prestige and property ownership they conveyed. However, the transfer of so much land and power to that group resulted in the wasting of capital resources and the placement of valuable land in the hands of owners who were largely exploitative and unproductive. This perpetuated an economic situation where wealth could not be generated in Asturias or in Spain. It also squeezed the less privileged by denying them opportunities for local offices, titles, and property ownership, which were the primary means for social mobility.[9]

Faya Díaz described a noble population that was a majority in Asturias, even though they lived on the verge of poverty. Travel to the Indies was the only alternative for the many Spaniards trapped in this archaic social and political system to seek the valued land, titles, and prestige, and the newly acquired colonies provided that opportunity.[10] As many Spaniards began to look for opportunities for self-improvement, some became so desperate that even venturing to the New World, still largely unknown, seemed a plausible choice. Certainly, the prospect of a dangerous voyage by sea and the unfamiliarity of the New World must have been daunting to the typical Spaniard of the time. As Faya Díaz observed, "The majority of those [Spaniards] who immigrated did so under great uncertainty, but were motivated by the possibility of prosperity, . . . commerce, exploitation of its extensive mineral resources, and agriculture."[11]

THE ASTURIAN SOURCE: LA POLA DE SIERO

In northern Spain is the small village of Siero, more commonly known as La Pola de Siero, or La Pola for short. The village lies roughly in the center of the province of Asturias on the northern coast of Spain and today has a population of approximately 12,000 people. It is about sixteen kilometers (almost ten miles) east of the better-known city of Oviedo, the capital of Asturias, and a similar distance south from Gijón, the largest city in the province.

In addition to being the capital of Asturias and its political and administrative center, Oviedo is also the cultural center of the province and the hub of its communication network. It is about 28 kilometers from Spain's northern coast and the Bay of Biscay (Golfo de Vizcaya), some 708 kilometers from Madrid. The only other major cities in the region are Gijón, a seaport, and the industrial city of Avilés. The heir to the Spanish throne assumed the title of Prince of Asturias, much like the heir to the British throne is known as the Duke of Cornwall.[12]

Among the notable cultural characteristics peculiar to this Asturian region (many of which found later expression in New Mexico) are some of the customs associated with the *vaqueros de alzuela* (high-range cowboys), who grazed their cattle in the mountains. The agrarian, pastoral, and farming economies of the provinces were similar to those introduced in the New World and, more specifically, in New Spain/Mexico and in New Mexico by the Spaniards, which provides some interesting parallels in foods and customs. The Asturian delicacy *morcilla* (blood sausage), made from the blood and intestines of freshly slaughtered (*matanza*) livestock, remains popular in New Mexico. The *fiesta de huevos pintos* (festival of the painted eggs), still celebrated in Siero on Easter Tuesday, bears a resemblance to the traditional *baile de los cascarones* until recently celebrated in New Mexico.[13] In the New Mexico version, colored eggshells filled with confetti are prepared ahead of time. On the night of the dance, two days after Easter Sunday, partygoers break the brittle eggshells on each other's head prior to engaging in a dance.

La Pola was founded in the thirteenth century under a charter granted by King Alfonso X in 1270 on a site that previously held a hostel that provided accommodations for pilgrims traveling the Camino de Santiago (Way of Santiago) and destined for Santiago de Compostela.[14] Siero is divided into twenty-four parishes, and although the Vigils are located throughout the city, the Montes Vigil clan hailed from the *feligresia de San Martíno* (parish of San Martíno). La Pola, while obscure in Spanish history, is famous as the village that produced one of the most prolific Hispanic families in New Mexico—the Vigils, the ancestors of Donaciano Vigil. The Vigil surname with various adjunct surnames in the tradition of Spanish culture is quite common in Asturias. In addition to La Pola, other nearby communities, such as Villaviciosa, Llanes, and Gijón, also contain families with Vigil surnames.

THE GENESIS, ASCENT, AND CONSOLIDATION OF ONE LINEAGE OF THE VIGIL FAMILY

Although an ancient town even by Spanish standards, La Pola, like the entire province of Asturias, was affected by the transcendental changes that occurred in Spain in the fifteenth and sixteenth centuries. The unification of the major provinces of Castile and Aragon under los reyes católicos and the discovery of the New World made Spain a world power. Internally, many of the factors that created the nobility and fostered its growth had reached down to the local municipalities, including La Pola, where some of the Vigil clan had reached noble status by providing mercenary armies that fought for the Crown against the Moorish adversaries. Some had expanded their wealth and power by the well-known system of mayorazgo and the establishment of marquesados. Some even benefited from the acquisition and purchase of municipal offices, titles, and estates through policies advanced by successive monarchs. As mentioned above, the same policies that benefited a few also created a large noble and middle class of landless and impoverished people who lacked opportunities for advancement, titles, land, and wealth.

In addition to shedding a general light on institutions such as mayorazgo and marquesado in Spain at large, some scholars have focused their study on the province of Asturias and the municipality of Siero. Juan Díaz Álvarez, a protégé of María Angeles Faya Díaz, was awarded the X Premio de Investigación "Padre Patac" in 2004 for his groundbreaking research on the Asturian nobility in his book *Ascenso de una Casa Asturiana: Los Vigil de Quiñones, Marqueses de Santa Cruz de Marcenado*.[15] Díaz Álvarez described how "La Casa de Vigil" (founded by Juan de Vigil, "El de Vigil") was established and created a mayorazgo. This genealogical line utilized established strategies of social mobility in Asturias to acquire through purchase, marriage, and inheritance for one member of the family, don Sebastian Vigil de Quiñones, the title of Marquesado de Santa Cruz de Marcenado during the reign of the last Austrian king of Spain.[16] Interestingly, the creation of this mayorazgo in 1580 occurred about the same time as the birth and early adulthood of Juan Montes Vigil II and provides a glimpse of the wealth of a segment of the Vigil family who were cousins of Juan Montes II.

THE PUSH AND PULL OF THE INDIES

The research of Faya Díaz and Díaz Álvarez affirms that the social and economic consequences of institutional norms and traditions, such as the mayorazgo and marquesado, and policies like the Austrian monarch's sale of public offices and titles can provide a new perspective on conditions in the sixteenth and seventeenth centuries that influenced Spanish migration. The lesser nobility and the commoners became the victims of a system that favored the firstborn male at the expense of the greater part of his lesser relatives. This was a "push" for those emigrants to escape from the discriminatory institutions and policies that robbed them of opportunities for their own wealth, progress, success, and social mobility as measured by titles of nobility in the mother country. They were forced to look elsewhere for those opportunities, and the Indias (Americas) became their destination of choice. As Faya Díaz wrote, "America offered for the *peninsulares* what were believed to be unlimited opportunities for Spanish emigrants to [achieve] unlimited wealth."[17] They even established a well-worn path for migration. As Faya Díaz observed, they would travel as "servant[s], ecclesiastical helpers, functionaries, military personnel, or merchants."[18] Juan Montes Vigil II would exemplify that migration.

In the centuries following the "discovery" of America by Columbus in 1492, the New World became a favored destination for adventurous Spaniards. The Spanish government sought to establish colonies free of the vices and corruption found in Spain and Europe of that period. The number of aspiring travelers was so great that the Spanish monarchs issued decrees instituting strict controls on those allowed to travel to the Indies. The structure of Spain's administrative organization for its colonial government began to be solidified in the latter half of the sixteenth century. The Catholic monarchs originally designated Juan Rodriguez de Fonseca, a theologian, to oversee the colonization process, and he laid the foundation for colonial bureaucracy. Referred to as the "president of the Indies," in 1524 he presided over the eight-member council that became known as the Junta de Indias (Council of the Indies), which exercised supreme authority over the Indies. Early archival records were kept in Simancas, but later these were removed to a permanent repository, the Casa de Contratación, which had been founded in 1503 at Seville as a customs storehouse for the Indies. In 1572 the original Market House of Seville was designated as the permanent home for the Archive of the Indies.[19]

SEVILLE: LA CASA DE CONTRATACIÓN

By the end of the sixteenth century, Seville had become the administrative headquarters for Spain's colonies in the New World. Spanish citizens desiring to travel to the Indies were required to obtain a *cédula real* (royal license or certificate) from the Casa de Contratación (House of Trade) granting such permission. The president and official judges of this body were required to carefully review and screen all applications for emigration, verify with documents and witnesses all information provided, and grant or deny a royal license. Among the requirements for travelers was proving they were capable of affording the costs of travel and of their own maintenance once they arrived at their destination. Married men had to prove that they were not leaving behind a wife and family that would be destitute because of their absence. The Crown prohibited conversos (Jewish or Muslim converts to Catholicism), Jews, Muslims, criminals, paupers, or any other people deemed "undesirable" from traveling to the New World. The Casa de Contratación archival records were meticulously documented and preserved, and they are housed in the Archivo General de Indias in Seville, chronicling the migration of Spaniards to the New World.[20] A thorough record of most of the early Spanish émigrés to the Americas thus exists, but no such records exist for other European countries, including England, France, Germany, Italy, Ireland, Russia, and Poland.

PASAJEROS A INDIAS

A cursory search of the records of the *pasajeros a Indias*, as the Spanish travelers to the Americas were called in the folios of the Casa de Contratación, revealed the names of three Vigils who migrated to the Indies. The earliest Vigil to travel to New Spain was Rodrigo de Vigil, a public notary for the king at Oaxaca. He was from Siero in Asturias and was in New Spain shortly after Hernán

Cortés's conquest of the Aztecs in 1520.²¹ No record has been located in the New World that details what became of Rodrigo, if and where he settled, what his occupation was, or if he married or had descendants. He may have been related or connected to other Vigils from Siero who later ventured to the New World. A second Vigil, identified simply as Juan Vigil, a son of Francisco de Vigil and María Hernandez and a resident of Salamanca, is listed as having received permission to travel to the Indies on 27 March 1540. No record of his actual presence in the New World has been located.²²

JUAN MONTES VIGIL II

The third Vigil who migrated is Juan Montes Vigil, whose record is found in Contratación number 5328, ramo 29, images 1–5, for 1611, Pasajeros a Indias. The following information about Juan II is derived from those archival records. Juan II was born in the village of Siero, more specifically in the parish (feligresia) of San Martíno.²³ Juan's birth date is not given in the Contratación petition, so we have had to rely on alternative sources. In a private genealogy, LaDeane Miller wrote that Juan Montes II was born in 1597. He married Catalina Herrera de Cantillana on 21 July 1619 in Zacatecas, New Spain/Mexico. However, this marriage record listed his age as nineteen, which would mean he was born in 1600. Catalina, according to the Miller genealogy, was born in the feligresia of San Martíno in Siero in 1602. Both dates are plausible even if it means that they would have been childhood sweethearts: he was eleven or fourteen years old and she was nine years old in 1611, when he departed for the Indies.

Juan II's parents were Juan Montes Vigil I and María de Vigil, who were both natives of Siero and *hijos dalgo* (untitled nobles) of the *casa y solar* (house and manor) of the Vigil family. Juan II's paternal grandparents were Lucas Montes de Vigil and Isabel de Vigil. His maternal grandparents were Francisco de Vigil and Catalina de Arguelles.²⁴ It is through his mother's family (Arguelles) that Juan II's genealogical connection is closest to that of Sebastian Vigil, the Marquesado de Santa Cruz de Marcenado. Although very little is known about Juan II, he is a principal figure in the genealogical records of the Donaciano Vigil family. He migrated to New Spain in 1611 and started the Montes Vigil lineage that eventually led to Donaciano. Although born in Siero, he at one point established residence in Madrid. In 1611, at the time his application was processed and he left Spain, he was listed as a resident of Seville. It is difficult to imagine the reasons that the youngster Juan II embarked on the onerous path to the Indies, including the obstacles of the rigorous qualification and screening standards to secure permission to travel. However, according to Faya Díaz, it was a well-worn path pursued by others from Asturias.

The archival records reveal that on 22 June 1611, Juan II appeared before the president and official members of Her Majesty's royal court of the Casa de Contratación in Seville, requesting a license to travel to New Spain. His petition indicated that he sought to accompany don Jacinto de Olmos as his *criado* (servant).[25] Olmos had appeared before the same body a week before on 14 June 1611, declaring that he had a cédula real (royal certificate) granting him license to return to the province of Peru. However, he indicated that there had been no *flota* (fleet) journeying to the province through *tierra firme* (the mainland), as was customary in the present year, and that he had a great need to return to Peru in a short time. The delay while waiting for a fleet to travel to the mainland would cause Olmos great loss. Accordingly, he requested a license to return to Peru via a fleet scheduled to depart for the Antilles (Caribbean) islands of New Spain.[26]

From the time of the first landing in the Americas, Spanish ships carried precious minerals back to Spain. In the 1520s, due to increasing acts of piracy by British and French ships seeking such treasures, Spain initiated the practice of organizing two distinct fleets with as many as ten ships heavily armed with cannons. The two separate fleets were scheduled for different departing times, departed first from Seville (and later Cádiz), and also had separate destinations, one to Vera Cruz in New Spain/Mexico and the other to Cartagena in today's Colombia in South America.[27] Moreover, at different times, some fleets stopped in one or another of the Antilles islands, known as Hispaniola (today's Dominican Republic or Haiti), while others went directly to tierra firme, Vera Cruz, or Cartagena. Consequently, some travelers had to take a less direct fleet in order to arrive at their ultimate destination if waiting for another fleet would cause them unreasonable or costly delay. Apparently, that was the situation that prompted Olmos to secure permission to join the next fleet available.[28]

On behalf of his majesty, on 14 June 1611, the president and official justices of the Casa de Contratación granted a license to Olmos to travel to New Spain by virtue of the royal certificate he had presented. Having received his royal license to return to Peru via New Spain, Olmos then turned his attention to securing a similar license for his criado Juan II. In his second appearance before the officials of the Casa de Contratación, Olmos presented Juan II as a witness on his behalf. Juan II, identified as a resident of Seville in the *collacion* (collar) on the Calle de las Palmas, testified that he had known Olmos for over five years, having traded and communicated with him and his father, don Diego García de Montalvo. He also said that he knew Olmos lived in the province of Peru and was unmarried. In addition to Juan II, Luis de Padilla, also of Seville, presented himself as a witness for Olmos, attesting that he had known him for many years and had interacted and conducted business with him and Montalvo. He also knew that Olmos had journeyed between Spain and Peru.[29]

The relationship between Juan II and Jacinto de Olmos is intriguing and bears some speculation. It is, of course, possible that the eleven-year-old Juan II was indeed a servant to the obviously affluent Olmos. It is more likely that Vigil was a friend or acquaintance or was merely posing as a servant for Olmos in order to secure the necessary licensure that would permit him to travel to New Spain. It might even be possible that the two engaged in a convenient business arrangement of mutual benefit. As Faya Díaz observed, the criado approach was a commonly used strategy in such circumstances.

In either case, before Juan II received his royal license, he had to convince the judges in the Casa de Contratación that he was indeed who he claimed to be, that he was not an undesirable, and that he was from a family worthy of such recognition. The process for securing permission was laborious, drawn out, and fraught with bureaucratic red tape. This was fortunate, however, for posterity's sake, because the extensive, detailed written documentation of the proceedings, testimony, and evidence provide a remarkable record of Juan II's family background.

Juan II formally began the process of securing approval to travel to America on 10 February 1609 when Bartolomé de Vigil, a resident and *regidor* (council member) of the village of Siero and Juan II's uncle, appeared before Judge Pedro Cote, also of the Council of Siero. He presented a petition attesting to the family background of Juan II and requested permission for him to journey abroad.[30] As the *curador* (guardian) for his nephew, who was also a native of Siero and now a resident of Madrid, Bartolomé affirmed, "He, my minor, requests leave to pass to the Indies in New Spain and other provinces [so that] he shall be regarded as a *hijo dalgo* [untitled nobleman] . . . representing descent through direct and legitimate lineage of the house and manor of Vigil."[31] Bartolomé attested further that Juan II was *limpio* (clean) of Moorish, Jewish, or mixed races nor was he obligated to church vows. Similarly, married people and clergy were especially scrutinized to ensure that they were not escaping from their obligations. Juan II's testimony confirmed that he was free and single, not subject to the bonds of matrimony or the church.

Bartolomé offered further testimony about the deceased parents of Juan II. His legitimate father was Juan Montes Vigil (I), and his mother was María de Vigil. His paternal grandfather was Lucas Montes de Vigil, and his grandmother was Isabel de Vigil (Juan I's parents). His maternal grandparents were Francisco de Vigil and Catalina de Arguelles (María's parents).[32] It is noteworthy that both of Juan II's parents came from the Vigil clan in Siero. Bartolomé certified that all of Juan II's parents and grandparents were married in the church and that his lineage was legitimate. Having presented his petition and request, Bartolomé next presented a series of fellow residents at Siero and from the vicinity to affirm his own testimony regarding Juan II. These witnesses included Martín García, Juan de Careses, Juan Gonzales, Juan Fernandez del Camino, Alfonso de Villar, and Diego de Villanueba. They all stated that they were acquainted with Juan II and his parents and grandparents, and all attested to the aforementioned details and specific issues relating to Juan II's line of direct and legitimate descent, the names of his parents and grandparents, the purity of his blood, and his noble status and that he was a free, single man "not subject to any order of matrimony or religion."[33]

Following the presentation of Bartolomé's and the witnesses' testimony, the judges certified the declarations and directed the clerk to issue a notarized transcript of the proceedings to Bartolomé. Bartolomé, in turn, gave the documents to his nephew, who then presented them to the officials at the Casa de Contratación along with his request for a cédula real. These documents were found together in the archive.[34]

Sometime after 21 June 1611, Juan II apparently embarked from Spain in the company of his sponsor and master, Jacinto de Olmos. By 1611, travel by sea vessel to the New World had become routine by the standards of the day, and while Columbus's initial voyage consisted of only three ships, the two fleets that normally sailed from Seville through the port of Cádiz now numbered a dozen or more vessels. The passengers and cargo included more women and children venturing to join husbands and fathers, along with diverse livestock and all forms of manufactured products. While not exactly a holiday excursion, the mix of diverse passengers and cargo together on the high seas for weeks at a time made for quite an adventure for all. At the same time, the normal perils of the sea itself, combined with many people living in close quarters for so long, created problems. The typically crowded conditions on such vessels afforded little privacy and attention to personal hygiene. Beyond the normal pitfalls of seasickness, more serious illnesses plagued the passengers, and some died en route and were buried at sea. Juan II survived the voyage, and although the cédula real he received listed Peru by way of New Spain as his final destination, he only got as far as New Spain, for the next record lists him as a resident of Mexico City, New Spain/Mexico.

CATALINA HERRERA DE CANTILLANA

It is not known if Juan II left a sweetheart back in Spain and later sent for her, as sometimes happened. Eight years after arriving in the New World, he married Catalina Herrera de Cantillana, also a native of the feligresia of San Martíno in Siero, Spain, in Zacatecas, Mexico, on 21 July 1619.[35] Catalina is somewhat a mystery. The marriage record of Catalina and Juan II reveals that she was a native of Spain born about 1600. This date is close to the birth date of 1602 in the Miller genealogy. Notwithstanding her young age, it is plausible that she could have traveled to the Indies after 1611, reunited with him, and married Juan II in 1619.[36]

JUAN MONTES VIGIL III

Juan II and Catalina had two children born in 1621 and 1623 in Mexico City, the capital of New Spain. They remained as residents of that city and died before 2 October 1682; their son, Juan III, declared in his will of that date that his parents were both deceased and had been natives of the *reynos de Castilla* and "*vecinos* [citizens] of Mexico City."[37] Although Juan III was born in Mexico City, he relocated to Zacatecas, the capital of Nueva Galicia, a province established in 1548 in New Spain/Mexico. Nueva Galicia was a rich mining area for gold, silver, and other minerals, which fostered rapid economic growth and development that led to the construction of ornate and elaborate churches, monasteries, palaces, and governmental offices. This progress probably attracted Juan Montes III to the region, and he soon became a prominent merchant and moneylender (or pawnbroker), an early predecessor of a modern banker. The two wills he prepared reflected a successful businessperson, who provided his son, Francisco, with a small fortune.[38]

The wills of 2 October 1682 and 25 April 1683 provide most of what is known about Juan III. He loaned money in exchange for valuable items. Among the items listed in his first will were silver *platillos* (saucers), candelabras, and salt shakers.[39] The declarations in his will reflected something of his character. He affirmed his Catholic faith. He requested that eighteen masses be held for the repose of his soul. Whether to cover all the bases or seek insurance for the afterlife, he spread the masses around: nine to be said in the chapel of Santo Cristo Milagroso in the parish of Zacatecas and another nine masses to be recited at the altar of Nuestra Señora de la Soledad in the Convento of San Agustín. As is typical of testaments of the period, Juan III asked for supplication from the apostles and from San Pablo and San Juan. He bequeathed from the sale of his possessions 500 pesos to Juan de Vargas, prior of the Convent of San Agustín in Zacatecas; 500 pesos to Captain Antonio de Salazar, *juez oficial* of the Real Hacienda y Caxa de Zacatecas; and 136 pesos to doña Gerónima Gutierrez. He also mentioned individuals, some of them merchants, who owed him a total of 3,770 pesos, ranging from 40 pesos to 1,590 pesos.

Two enslaved people are named as part of his property: a mulatta named Tomasa and her one-year-old son named Miguel. He sold a third mulatta slave, Nicolasa, to Tomás Hernandez, a resident of Zacatecas, for 115 pesos. He directed that when Hernandez paid the balance of 100 pesos, the papers for Nicolasa in his personal file would be transferred to him.[40]

FRANCISCO MONTES VIGIL

Nicolás Díaz Caballero, apparently Juan III's brother-in-law, was named as executor of Juan III's estate in the first will. Although he never married, Juan Montes III acknowledged one *hijo natural* (a son of unmarried parents) named Francisco Montes Vigil, who was born about 1666 in Zacatecas. Juan III left the bulk of his estate to Francisco, who was sixteen years old and was placed in the care of Díaz Caballero, his uncle. Juan III also directed that if Francisco died before coming of age to acquire his inheritance, everything would go to Juan III's sister, María de Herrera Cantillana. Interestingly, he declared that if his son, Francisco, or sister, María, did not survive him, his estate would pass to an orphan child, Carlos Vigil, age two, who was being reared by Juan and his sister.⁴¹ He also placed this boy in the care of Díaz Caballero. In his second will of 25 April 1683, Juan Montes III named Francisco Montes Vigil as executor of his estate and described him as being seventeen years old and married to María Jiménez.⁴² In this will, he was a bit more forthcoming. He stated that he was a single man and had never married, but that he had a natural son by a single woman (whose name and ethnicity he still failed to reveal). The issue of the racial makeup of the Montes Vigil clan had not yet arisen because, presumably up to Juan Montes III, they were regarded as white. As indicated above, both of Juan Montes III's parents were natives of Spain (*peninsulares*) and white, and although he was born in New Spain (criollo), he was also white.⁴³

Every record uncovered thus far indicates clearly that Francisco Montes was a hijo natural born to Juan Montes III and an unknown or unidentified mother. Juan Montes III was known to have held more than one enslaved person and sold female slaves on at least two occasions, including Nicolasa, described above. Nicolasa was born about 1653, which would have made her about thirteen years old when Francisco was born about 1666. The fact that Francisco was described as mulatto suggests that Nicolasa could have been his mother. She was mulatta, thirteen years old, and a slave of Juan Montes III, and he refused to identify Francisco's mother.⁴⁴ Although slavery was common in the Spanish colonies, it was illegal under Spanish law and the Laws of the Indies. The fact that Juan Montes III held and sold enslaved people suggests he was a person of questionable character. If indeed, as we have speculated, he had one or more children with an enslaved thirteen-year-old in his household and later sold her, he was a scoundrel, even by the lax standards of the period.

There is some indication that Francisco Montes Vigil may have been of mixed race, a mestizo (of mixed Indigenous and Spanish blood) or mulatto (of mixed African and Spanish blood). According to María Martínez, who discussed the racial/ethnic origins of Francisco Montes Vigil, "The baptisms of his [Francisco's] children . . . that of his son, Juan, and daughter . . . María Montes [are why] we have insight [in]to the mother's race. In one [Juan's] case, the father, Francisco, and daughter are referred to as mulatto, while the baptism of María lists her as *morisca* [Moorish]."⁴⁵ This could possibly account for why Juan Montes III did not marry Francisco's mother, yet acknowledged and raised his son.⁴⁶ New Spain in the seventeenth century was characterized by a rigid, stratified class structure. At the top of the social ladder were the Spaniards with blood connections to one of the royal families; next were the nobles with or without title, followed by the peninsulares (Spaniards born in Spain), the criollos (people born in the New World of two Spanish parents), the *castizos* (people born of one Spanish and one mestizo parent), the mestizos (people born of one Spanish and one Indigenous parent), and the mulattos (people born of one Spanish and one Black parent). Although this caste system was formally recognized and superficially adhered to in governmental and social circles, the practical reality of everyday life created a more complex and confused picture of racial diversity.

From the beginning of Spanish exploration, Spanish soldiers mixed freely with female Natives, leaving a progeny of mestizos. Even later in the colonial period, when Spanish women were allowed to travel to the Indies, they still comprised only a small percentage of the population. Consequently, Spanish men, whether of peninsular, criollo, or even castizo character, often took mestizo or Native wives. Even though some families took pains to preserve their "racial purity," the effort proved fruitless over decades. Moreover, because status in the colonies was dictated as much by economic wealth as by birth, people of mixed racial origins, such as mestizos or mulattos, were deferentially regarded as *españoles* (Spaniards) and treated as equals because of their economic status. In other words, as the skin pigmentation of the population darkened, more and more people accepted this as the normal skin color of españoles. Therefore, in New Spain, economic status more than race dictated one's social position. An economically prosperous mestizo could be regarded as español, while a poorer one would be lower on the social ladder. The term "mestizo," though it eventually applied to the majority of the population, was rarely used because it carried a stigma of illegitimacy.[47]

The records regarding Francisco Montes Vigil's ethnicity present an interesting paradox. Francisco Montes is described in his son Juan Carlos's birth records as mulatto, as is his son. In her birth records, his daughter María is described as *morisca*, which meant "Moorish" or dark-skinned.[48] The uncertainty is exacerbated because Spanish priests were notorious for ascribing race in their records based on personal impressions rather than facts. Further, when Francisco Montes and his wife, María Jiménez de Ancizo, enlisted as participants in the Juan Paez Hurtado expedition to New Mexico on 12 January 1695, both were identified as españoles, even though others were listed as mestizos or mulattos. Francisco was specifically described as being a Spaniard, a native of Zacatecas, thirty years old, able-bodied, having somewhat curly chestnut hair, and a scar below his left eye. María Jiménez de Ancizo was described as being a Spaniard and a native of Zacatecas.[49]

Although it is not known when Juan Montes III died, his second will indicated that he was ill and bedridden, so it is likely he died shortly after writing it in April 1683. His son, Francisco Montes, served as executor and inherited the bulk of his father's estate, as mandated by Juan Montes III. Francisco married María Jiménez de Ancizo in 1683. María was described as a Spaniard (probably criollo) woman in the birth records of her children. Thus, Francisco's mixed race was not a detriment in the marriage. Francisco remained a resident of Zacatecas (in the region of La Ciénega de Mata Ojuelos) for the next twelve years, administering his father's affairs. During that time, he and María had five children.

Birth records have not yet been located for all the children, but the eldest was María de la Concepción, who was born on 3 September 1685. Their second child, María de las Nieves, was nine years old in the same year, so she must have been born in 1686. The third child, a son named Pedro Policarpio, was listed as eight years old and must have been born in 1687. The birth record for the fourth child, Juan Carlos, indicated that he was born on 20 March 1689 in Zacatecas; he was described as mulatto, as was his father, Francisco. His mother, however, was described as española. Juan Carlos was listed as six years old in 1695. The fifth child of Francisco Montes Vigil and María Jiménez de Ancizo was Domingo, who was listed as two years of age in 1695 and must have been born in 1692 or 1693.[50] Thus by 1695, the Montes Vigil progeny of Juan II were established and, while small in number, presented the potential for future growth in New Spain.

2

NEW MEXICO BECKONS

Restoring the Colony

Francisco Montes Vigil; his wife, María Jiménez de Ancizo; and their five children eventually moved to New Mexico. In the decade or so after the death of his father, Francisco apparently exhausted the considerable estate he had inherited and grew his family just as rapidly. By 1694–1695, he was searching for new opportunities. The appropriate circumstances would present themselves shortly, and Francisco would seize the opportunity.

The first Spanish permanent settlement of New Mexico had occurred in 1598 with a colonizing party under Juan de Oñate, the first governor of the province. Although he did not find the great wealth in precious minerals he had sought, Oñate established the first colony in San Gabriel and explored the southwestern territory extensively.

In the seventeenth century, twenty-five other Spanish governors served in New Mexico. Colonization continued during this time, new communities (Santa Fe, Santa Cruz, Albuquerque, Taos, and San Miguel) were established, the conversion of the Pueblos to Christianity continued, a semblance of commerce was initiated, and the agricultural economy began. However, relations with the Pueblos deteriorated after 1640, culminating in the Pueblo Revolt of 1680 under the leadership of Popé. The revolt united many of the Pueblo tribes and resulted in the expulsion from New Mexico of the Spaniards, then under Governor Antonio de Otermín. The remnants of the New Mexico colony remained in San Lorenzo, six miles south of present-day Las Cruces. Otermín was ordered by the viceroy to retake New Mexico, but his failure to do so led to his removal, and a new governor, Domingo Jironza Petriz de Cruzate, was named. Cruzate established El Paso as his headquarters and the capital of New Mexico and sent two expeditions to recapture the province, but both ended in failure. In 1692, the newly appointed governor, don Diego de Vargas Zapata y Luján

Ponce de León y Contreras with 200 Spaniards and 100 Natives, reconquered the territory and reestablished Spanish control over New Mexico.

DIEGO DE VARGAS AND THE RESETTLEMENT OF NEW MEXICO

Following the reconquest, Vargas realized that he would need more settlers to complete the colonization process. Accordingly, he dispatched two of his top associates back to New Spain/Mexico to recruit more colonists. The Velasco-Farfán expedition, led by Cristóbal de Velasco and Fray Francisco Farfán, recruited 800 people. This included 100 soldiers and 17 priests from the vicinity of Mexico City and Zacatecas, who joined Vargas in the New Mexico colony in 1693.[1] Still, Vargas felt the need for more people to build a more resilient colony so he requested permission from the viceroy for a second recruitment of settlers. On 23 March 1694, the *audiencia* (governing council) and viceroy of New Spain "directed Vargas to appoint a qualified person to recruit families of colonists in the vicinity of Zacatecas and then accompany them to New Mexico. The viceroy ordered royal officials to furnish money for the sustenance and transportation of the colonists who might be recruited there."[2] Vargas turned to his most trusted military officer, Juan Paez Hurtado, a native of Los Palacios y Villafranca (south of Seville) in Spain, who had been named *capitán cabo y caudillo* by Vargas in 1692. He became a close associate and an integral partner in Vargas's resettlement of New Mexico, assisting "Vargas in reconquest military operations from Acoma to Zuni and Moqui."[3] John B. Colligan's research is the basis for our narrative of the Juan Paez Hurtado expedition.

Vargas wrote to the viceroy on 2 June 1694 that in compliance with the directions of 23 March 1694, he had appointed Paez Hurtado as "captain and quartermaster" of the recruitment expedition. Vargas noted in his letter that he had "granted Paez Hurtado the power and authority to recruit families in the various mining camps in Nueva Vizcaya and Nueva Galicia, such as San José de Parral, [and] the villages of de Llerena, Sombrerete, and Zacatecas."[4] Vargas outlined to the viceroy the instructions he had given Paez Hurtado, which were to "recruit and assist families with persons of *calidad* [good character] and social standing, and pay the entire cost of the trip to Santa Fe, including supplying them with meat, flour, and corn. He was to supply them with saddles and pack animals so that they could transport their possessions."[5]

The task that Paez Hurtado faced was quite formidable, but his greatest frustration was not in the actual recruitment, but in securing government reimbursement for his expenses for the expedition. The directive Governor Vargas had received from the viceroy (the Count of Galve) and the audiencia authorized payments for the sustenance of each family recruited. However, the loosely worded directive enabled local officials in Durango, Sombrerete, and Zacatecas to shortchange Paez Hurtado, shirk their responsibility, and shift blame to one another. Paez Hurtado was frustrated in his effort to secure the promised financial support and resorted to fraudulent means to secure reimbursement for his and the colonists' expenses. We do not know whether Paez Hurtado was personally dishonest or whether he acted that way due to the intransigence of the officials he dealt with, but the Paez Hurtado expedition was forever tainted by the fraudulent practices.

After receiving his orders from Vargas, Paez Hurtado proceeded to Durango and Parral, but he was unable to secure any colonists, so he traveled to Zacatecas, where he enlisted the first recruits on 7 December 1694. He had been rebuffed in securing reimbursement for his expenses by government authorities in Durango and Parral. He presented a bill to accountants in Zacatecas for 820 pesos for expenses for himself, twenty-one soldiers, four civilians, and twenty-one Natives, who were acting as herders for the cattle and sheep he secured for the expedition. The accountants disallowed most of the bill and only authorized the payment of "320 *pesos de oro común en reales*."[6] Since oro común carried less value than, for example, *oro fino*, offering the payment in reales of oro común was a way of shortchanging the already reduced payment.

Concerning the enlistees, it was determined that each person would receive an allowance of one and a half reales per day on a weekly basis for sustenance from the day they enlisted to the date of their departure for New Mexico on 16 February 1695 (they actually received the allowance from 14 February). Thus, Francisco Montes Vigil's eight-member family would have qualified for a maintenance allowance of twelve reales per day, or eighty-four reales per week. After enlisting, each family was taken to "the royal treasury office where they were supposedly given their allowances, followed by a visit to a store where they received articles of clothes, yardage of materials and supplies."[7] Spanish officials prepared the official muster roll of families enrolled in the expedition. The muster roll by Colligan listed forty-six families, although Clevy L. Strout, who discovered the muster roll, consistently mentioned forty-five families.[8]

The viceroy also directed that for the trip to New Mexico, most families would receive reimbursement of 320 pesos, while families with three or fewer members would receive 300 pesos. This requirement apparently prompted Paez Hurtado and some of the family heads to conspire to receive more money. Francisco Montes Vigil's family, for example, was split to access the larger 320-peso stipend twice. Francisco Montes, his wife, and two sons, Pedro Policarpio and Juan Carlos, qualified for the higher 320-peso allotment. The next entry in the roster was Juan Antonio Romero, who by other accounts was not married and later testified that he enlisted alone. However, he was listed as a head of household with three children described as his nieces and nephews.[9] The children—María de la Concepción (age eleven), María de las Nieves (age nine), and Domingo (age two)—were actually Francisco Montes Vigil and María Jiménez de Ancizo's children. Another child in Francisco's family, Juan Eugenio Montes Vigil, listed as a muleteer, had been enslaved by Francisco and his wife, but was now free. The act of splitting his family to qualify for higher stipends, even if it was encouraged or sanctioned by Paez Hurtado, casts a negative light on the character of Francisco. He was complicit with Paez Hurtado and benefited financially from the illegal arrangement. Moreover, the status of the five-year-old Juan Eugenio, listed as a mulatto and freed slave, raises more issues. Not only does it identify Francisco as a slaver, but he had Juan Eugenio assigned to a separate family group and working as a five-year-old muleteer.[10]

NORTH TO SANTA FE

Francisco Montes Vigil, María Jiménez de Ancizo, and their five children were among the 200 colonists who departed from Zacatecas and proceeded north toward Santa Fe over El Camino Real on 16 February 1695. En route, they stopped in places like Sombrerete, Parral, El Tule, and El Paso. The journey was difficult, especially for those with young children, like the Montes Vigil family, but uneventful. They were given a food ration of "a *jicarita* or small gourd full of flour daily. . . . Cattle were butchered and meat given out weekly, the usual ratio being a quarter of beef divided among four persons."[11]

The caravan arrived in Santa Fe on 9 May 1695, and as Vargas directed, the settlers were quartered in lodgings vacated by the Velasco-Farfán colonists, who had been relocated to Santa Cruz de la Cañada.[12] Thus, Francisco Montes

HISTORIC TRAILS

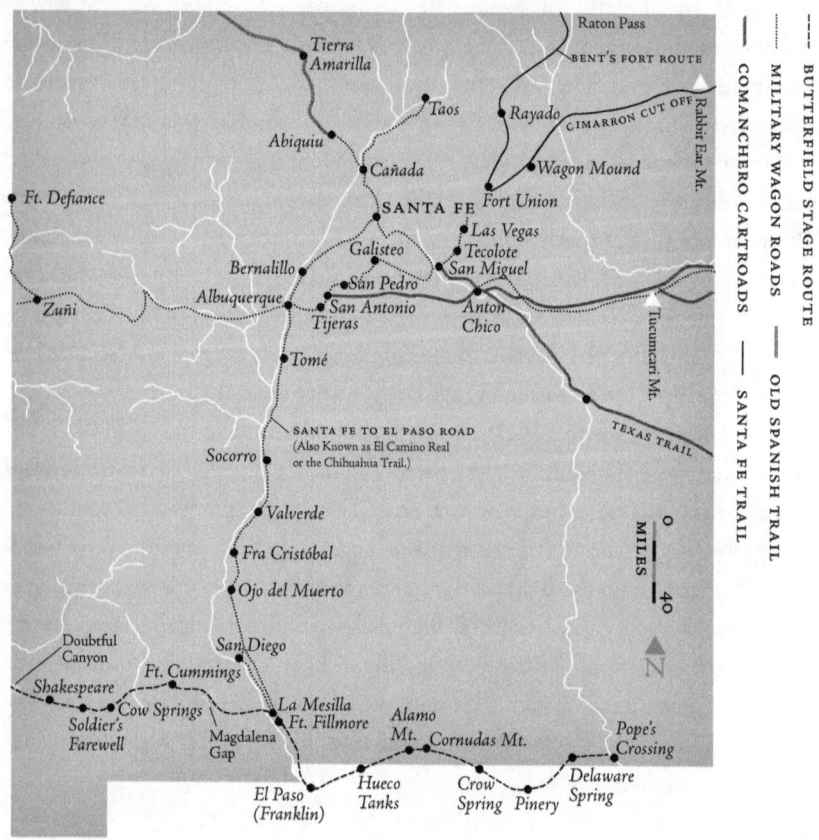

MAP 1. Historic trails and roads of New Mexico and how they connected to national and international trails and to the principal towns and villages. Source: Warren A. Beck and Ynez D. Haase, *Historical Atlas of New Mexico* (Norman: University of Oklahoma Press, 1969), map 34, "Historic Trails." Reprinted by permission of the publisher. Map modified and adapted from the original by Mindy Basinger Hill.

Vigil planted the seed for the Vigil family surname in New Mexico. That seed would grow into the thousands of Vigils that live in New Mexico and other southwestern states today.

Almost from their arrival in Santa Fe, the colonists faced hardships. Lack of food brought on by drought, failed crops, and insect infestation resulted in the authorities raiding the nearby Pueblo villages for badly needed corn and grain to feed the increased settler population. This only exacerbated conditions, as the Pueblos resisted and retaliated in the Pueblo Revolt of 1696. Santa Fe was like an armed camp with the male colonists serving in campaigns against the Indigenous people or defending the presidio against possible attacks. Understandably, this was not the life that the colonists had imagined. Food was scarce, and it was up to Vargas to remedy the dire condition. He commanded a force to Picuris and Taos to steal food from the Natives. He seized 800 bushels of corn at Taos and then attacked Jemez and took 600 more bushels of corn.[13]

Such were the conditions that Francisco Montes Vigil, María Jiménez, and their children encountered in Santa Fe. Amid their frustration and anguish, there must have been concern about whether they had made the right choice in coming to New Mexico. Francisco must have pondered his current situation and wondered if the frustrated dreams of his grandfather Juan II for a better life, land, title, and wealth in the New World were now being repeated in his own life. Francisco was soon awakened to the reality that his family now faced a life-or-death struggle for survival.

Vargas issued a call to the recent immigrants in Santa Fe for volunteers to join the New Mexico militia. Their mission was to secure food supplies by peaceful means or by force from the Pueblos, who had the only corn and grain available for the survival of the colony. Francisco was among the first to enlist. In addition to helping solidify the Spanish colony in Santa Fe, he participated in various campaigns against the Pueblos following the Pueblo Revolt of 1696. It was a fortuitous decision that foreshadowed his and his descendants' lives as military leaders in New Mexico.

Colligan described how the latest immigrants (and surely Francisco de Vigil) in New Mexico quickly realized that life would be lived as if in an armed camp. The men were often away on campaigns or concerned with the protection of their families. Gardens were not planted, and crucial harvests were lost. The adversities they faced resulted in ill feelings toward the Spanish officials.[14]

With time, Francisco and his family adapted and became pioneering Hispanic New Mexicans. Not known for a particular trade, Francisco applied himself to planting and harvesting crops, working his land, maintaining the community ditches, and tending to the goats, sheep, horses, and cattle that sustained his family. At the same time, he found his calling as a career militia soldier with swift promotions in rank. On 27 January 1710, in recognition of his service in the militia, Francisco received a grant of land, the Alameda grant, from the Marquis de Penuela on behalf of King Philip V of Spain. The award consisted of 89,000 acres lying north and west of the village of Alameda. The grant crossed present-day Bernalillo and Sandoval Counties off the old US Highway 85, about seven miles north of Albuquerque.[15] Francisco sold the grant to Captain Juan Gonzales Bas, the alcalde (mayor) and war captain of the town of Bernalillo, because he could not settle on the land since he was in the royal service in Santa Fe.

By 1712, Francisco had risen to the rank of assistant captain of the Santa Fe presidio. He and María added four more children to their already large family: Francisco Montes (born about 1699–1700), Manuel Montes Vigil (born about 1702), Gertrudes Montes Vigil (born about 1704 or 1705), and Elena Montes Vigil (born about 1707). Francisco and María had moved around 1700 to Santa Cruz de la Cañada, where the four children were born. However, Francisco's service in the militia in the Santa Fe presidio required his continued residence there. In 1715, reflecting on the modest estate he had accumulated in twenty years in New Mexico, he and his wife distributed forty cattle (including oxen and calves) among their children María de las Nieves, Gertrudes, Elena, Domingo, Francisco, and Manuel. The portion of the bequest intended for the (probably deceased) María de la Concepción Romero was given to her son Antonio Romero.

Francisco had retired from the militia in 1712, but returned to active service later and continued to answer the call for special assignments. Governor Juan Ignacio Mogollón made him a member of the War Council between 1712 and 1715. In 1716, Francisco participated in a Moqui campaign under Governor and Captain General Felix Martínez.[16] By 1720, Francisco was a permanent lieutenant in the Santa Fe presidio militia. In that year, Francisco was recruited as a member of a military expedition organized and led by Lieutenant General Pedro de Villasur, which was charged with checking the growing French influence in the Great Plains of North America. Spain had claimed all of the area as part of its domain, but French Canadian trappers had increased their trapping and commerce in the region. Villasur led a party of 120, including mounted soldiers, Pueblo allies, and Apache scouts. The party was attacked in present-day Nebraska by a group of Pawnees and Otoes near the Platte and Loup Rivers where Villasur was killed along with thirty-five of his soldiers and ten scouts. Juan Archiveque, a close friend of Francisco from their days in Zacatecas, and Captain José Naranjo, a noted Indigenous guide, were also casualties. The survivors of the expedition were forced to retreat and return to New Mexico, thus ending Spanish influence in the Midwest. Francisco was one of the fourteen survivors of this campaign, and he continued to fight the Natives and protect the Santa Cruz garrison. One biographer described Francisco as a humble man who was true to his word. He was a natural leader and was noted for saying, "Fight the enemy, till the soil, work the irrigated ditches, tread the mill, grind corn and flour, chase Indians, marry, and give in marriage."[17]

Francisco Montes Vigil certainly set a standard for his immediate and later descendants to follow by his exemplary service as a pioneer settler and militia soldier in New Mexico. He may have been the last of the Vigil patriarchs who insisted on retaining the full surname of Montes Vigil. The Vigil clan dropped the Montes prefix and became known simply by the surname Vigil sometime in the 1730s. Francisco Montes Vigil died on 11 September 1730 at Santa Cruz de la Cañada. Based on his estimated birth date of 1666 in Zacatecas, New Spain, he was sixty-four years old at the time of his death.[18]

PROGENITORS OF THE VIGIL FAMILY OF NEW MEXICO

In addition to a remarkable legacy as a connecting link between the Montes Vigil family from Spain and the Vigil family of New Mexico, along with his military career, Francisco Montes Vigil and María Jiménez de Ancizo left a large family, which continued to spread the Vigil surname through all parts of New Mexico and the southwestern United States. Because theirs was the original Vigil family, it is worthwhile to recount the evolution of the Francisco Montes Vigil and María Jiménez de Ancizo children in that first New Mexico generation.

María de la Concepción Montes Vigil, the eldest of Francisco's children, was born about 1683 or 1684 and was eleven years old when the family enlisted with the Paez Hurtado expedition. She traveled to New Mexico as a member of the Juan Antonio Romero family, as described above. María de la Concepción apparently married Martín Romero after their arrival in Santa Fe. María might have died by 1715 when Francisco and his wife divided the livestock among their children because María's share was given to her son Antonio Romero, who was described by Francisco as "our *nieto*" (grandson). However, one source lists her as marrying José Tenorio in 1722 when she would have been thirty-eight years old.[19]

María de las Nieves Montes Vigil, the second child of Francisco and María, was born on 3 September 1685 in Zacatecas. The only other record lists her as marrying Sebastian Martín in Santa Cruz on 2 September 1733, when she would have been forty-eight years old.[20]

Pedro Policarpio Montes Vigil came to be known as Pedro Montes Vigil de Santillana, the latter surname referring to the maternal line of Catalina de Cantillana, his maternal great-grandmother. His younger brother Francisco Montes II and Francisco's son Francisco Montes III also chose to use the Santillana surname. Why they chose this identification is unknown, but they used the surname in all of their official records. The use of *s* as the first letter instead of the correct form with a *c* could have been an error, given that Cantillana was a rare name in New Mexico, while Santillana was more common. It illustrates that they were aware of and chose to retain their ancestral Spanish surname associations. Pedro originally resided in Santa Fe but in the early 1700s moved to Santa Cruz with his wife, Juana Trujillo, a daughter of Mateo Trujillo and María Tapia. Pedro and Juana had one child, Manuel, who died as an infant. Pedro was credited for his work on the restoration of the San Miguel Chapel in Santa Cruz. The 1750 Territorial Census for New Mexico lists Pedro and his wife as residents of Santa Cruz, childless, but in a household of five adults. Pedro's younger brother Domingo was his neighbor, and they shared a land grant. Nephews Juan Bautista and Cristóval Vigil were also neighbors.[21]

Juan Carlos Montes Vigil, born on 20 March 1689, was a soldier. Although his birthplace in one source is given as Mexico City, this is unlikely since the Francisco Montes Vigil family was living in Zacatecas at that time. Juan Carlos remained in Santa Fe when the family moved to Santa Cruz. He married Ynes López in 1733, and they had three children, Manuela, Juan, and Ynes, who all died at a young age. Their mother, Ynes, died about 1745. Juan Carlos then married Antonia Nicolasa Luján, and they had two children, María de Luz and Antonio Vigil. Juan Carlos remained in Santa Fe until his death on 18 May 1762.[22]

Domingo Montes Vigil was born in 1692 or 1693 in Zacatecas. He was the youngest of Francisco Montes and María Jiménez's children who were born in New Spain. After a short stay in Santa Fe, Domingo moved with the family to Santa Cruz in the early 1700s. Domingo married his first wife, Pascuala Salazar, in 1715, and they had three children: Juan Bautista, Juan Cristóval, and Salbador Vigil. Pascuala died in 1724. Domingo and Pascuala are noteworthy in our context because they are the great-grandparents of Donaciano Vigil. After his first wife died, Domingo married María Estela Márquez in 1725, and they had six children: Barbara, Francisco Antonio, Julian, Gregorio Pablo, Nicolasa, and Rosalia Montes Vigil.[23] Domingo also served in the New Mexico militia with the Santa Cruz contingent. He used his service in the militia as a springboard to public life, as he later became alcalde of Santa Cruz. A New Mexico alcalde combined both political leadership similar to a mayor and judicial power similar to a local magistrate. One of his sons and some of his grandsons would follow a similar career route.

Domingo must have made a notable impression on his peers and community. One biographer wrote that he was referred to as Captain Domingo Montes Vigil on 17 April 1732 when one of his daughters was baptized.[24] Charles C. Chapman in "New Mexico Generations" quotes Stanley Crocchiola in *Giant in Lilliput*, who refers to Domingo Montes Vigil as the alcalde of Santa Cruz who dedicated his life to protecting the Indigenous people in his jurisdiction against the *ricos* (privileged, wealthy, landholding class) and others who sought their land and used them as quasi-slaves. If the settlers continued to exploit them, they would unite with the Navajos, Utes, and Apaches against the province and repeat the "uprising of 1680."[25] Another biographer acknowledged that Domingo "had a deep empathy for the plight of the Native Americans and made every effort to protect all who were living within his domain."[26] Domingo Montes Vigil's sympathy toward the Pueblos affirms that there were some Hispanos in the colonial period of New Mexico who objected to the oppressive treatment of the Pueblos under Spanish policies and institutions, such as the encomienda (forced labor) system, which exploited them and their land. Such policies were a direct cause of the various Pueblo revolts against the Spaniards.

Francisco Montes Vigil II was the first child of Francisco and María born in New Mexico. He was born about 1699 or 1700 in Santa Cruz and later chose to be known as Francisco Montes Vigil de Santillana. Francisco Montes II married Antonia de Castillo in 1730 in Santa Cruz, and there they raised eight children (names unknown). He is referred to as a recipient of the Francisco Montes Vigil land grant.[27]

Manuel Montes Vigil was the second of Francisco and María's children born in the province of New Mexico. He was born in 1702 in Santa Cruz de la Cañada. In 1719, he married Manuela Sánchez, daughter of Pedro Sánchez de Inigo (her mother's name is unknown), and they settled in Santa Fe. Like his father, Manuel was a farmer and enlisted in the Santa Fe branch of the New Mexico militia, where he served for twenty years. Manuel and Manuela had four children: Joséfa, Ysabel, Juan Luis, and Mario Antonio Vigil. Manuel Montes Vigil died on 31 March 1732 in Santa Fe.[28]

Gertrudes Montes Vigil was the third child and first girl of Francisco Montes and María Jiménez born in New Mexico, and she was born in Santa Cruz about 1704 or 1705. She married Francisco Xavier de Herrera, had two children, and resided with the Vigil family in Santa Cruz.

Elena Montes Vigil, born in 1707 in Santa Cruz, was the fourth child born in New Mexico to Francisco Montes Vigil and María Jiménez. Elena married Diego Gonzales II, and they resided in Chimayo. Diego served in the New Mexico militia, rising to the rank of *alférez* (second lieutenant). They had three children: Ygnacia, Francisco, and Miguel Gonzales. Elena died in 1772 in Santa Cruz.[29]

Thus, with nine children, five born in New Spain/Mexico and four born in New Mexico, we have the first generation, which went on to produce the sizable Vigil family of New Mexico and later spread through all parts of the Southwest and eventually the United States. Each new branch of the Vigil family tree not only reflected the growing numbers of people with the Vigil surname, but the extensive social, cultural, economic, and political networks of familial associations.

JUAN CRISTÓVAL MONTES VIGIL I

As mentioned above, Domingo Montes Vigil was married twice. His first marriage was to Pascuala Ynez de Salazar, and this marriage in 1715 produced three children: Juan Bautista Montes Vigil, Cristóval (or Juan Cristóval) Montes Vigil, and Salbador Vigil. The middle child, Juan Cristóval I, was born about 1721. Because there has been confusion as to his exact name, which is alternately given as Cristóval or Juan Cristóval and alternately spelled Cristóval or Cristóbal, we note that here we refer to him as Cristóval, since he was known by that name in life, and it reflects the correct spelling in Spanish of the name. Cristóval Montes Vigil was born and lived most of his early life in Santa Cruz de la Cañada. Like his father, Domingo, and grandfather Francisco, he embraced a career in the New Mexico militia while also engaged with farming and ranching in the Santa Cruz area. Cristóval married María Teodora Medina about 1742, and they had thirteen known children. Ten of them were boys, which makes him perhaps the most prolific in spreading the Vigil name. He was a lifelong member of the Santa Cruz militia and in later life moved to Taos. On 9 August 1742, Cristóval, his brother Juan Bautista, and uncle Pedro Montes Vigil petitioned for and were awarded land near Taos. The grant, known alternately as Los Luceros or the Antoine Leroux grant, was apparently utilized by Cristóval and his relatives.[30]

Cristóval's military career shows that he was an officer, rising through the ranks to alférez (second lieutenant) and *teniente* (lieutenant) by 1777. At the same time, he became active in public affairs, serving as alcalde of the village of Santa Cruz. Cristóval's residency in Santa Cruz accommodated him well because he was able to farm his land and raise livestock to support his large family. At the same time, he was able to perform his duty as a member of the militia, which is why he vehemently objected to a proposal by Governor Juan Bautista de Anza in 1780 to centralize the militia, forcing soldiers like him to move into more compact defensible plazas and away from the river valleys where they lived and farmed.[31]

During Cristóval's tenure as alcalde, a Comanche raiding party had been continually attacking villages in the area of Taos, New Mexico. In one such attack in 1768, 500 Comanches led by the notorious chief Cuerno Verde (Green Horn) attacked Ojo Caliente and carried away firearms, food supplies, and animals. However, Cuerno Verde was killed in the cross fire between Natives and villagers. His son picked up the chief's headdress and adopted his father's name of Cuerno Verde, becoming the new leader of the Comanches and continuing the raids.

In 1777, Teodoro de Croix, commanding general of the Spanish internal colonies, appointed Juan Bautista de Anza as governor of New Mexico. Anza, a native of New Spain/Mexico, was a military officer serving as the commander of the presidio of Tubac in Arizona, near present-day Tucson. Anza gained fame in the 1770s when he discovered an overland desert trail to the California mission at Monterey, and he later established the mission (Dolores) that would become the presidio of San Francisco. In selecting Anza as governor of New Mexico, Croix hoped that Anza could address the perennial Comanche raiding problem in the province. In 1779, Anza led a force of 800 New Mexico militiamen accompanied by Ute and Apache warriors through what is today the San Luis Valley of Colorado. He selected a new route, avoiding detection near present-day Manitou Springs in Colorado, and proceeded east toward what is now Colorado Springs. There he attacked a small party of Comanches at their headquarters and pursued them south through present-day Fountain Springs. Crossing the Arkansas River near present-day Pueblo, Colorado, he encountered and attacked at Greenhorn Creek the main force of Comanches returning from a raid on Taos. His forces routed the Comanches, killing the young Cuerno Verde and other Indigenous leaders.[32] Among Anza's forces were three of Cristóval Vigil's sons, Cristóval Faustin (thirty-one), Salbador (twenty-seven), and José (twenty-three), who had followed their father into the New Mexico militia.

In addition to his service in the militia and as alcalde, Cristóval was a successful farmer-rancher, attending regional trade fairs to buy and sell livestock and other products. He was also a benevolent leader of the Santa Cruz community, "credited with payment for the cost of building the main altar of the church in Santa Cruz," and he was instrumental in the completion of the church of the pueblo and mission of Nuestra Señora de los Dolores de Sandia.[33] Cristóval and his wife, Teodora, relocated to Taos and are found in the 1790 Taos Census.[34] María Teodora Medina Montes Vigil died soon after at about age sixty-one. Cristóval Montes Vigil, reflecting his continued vigor at age seventy-one, married Juana de Luna, age fifty-one, the mother-in-law of two of his sons, on 24 August 1791 in Taos. Cristóval was reputed to be a well-educated man and a "firm believer in education," who insisted that his children, particularly the boys, receive the best schooling available in the remote province of New Mexico where public education was nonexistent and books were rare.[35]

JUAN CRISTÓBAL MONTES VIGIL II

The ninth child and the seventh son born to Cristóval and Teodora was Juan Cristóbal Montes Vigil II, born in 1760 in Santa Cruz de la Cañada. Like his older brothers, Juan Cristóbal followed his father into a career in the militia in the garrison of Santa Cruz, although he did not participate in the Anza expedition.[36] He was known as a studious young man, tutored by his father and guided toward books and reading. Philip Vigil wrote that Juan Cristóbal Vigil II (who would later become Donaciano's father) claimed that he was required to read for one hour each day from the Bible, philosophy, spiritual works, and any other material he could acquire from the friars. When he had the opportunity to travel to the trade fairs in Chihuahua or Durango with his father, he was always eager to return with new books, paper, and pencils.[37]

While most of Cristóval Vigil's sons and daughters remained in Santa Cruz into adulthood and lived in close proximity to their parents and each other, Juan Cristóbal, for some reason, struck out on his own. Perhaps it was a desire to break away from family in a small village and explore a new life and possibilities in the "big city" (Santa Fe); perhaps it was the same adventurous spirit that motivated his ancestors Juan Montes II or Francisco Montes Vigil. At the age of twenty-one on 1 September 1781, he established residency in Santa Fe, where he enlisted in the militia presidial company. His enlistment papers record his prior occupation as a farmer. He was "5' 4" tall, with dark eyes, black hair and eyebrows, ruddy skin, a sharp nose, thin beard, with five moles on the right side of his chest."[38] A little over a year later, on 19 November 1782, he married María Antonia Andrea Martínez in the Castrense (Military) Chapel in Santa Fe. Antonia was the daughter of Miguel Martínez and Ane María Moya. Antonia had been married before to Juan Francisco Trujillo, and they had one child, Gregorio Trujillo. Therefore, she had a three-year-old son when she married Juan Cristóbal. Juan Cristóbal established a close relationship with his stepson, Gregorio, who would later be very close to his half brother Donaciano Vigil. Juan Cristóbal and Antonia Andrea had six children: daughters Ana María (born about 1786), Juana María (born about 1787), Paula (birth date unknown), and María Ygnes (birth date unknown), and sons Donaciano (born 1802) and Juan Bautista (born 1808).[39] Ana María, Paula, and Juana María predeceased their mother, but María Ygnes survived to adulthood and lived on property with a house willed to her from her parents' estates.[40]

Sometime between 1782 and 1800, Juan Cristóbal purchased a parcel of property west of the Santa Fe Plaza that was commonly referred to as *los altos* (the heights). It lay above a *barranca* (ravine) that separated the high ground from the valley floor of the Santa Fe River, which flowed east to west several hundred feet north of the ravine.[41] The site of the property Juan Cristóbal purchased is today listed as 518 Alto Street, and it may have been attractive to him because of the rich bottomland adjacent to the Santa Fe River. This ideal farmland could be readily irrigated by ditches from the Santa Fe River. The area contained large cultivated tracts that had been used for both *temporales* (dry farming) above the ravine and early *regadillos* (irrigated) farmland below it. Juan Cristóbal planted five fruit trees known in the neighborhood as the *arbolera* (orchard), a small garden near the house, and a larger *huerta* (vegetable plot) near the river.

The area was in an early stage of urban development as houses were already being constructed, and a license was issued on 14 October 1795 by the authorities for building what became the Chapel of Our Lady of Guadalupe.

The church is the oldest shrine in the United States dedicated to Our Lady of Guadalupe and is located about 300 feet east from the Vigil property.[42] That neighborhood was known as the Barrio de Guadalupe. After purchasing the property, Juan Cristóbal built an adobe house. As was typical of the day, the house was built in stages, originally with a main room, a kitchen, and a combination living room and bedroom; other rooms were added as the family grew. The architectural style, today referred to as "Spanish colonial," was a single story, and the rooms created an inner central *placita*. The restored Donaciano Vigil House today is owned by the Historic Santa Fe Foundation and is featured in yearly foundation-sponsored tours.

By 1832, when Juan Cristóbal wrote his will, he described the home as follows: "I declare for my goods the house of my abode [*morada*] which is composed of four parts and an orchard with five fruit trees, and in addition to this a plot of land close by and contiguous to the said land a large room and another structure which because they are old have been assigned as a stable for the animals and a barn."[43] The Guadalupe Barrio had grown rapidly following the construction of the church, and by 1832, according to a Mexican census, fifty-seven families were living there. Most of the heads of household in the area were listed as having occupations as farmers and laborers, with some working as shepherds, masons, cobblers, tailors, and silversmiths.[44]

Juan Cristóbal's formal demeanor and education obviously served him well in his career, and he rose quickly through the ranks of the Santa Fe garrison. By 12 July 1800, Juan Cristóbal had retired from active service in the militia, listed in the Santa Fe presidial roster as *inválido*.[45] Nevertheless, he continued to serve in various public offices locally and at the provincial level.[46] This work was climaxed by his service as alcalde for the town of Santa Fe from 1815 to 1821.[47] Juan Cristóbal Vigil died on 21 September 1832 and was buried the next day in the cemetery of the Castrense Chapel. Unfortunately, neither he nor his wife, Antonia Andrea, lived to see the rise in prominence of their son Donaciano.

3

CONDITIONS IN SANTA FE
DURING DONACIANO'S YOUTH

New Mexico at the dawn of the nineteenth century was a poverty-ridden territory. Although there was a small privileged class of *ricos*, who possessed great wealth, vast landholdings, and large herds of livestock in the form of cattle, sheep, and horses, these few wealthy people were outnumbered by the greater population of the servant class of *peones* or *pobres*. The ricos often used their wealth to engage in commercial operations that yielded further wealth. However, the larger segment of the Spanish/Mexican population was mired in poverty and working as small farmers, shepherds, cowboys, or day laborers in the fields, mines, or commercial establishments. Most New Mexicans were living in conditions much like those in which their ancestors had lived for over a hundred years.[1] One writer observed, "Santa Fe was the center of government, culture, and commerce.... [Aside] from nomadic and Pueblo Indians, the majority of people lived in *estancias* [settlements].... A small middle class of farmers and artisans peddled their produce and worked for wages. New Mexico was essentially a feudalistic society."[2]

The Spanish population of New Mexico increased very slightly in the period 1800–1821. The census compiled by Governor Joaquín del Real Alencaster on 20 November 1805 recorded the Spanish population as 26,835 and the Indigenous population as 8,172, totaling 35,007. In 1821, the *custodio*, José Pedro Rubi, stated that there were 9,000 Natives and 34,000 Spaniards in New Mexico for a total population of 43,000, which indicated an increase of 7,993 people (23 percent) in the sixteen-year period.[3] Santa Fe's population increased by more than 50 percent: from 3,963 in 1805 to 6,038 in 1821. Santa Cruz de la Cañada also increased from 2,188 in 1805 to 2,633 in 1821. However, Albuquerque declined from 4,294 in 1805 to 2,564 in 1821. Taos also lost population, declining from 1,337 in 1805 to 1,252 in 1821.[4]

A major factor for the stagnant population and the depressed economy was the lack of exportable commodities (food, livestock, or manufactured goods) that would launch and sustain a healthy balance of commerce. Under Spain, New Mexico's trade was severely restricted and limited to Spain and its colonies. As a result, in 1804 New Mexico's primary imports were manufactured goods from Chihuahua, Mexico, totaling $112,000. Exports, mainly of hides, wool, and wine, totaled about $60,000 in the same period. The only internal trade of any consequence was with the Natives, a barter system for perishable and nonperishable foods, grains and hay for livestock, and animal pelts for woven wool products. Although the bartering of some goods with the Plains people may have taken place, trade with the United States was prohibited. In 1804, the first significant enterprise of copper mining began in Santa Rita del Cobre. Still, commercial conditions were so bad that a council convened in Santa Fe in 1805 to consider measures for developing New Mexico's economy.[5]

Conditions among the people were also symptomatic of the depressed economy. The dwellings of New Mexicans were constructed of sun-dried adobe bricks with flat roofs supported by vigas (hewed logs). Ricos had more elaborate homes (sometimes two stories) on larger lots, sometimes called haciendas. Most of the common people had two- to four-room adobe homes. Dirt floors were common, but the ricos sometimes had carpets or wood floors. Wool-stuffed mattresses and pillows were the norm; they were piled together to serve as a divan in the day and spread over the floor for sleeping at night. Chests were used for storing clothing, although ricos sometimes had closets. Interior walls, inherently a drab brown from adobe construction, were whitewashed or draped with calico cloth. The typical daily diet consisted of tortillas, frijoles, chile con carne, and atole (corn gruel). The main sources of meat were pigs, sheep, goats, and wild game, usually prepared as stews for greater yield. Ricos had more variety and were more likely to have more meat at a single meal.[6]

The masses of the people were described as "ignorant, superstitious, [and] largely illiterate" due to the lack of schools; "there were few schools worthy of the name."[7] Relations between the government and the people were based on suspicion and distrust for centuries. The barren and arid climate of many parts of New Mexico did little to encourage much optimism among the sparse population. Reflecting the elitist mentality of the Mexican-appointed administrators, Governor Joaquín del Real Alencaster (1805–1808) complained that the inhabitants were "unprogressive and unruly, generally contemptuous of government and largely uncontrolled."[8]

New Mexico was an isolated, archaic, underdeveloped, and remote province in the northernmost territory of New Spain, itself governed by its remote European sponsor, Spain. Most of the social and economic conditions in New Mexico were attributed to its isolation from any form of developed civilization. New Mexico was isolated from New Spain/Mexico, its closest link to Spain, and even Mexico was mired in underdevelopment due to Spain's trade restrictions. New Mexico did not begin to emerge from its chronic underdevelopment until after Mexico gained its independence from Spain in 1821 and the yoke of trade restrictions was lifted, thus opening the Santa Fe Trail and commerce with the United States.

These economic and domestic descriptions might seem bleak, but others who visited New Mexico during the period offered a more balanced view. Lansing Bloom focused his work on New Mexico under Mexican administration and offered an interesting perspective from documented contemporary accounts of the period. He observed that in 1822 the people were industrious and content with simple wants and an appreciation for celebratory events; fairs and fiestas were commonplace. New Mexicans' small provincial world dictated their ambitions and principles, and they were not yet aware of the world existing beyond their margins. "They met oppressive conditions with hardihood and patience; and it must be admitted, they so adjusted themselves to their environment that life repaid them with a good measure of enjoyment."[9]

Antonio Barreiro, an *asesor* (legal advisor), was selected under a decree by the Mexican Congress in 1829 to report on the conditions in New Mexico. The asesor "was expected to be consulted on civil and criminal cases and, in fact, was the legal advisor representing the central administration."[10] Barreiro was well suited for the position of asesor and deputy since he was an attorney. Barreiro's presence in New Mexico in the 1830s was significant because it provided an informed and articulate outsider's view of New Mexico in the midst of the province's tenure under Mexico. In 1832, his report was first published in a book titled *Ojeada sobre Nuevo Mexico*.[11] Barreiro wrote an interesting and lucid perspective of the New Mexico where Donaciano grew up, including a historical sketch and descriptions of the people, towns, climate, and geography of the isolated province. Barreiro estimated the population of New Mexico at 41,458, although other estimates reported the population to be as high as 57,176.[12] The principal towns in the province were Santa Fe, Albuquerque, Taos, and Santa Cruz de la Cañada. Barreiro was impressed with the geography, including the majestic mountains, the forests, and plains, which provided habitats for abundant wild game, such as buffalo, deer, wild horses, Cimarron sheep, and turkeys.[13]

Barreiro also wrote about the towns, and Santa Fe, in particular, did not escape his scrutiny. The Palace of the Governors, which housed the offices of the governor, deputation, commissary, barracks, paymaster, and guardhouse, was in the "very worst state imaginable."[14] The buildings were spacious but partly in ruins and disrepair. Barreiro described the private residences as being "low and built of adobes," but nevertheless "roomy and quite attractive." He also admired a "public promenade" that had been landscaped with cottonwood trees.[15] Barreiro observed that "agriculture [was] utterly neglected" except for corn, wheat, and beans, which were the primary subsistence products. Fruits, such as apples, apricots, chokecherries, and plums, were grown but mainly for local consumption and certainly not in sufficient quantities for commerce.[16]

Equally distressing to Barreiro was the condition of education. The private home of the vicar general, don Juan Rafaél Rascón, served as the only school in Santa Fe. The sole instructor was the young Guadalupe Miranda whose "constancy and devotion" deserved praise, even if he suffered from a lack of books and resources. In Barreiro's view, "although nothing was better provided for [than the school] nothing was in more distressing condition than this."[17]

A commentary on and analysis of the commercial and economic activities in New Mexico were also included in *Ojeada sobre Nuevo Mexico*. Barreiro wrote that trade carried over the Santa Fe Trail was good and profitable for the merchants, both Anglos and Hispanos, and beneficial to New Mexico because it stimulated the local economy and provided manufactured goods while creating a market for locally produced items. The tenuous New Mexican economy was still based on barter and a necessity for credit. Barreiro wrote that New Mexicans were largely isolated from the "comforts of civilized life; fall prey to lawlessness due to a weak legal system; [and practiced] a religion that engendered corruption from its clergy. The governors cared only about increasing their own individual power and wealth. . . . The region's individuals could find neither legal nor spiritual relief from their travails."[18]

Concluding the ojeada, Barreiro observed that he had felt "extraordinary delight" in discussing the rich natural resources and land New Mexico held, while at the same time glancing over the decadence of the "political conditions and disorganized administration." Only an "extraordinary effort" and the attention of government would elevate the province to the "pinnacle of her good feelings." Barreiro felt that ignorance was the primary cause of the "moral ills" of the territory, and its only solution was the "propagation of culture," which would be the primary object of a government's "beneficence."[19]

Barreiro's insightful and provocative observations and the publication and wide circulation of his book in New Mexico and Mexico ensured that conditions in the province were well known. Barreiro proposed a series of reforms that would benefit the people of New Mexico, while providing a recurring source of income for the mother country. His proposals were largely ignored.[20] Barreiro amazingly foreshadowed the American invasion two decades before it occurred, as he concluded, "The stars of the capital of the north will shine without a doubt even more brightly in New Mexico where the darkness is most dense due to the deplorable state in which the Mexican government has left it."[21]

Even before Mexican independence in 1821, Spain should have been similarly apprised of the situation in New Mexico because of Pedro Pino's representation of the province in Spain's *cortes* (legislative assembly) in 1811. On 14 September 1810, the Council of Regency, established by the Spanish cortes, issued a decree providing for the election of American deputies to the cortes. In the same year, Pedro Bautista Pino was selected by a ten-member committee appointed by Governor José Manrique to be New Mexico's representative to the cortes, the only person ever to be so designated. Pino was a good choice; he was one of New Mexico's wealthiest men and could afford to pay his own travel expenses, and he was a capable delegate. Pino left New Mexico on 14 October 1811, accompanied by his eleven-year-old grandson, Juan Pino.

They arrived in Cadiz on 12 August 1812, too late for Pino to participate in the drafting of a constitution. Pino published a report called *Exposición* describing the conditions and needs of New Mexico, which he presented to the cortes.[22] Pino's report dealt with many issues facing the province. In 1812, peace existed with the Navajos, Utes, and Comanches, but the Mescalero Apaches were still waging war. Pino summarized the New Mexican economy as follows: "Agriculture, industries, and commerce are the bases of their prosperity; but in no one of them does the province amount to anything [due] to the neglect [with] which the government has thus far treated her, and because of the pillage yearly suffered by those who might prosper by their products and manufactures."[23]

In the report, printed in Cádiz in November 1812, Pino recommended an improved military effort to protect New Mexico from invasion by the United States. This approach ensured he would get the attention of Spanish officials more readily than if he had asked for protection from the Natives. He also recommended the creation of five new presidios on the frontier regions for the same purpose. Finally, he called for the creation of an audiencia in Chihuahua, which would be closer and more responsive to New Mexico than the audiencia in Guadalajara. Some reforms under the Spanish cortes seemed to improve the local government in New Mexico, such as expansion of ayuntamientos, but there is no evidence of major reforms as recommended by Pino.[24] In the end, Pino's singular accomplishment was recorded back in New Mexico by a familiar Spanish *refrán* (ditty), "Pedro Pino Fue, Pedro Pino Vino," signifying that Pino had gone all the way to Spain and returned, but nothing much changed in New Mexico.[25]

Such were the conditions in New Mexico when Donaciano Vigil was born on 6 September 1802 and that he would face growing up in Santa Fe over the final two decades of Spanish rule. His birth home was described as a "retired, quiet retreat, [amid] a boundary [of] magnificent trees" on the south bank of the Santa Fe River near the Chapel of Our Lady of Guadalupe.[26]

Donaciano personally experienced conditions of poverty owing to the trade restrictions and isolation from the central government. In particular, he was aware of the dearth of educational opportunities available to young children in New Mexico. Donaciano's own description of conditions is quite revealing. In two different autobiographical sketches prepared later in life, he discussed his education. In the first, Donaciano attributed his limited education to two principal causes. One was the "religious fanaticism of the period." The government sustained the Catholic religion without tolerance for any other. The second was that the teachers, if there were any capable ones at all, were restrained by the law of the land from bettering education and extending it to a higher level.[27]

While a few public schools existed in 1808–1810, the teaching was limited in the sciences, and it was mainly in writing and arithmetic that Donaciano received instruction. Unfortunately, the compensation for teachers was inadequate to provide for subsistence, which forced teachers to leave their positions to obtain other means of employment. Donaciano's father received eight pesos a month for his retirement from service in the militia. This was a modest sum, and Donaciano left his studies to help his parents.[28] Although his father lacked advanced knowledge of the arts, sciences, philosophy, and language, he did teach Donaciano to read and write and instilled in him an insatiable thirst for knowledge that would manifest throughout his life.

Donaciano's father, Juan Cristóbal, was an impressive man, well educated, capable, and respected among the soldiers and officers of the garrison, as well as by private citizens in the community. However, probably owing to Cristóval's large family, Juan Cristóbal was of limited means, and his enlistment as a soldier in the Santa Fe presidio provided a meager, although reliable, source of income to augment his life as a farmer. Still, he was a strong influence on and role model for Donaciano.

In 1803, the government under the leadership of Comandante General Nemesio Salcido sought to address the lack of formal schools in the province by organizing a public school that could at least serve the soldiers' male children, twelve years of age or older. Educated people were sought as teachers, either as volunteers or for a small stipend, to provide instruction that included Christian doctrine, reading, writing, and arithmetic. Two teachers were selected to serve under Juan Cristóbal's direction. The local town council (*cabildo*) was encouraged to assume permanent sponsorship of the school.[29] However, this effort was short-lived as the public school experiment folded, and Juan Cristóbal was back to personally tutoring his boys in the privacy of his home. His own father, Cristóval, had made Juan Cristóbal "so obsessed" with education that his home schooling involved a daily regimen of assigned reading, writing, composition, oral discourse, and problem solving that was combined with homework. Clearly, Juan Cristóbal fostered greater ambitions in his sons than was typical for a young man living in an adobe dwelling while performing farming and ranching chores. Since he could not afford to send his sons to private or public schools in Mexico or the United States, as some ricos were doing at the time, he had to be the stern teacher and his house the classroom.[30]

Twitchell wrote that Donaciano's family was "of limited means, and without the power and influence that accompanied wealth," but his father, Juan Cristóbal, was well educated and "fully appreciated the advantage of education," which he imparted to his children.[31] Twitchell further noted that Juan Cristóbal served not only as his children's tutor, but also as the overseer of their instruction as they advanced in age. As a result, Donaciano, his brother Juan, and their cousin Juan Bautista Vigil y Alarid developed a liking for books and study and actively pursued every opportunity for advancing their knowledge. The education that the boys received was such that Donaciano and Juan Bautista (his cousin) were later regarded by many, including American observers, as among the educated men in the territory.[32]

4

THE SOLDIER

At the age of twenty-one on 1 March 1823, Donaciano made the first and most momentous decision in his young life: he enlisted in the militia of the presidio of Santa Fe.[1] Perhaps he did this at the urging of his father, Juan Cristóbal, who had served honorably in the New Mexico militia, or possibly because of the limited career opportunities for young men in New Mexico. As Lansing Bloom observed, "Mexico was weak economically, nowhere in the world were there greater contrasts of wealth and poverty.... An active life was to be found only in one of four careers: cleric, lawyer, soldier, or government official."[2]

A PRIVATE IN THE SANTA FE PRESIDIO

Donaciano thus became another in the series of his ancestors who joined the military. In his biography, Father Stanley Crocchiola wrote that the Vigil men were a "warrior clan" dating back to the Middle Ages in Spain.[3] According to Crocchiola, the "Vigils engaged in some sort of struggle or other in the Crusades, the ousting of the Moors, battling the enemies of Castile.... Their watchfulness and alertness as sentries earned for them the name that became part of their heritage."[4] The New World tradition of the Montes Vigil military clan did not include Donaciano's fifth or sixth great-grandfathers, for neither Juan Montes II, who came to the New World from Spain, nor his son Juan Montes III were military men. Notwithstanding Crocchiola's assertion that he had been the "son of a military captain commanding the garrison at Zacatecas,"[5] Francisco Montes Vigil, who came from Zacatecas in 1695, had not been in the military prior to enlisting in the Juan Paez Hurtado expedition to help colonize New Mexico.

However, after arriving in New Mexico, Francisco enlisted in the militia and served over two decades. He rose to the rank of captain while serving in the Santa Cruz unit and established the tradition of military service for the Montes Vigil clan in New Mexico. Francisco's example would be emulated by Francisco's son Domingo (also a captain of the militia), his son Cristóval, and Cristóval's son Juan Cristóbal (Donaciano's father), who also held the rank of captain of the Santa Fe unit of the militia. It was natural that Donaciano would follow the path established by these immediate ancestors, who started in the military and used that as a springboard to political careers. Two years after enlisting in the militia, on 10 October 1825 Donaciano married María del Refugio Sánchez, a native of Santa Fe and daughter of Diego Antonio Sánchez and María Manuela Gallegos. The marriage took place in the old *parroquia* church, site of the later St. Francis Cathedral. It was celebrated by the Reverend Vicar Juan Felipe Ortíz with Teodocio Quintana and Diego Padilla as witnesses. From the date of their marriage, Donaciano and María resided in the Alto Street home of his parents.[6]

There were very few career paths available to New Mexicans in the early 1800s, particularly for those in the middle or lower classes. The sons of the ricos, such as the Perea clan of Bernalillo, or landowners with substantial herds of sheep on large sections of irrigated farmland, such as the Pino clan of northern New Mexico, apprenticed in their fathers' enterprises. Others, such as Antonio Martínez of Taos and José Manuel Gallegos, joined the priesthood, which led to prominence and political careers. For the Montes Vigil clan, including Donaciano, military careers also would lead to prominence and culminate in careers in public office. Although the militia in New Mexico was notoriously undertrained and underpaid, it was the only organized military force in the territory and did provide a modest salary.

Donaciano's ability to read and write led to added responsibilities as a company clerk and promotions in rank. He worked closely with territorial governors, such as Manuel Armijo, and in several respects Armijo's own rise as a military leader and governor during the Mexican regime served as a model for Donaciano to follow since he was a native of New Mexico. Almost from the time of his enlistment in 1823, Donaciano served under and associated with several New Mexican military and political leaders, such as José Antonio Viscarra, Francisco Sarracino, Bartolomé Baca, Antonio Narbona, and Albino Pérez, who reinforced Donaciano's career ambitions.

What were the conditions for the New Mexico militia at the time that Donaciano enlisted? Twitchell wrote that in that era, "at no time . . . did Mexico provide military protection to the people of the territory. . . . The inhabitants were compelled to protect themselves from the . . . incursions of the war-like [Indigenous people] as best they could. Poorly armed [they] were practically helpless. Murders were committed, ranchos burned, and stock driven away."⁷ Twitchell also wrote that under Mexico between 1821 and 1839, New Mexico was partially under "the rule" of a *comandante*, who was suffixed with one of the descriptive terms: *militar*, *principal*, or *de armas*. This officer reported to the comandante general of Chihuahua. "At times, the military and civil commander was the same individual."⁸ During the administration of Bartolomé Baca, for example, Baca was the *jefe político* and was in command of the company.

Although there were units of militia located in various communities throughout the province, such as Bernalillo and Socorro in the Rio Abajo and Santa Cruz and San Miguel in the north, these were mainly useful for protecting the distant and isolated villages. The main force of the militia was concentrated in the presidio or capital of the province in Santa Fe. Protection fell to the "veteran" company of Santa Fe, which "mustered only one hundred and twenty-one men . . . but the pay of the men was very irregularly provided for." Consequently, "the settlers, at their own cost, maintained some militia" during the Spanish and Mexican regimes, since neither administration was effective at protecting New Mexico from hostile Indigenous tribes. In 1824, when Baca was in command, the cost of the maintenance of the presidial company was $35,488.⁹ Twitchell noted that the general government in Mexico had enacted a law providing for three "permanent troops of cavalry and troops of active mounted militia, in all a force of five hundred men, at an annual cost of $439,110, but as late as 1832, there was only one company of regular troops stationed in New Mexico."¹⁰

From the time of his enlistment in 1823, Donaciano's education proved to be an advantage that set him apart from his peers in the presidio company. Higher-ranking officers, including and most important the governor or comandante militar, came to rely on the ambitious recruit to read, interpret, or analyze edicts or directives from superiors in Mexico. He also maintained financial accounts, kept roster files and logs of militia activities and campaigns, and generally maintained clerical records for the military unit or the governor's and comandante's offices. Not only did his education and clerical skills provide a distinct advantage for future promotions, but on more than one occasion, they enabled Donaciano to get out of trouble.

After he enlisted, the first challenge for Donaciano was to acclimate to a new regimen as a presidio soldier. The military role of the presidio was not only to protect the capital of Santa Fe, but also to play a major defensive role for the population of the entire province. The limited resources to compensate the officers and soldiers show that militia members, most of them with families to support, could not live on their military pay alone, and most had to farm or raise livestock to augment their salaries. This was difficult given that the soldiers were often on patrols to interdict or chase raiding parties, providing escorts to wagon trains, or carrying out similar missions in the distant regions of the province. Robert Torrez offered a glimpse of the Santa Fe presidio and its soldiers about the time that Donaciano enlisted and served. The salaries that the soldiers received constituted much of the hard currency in New Mexico. The *reglamentos* of 1729 had set the salaries and the number of men for each of the presidios in New Spain. The reglamentos were changed by 1796 to include 126 officers and men, and although the officers' salaries increased, the salaries of the enlisted men decreased from 400 pesos to 240 pesos a year.[11]

The 1796 reglamento was still in effect when Donaciano enlisted, and he earned 240 pesos a year.[12] In addition to the monthly salary of 20 pesos, married soldiers twice a month also received rations, including eight *almudes* (2.48 bushels) of corn; one almude (0.31 bushel) of beans; three *reciles* (0.30 peso) of soap; four reales (0.40 peso) of cigarettes; one real (0.10 peso) of salt; and one *calsado* (stocking) per month. A single man was paid less of each ration, but was allocated 1 peso (if needed) for housekeeping services.[13] The salary of 20 pesos per month, while not lucrative, was fair, especially when compared to American soldiers, who received five dollars a month.[14]

Until 1790, officers and soldiers of the presidio resided in scattered homes at or near the Santa Fe Plaza. In 1788, Governor Fernando de la Concha had implemented a plan that "called for construction of new buildings in which to consolidate housing for the *presidio* troops and their families outside the plaza area.... By November 1790, the project was nearly completed ... [and] ninety-eight of the planned 114 houses were soon inhabited by *presidio* soldiers."[15] While the massive building project enhanced the living accommodations and drastically altered the appearance of the north side of the Santa Fe Plaza, subsequent events indicate that the overall conditions facing officers and soldiers hardly changed and even worsened. The original *cuartel* construction project, according to the Plano de el Presidio de Santa Fe, 1791, created a rectangle with dwellings forming the north-south and east-west perimeter walls, which enclosed a central courtyard accessed by a south wing entrance. Each wing consisted of a series of twin dwellings that comprised the inner and outer sections of the walls. The large central courtyard was the earliest headquarter offices of the presidio. The only surviving section of the cuartel is the southeast section, which now is a part of the Palace of the Governors fronting the Santa Fe Plaza.[16]

In 1821, Mexico gained independence from Spain and the presidio's official name was changed to Compañía Veterana de Caballería, Presidio Nacional de Santa Fe, consisting of ninety-nine officers and men, five interpreters, and inválidos (retirees). However, "military records and musters show little indication of change[s] in structure, organization, or routine of the *presidio* during the months following independence.... Every indication is that the duties and command structure of the *presidio* changed little with the transfer of sovereignty from Spain to Mexico."[17]

The circumstances at the presidio and for its soldiers deteriorated, and the central government in Mexico, facing fiscal woes, was unable to sustain even the meager allocation of funds provided under Spain. Garrison payroll accounts for 1822, a year after Mexican independence, show that salaries for all officers and soldiers were budgeted at 26,400 pesos annually (2,200 pesos per month), but these meager salaries were seldom paid and thus failed to meet the needs of the troops. Late in 1823, the military commander sought assistance from Governor Bartolomé Baca for immediate pay for his troops. He then directed the matter to the diputación, but to no avail as it was suggested that the concern be redirected to government officials in Mexico. At the end of 1824, the situation had deteriorated even further, causing the diputación to consider a proposal to abolish the garrison, retaining only thirty men who would be assigned to different outposts in the territory for basic defense.[18]

In the 1830s, authorities regularly dealt with salary budget shortfalls that led to reductions in force. In 1835, Captain José Caballero reported a muster list of forty-one soldiers on leave without pay. The soldiers had been sent home to fend for themselves because the government could not fulfill its financial obligations. In 1837, Governor Albino Pérez was similarly frustrated. He reported that "the commissary was completely devoid of funds and goods and [he] had been unable to pay for the crops distributed to the troops.... Circumstances had worsened to the point where he had been forced to release all the troops except for two *cabos* [corporals] and seven soldiers, which were all he could support on his own account."[19] As the governor and military leaders were facing these exasperating conditions and financial obstacles just to maintain a skeletal military force to protect the province, the various Indigenous enemies were not wavering in their continued assault on the Mexican colonists. This period was one of the most devastating of the "Navajo wars" of the nineteenth century in New Mexico. Torrez wrote, "Relations with the hostile frontier tribes consumed New Mexico during the Mexican period, 1821 to 1846 ... with almost continuous warfare with the Navajo."[20]

From the time that he enlisted in 1823, Donaciano adapted to the regimented lifestyle of the military, even if it was more in the manner of a citizen-soldier. Donaciano continued to reside in his parents' house on Alto Street after his father, Juan Cristóbal, died on 21 September 1832 and his mother, Antonia Andrea Martínez, died on 24 January 1839. In his will dated 31 May 1832, Juan Cristóbal left the house, properties, and furnishings to his wife, Antonia Andrea. In her will dated 27 May 1834, Antonia Andrea decreed, "The furnishings of the house, both within and without, be divided among my children equally so that they may enjoy it with the blessings of God."[21] She noted in the will that her daughters Ana María, Paula, and Juana María had predeceased her, and that Juana's only heir, her son Agapito, would share in the house. Another daughter, María Ygnes, would not share in the main house since she had been given her own house by her father, Juan Cristóbal. In his first will, prepared in either 1842 or 1843, Donaciano stated that he had acquired by inheritance from his parents and also purchased from his brothers Gregorio and Juan, niece Ana María, and nephew Agapito portions of the house and property originally belonging to his parents. Donaciano added rooms and other improvements to the house and property to accommodate his large family, and they resided there until 1855 when they moved to Pecos. In 1856, he sold the house and property to Vicente García.[22]

Garrison duty in the Santa Fe presidio consisted of a standard daily routine, including roll call in formation followed by the reading of orders for the day, special orders, drills, and some physical training and other training sessions. Inspections and the review of troops were scheduled as necessary. Variations of the daily routine occurred on special fiesta days or when dignitaries or higher-ranking Mexican officers visited.[23]

The formal military training Donaciano received was limited to standard military operating procedures, including drills, use and care of weapons, tactical deployments, horsemanship, and the care of horses taught by more experienced noncommissioned officers (sergeants and below). Much of the training occurred in the form of on-the-job experience, where soldiers learned by emulating veterans or carrying out the directives of noncommissioned officers. Typical

FIGURE 2. Donaciano Vigil residence in Santa Fe (ca. 1890). Donaciano's childhood home was built by his father, Juan Cristóbal Vigil, in the early 1800s. Acquired by inheritance from his parents and through purchase from his siblings, it remained his home until he moved to Pecos in 1855. The house went through several major renovations in the 1940s and 1970s. In 2020 it was renovated by Lightfoot, Inc., and won the Grand Hacienda Prize during the Santa Fe Parade of Homes. It was listed in the New Mexico Register of Cultural Properties in 1969 and in the National Register of Historic Homes in 1972. It is a prominent stop on the Historic Santa Fe Foundation tours of Santa Fe. Source: Palace of the Governors Photo Archive, NMHM/DCA, negative no. 035854.

training sessions involved the soldiers sitting in groups, listening to readings of laws or regulations, followed or accompanied by noncommissioned officers providing instruction on military organization and procedures, self-defense, and small- or large-unit tactics.[24] In addition, garrison soldiers had regular duties on rotation, such as guarding and caring for the *caballada* (horse herd); guarding the commissary, jailhouse, and weapons arsenal; mail service; and security detail for the governor, comandante, and senior officers.[25]

Notwithstanding the general lack of training of the soldiers, there were exceptions, and a few men were fortunate to acquire advanced training as part of their military service. Román Martínez, a drummer, trained for his position under the drummer at the presidio of Chihuahua, Mexico. In 1841, Governor Manuel Armijo, noting the lack of preparation of his troops, received permission to send eight of the most promising young men to military colleges in Mexico. Donaciano's eldest son, Antonio Basilio, was one of those eight cadets. In March 1843, Cadet Gáspar Ortíz and Sergeant Jesús María Silva attended the Colegio Militar de Méjico, and Teniente Juan Ortíz, Sergeants José Tenorio and Román Sena, and Cadet Jesús Jaramillo attended the Escuela Normal de Méjico. In 1844, two cadets from each garrison headed to the Academia Militar de Chihuahua: Jesús María Sena and Julian Sánchez from Santa Fe, Ignacio Sena and Andrés Tapia from San Miguel del Bado, and Juan José Silva and José Rafaél Chacón from Taos.[26] Antonio Basilio Vigil attended the military school in Mexico City and was commissioned as a second lieutenant in the Mexican army at fourteen years of age. When hostilities erupted against the United States, he was part of General Mariano Arista's army and participated as a Mexican soldier in the Battle of Palo Alto in 1846. To help pay his expenses at military school, Donaciano had signed a voucher in 1842 allowing for a deduction from his military pay to defray Antonio's expenses. Surely when these young men returned to their respective garrisons in New Mexico, they were able to impart to their peers some of their training. Still, this was certainly not enough to prepare the regular soldiers for combat against the guerrilla-type warfare of the Natives or even conventional warfare, such as with the American army.

Soldiers enlisted for a term of ten years, although there does not appear to have been fixed periods of overall service in the militia. Often, those who chose to leave the service could do so at the completion of their initial or subsequent enlistment term. The companies had a fixed allocation of funds, and roster sizes were set to conform to the allocations, so it appears that an initial enlistment required that there be an existent vacancy in the company, and new enlistees had to compete for the vacant slot. Therefore, garrison troop levels and financial resources played a role in the company rosters.

Despite the persistent problems with compensation, the lack of training, and the concomitant dangers of serving in campaigns against Natives, there was no shortage of volunteers to enlist. The extreme poverty of most *vecinos* in New Mexico and the dearth of jobs available made the militia attractive since soldiers were provided a monthly salary along with food, clothing, and other supplies, even though these were meager and unreliable. Military life was no more dangerous than the risks taken by the stockmen and farmers living unprotected within the perimeters of smaller communities. Soldiers generally survived their ten-year service, and twenty and thirty years of service were not unusual. Many soldiers continued to serve until old age. Tomás Jasco, for example, claimed benefits for fifty years of service.[27] As Tyler noted about Donaciano, "It was hard to get one's foot in the door without leadership and literacy qualifications, but an enterprising soldier like Donaciano Vigil could serve as a soldier and volunteer his services as '*compania escribiente*.'"[28]

Naturally, because the monthly stipend and rations were not sufficient to support the soldiers and their dependents, they had to augment their compensation by planting domestic gardens that could thrive in the high elevation of Santa Fe (7,199 feet) with its short growing season. They kept domesticated animals for food supplies and work animals to haul an assortment of goods for sale or for use on various jobs. They performed work for others for money or barter. There is evidence at the Alto Street home of Donaciano that early owners planted large gardens and several fruit trees since the Santa Fe River flowed in a valley just north and below the residence. The records show that Donaciano and his father planted a large huerta on land fed by an irrigation ditch fed by the river. It was also customary for soldiers to work either full- or part-time jobs as clerks, wood haulers, day laborers, freighters, or storekeepers. Donaciano applied for and received a dram shop license that authorized him to sell liquor, perhaps as part of a neighborhood grocery store operated from his home. Donaciano had worked as a clerk in a general store in Santa Fe, and it is logical that he may have opened his own neighborhood shop in addition to his military duties.[29]

Noncommissioned officers were the backbone of the presidio company. Generally, the sergeants were the most experienced and longest-serving of the soldiers, which explains why the promotion to sergeant took at least a decade to achieve. In 1821, of the fifteen men who occupied positions of sergeant and *cabo*, three had served more than forty years, and eight had served more than thirty years in the militia. Sergeant Ramón Sánchez, seventy-six years of age; Cabo José Armijo, eighty-three years of age; and Sergeant José Alarid, fifty-nine years of age, each had forty years of experience. This means that all of these men probably served with Juan Cristóbal Vigil (Donaciano's father) when he was captain of the Santa Fe garrison in the 1790s.[30] When a militia soldier retired, voluntarily or not, after completing twenty years of service, he was referred to as "inválido," which literally meant that he was retired due to disability. A soldier on active duty was referred to as *habilitado*, or qualified for regular duty.

Profiles of individual soldiers in the militia are available owing to the permanent enlistment record requirements, which mandated a description of each enlistee's religion (usually Catholic), marital status, hair color, skin features, nasal form, scars, and beard.[31] In 1845 the tallest soldier was recorded as five feet eight inches, and the shortest was five feet one inch with the average height between five feet five and five feet six. By comparison, Donaciano was a giant, reported to be six feet four inches. In terms of literacy, five of the ten sergeants, including Donaciano, could read and write, while five could not. Of the sixty-two noncommissioned officers and soldiers of the Santa Fe garrison, thirty-two were married, three were widowed, and twenty-seven were single. Sixteen soldiers listed minor children or a mother they supported.[32] Donaciano was single when he enlisted in 1823.

Donaciano's baptism into combat came immediately after his enlistment and under perhaps the most capable military commander of that era, Captain José Antonio Viscarra. During that period, Navajo warfare in the form of surprise attacks and raids on Spanish and Pueblo villages was commonplace. It should be noted that the atrocities were not one-sided. Mexican soldiers were equally violent in their attacks on the Natives, killing entire bands and capturing children and women to be enslaved. On one occasion in the 1820s, a band of Navajos assembled at the Pueblo village of Cochiti on the invitation of Mexican authorities to conduct peace negotiations. Shortly after their arrival at the camp, the Mexicans, infuriated by the recent Navajo depredations, fell upon the outnumbered visitors and killed them all.[33]

The Navajo raids followed a familiar pattern. During the spring, the Navajos were generally peaceful, sowing their crops while disposing of or exchanging the booty they had stolen from the Mexicans and Pueblos during the winter. Then in the fall, following the harvesting of crops, they would resume their pillaging raids until the next spring. During 1823 Colonel Viscarra led a punitive expedition against the Navajos during the months of June–August with Donaciano participating as a recent recruit. This campaign resulted in the deaths of fifty Navajo warriors and the capture of thirty-six prisoners.[34] Twitchell wrote, "Of the Spanish and Mexican commanders in New Mexico at that time, Colonel Viscarra seems to have been the most successful in his efforts to punish and pacify them."[35]

The discussion of Donaciano's participation in routine campaigns against the Navajos might seem callous to contemporary readers. To New Mexicans, these campaigns were necessary, but the victims of these attacks suffered atrocities. On 18 June 1846, Donaciano wrote about a tragedy that was playing out: "I have heard reports of the number of Mexican captives and especially ... of young women who serve the ... pleasures of the ... Indians [and] of the brutal treatment they receive."[36] It is not surprising that Donaciano was observing the conflict through the lens of a Mexican man and not from the wider cultural perspective of how young Indigenous women and boys were suffering similar treatment at the hands of soldiers like him and his peers. History is written not in the present but in the future of the time when events occurred. James Brooks wrote about that period with the hindsight of a modern historian. In his widely acclaimed book, Brooks accurately described the "intellectual exchange network that is treated as a borderland's political cultural economy.... Native Americans and New Mexicans, despite their cultural differences, shared an understanding of the distribution and production of wealth as conditioned by social relations of power."[37] What has been regarded by many writers as a form of slavery was described by Brooks as a complicated social and economic system in which vulnerable segments of diverse populations of Hispanic New Mexicans and Indigenous groups, such as Navajos, Utes, Apaches, and Comanches, mutually engaged in a form of barter economy where people were treated as commodities, like buffalo fur, deerskins, other pelts, and livestock. In the scheme of the borderland economy, raids by one perpetrator against another and in reverse occurred because the vulnerable people in all groups were seen as targets to be captured for sale, exchange, ransom, or reward. The outcome of the exchange became more complicated as captured victims were forcibly integrated into their new social milieu. Captives evolved into kin as cousins of the group they came from and of the group they now belonged to. For example, in New Mexico, Indigenous criados in a Mexican household over time were integrated into the host society, where they were called *genízaros*. In Donaciano's time, this was not considered slavery because slavery was illegal under Spanish and Mexican law, but it must have seemed like slavery to the people, whether Mexican or Native, who were carried by their captors away from their family to a new life in a strange new world. It was a tragedy.

In mid-1830, Donaciano was appointed *escribiente* (company clerk), starting at a salary of fourteen pesos per month and serving under the comandante militar in the Santa Fe garrison.³⁸ Donaciano's superiors valued his ability to read and write. Most historians concur that the company records for his period of service between 1823 and 1840 are among the best organized and chronicled.³⁹

In 1828, Colonel Viscarra had returned to New Mexico and again briefly served as comandante principal. In 1829, he led a detachment of Mexican troops escorting a caravan of wagons returning from New Mexico to Missouri on the Santa Fe Trail (see map 1). A group of wagon masters had appealed to the American and Mexican governments to provide such military escorts after a series of attacks by Natives on the caravans on the trail. In 1829, the Americans dispatched Major Bennet Riley and an infantry battalion to protect the caravans on the American side of the border. Major Riley's force, on foot, escorted the caravans in the spring and then remained near the Arkansas River awaiting the return of the caravans in the fall. In the meantime, mounted Natives constantly harassed the horseless troops. That fall, Colonel Viscarra led the Mexican detachment escorting the returning caravans east.

When Viscarra's caravan met up with the American troops at a place on the Arkansas River known as Chouteau Island (near the present town of Hartland in Kearny County, Kansas), Captain Clifton Wharton invited Viscarra and his officers Captains Obrazo and Lobato to dine at his tent. Twitchell noted that this was "in all probability the first time the Mexican officers, on duty, and in command of Mexican troops ever partook, on American soil, of the hospitality of an American officer."⁴⁰ Lieutenant Philip St. George Cooke (later a general in the US Army) recorded an account of the dinner in his journal.⁴¹ During the dinner, the guests "were treated to a feast of bread, buffalo meat ... and as an extraordinary rarity some salt pork ... and crowning all were several large raw onions of the El Paso variety. ... Accompanying this delicious repast and served in a tin cup was a liberal allowance of whiskey which like the salt pork had been reserved for an unusual occasion."⁴² According to Twitchell, there assembled the most peculiar assortment of "men and animals ... creoles, polished gentlemen ... in Spanish costume; grave Spaniards, exiled from Mexico ... with property in stock and coin ... in a company of Mexican regulars ... tribes of Indians ... [and] the American command. ... Four or five languages [were] spoken ... and the *caballada* of more than two thousand horses, mules and burros [produced] an incessant braying."⁴³

Donaciano was in the group of Mexican soldiers led by Viscarra on this occasion, and he later recorded a commentary in a general summary of his military career. Donaciano wrote in the third person, "Concurrió a la expedición que escoló una carabana de comerciantes de los Estados Unidos del Norte America hacia el Rio Arkansas a las órdenes del Capitán y Comandante, José Antonio Viscarra, regresando en 6 Noviembre 1829."⁴⁴ Surely the occurrences and circumstances surrounding this unique event were unprecedented in the history of the Southwest.

The 1830s was a transitional period in the career of Donaciano Vigil. As he entered the second decade of his military career, promotions came quickly as did his responsibilities in the presidial company. His close association with political leaders of the territory seamlessly transitioned him to greater involvement in public and political affairs. In December 1832, after serving nine years and eight months as a *soldado* (regular soldier), Donaciano was finally promoted to sergeant.⁴⁵ The promotion filled a vacancy in a newly created company of militia in San Miguel del Bado. The commander of that company was Captain José Miguel Zuloaga. In addition to his duties as sergeant, Donaciano also served as company clerk, keeping personnel and other records and financial accounts for the company.⁴⁶ Of course, his assignment to San Miguel meant that he would be away from his family in Santa Fe. Donaciano served a total of seven years, three months, and three days in the new position. It was perhaps during that seven-year period that his eldest son, Antonio Basilio, born on 13 June 1827, met his future wife, María de la Luz Rowland, the daughter of longtime merchant Thomas Rowland (aka Tomás Rolenes) in San Miguel del Bado.⁴⁷ Antonio Basilio was about thirteen years old at the end of his father's service at San Miguel and might have stayed with his father during part of his assignment there.

In 1834, Sergeant Vigil participated in another military campaign against the Navajos, this time led by Captain and Comandante Principal Blas de Hinojos. These operations were always the most dangerous because the Mexicans were carrying the war to the very doorstep of the Navajos. Traveling on unfamiliar trails with canyons and hills that provided easy cover for Indigenous people, the Mexicans proceeded with a minimal knowledge of the terrain. The Natives, on the other hand, were familiar with their own land and could plan their campaigns for maximum advantage. One tactic was to stage an ambush against the unsuspecting Mexican troops as they proceeded through the gorges or canyons.⁴⁸ Lasting approximately a month from 13 October to 17 November 1834, the Hinojos campaign ended with the deaths of sixteen Navajos and three enemy captives.⁴⁹ Hinojos was killed by the Navajos in a carefully orchestrated ambush.⁵⁰

Just before or in preparation for the Hinojos campaign, Donaciano was involved in an incident mocked by Americans, including Josiah Gregg, who first reported on it. As Gregg described it, Captain Hinojos had commanded an orderly, Sergeant Vigil, to fill a powder flask from an unbroached keg of twenty-five pounds of gunpowder. The sergeant bored a hole with a gimlet, but found the hole to be too small. He looked around for a tool to enlarge the hole and spied an iron poker near the fireplace. Obviously inexperienced in dealing with gunpowder in bulk form, Donaciano unthinkingly warmed the poker and tried to use it to widen the hole. The resultant explosion blew out the roof and the upper part of the building, tearing everything to pieces. Donaciano and the captain, who witnessed the disastrous blunder, although bruised and scorched, were more frightened than hurt. The "ingenious sergeant," reported Gregg, was "later secretary of the territory."[51] This incident was widely discussed and seen as humorous among those in the territory, and the Americans saw it as an example of the ineptness of the Mexican people. In reality, it reflected the ignorance, inexperience, and lack of training of the Mexican soldiers regarding the handling of dangerous explosive materials.

MEXICAN CENTRALIZATION OF POWER: PRELUDE TO INSURRECTION

In 1836, a general reorganization of the government in Mexico led to a change in the governorship of New Mexico implemented by Antonio López de Santa Anna. He instituted a centralized form of government that replaced the former largely autonomous states of Mexico (very similar to American states) with new departments that were headed by a governor appointed by the Mexican president and directly responsible to him. Desperately in need of cash, Santa Anna required his governors to impose new taxes and turn the revenues over to him. Santa Anna's reforms met with uprisings in Zacatecas, Texas, and California. The reforms created the Department of New Mexico with the comandante principal, Colonel Albino Pérez, a distinguished career army officer from Mexico, appointed as governor. Governor Pérez was responsible for implementing Santa Anna's administrative and fiscal reforms in New Mexico.

Pérez's immediate problem, however, was the continuing Navajo raids in the territory. He quickly organized a militia force, and Donaciano, as second sergeant, occupied his highest level of command in this successful operation under Pérez. The Mexican force encountered a raiding party of seventeen Navajos. Seven Navajos were killed, an additional seven prisoners were taken, and a sizable herd of 6,000 sheep (*ganado*) were seized in the operation, which took place between December 1836 and January 1837.[52]

Around this time, an incident occurred between Donaciano and a superior officer, Esquipula Caballero, which resulted in charges of insubordination and the incarceration of Donaciano. Sergeant Vigil, it should be noted, had experienced prior differences with Caballero, a haughty career soldier from Mexico, who regarded himself as superior to the militia soldiers in New Mexico. Sometime in 1835, Second Lieutenant Caballero had encountered Donaciano at a social function. Their words were heated, and Caballero filed charges of insubordination against Donaciano, but at the 2 January 1836 trial, Sergeant Vigil was exonerated.

Later in 1836, Donaciano, along with other militia soldiers, was furloughed from his military duties due to the government's inability to pay wages, so the soldiers had to fend for themselves. Donaciano had obtained employment as a clerk in the grocery, dry goods, and liquor store of Tomás Valencia. One day, Caballero, who was serving as the commandant of all military forces in the department, entered the store and insisted that Donaciano issue a bottle of aguardiente (a form of rum) on credit. Donaciano refused, saying that his explicit instructions from Valencia were that all sales were cash, and no form of credit would be accepted. Caballero became abusive, forcing Donaciano to remove the commandant bodily from the store. During the scuffle, Caballero's wrist was bruised. Caballero, exercising his authority as the military commander, arrested Donaciano and placed him in the guardhouse jail in the Palace of the Governors.[53]

REBELLION IN RIO ARRIBA

Albino Pérez's administration was hampered from the start in 1836. He was seen as an outsider imposed on New Mexicans by the new president of Mexico, Santa Anna. Pérez struggled to maintain an active militia, even exhausting his personal financial resources, and was forced to furlough, at least temporarily, the remaining militia soldiers.

In 1837, the government of Mexico imposed a national tax to be collected at the departmental level, which placed an already unpopular Governor Pérez in the position of having to collect an unpopular tax. Rumors spread of new taxes on poultry and even on men for sleeping with their own wives.[54] Pérez was seen as the enforcer of Santa Anna's unpopular departmental reforms and new taxes, even if none had yet been introduced.

In December 1836, Pérez had dissolved the ayuntamiento (council) of Santa Cruz de la Cañada. Some saw this as a step in implementing the departmental plan, which also called for abolishment of the legislature. In 1837, the alcalde of Santa Cruz, Juan José Esquibel, disobeyed the governor on several issues. The unrest grew into a minor insurrection in June 1837 when the alcalde was arrested and imprisoned by a local prefect of the northern district, Ramón Abreu, who acted under the orders and authority of the governor. Alcalde Esquibel was then released by a mob, and he proceeded to form a new governing council of twelve members and called the insurgent body a *cantón*, the slang word for home or region. The rebels were composed primarily of Hispanic vecinos (residents) and Pueblos of the Santa Cruz region, commonly referred to as Río Arriba (the northern Rio Grande region). It is apparent that the rebels chose the word "cantón" to indicate a political connection to a regional movement involving a group beyond the towns of Santa Cruz and Taos, as well as a broader group of Hispanics and Pueblos. The rebels issued a proclamation opposing the departmental reforms and new taxes.[55]

Pérez thus had an armed rebellion on his hands, but no military troops to combat it. He hastily mobilized a small force of officers and soldiers still in the ranks, along with a few Pueblo volunteers from Sandia, Cochiti, and Santo Domingo. Donaciano was still in jail from the Caballero incident, and the governor released him. Donaciano then joined the governor's force of about 200 volunteers and irregulars. On 7 August 1837, Pérez and his troops, led by a few presidial officers, marched north toward Santa Cruz to confront the rebels. But he never reached Santa Cruz. At La Mesilla near San Ildefonso Pueblo, the governor and his small force encountered four bands of rebels numbering between 1,500 and 2,000 men. One of these immediately attacked Pérez's group as he tried to begin negotiations, creating a wild, chaotic scene. The Pueblos, two militia officers, ten soldiers, and two citizens deserted Pérez's force and joined the rebels, taking one of the cannons with them. Francisco Sarracino, ahead of the governor's troops, retreated to the remaining cannon, which Sergeant Vigil had positioned on top of a hill. This is the last mention of Donaciano in the report of the initial battle. Apparently having positioned the cannon atop the hill, as would be logical, Donaciano had left his friend Sarracino in charge. As a sergeant, Donaciano may have left to rally the other forces amid the chaos.

Why Donaciano did not initiate artillery fire immediately, given that the cannon was their strongest weapon since they were outnumbered, is unknown. The situation deteriorated rapidly. Pérez yelled at Sarracino, "Don't abandon the cannon." Sarracino replied that he "would sooner abandon my life than the cannon."[56] However, the disorder was now so great that no one loaded or fired the cannon. Pérez and a few of his men took positions near the cannon, firing their muskets, but they soon were overrun, and the rebels killed six men guarding the cannon. At that point, Pérez and a small escort of troops retreated to Santa Fe to plan his escape to the Rio Abajo. A contingent of men remained at the scene of the battle to cover the governor's retreat. The soldiers Alférez Ramón Baca, Sergeant Donaciano Vigil, Corporal Tomás Martínez, Manuel Maldonado, José Sena, Nepomoceno Jiménez, Juan Sandoval, and the wounded Francisco Sarracino and the civilians Agustín Durán, Felipe Sena, and Juan Bustamante were soon overrun by the rebels. The prisoners were disarmed, stripped of clothing and property, manacled with rawhide, marched on foot to the Santa Cruz prison, and held for the next six days.[57] Sergeant Vigil was the only captive not manacled and held in jail because the rebels had other plans for him. Antonio Abad Montoya recruited Donaciano to act as the secretary and scribe for the cantón rebels. Seeing little choice, he agreed to do so.

Pérez had retreated to Santa Fe and arranged for an escape to the Rio Abajo. However, a group of rebel sympathizers from Santo Domingo Pueblo captured him and a small group of his supporters that evening. Pérez was decapitated, and a number of his supporters, including Santiago, Mariano, and Román Abreu, were also killed. The insurrectionists then set up camp in Santa Fe near the Rosario Cemetery, where they organized a provisional government with José Gonzales from Taos as governor.[58] One mystery that immediately surfaced after the rebel victory was why the rebels had recruited Donaciano as their secretary. The illiterate José Gonzales, a Mexican *cibolero* (buffalo hunter), certainly needed a capable secretary and advisor. He also knew of Donaciano's record in the militia. Therefore, he had ordered Donaciano released to serve as secretary of the rebel government.

Donaciano had to consider the possibility that by associating with Gonzales, he would be implicated in participating or collaborating in the rebellion against Governor Pérez and the legitimate New Mexico government. Since Governor

Pérez had been killed, he could not personally attest to the fact that he had ordered Sergeant Vigil to accompany his forces to confront the rebels at La Mesilla. Donaciano had remained with the government forces throughout the battle and with Sena and a few other men to cover the retreat of Governor Pérez and his party. Accordingly, Donaciano later secured sworn written statements from witnesses (both fellow soldiers and rebels) to the effect that he had comported himself honorably as a soldier for the government in the engagement against the rebel forces.[59]

The rebellion of 1837 presented a very real personal and ideological dilemma for Donaciano. Phillip Gonzales posited the interesting concept of *hombre de bien* (figuratively meaning a man who seeks good). The concept was somewhat associated with New Mexico priests who, as politicians, advocated for the public good, but it was not limited to priests. Some laypeople were considered hombres de bien. It is apparent that Donaciano considered himself and was considered by others as such, which he later described in a letter to the newspaper *El Republicano*.[60] Such men were rational and moderate in orientation. While harboring an understanding of the underlying populist cause of the rebellion, hombres de bien were opposed to the violation of the rule of law and the ruthless violence perpetrated by the rebels. Thus, Donaciano's role as secretary to the rebels was to encourage them to follow a legal path to the resolution of their grievances.

Governor José Gonzales hoped to lead a moderate ad hoc government that would advocate for the rebels' objectives. Although serving under duress, Donaciano advised Gonzales to follow a temperate approach. Seeking to gain legitimacy for his rebel government, the governor called for a *junta popular* (popular assembly), invited moderates Manuel Armijo and Padre Antonio José Martínez to participate in his government, and proposed sending representatives to Mexico to convey the rebels' grievances and gain legitimization of his government. Clearly, any representatives sent to Mexico would have found it difficult to convince a centralist Mexican leadership that a faction (cantón) that had rebelled and murdered the government-sponsored governor and other officials was serious about pledging allegiance to the central government. The blood on his hands made Gonzales's appeal impossible. The deputies were never sent to Mexico.[61]

Meanwhile in the Rio Abajo (Bernalillo and Valencia Counties in the lower Rio Grande region), a group of prominent citizens under the leadership of Tomé priest Ignacio de Madariaga convened and drew up a pronouncement known as the Plan de Tomé on 8 September 1837. They declared their opposition to and "fear of the anarchy and abuse of property threatened by the *cantón* of La Cañada."[62] Manuel Armijo, perhaps inspired by the Plan de Tomé, now made an about-face and condemned the insurrection for bringing "anarchy and destruction" to the country in place of the peace and security that had existed before. The organizers of the Plan de Tomé recruited a force of some 400 men and placed them under the leadership of Armijo as commander and Mariano Chávez as second-in-command. Back in Santa Fe, Captain José Caballero and the former militia members had organized themselves into a volunteer company of 200 men to oppose the rebels and protect the capital. When Caballero received word of the developments in the Rio Abajo, he marched south with his force and joined Armijo's camp.[63] In addition, the supreme government in Mexico dispatched a contingent of 400 troops from Chihuahua and Zacatecas to assist in quelling the rebellion. Manuel Armijo, now in command of a force of over 1,000 men, returned to Santa Fe to prepare to engage the rebels.[64]

In September 1837, Governor José Gonzales, having fallen out with his rebel army leaders, returned to Santa Fe, and when informed of the Plan de Tomé, he embraced and signed the plan. On 14 September, Armijo, having returned to Santa Fe with his army, met with his officers and offered to step down as commander if anyone preferred another commander or a different plan of action. He offered the command to Juan Estevan Pino, who declined. Armijo began preparations for the encounter by soliciting funds to support the troops, arranging to train the volunteers, mounting the artillery, repairing arms, and securing ammunition. He then had his officers seize three privately owned large wagons to carry the provisions and supplies for the armed force.[65]

With Gonzales in jail in Santa Fe, the rebel army was now under the command of Pablo Montoya, the leader of the Taos faction of the cantón. A former alcalde of Taos and a colonel of the Taos militia, Montoya had a reputation as a troublemaker. Donaciano later called him a "mischievous fool" and a "brigand." While Armijo's troops were undergoing preparations, reports reached Santa Fe that the rebel army, numbering about 3,000, was approaching the city and taking favorable positions. Armijo, obviously a better diplomat than a combat commander, initiated correspondence with Montoya because, as he wrote in his report to Mexico later, "he meant to avoid battle and bloodshed, if possible, for he knew that most of the rebels had joined the force out of ignorance and fear."[66] Armijo's strategy worked, and he persuaded Montoya to come to Santa Fe for negotiations. Montoya and Armijo drafted an agreement whereby the

FIGURE 3. Governor Manuel Armijo (ca. 1840, artist unknown). Armijo served as governor in 1827–1829 and after the Santa Cruz rebellion (1837–1844). He also was governor in 1846 on the eve of the American occupation of New Mexico, when he fled to Mexico. Source: ZIM, UNM, CSWR PICT COLLS 000-742-0001.

rebels would dissolve the cantón and recognize Armijo as the political and military head pending approval from Mexico. The rebels agreed to Armijo's terms, including the surrender of four of the instigators of the initial rebellion, who would be indicted. In accordance with the agreement, the four leaders turned over to Armijo—Juan (El Chopón) Vigil, Juan José Esquibel, and the brothers Desiderio and Antonio Abad Montoya—were housed in the Santa Fe jail.[67]

Various explanations were later offered as to why Pablo Montoya and the other rebel leaders so readily capitulated to Armijo's terms. It has been suggested that they lacked leadership, arms, ammunition, discipline, and organization. However, none of those reasons deterred them from their original actions. It is more likely that Armijo's persuasive arguments and threats that his troops would prevail in a battle, along with the fact that he had previously been their trusted ally, convinced them to disband under his terms. The insurrection was over, at least temporarily. Armijo made his reports to Mexico and was appointed governor, probably because he was the most logical candidate at that time.

Armijo issued a series of circulars on 24 September directed to all alcaldes, threatening to do whatever was necessary to maintain order and instructing them to report any suspicious activity. Indeed, on 18 October, a messenger from the alcalde of Santa Cruz reported news of rebel factions whipping up unrest near Las Truchas. A day later, a report from the alcalde of La Cañada stated that the same rebels were planning an attack on Santa Fe from two different directions. It was suspected that the four rebel leaders in the Santa Fe jail had been inciting the rebels. Armijo, who had returned home to Albuquerque and left Caballero in charge in Santa Fe, sent orders to execute the four prisoners by decapitation.[68] However, Caballero and other officers in Santa Fe expressed doubts about the executions and delayed their implementation. Meanwhile, Armijo, fearing a resurrection of rebel activity, wrote to Mexico requesting federal troops in the event of a new rebellion. General José Calvo replied on 15 November that he had José Gonzales dispatch a squadron of Vera Cruz dragoons from Zacatecas under Captain Tomás Zuloaga and another contingent of troops under Colonel Cayetano Justiniani. Although both José Calvo and Mariano Arista promised they would join their troops, neither actually did. The two detachments under Zuloaga and Justiniani merged in El Paso and proceeded north, arriving in Santa Fe in January 1838. The 167 well-trained and -equipped Mexican troops did not have to wait long for action. On 19 January, Antonio (El Coyote) Vigil, a rebel leader, issued a call for rebels from various northern villages to meet for possible action to free the four prisoners in the Santa Fe jail. On 22 January, Juez, a Cochiti Pueblo, sent Armijo a warning about a possible alliance between Cochitis and the rebels under Antonio Vigil. Governor Armijo sent a reply warning the rebels to turn over José Gonzales (who had been released from jail) and Antonio Vigil within twenty-four hours or the prisoners would be executed. On 24 January 1838, the prisoners Juan (El Chopón) Vigil, Juan José Esquibel, and the brothers Desiderio and Antonio Abad Montoya, were decapitated per Armijo's orders.[69]

On 27 January, Armijo marched with a force of 582 men, including the Vera Cruz dragoons, under the command of Colonel Justiniani. Justiniani, an energetic and skillful leader, courteously offered to cede his command to Armijo, even though he was by rank superior to the governor. With Armijo as commander, the Mexican troops marched toward Santa Cruz de la Cañada to engage the rebel forces. At the *puerto* (pass) of Pojoaque, seventeen miles north of Santa Fe, 1,300 rebels had positioned themselves at the outpost to defend against Armijo's forces. As his troops faced off with the rebels, Armijo was perturbed and on the verge of retreating when Captain Pedro Muñoz of the Vera Cruz dragoons cried out, "What's to be done, General Armijo? If your Excellency will permit me, I will oust that rabble in an instant with my little company alone." Armijo consented, and the captain and his troops rushed on the insurgents, who yielded and fled precipitously.[70] Twenty rebels were killed, eight were captured, and many more were wounded. Among the rebels retreating, the deposed Governor José Gonzales was caught and shot instantly without a trial.[71]

The battle at Pojoaque ended the rebellion, and the toll was heaviest on the rebels, who lost their lives and the cause for which they fought. After this last battle, some of the rebels were granted amnesty.[72] Pablo Montoya, for example, returned to his home in Taos, only to reemerge as a leader of another insurrection, this one against the American government, ten years later. Armijo took possession of the Palace of the Governors and pronounced himself governor and comandante general. He then reported to President Santa Anna, obviously extolling his role in the restoration of Mexican control and seeking and receiving Santa Anna's blessing to retain the governorship, which he did until 1846 and the American occupation. Governor Armijo then sent for Donaciano, appointed him as his military secretary, and told him to "let Caballero and all his enemies do their best that he [Armijo] would stand by him."[73]

ELITE GROUP INVOLVEMENT IN THE INSURRECTION OF 1837

Historian Andrés Reséndez confirmed that the revolt of 1837 in New Mexico began as an effort to dislodge the centralism mandated by the Santa Anna government in Mexico. The appointment of Albino Pérez was part of that centralization since he was the first non–New Mexican appointed as governor in a decade. Moreover, Pérez came to the office with distinct orders to implement greater central control and new taxes. Pérez complied by altering the legislative role of the assembly and making it more of an advisory body to the governor. He also ordered prefects to report directly to him and even downsized the local militia, although this was more a result of the lack of finances than a direct intent. The incident that triggered the revolt was his intervention, through the prefect Abreu, to arrest the local alcalde. The revolt led to the death of Pérez, but did not end centralism. Instead, Reséndez argued, the rebellion solidified three main groups that already had existed but that became more prominent in New Mexico politics in the next decade. The ricos were landed elites whose control over the land produced wealth from farming and ranching and usually spilled over into commerce and trade. The Catholic clergy had influence over the spiritual life of their congregations, which empowered the clergy to participate extensively in governmental and political affairs. The *letrados*, or literate political and governmental leaders, such as Armijo and Donaciano, had the ability to interpret and speak for the masses, which yielded a unique power to influence politics. According to Reséndez, these three groups were instrumental in determining political outcomes in the next decade over such issues as loyalty to or separation from Mexico; republican versus centralized control; and ultimately the future of New Mexico as a colony of Mexico, an independent entity, or a territory of the United States.[74]

In 1838, with Manuel Armijo in the governorship of New Mexico, Donaciano was restored to good standing in the Santa Fe presidio and returned to his roles as sergeant and company clerk. The Navajos resumed their raiding on the isolated northern villages. Governor Armijo, determined to avoid Pérez's failings, ordered a retaliatory expedition against the Navajos for a recent raid. Donaciano once again found himself as second sergeant in command of the militia force that engaged the Navajos in their own territory, killing two and capturing sixteen prisoners. Equally important, the Mexican forces seized 226 horses, 2,000 head of sheep, 160 animal hides, and 6 serapes, among other valuable booty. The soldiers destroyed over 1,200 corn stalks.[75] The success of this operation surely helped discourage incursions by the Navajos and restored some confidence in the soldiers and villagers about the ability of their militia to successfully engage the Navajo raiders, recover lost property, and deter future attacks.

On 4 April 1840, perhaps due to Donaciano's role in the 1838 Navajo operation, Governor Armijo recommended Sergeant Vigil for a promotion to alférez (second lieutenant). This promotion came at the expense of Donaciano's archenemy, Esquipula Caballero, who had been suspended, vacating his position as second lieutenant.[76] This promotion ended his tenure as a sergeant in the company of San Miguel de Bado; he had served from 31 December 1832 to 3 April 1840. This new assignment required Donaciano's relocation to Taos, as the vacancy he filled was in the Taos company.[77]

TEXAS DESIGNS ON NEW MEXICO

Just sixteen months later, on 17 August 1841, Second Lieutenant Donaciano Vigil was promoted to first lieutenant of the company at San Miguel del Bado.

This served to fill a vacancy created by the promotion of José Silva from first lieutenant to captain of the company. A copy of Lieutenant Donaciano Vigil's certificate of promotion, signed by Mexican president Anastasio Bustamante, is in Donaciano's military record in the Mexican Archives of New Mexico, a copy of which is in the Donaciano Vigil Collection.[78]

Donaciano's assignment to San Miguel was fortuitous, for it placed him in the throes of the next great challenge to New Mexico. This occurred in what some historians have called the Texan–Santa Fe expedition, but in New Mexico it was called the "Texas invasion of New Mexico." The Santa Fe Pioneers, as the group was called by the Texans, was officially termed the "political-military commercial expedition of 1841."[79] President Mirabeau B. Lamar of the newly independent Republic of Texas was described by Joe Frantz as "broke and not getting any better off financially. . . . [He] was desperate for trade." Lamar eagerly believed that New Mexicans were "ripe for new leadership," and he sent a "bold" and "ill-advised letter . . . inviting them [New Mexicans] to join the Republic of Texas." He claimed that "Texans would soon arrive to work out a union." In reality, Lamar sought to capture some of the lucrative trade that had developed over the Santa Fe Trail between Independence, Missouri, and Santa Fe. Texas had previously harbored designs on the eastern half of New Mexico. After independence from Mexico was secured in the two Treaties of Velasco, Texas formally reasserted its prior claims to New Mexico. The actual demand was for lands east of the Rocky Mountains and north and east of the Rio Grande (see map 2). President Lamar felt that Texas needed trade for its growth and sought to use those claims as a basis for usurping the Santa Fe trade. Lamar was so naïve about New Mexicans' true sentiments and suspicions toward the Texans that he felt that his plan was "such a good idea that the offer could hardly be refused."[80]

In 1840, an American residing in Santa Fe who had traveled to Texas, William G. Dryden, had been approached by Lamar, who offered him a role as a commissioner for Texas in an attempt to influence the people of New Mexico (or, at least, eastern New Mexico) to approve a change in government. John Rowland and William Workman, Americans and merchants in New Mexico, also agreed to serve as commissioners for that purpose.[81] On his return to Santa Fe, Dryden, carrying a letter of instructions for the commissioners outlining the "benefits which would accrue to New Mexicans on joining the Texas Republic," was able to encourage the other commissioners to lobby for this outcome.[82]

THE TEXAS CLAIM

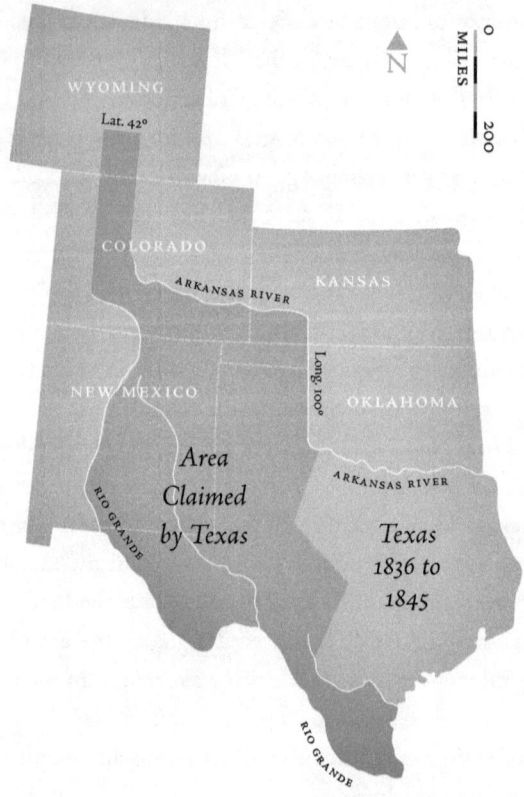

MAP 2. Texas land claim. The land claimed by the newly independent Texas Republic at the end of the Mexican War included everything east of the Rio Grande (more than half of present-day New Mexico). Texas made several attempts to forcibly occupy this disputed territory, including the notorious Texan–Santa Fe expedition of 1841. Source: Warren A. Beck and Ynez D. Haase, *Historical Atlas of New Mexico* (Norman: University of Oklahoma Press, 1969), map 30, "The Texas Claim after the Conclusion of Peace with Mexico." Reprinted by permission of the publisher. Map modified and adapted from the original by Mindy Basinger Hill.

The proposal did not sit well with New Mexico's Hispanic leaders and population, while it may have been welcomed by some American merchants in the territory. Native New Mexicans harbored a mistrust for Texans and were suspicious given Texas's designs on New Mexico land. Governor Manuel Armijo, alerted by the rumors of agents on behalf of Texas encouraging Texan intervention in New Mexico, ordered the arrest of those agents who advocated for insurgency. At the same time, he ordered the commanders at San Miguel del Bado to be on the alert, send out patrols to intercept any possible infiltrators from Texas, and prepare their troops for a defense of the territory.[83] Apparently, the lobbying carried out by Rowland and Workman had placed them in such danger of arrest for conspiracy against the Mexican government that they quickly organized an expedition of twenty-five people. They then exited the territory in September 1841 and traveled to California on the Old Spanish Trail.[84]

Anxious to advance his project, Lamar apparently did not wait for feedback from his commissioners, or else he ignored it. He sought but was unable to obtain congressional approval for the project. Thus frustrated, he decided to proceed alone. He issued a call for volunteers for a military force. After securing military support, he enlisted the merchants William Cooke, Richard Brenham, José Antonio Navarro, and George Van Ness to serve as commissioners (civilian spokesmen). The military contingent was headed by Commander Hugh McLeod with George Thomas as second-in-command. It was organized into five companies of infantry and one company of artillery. The contingent of merchants, guests, teamsters, and soldiers consisted of 321 people. Twenty-one ox-drawn wagons carried supplies and $200,000 in merchandise, which the traders hoped to exchange in Santa Fe.[85] The party, dubbed the Santa Fe Pioneers, departed on 19 June 1841 from Kenny's Fort on Brushy Creek, some twenty miles north of Austin, Texas. They traveled north, crossed the Brazos River on 8 July, and reached the Western Cross Timbers on 21 July. They then pursued a northwesterly course to the site of present-day Wichita Falls, Texas, where they mistook the Wichita River for the Red River and proceeded through the Wichita Valley until 17 August, when their Mexican guide deserted them.[86] They then realized their error and sent a company north to search for the Red River. On 20 August, a guide from the advance party returned to lead the Santa Fe Pioneers toward New Mexico. They incurred harassment from hostile Natives and began to feel the effects of the lack of water and dwindling provisions. Continuing north, the party reached the eastern edge of the Llano Estacado (Staked Plains).[87]

The Llano Estacado is one of the most desolate and forbidding regions of arid land in the United States. It is the southernmost portion of the high plains of North America, lying south of the Canadian River in northeastern New Mexico and northwestern Texas. The region was named for the precipitous bluffs formed by the erosion of the cap rock and slumping of the rough terrain.

Unable to continue through a rise in elevation due to the impervious cap rock, McLeod split his command, sending a party of horsemen to seek the nearest New Mexico settlements while the main group waited. The advance party experienced difficult travel and hardship through the barren desert terrain, but finally encountered some Mexican traders on 12 September. They sent some men back to guide the main party to the Mexican settlement. The Texans had naïvely expected to be welcomed by the citizens of New Mexico and did not expect armed resistance. However, Governor Armijo had been informed of the approaching military expedition and ordered the commanders at San Miguel to search for and attack the invaders. The first contact the Mexican soldiers had with the Texans was with the advance party.[88]

One leader of the Santa Fe Pioneers, Captain William G. Lewis, later reviled as a traitor by the Texans, probably saved lives by persuading the advance party to surrender on 17 September rather than fight, given their haggard and exhausted condition. Captain Lewis then led the Mexican soldiers to a site called Laguna Colorada (Red Lake) near present-day Tucumcari, New Mexico, where the main force was camped following the grueling journey through the barren Llano Estacado. Again, Lewis persuaded the main party to surrender, and given their weakened condition, they promptly did.[89] A commentary in the *Handbook of Texas* by the Texas State Historical Association described the outcome as follows: "Thus without the firing of a single shot ... the Texans ... had been conquered by the arid plains.... The Texas prisoners were marched to Mexico City ... [and] subjected to many indignities.... The affair became the subject of a heated diplomatic controversy between the United States and Mexico before the prisoners were finally released in April 1842."[90]

According to George W. Kendall, a member of the expedition who later wrote an eyewitness account of the events, the capture of the advance party occurred near the eastern New Mexico village of La Cuesta, near present-day Ribera. Kendall wrote that on 16 September 1841, the advance party of five men—Van Ness, Lewis, Howard, Fitzgerald, and Kendall—was surprised and surrounded by "more than a hundred soldiers, armed with lances, swords, bows and arrows, and old-fashioned carbines [*escopetas*]."⁹¹ Captain Damasio Salazar, who would subsequently be vilified for his cruel and inhumane treatment of the Texans, led the Mexicans. Salazar feigned initial friendliness toward the Texans, but once they were in captivity and relieved of their weapons, he prepared to execute them on the spot. Only the intervention of don Gregorio Vigil, later an alcalde in San Miguel, prevented the execution.⁹² Kendall described what transpired as the Texans were lined up for execution: "a motion from Salazar, as if to give the command for our execution ... [and then] an altercation ensued between Damasio and a Mexican named Vigil ... interfering for our lives. ... Vigil prevailed over the bloodthirsty captain and thus were our lives spared."⁹³ Salazar was reviled for his mistreatment of the prisoners and also the main party when they were captured and imprisoned in San Miguel del Bado until orders arrived from Armijo to march them to Mexico City. Salazar was also involved in escorting the prisoners to Mexico, where he perpetrated further atrocities against the Texan prisoners.⁹⁴

In his early account, Ralph Emerson Twitchell recognized that New Mexicans harbored some discontentment due to Armijo's exploitations as governor and the treatment they received from Mexico, but this did not predispose them to an acceptance of a Texan invasion. Twitchell wrote, "The Mexicans and Armijo have been the subjects of great abuses for their conduct and treatment of the Texans, but generally speaking, all fair-minded people must admit that the invaders ... received the same sort of treatment that would have been accorded by their own people had Texas been invaded by a hostile force."⁹⁵

For Texas, the Texan–Santa Fe expedition was an unmitigated defeat that caused great rancor and hostility toward New Mexicans. However, a more balanced perspective would logically account for Lamar's highly questionable actions in this affair. The object of the expedition was to conquer a territory in order to exploit its trade and commerce for the victor. That New Mexicans would embrace an oppressive invader was inconceivable. The military intent on the part of President Lamar and Commander McLeod is evident in a description of the military force, which was organized into five companies of infantry and one of artillery.⁹⁶ To send a force composed primarily of foot soldiers and some with cannons to travel hundreds of miles through unknown arid terrain to conquer an unknown enemy in another country without a capable and reliable guide was an extreme form of folly. The fact that the expedition was dependent on a single Mexican scout, who abandoned them, leaving them in jeopardy of starvation given their intended route, doomed the Santa Fe Pioneers long before the expedition reached the Llano Estacado. The benevolence of men, such as Gregorio Vigil and perhaps some of the other Mexican soldiers and officers, was what kept the invaders from disaster. Captain William G. Lewis saved the expedition by persuading the advance party and the main party to surrender, given their weakened condition, rather than carry out their ill-conceived mission. According to Kendall's account, Lewis went beyond the role of peacemaker later when he actively collaborated with Armijo as the governor implemented plans for the removal of the captured Texans to Mexico. Still, it is safe to say that rather than face embarrassment for their capture and endure the harsh treatment they received under Salazar, the majority of the Texans would have surely perished had they chosen to fight rather than surrender.

The Mexican army was prepared if the Texans attempted to fight or resist capture. While Donaciano's role in the Texan–Santa Fe imbroglio is not clear, we can piece together some of his involvement. At the time the events of the Texas expedition unfolded in the summer of 1841, Donaciano was stationed in Taos after his appointment as second lieutenant (alférez) of the Taos company. On 17 August, he was promoted to lieutenant of the company at San Miguel del Bado. His first assignment was to secure volunteers from the Taos/Rio Arriba region to augment the Bado company's regular forces. He and the volunteers he recruited then joined Governor Armijo's regular forces, now numbering some 1,500 troops, which Armijo led to reinforce the Bado company. When Governor Armijo arrived in Bado, he was inclined to deal harshly with the Texans who had been captured and detained by Captain Salazar. However, when some of his officers objected, it is said that he agreed to hold a vote among his officers on the prisoners' treatment. The approval of leniency was carried by one vote, and the decision was made to detain and transfer the captured Texans to Mexico. It can be assumed that the mild-tempered Donaciano was one of the officers who argued and voted for restraint and leniency. Unfortunately, the Mexican military record of the capture of the Texans only tells us that Lieutenant Donaciano Vigil was one of the high-ranking officers in charge of the Mexican troops. It does not tell us the specific role he played.

What is known is that Lieutenant Vigil was awarded, along with other high-ranking officials, including Governor Manuel Armijo, an Escudo de Honor, largely equivalent to the American Congressional Medal of Honor.[97] President Santa Anna granted the awards on behalf of the Mexican government, which indicated that the successful defense against the Texan army was considered an important victory for Mexico. In addition to receiving the award, Donaciano was temporarily promoted to captain. And on 18 April 1842, Donaciano was promoted to the permanent rank of captain of the company at San Miguel del Bado.[98]

In 1845, Donaciano was dispatched to Chihuahua, Mexico, by Governor Manuel Armijo to purchase *remonta* (horses to remount the cavalry) and other equipment and supplies to better equip the New Mexico militia for the possible defense of the territory against the United States. Given that at the time Donaciano was an active member of the legislative assembly as a *suplente* (substitute delegate), the assembly issued a strong protest against the governor for deploying Donaciano at that time. Rumors of an American invasion had been rife following the rebellions in Texas, California, and New Mexico. Donaciano's appointment for this task reflected Armijo's growing apprehension about a possible American invasion of New Mexico and the unpreparedness of his troops to repel such an invasion. He had confidence in Donaciano's persuasive ability to acquire much-needed replacement horses and military equipment from the intransigent commanders in Mexico.

However, Donaciano failed in this mission because it coincided with a change in leadership of the central government in Mexico. The Mexican government was unwilling both to provide money for the purchase of more modern weapons and to provide suitable surplus arms from its own meager supplies. It is interesting that with the Mexican republic's northern provinces imploding and the rumors of an imminent American invasion, Mexico would not provide so much as surplus munitions to a northern province begging for such supplies. The fact that New Mexico was in the cross hairs of the invader did not seem to make much difference. Perhaps the Mexican leaders were already anticipating their own future invasion by the formidable northern adversary.

While Donaciano was in Chihuahua, the comandante militar of the garrison there became seriously ill, and Governor Angel Trías of that department appointed Donaciano Vigil, the ranking officer present, as *comandante interino de las armas* (interim commander of arms). Donaciano served several months in that capacity until relieved by a permanent commander.[99]

A POLITICAL LEADER IN THE DEPARTMENT OF NEW MEXICO UNDER THE MEXICAN REGIME

In the 1830s, Donaciano evolved in his role as a military officer in the Mexican army with added responsibilities and higher ranks. He came to understand the linkage between the day-to-day duties and circumstances of the ordinary soldier and the political world that largely dictated those circumstances. He also came to appreciate how his father, Juan Cristóbal, had made the natural transition into politics as an alcalde. Undoubtedly, Donaciano's close association with the most important jefes políticos (political bosses) in New Mexico in the 1820s and 1830s provided mentorship to the ambitious young soldier. Men such as José Antonio Viscarra, Antonio Narbona, Blas de Hinojos, Albino Pérez, and Manuel Armijo were capable leaders and occupied the joint positions of governor and comandante principal. These men dealt with the formidable challenges of overseeing the operations of government and encouraging growth and development, while providing internal military security for the struggling frontier colony. All of these leaders, in their own times and ways, contributed to the history of New Mexico and thus merit more consideration than they have received. Donaciano came to appreciate how each of them had struggled with a central regime in Mexico that governed with a firm hand, controlling commerce and trade while neglecting to provide sufficient funding for the necessities of local government, particularly the defense of the territory.

It has been a widely held assumption that Hispanic people in the Americas rarely, if ever, showed interest in or participated in governmental matters. Lansing Bloom wrote, "It is universally admitted that the Mexican people as such never exercised a voice in their governmental affairs.... Many will doubtless attest to this sweeping assertion, but there are others who have studied back to the theory and practice of Spanish government who see Spanish-American history differently."[1]

Bloom argued that in New Mexico, whose emergence as a Spanish colony coincided with the founding of the thirteen American colonies of the Atlantic seaboard, "there were beginnings of representative government from that earliest time to 1846."[2] In January 1822, according to Bloom, an "electoral *junta* assembled in the *sala de cabildo*" of the ayuntamiento in Santa Fe, electing seven deputies and three alternates to constitute the first provincial diputación. "This little group was the first of an unbroken succession of legislative bodies that functioned throughout the Mexican period, 1822–1846, while New Mexico was a province, territory, department, and again territory of the Mexican nation."[3] Although it was far removed from matters of national interest and received "pitifully small assistance" from Mexico, "the *diputación* operated in the wider sphere for New Mexico as a whole, and no one can read the minutes of its sessions during its twenty-five years without realizing that its deliberations and legislative enactments affected every life of the commonweal."[4] When we consider this evolution of representative institutions in New Mexico, we can more readily understand the events that took place there between 1821 and 1846.

SANTA ANNA AND THE CENTRALIZATION OF POWER IN MEXICO

One person, Antonio López de Santa Anna, dominated center stage in Mexican politics between 1824 and 1846, and his influence was felt well beyond the confines of the Plaza de la Constitución or Zócalo, as the central government square in Mexico City is known. His popularity or notoriety, depending on the various stages of his career, was felt equally in the northern provinces as in Mexico. Antonio de Padua María Severino López de Santa Anna y Pérez de Lebrón, most commonly known as simply Santa Anna, has been referred to as the "Napoleon of the West." He is among Mexico's most prominent personalities, having served several terms as president, and is one of its most storied military leaders. Depending on the source, Santa Anna has been vilified as a tyrant, traitor, and villain, or praised as a patriot and hero of the Mexican republic. He was the preeminent Mexican leader in the mid-nineteenth century and intimately affected New Mexico in the heyday of Donaciano Vigil's roles as both soldier and political leader.

Santa Anna was born in the town of Xalapa, Vera Cruz, Mexico, on 21 February 1794.[5] He joined the Spanish army as a cadet while still a teenager (age sixteen) in July 1810, two months before the Mexican War of Independence from Spain broke out on 16 September 1810. He quickly advanced to the rank of captain while fighting on the Spanish royalist side.[6] He later joined the rebels led by Agustín de Iturbide, who also had fought for the Crown before becoming the commander of the Mexican revolutionary forces. By the time independence was declared with Iturbide's march into Mexico City on 27 September 1821, Santa Anna was a hardened twenty-seven-year-old colonel, having spent his young manhood fighting in the bloodiest and most violent period in Mexican history.[7] Iturbide led the fight for Mexican independence and later became emperor of Mexico. Santa Anna then emerged as the leader of the forces that deposed Iturbide and banished the monarchy in 1823. Consequently, he became known as the founder of the republic for his support of the liberal reforms that led to the Mexican Constitution of 1824. In 1829, Santa Anna led the Mexican forces that quashed Spain's attempt to reconquer Mexico, and he was hailed as the "hero of Tampico," which vaulted him to the Mexican presidency in 1833.[8] For the next two decades, he was the on-again, off-again president of Mexico.

Santa Anna's roles as a successful military leader for Mexican independence and as one of the leading advocates of the liberal 1824 Mexican Constitution, modeled after the US Constitution, made him wildly popular in New Mexico, where he was viewed as a combination of the American founders George Washington and Thomas Jefferson. In the decade between 1824 and 1835, New Mexico experienced unprecedented economic growth owing to the opening of trade with the United States over the Santa Fe Trail and a greater sharing of power between the governor and the resurgent assembly. In this context, the more conservative turn toward a centralization of power in Mexico beginning in 1835 was seen by New Mexicans as a betrayal by Santa Anna of the liberal reforms they had enjoyed since 1824. The imposition of Albino Pérez as governor and his effort to implement the new centralist agenda were seen as the causes of the 1837 Rio Arriba rebellion.

While Santa Anna enjoyed the title of president, he had little interest in governing, and he permitted his vice president, Dr. Valentín Gómez Farías, to rule the nation during his first presidency. Gómez Farías implemented radical liberal reforms that challenged the influence of the Catholic Church and the military, two of the most powerful interest groups in the country. When opposition from conservatives surfaced, Santa Anna relieved Gómez Farías and through the Plan of Cuernavaca, published on 25 May 1834, took control of the government and replaced the 1824 constitution with the Siete Leyes (Seven Laws). He dissolved the federal congress and established himself as a dictator with the title of president and the full backing of the military.

Santa Anna in October 1835 established his own selected congress, which began implementing a centralized structure with power concentrated in the national government in Mexico City. The implementation of the Siete Leyes was met with resistance in New Mexico where they were referred to as the "seven plagues." Donaciano wrote of this period, "In the year of 1836 the government in Mexico was centralized by virtue of the seven laws ... [and] taxation laws were decreed.... During the period ... there were enmities in the country, accusations by influential citizens against the fiscal authorities ... of the dissipation of the money collected and bad mismanagement."[9]

These and other related reforms only exacerbated the situation. Over the next two decades, Mexican politics "teetered between simple chaos and unmitigated anarchy," and the Mexican presidency "changed hands thirty-six times between May 1833 and August 1855."[10] Biographer Will Fowler mounted a noble effort to rehabilitate Santa Anna, and while he succeeded in restoring Santa Anna's reputation as a worthy and patriotic military leader, his defense of Santa Anna as a political leader is less convincing. For example, Fowler wrote that "considering the little time he actually spent at the head of the nation between 1833 and 1835, it is surprising that he [was] blamed for so many of the problems that surfaced at the time. He was not present in Mexico City long enough to give the country a direction that could be described as his own."[11] In other words, Santa Anna should not be blamed for the 1833–1835 constitutional and legal changes toward centralization since he was not actually present in the deliberations that led to the abolition of the federalist charter of 1824 or its replacement by the blatantly centralist 1836 constitution. However, Santa Anna was the designated president at the time, and he empowered surrogates, such as Valentín Gómez Farías, José María Tornel, and José María Bocanegra, to govern in his stead. Fowler admitted that "the great irony or paradox of Santa Anna's success is that he was able to rise to power on repeated occasions.... The cause of his repeated fall from grace: his absenteeism.... His repeated absences were responsible for the undoing of his governments. He was never there long enough to consolidate his hold on power. He was not interested in doing so."[12]

Santa Anna's failures in rising to the occasion to provide the leadership his country badly needed ultimately helped seal the fate of Mexico and its failure to evolve to the status of a greater nation. That failure of leadership also had very real consequences for the far-flung northern territories, like New Mexico.

The dramatic alteration of the distribution of power in the Mexican government under Santa Anna can only be understood by comparing it with how New Mexico fared under the progressive federalism that had initially developed under the Spanish constitution of 1812, established under the Spanish cortes, which Weber said "continued to influence Mexican political structures on the state as well as the federal level."[13] That system was in place under Spain until 1821. Six assemblies were authorized for all of Mexico, and one, the Provincias Internas del Oriente (including Sonora, New Mexico, and Texas), introduced a semblance of national representation for New Mexicans. In this period the first deputation was created in New Mexico.

The liberal reforms continued under the Mexican Constitution of 1824, established after Mexican independence and the overthrow of Emperor Iturbide. That new constitution was a progressive document that eliminated class distinctions, made all people citizens (including Natives), provided for a system of elections, allowed representative institutions, and revitalized municipal government, allowing for local ayuntamientos.[14] Like the US Constitution after which it was modeled, it created a federal system with states and territories as political subdivisions. The states/territories fostered their own legislative bodies vested with deliberative and policy-making powers. The country was even referred to as the Estados Unidos de Mexico. Weber wrote, "Under the 1824 constitution, most Mexican provinces became states. They drew up their own constitutions, converted their deputations to legislatures, and became sovereign political entities with control over their internal affairs."[15] However, New Mexico was not an original state, so it fell under the control of the Mexican Congress, which in 1824 had designated New Mexico a territory. New Mexicans retained the tradition of the *asamblea*, which continued to meet, deliberate, and enact legislation and policies while also providing advisory opinions to the governor. New Mexico politicians in the deputation remained quite active by seeking more autonomy and meeting regularly. It was, however, frustrating, as Melquiades Antonio Ortega of New Mexico pointed out in 1831: "The old Spanish laws are [still] seen in force, many of them incompatible with our present federal system."[16] In short, New Mexico politicians actively sought to exercise the freedom of representative bodies that they had recently enjoyed under both Spain and Mexico.

The new order established by Santa Anna in 1835 contrasted with the past by the establishment of the departmental system to replace the former states or provinces, which had experienced some level of autonomy. The Mexican territory was divided into departments, each headed by a governor appointed by the president under the new system. To implement the change, Mexico designated Albino Pérez as governor of New Mexico.

The restructured departmental system would provide a clear chain of command from the national to the local level and thus "forge a more unified nation" responsible primarily to a strongman president, such as Santa Anna. Each department was an administrative unit of the central government, which was designed to curb the "centrifugal excesses of federalism."[17] Every department was divided into *distritos* (districts) headed by a prefect directly responsible to the governor. Each district was further subdivided into *partidos* headed by subprefects responsible to the prefect. The lowest level of government, the ayuntamiento, was abolished except for towns over 8,000 people. In New Mexico, only Santa Fe, the capital of the department, qualified for an ayuntamiento. The governor, no longer called jefe político, was appointed by the Mexican president, albeit with the assembly's role in nomination, and was directly answerable to the president.

The legislature of each state or province was replaced by a diputación that would be less of a legislative body and more like a junta, serving solely as an advisory body to the governor. Congressional enactments would later determine further subdivisions, such as local governments. In addition, departmental governments would enforce the collection of a new national tax for the central government. Donaciano observed, "Pérez, expected to do justice for the people's complaints, [instead] protected the employees so that hatred descended heavily upon his own position."[18] The new departmental structure and the proposed new taxes were vehemently opposed in most of the former provinces and led to open rebellions in Texas, California, and New Mexico. Fortunately, the new structures and tax policies were not rigidly enforced because of this opposition.

THE FIRST POLITICAL STAGE:
A *VOCAL* IN THE NEW MEXICO ASSEMBLY

During the period 1836–1846, the deputation consisted of seven regular members called vocales, who were chosen in indirect elections for terms of two years. New Mexico did not have a system of direct popular election. Consequently, public officials, such as provincial delegates to the Mexican Congress, vocales for the assembly, and local ayuntamientos, were elected indirectly by a *junta electoral* (electoral committee), much like the US Electoral College. Members of the powerful junta electoral were appointed by the governor by districts and consisted of wealthy, landed, or otherwise influential leading citizens.[19] Such an electoral process obviously favored elites and propagated a system where non-elites were disadvantaged. Under this system, the man who received the most votes or had served longest was the *vocal mayor* (senior deputy), presiding over sessions and serving as acting governor when the governor's office was vacant or in other emergency circumstances. In cases of death, resignation, or the absence of a regular member, a suplente (alternate), sometimes appointed by the assembly, took his place. Not a rich man, Donaciano was fortunate to serve and later professed support for direct popular elections. Serving in the assembly was regarded as an honor and duty, and most vocales were diligent about attendance at sessions. Still, because some vocales lived in distant parts of the territory, absences were common, and suplentes often took their place, acting as junior members. Sessions of the assembly were held weekly in designated rooms of the Palace of the Governors. Members were supposed to be paid for their service, but the treasury department was typically short of funds, so they were sometimes reimbursed in public goods (food or clothing), and even land served as remuneration.[20]

The elections of 1836 in New Mexico brought into the deputation several well-educated, skilled, and independent-minded members, who made the body a stronger institution than it was intended to be. A priest, Antonio José Martínez, was president of the seven-member deputation, and he and the other members had no interest in being an advisory body exempt from any power to legislate. Gonzales wrote that the assembly led New Mexico toward a "robust local government," creating three New Mexico *prefecturas* (prefectures)—the north, central, and southwestern—and *alcaldias* (townships), each governed by an ayuntamiento, and partitioned New Mexico into two distinct civil districts. The Rio Arriba and the Rio Abajo districts placed the Rio Grande as the centerline, running north to south. The deputation also fought against a centralization of power and their own diminution by federal decrees. Journal proceedings of the assembly showed an increased tendency of the members to assert their autonomy by securing the "guarantee of the appointment of New Mexicans to federal jobs and military leadership" and embracing an "independent treasury" by setting, collecting, and expending commercial tariffs from the Santa Fe Trail trade for the benefit of the territory.[21]

In addition, the deputation exercised its mandated duty of *quinterna* (a form of lottery) to nominate three candidates for the governorship to be selected by the Mexican president. In 1836, the members purposely excluded Albino Pérez, who had already been designated by Mexico to serve in that post.[22] This tradition of selecting strong-willed and independent-minded men to serve in the deputation continued through 1838 when Donaciano was elected to his first two-year term in the legislative assembly. He was again elected to the assembly in 1843 and continued as a regular member of that body until 1845 when he was dispatched to Chihuahua for military supplies. On Donaciano's return to New Mexico in 1846, he was elected as a suplente member of the assembly and was a frequent participant during the most important period for New Mexico under Mexican rule.

For New Mexicans, the experience of a semblance of democratic government, albeit through indirect elections, from 1824 to the mid-1830s was a good one. Once they became accustomed to being represented by a local territorial assembly, a delegate to the national congress, and an ayuntamiento, they cherished that right. The territorial assembly, whatever name it was given or form it took, thoroughly relished its privilege to debate the issues of the day and embraced its participatory power to make and recommend public policy. Bloom observed, "The citizens of New Mexico during the Spanish and Mexican period, were thrown almost to their own resources ... [but] the results ... they obtained loom up impressively, nor is it so material that they received the forms of government ... from [the] king ... as is the fact that they made these forms their own by adaptation and use."[23]

The New Mexico deputation defied Mexico's intent of centralization in several ways. Instead of calling itself a *diputación provincial*, it preferred the name *diputación territorial*. The deputation met regularly and addressed matters such as apportioning the uncultivated lands of the Pueblos. However, their actions on apportionment were later reversed in favor of the Natives when the latter complained, and the authorities in Mexico supported their claims. The deputation also encouraged the establishment of ayuntamientos in the territory, and most towns and even pueblos had these local governing bodies.

The deputation also defied national authority by ignoring or refusing to adhere to some federal regulations, such as submitting annual reports or seeking congressional approval for local rules and regulations pertaining to tax assessments or tariff regulations.[24] Clearly, the deputation played an important role in New Mexico despite efforts from the central government in Mexico to downplay and minimize its role to an advisory capacity. In 1843, continued political inversions in Mexico resulted in changes in the centralized government's structure, and a new constitutional order was decreed as the Bases Orgánicas (Organic Bases). In June 1843, the Bases eliminated the supreme conservative power, a conservative coalition of political (the president), military, and church interests; expanded the power of the president; and retained the centralization of the previous decade. Santa Anna was elected as president in January 1844, but when he tried to dissolve the congress, he was ousted from power and replaced by José Joaquín de Herrera, one of a long succession of short-term presidents. Herrera served nine days before being ousted by Valentín Canalizo, who served two and a half months until he was ousted and replaced by Herrera. Herrera served three months before being ousted by a coup led by General Mariano Paredes, who vacated the presidency by yielding to Vice President Nicolás Bravo, and then Paredes left office to fight the American invasion.[25]

While Santa Anna was only one of the several presidents who served at this time, he was clearly the most influential. Lucas Alamán, a conservative intellectual, observed that "the history of Mexico since 1822 might accurately be called 'the history of Santa Anna's revolutions,' [since] his name plays the major role in all the political events in the country and its destiny has been intertwined with his."[26] The Bases, although proclaimed as republican, were even more conservative and centralized than their predecessors and ushered in three chaotic years described by Weber as the "most turbulent period of Mexican history."[27]

THE NEW MEXICO ASSEMBLY EMERGES
AS A FORUM FOR DISSENT

On 1 January 1844, the first New Mexico deputation convened under the Bases. The assembly opened with "grave ceremony" and adopted a *procunciamento* (resolution) that dutifully conveyed the members' continued loyalty to Mexico, but also stressed their resistance to the increasing centralization in the federalism of Santa Anna's regime. The pronouncement, directed to the vecinos of the department, declared, "Intimately united with the Mexican Republic, we continue to be free and independent." On behalf of New Mexicans, the deputation vowed to "hold religion, country, and glory over slavery."[28] The pronouncement went on to assert, "We have from you the conviction that when our enemies have assembled, when you [Santa Anna] triumph on the field of battle, you will have shown that for New Mexicans, the sweet words of 'country and honor' have real significance."[29] The *pronunciamento* was an important breakthrough for the assembly that, perhaps at first, had not taken "itself seriously ... which might account for the sketchy records it kept. However, as the year progressed and ended, members began to understand the nature of their authority."[30]

On 15 January, the assembly handled its first major problem as Governor Armijo resigned, claiming that he "wished to retire from the capital in order to take a rest and cure."[31] Clearly, Armijo felt that he had been betrayed by Santa Anna having a lower-level minister appoint a new military commander for New Mexico. Armijo named the president of the assembly, Mariano Chávez, a wealthy landowner and merchant from the Rio Abajo region, as acting governor until the confirmation of the next permanent governor.[32] Perhaps the most flagrant example of the deputation's independence and defiance of federal authority was the allowance and toleration of dissent. Chávez used his dual position as president of the assembly and acting governor to give a lengthy address conveying ambiguous patriotism—alluding to New Mexico, Mexico, or both—and reflecting what most of his colleagues and fellow New Mexicans felt. Chávez lamented that New Mexico had never lived up to the prosperity promised by its many resources or "the valor of virtues of its sons." Instead, "hopes and promises are only what it [New Mexico] has received ... in place of aid from its mother country. We are surrounded on all sides by lurking threats ... renegades ... almost perishing ... and our brothers instead of helping us are at each other's throats with the festering civil wars." Chávez promised, "Not a single foreigner will rule this territory [except] over our dead bodies [in this country whose] highest honor ... consists in being all Mexican." However, Chávez also cautioned that he was "convinced that we will receive a remedy for our troubles because as [Alexis de] Tocqueville says, 'there are certain necessities of the people that to disregard a single one will cause the ruin of empires and republics.'"[33] Perhaps, as Weber wrote, Chávez also delivered "thinly veiled" conditions for loyalty and support, which could only be expected if reciprocity governed Mexican and New Mexican relationships in the future.[34]

The assembly's pronunciamento, Chávez's address, and later Donaciano's speech to the assembly clearly conveyed the exasperation New Mexico's leaders were feeling toward Santa Anna, whom they had idolized as a champion of liberal reforms, such as the Mexican republic and the constitution of 1824. However, now Santa Anna was the leading force in the dismantling of those progressive reforms in favor of the more autocratic Siete Leyes and Bases Orgánicas. The liberal Lorenzo de Avila wrote of Santa Anna, "He is a man who within him has some force to take action, but he has no fixed principles ... or code of public behavior.... [He] moves to extremes ... and contradicts himself."[35] Santa Anna's contradictions had very real consequences for Mexico and its northern provinces. He was the dominant political actor in Mexico at the time, even if he was not actually occupying the presidency.

ANOTHER "OUTSIDER" AS GOVERNOR OF NEW MEXICO

It is noteworthy that the preceding 1 August 1843 session of the assembly had submitted a list of names for the governorship of New Mexico, who would be selected by the Mexican president as required by quinterna. Manuel Armijo, the sitting governor, was first on that list. By the time the assembly convened for its January 1844 session, the situation had changed dramatically. First, General Mariano Martínez de Lejanza had been appointed by General Mariano Monterde to serve as comandante militar of New Mexico. Prior to this, the office of comandante militar had been held simultaneously by the governor of the department. This appointment signaled a separation of the offices and a loss of support for Governor Armijo; this is why he asked to be relieved of the governorship. Thus, in January 1844 the assembly submitted an updated list of five names for governor in order of priority: Mariano Martínez, Manuel Armijo, Mariano Chávez, José Chávez, and Donaciano Vigil. The placement of Martínez at the head of the list was an acknowledgment that since he had been designated as comandante militar, Mexico likely considered him to be the next governor of the department. This was also the first time that Donaciano received mention as a potential governor.[36]

Governor Armijo spoke to the delegates when they convened in January, and while he was by then considered a lame duck, he did present himself with some dignity as he delivered, according to Minge, "the fate of the department into the hands of the assembly." Armijo commended the assembly, "To you who are the flowers of New Mexico [and] know its needs so well, nothing can be raised that needs remedying, that has not been foreseen by your wisdom.... I see finally, this honorable assembly, animated by the highest hopes and consequently I am certain of peace, happiness, and progress. Courage gentlemen!"[37]

Mariano Chávez continued to serve as acting governor until 9 April when he departed for his hacienda, Bosque de los Pinos near Albuquerque, to deal with private affairs. He submitted a letter to the assembly dated 10 April, asking to be relieved of the governorship for health reasons. The assembly voted to summon Manuel Armijo to resume his duties by 29 April. They appointed don Felipe Sena, the *vocal mas antiguo* (longest-serving assemblyman), to serve as acting governor. They informed General Mariano Martínez, the comandante militar who had arrived in the territory, and he concurred with their actions. The decision to recall Armijo underscores the fact that to a majority of the assembly, Armijo was still considered the legitimate governor.[38]

The assembly's January nominations for governor arrived in the Mexican capital in February 1844. Substitute president Valentín Canalizo sent General Martínez a letter informing him that "taking into consideration the patriotism and commendable virtues which are present in Your Excellency as also the nomination made in your favor by the Excellent [New Mexico] Departmental Assembly, [the president] has decided to name you the Constitutional Governor of the Department of New Mexico—March 30, 1844."[39] The notification reached Martínez by special courier on 28 April, and he notified the president of the assembly the next morning. Manuel Armijo had not acted on the assembly's request for him to resume the governorship on 29 April, so Felipe Sena, the vocal mas antiguo and acting governor, replied to Martínez. Sena congratulated him on his appointment by the supreme government and offered his support and readiness to hand over the reins of the governorship as "soon as agreeable" to Martínez.[40]

Once again, New Mexicans had a non–New Mexican imposed on them as governor of the department. Mariano Chávez, the previous assembly president and acting governor, had declared that reciprocity in relations between New Mexico and the mother country had been completely ignored. According to Weber, Chávez's "thinly veiled" conditions meant that "if Santa Anna wanted the cooperation of New Mexicans, he had to give something positive in return. What New Mexico got instead was another outsider to lead them."[41]

Mariano Martínez assumed the office of governor of the Department of New Mexico on 29 April 1844. His first important action was to recommend to the assembly the division of the territory into three districts—central, north, and southeast—for more efficient administration; the assembly promptly approved. Each district was further subdivided into seven partidos (counties). The population of the entire department at the time was 67,736, including the Pueblos, which made New Mexico the most populous of Mexico's northern territories. Martínez made his mark with improvements at the capital. He had trees planted in the *plaza de armas* along the road leading to the Rosario Cemetery, and a ditch was dug to provide water for the landscaped area. He installed a bullfight arena with stalls on the plaza. Finally, he borrowed a printing press and commenced publication of a government-run newspaper, which continued under his successor, José Chávez y Castillo.[42]

Governor Martínez's grave mistake, however, was assuming control of the collection of import and export taxes, which were the most important revenue sources for the department. Tax and fiscal issues were the Achilles' heel that had undermined the regimes of Pérez and Armijo. In Martínez's case, charges were brought against him for mismanagement of the custom taxes, and a year later he was relieved of the duties of governor.[43] Martínez had acquired "a reputation for arbitrariness and incompetence." According to Donaciano, "his subjects would have rebelled . . . if his administration had lasted a bit longer."[44] Don José Chávez y Castillo, the most senior deputy, assumed the office of governor on 1 May 1845. The assembly then submitted a new list of five nominees, this time headed by Manuel Armijo, and his appointment by the central government was received on 1 November 1845. Armijo assumed the governorship on 17 November 1845.

DONACIANO AND *LA VERDAD* NEWSPAPER

As mentioned above, Donaciano was first elected to the assembly in 1838 and reelected in 1843. The record of proceedings of the assembly indicates he was more active during his second term, particularly in 1844 when he was the first suplente of the assembly and was in almost constant demand as an alternate for absent vocales.[45] By this time, Donaciano was also the secretary for the assembly. For the not so affluent members, it was a sacrifice to serve; they depended on the meager salary it paid, and this sometimes created problems.

In 1844, the cash-strapped department during the tenure of Governor Mariano Martínez had problems meeting expenses, and funds were inadequate to pay its salaried officers (including vocales) and the troops. The frontier ports of entry for Santa Fe Trail merchants, which had been closed in 1843, were reopened in March 1844, and everyone had hoped that the infusion of revenues from custom duties would alleviate the shortfall in the treasury. In October, secretary of the assembly and vocal Donaciano objected to being paid in produce or goods because the fixed prices were too high. On 6 November, when he again demanded his salary, he was relieved of his position and ordered to take his issues to the governor. He was replaced by Tomás Ortíz, but when he took a leave, Donaciano returned as secretary. Donaciano then sent a letter of complaint to the assembly, which offended the members, and they referred him to the governor for punishment. He retaliated with a more offensive message on 27 November and was then expelled. This necessitated a meeting on 30 November between the assembly and Governor Martínez, where he advised the vocales that their action was arbitrary, and they had no power to expel a deputy. The matter was then referred to a committee, where it was permanently tabled.[46] This incident shows how sometimes assembly relations boiled over into heated disputes, and often these were due to financial issues.

It was perhaps in his role as assembly secretary that Donaciano felt a need for some kind of forum that would communicate to the public the ongoing debates and discussions of the assembly and the general activities of the government. He had been impressed with an effort by Ramón Abreu, a previous assembly secretary, who had briefly edited with the help of printer Jesús María Baca a short-lived Spanish-language weekly newspaper titled *El Crepúsculo de la Libertad* (The Dawn of Liberty). That newspaper was conceived and published by Antonio Barreiro to aid his campaign for reelection as a deputy to the Mexican Congress. As already stated, Governor Mariano Martínez had also briefly operated a government-run newspaper, and in January 1844, Donaciano revisited that idea. He suggested that the assembly purchase the press and publish a government-sponsored newspaper. Donaciano agreed to edit and publish it, circulating the first issue on 8 February 1844 with the title *La Verdad* (The Truth).[47] The timing and title of the new publication may have been related to certain clandestine sessions of the assembly that took place in the first week of February 1844, during which the quinterna was submitted to the Mexican government for its selection of governor. In its previous quinterna in November 1843, the assembly had listed Manuel Armijo as its first choice. However, in the secretive February meetings "those who favored Martínez for governor had overcome the other candidates and secured for him the coveted first place on the list of five. If there was any effort to re-nominate the list that the departmental *junta* had put through on 1 November, it failed."[48]

It was Donaciano's duty as secretary of the assembly to submit the names of the nominees to the Mexican government during the first ten days of February. However, he delayed and did not submit the quinterna to the Mexican minister of relations until 15 February, even though he had published the results in the initial 8 February issue of *La Verdad*.[49] In selecting the title *La Verdad*, Donaciano might have intended to expose the clandestine nature of the meetings and the nefarious means that were used to secure the top position for Martínez. It was already apparent that Donaciano was opposed to the selection of an outsider for the governorship. *La Verdad*, a Spanish-language newspaper, was published weekly for more than a year in 1844–1845 and was thus the longest-running newspaper of that time. Donaciano continued to serve as secretary of the assembly until 20 May 1845, and he used the newspaper as the official organ (*imprenta del gobierno*) of the departmental government.[50]

The printing press that Donaciano used to publish his newspaper is itself a monument to the efforts to provide enlightenment at a bleak period of scholarship in New Mexico. There are two stories, not necessarily contradictory, as to the origin of the press. Weber wrote that the press first came to New Mexico over the Santa Fe Trail as "part of the cargo of Josiah Gregg."[51] Gregg later sold it to Ramón Abreu, who as secretary of the assembly published the governmental proceedings. An alternate view about the origin of the printing press was provided by Bloom, who said that the press was brought to New Mexico by Antonio Barreiro, a Mexican attorney who lived in New Mexico for a short time in the 1820s and 1830s. He was elected twice as a deputy to the federal congress in 1832 and 1834, and he reportedly brought from Mexico to New Mexico a professional printer, Jesús María Baca, and the small press on which was printed the first newspaper in the province, *El Crepúsculo de la Libertad*.[52] Although only a few issues of *El Crepúsculo* were published, Barreiro was recognized as a visionary for introducing the press and for his critical commentary on New Mexico in his book, *Ojeada sobre Nuevo Mexico*.

In "Bilingual and Spanish Language Newspapers in Territorial New Mexico," Annabelle M. Oczon shed light on the earliest newspapers in New Mexico and clarified some of the conflicting accounts on the press. She wrote that the "illiteracy of the Spanish population" precluded the emergence and then limited the success of the earliest newspapers.[53] Oczon confirmed the account that Josiah Gregg brought the first printing press to New Mexico in 1834 and then sold it to Ramón Abreu, "a Santa Fe resident." In August or September of that year, she wrote, Barreiro published *El Crepúsculo de la Libertad*. Baca, a printer of "unknown origin," assisted Barreiro in the publication of the paper for his campaign for reelection as New Mexico's deputy to the Mexican Congress. The newspaper was issued weekly to fifty subscribers for one month. After Barreiro's reelection, the newspaper was discontinued because his goal of reelection had been achieved. Oczon's account does not dispute Bloom's report that Barreiro had recruited Baca in Mexico and brought him to New Mexico as the printer for the newspaper nor that Baca may have also worked with assembly secretary Abreu in publishing the government journal in the same year.[54] All sources concur that the press was also at some point in the possession of the priest José Antonio Martínez, who moved it to Taos from 1839 to 1840 to print religious tracts, pamphlets, and other educational materials for students in his private school.

After the demise of *La Verdad*, Governor Mariano Martínez and his successor, José Chávez y Castillo, acquired the press and used it to print governmental publications. For a short time in 1845, the press was used to publish a third newspaper in Santa Fe, *El Payo de Nuevo Mexico* (New Mexico Countryman).[55] According to Oczon, the first major newspaper published in New Mexico after the American occupation was the *Santa Fe Republican*, a bilingual periodical published by former American soldiers Oliver Hovey and Edward T. Davies, with George R. Gibson as editor.[56] As governor, Donaciano Vigil was a frequent contributor to that newspaper under both his real name and his pen name, CEMAPA.[57]

The two terms Donaciano served in the deputation, 1838–1840 and 1843–1845, were during the time when he was still in active service as an officer in the New Mexico militia. Apparently, election to and service in the legislative body were not prohibited to active military members. By the time he began his public and political career in the late 1830s, Donaciano had served close to two decades in the military and once as secretary of the territory under Governor Armijo. Donaciano became increasingly more outspoken about the central government's neglect, lack of support, and general mismanagement of the isolated colony, which was a major cause of the territory's problems.

Following the dismissal of Mariano Martínez, Manuel Armijo returned to the governorship on 17 November 1845. Donaciano was absent from New Mexico during the last part of 1845 due to his assignment in Chihuahua and did not return until the spring of 1846. When he returned, he found that matters had not changed much relative to the most pressing Native problem. Plus, the unpreparedness of the militia had become more of an issue as the province now faced the additional threat of an imminent invasion by the United States. Donaciano had anticipated the looming specter of the United States over all of the Mexican territory north of the Rio Grande, given the Texas independence movement, Texas's annexation by the United States, the unrest in California, and the deteriorating relations between American merchants and the government in New Mexico. His participation in the assembly had increased before his departure because he sensed that the body would likely play a role in the future of New Mexico, regardless of which wind would prevail. Given these developments, on his return to New Mexico he resumed his active role in the assembly, and his colleagues embraced his participation as a voice of reason and logic, even though he was acting as a suplente.

Donaciano was elected as the first suplente a third time for what would be the final two-year term of the departmental assembly beginning on 1 January 1846. The regular vocales elected were José Chávez, who would serve as *vocal mayor*, *cura* (priest) José Manuel Gallegos, cura Antonio José Martínez, Tomás Ortíz, Juan Perea, Juan Cristóbal Armijo, and Felipe Sena. Serving along with Donaciano as suplentes would be cura José Francisco Leyva, Antonio Sena, Pedro Otero (who would be replaced by Manuel Doroteo Pino), Serafin Ramirez, and Santiago Armijo. Like Donaciano, several suplentes would be called to serve due to the absence of the regular vocales in what would be the most eventful term of the assembly.[58]

The newly elected assembly, which still met in one of the rooms of the old Palace of the Governors, convened in January 1846. Things were different now. Perhaps because of his absence from New Mexico for a short time, Donaciano returned with a new resolve to try to make things better. He had matured and with that maturity came the realization that the only way things would improve would be if he and New Mexico followed a different course. It was becoming clear to him that the old approach under Mexico would not lead to a different and more favorable outcome for New Mexico. He had sensed in the previous sessions of the assembly that some of the older, wiser vocales, such as Mariano Chávez in his "hopes and promises" speech, were becoming skeptical and frustrated with Mexico's continued intransigence in trying to centralize power, the imposition of outside officials as governors, and its general neglect of the territory. In the past, Donaciano had listened and observed silently, as was the custom for newer and younger members. His elder colleagues, such as Chávez, the priests Martínez and Gallegos, his cousin Juan Bautista Vigil y Alarid, and Manuel Armijo, had made impassioned, eloquent speeches to the assembly about the future of New Mexico. Donaciano came to appreciate that this assembly in the old palace was their forum for expressing their frustrations, fears, and hopes for the province.

The context in which Donaciano presented his proposals to the assembly was highlighted in Charles Robert McClure's master's thesis. McClure maintained that "despite some progress in trade and commerce from the Santa Fe Trail, economic conditions had deteriorated even further by 1846." He wrote that Donaciano "moved that the assembly allow all munitions to come into the department duty free, and also moved that . . . some of the outstanding bills might be paid with the revenues expected from the first trade caravans." That measure passed in May 1846.[59]

In June 1846, Donaciano could be silent no more. This was his time, and this was the place. The approach he decided on was two major proposals, which he would present in speeches and follow with printed copies that could be reviewed and debated by the full assembly for further action. He began to write in the privacy of his home on Alto Street. He carefully selected the most appropriate words, phrases, and arguments, and prepared to present his two major resolutions to the assembly. Weber speculated that the preparation could have taken weeks as Donaciano honed and edited his work. His proposals, as the poet Thomas Gray wrote, would convey "thoughts that breathe and words that burn."[60]

It is significant that the two main speeches Donaciano Vigil made to the deputation came shortly after he returned from his failed mission to Chihuahua at the behest of Governor Armijo to secure drastically needed military supplies for the impending invasion of New Mexico by the United States. Donaciano's frustration and disillusionment with the mother country, already great, must have boiled over as he prepared the proposals. Moreover, his status as an alternate member suggests that the majority of the deputation would have had to approve his legitimacy as an acting delegate and embrace his arguments if they were to become the official declaration of the assembly. Perhaps Donaciano had suggested and the delegates concurred that he had an urgent message to deliver to the assembly.

DONACIANO VIGIL AS A DISSIDENT *VOCAL* AND ADVOCATE FOR NEW MEXICO: "ARMS, INDIANS, AND MISMANAGEMENT"

Donaciano wrote two speeches containing his proposals for consideration and action by the New Mexico Assembly. The first was titled "Vigil Opina sobre Armas, Municiones, Comercio, Norteamericanos, y Indios Bárbaros" (Vigil on Arms, Munitions, Trade, North Americans, and Barbaric Indians). The second was titled "Vigil Opina sobre la Maladministración de Nuevo México bajo los Gobernadores Pérez y Martínez y bajo el Comandante General García Conde" (Vigil on the Maladministration of New Mexico under Governors Pérez and Martínez and under Commanding General García Conde).[61]

David Weber so appreciated the seminal importance of Donaciano's speeches as rare examples of the writing of one nineteenth-century Hispanic figure that he took the time to research, transcribe, translate, and edit the book *Arms, Indians, and the Mismanagement of New Mexico*. In his introduction, Weber offered his justification for this unique approach to presenting a historic document: "First-hand accounts of conditions in New Mexico have almost entirely come from the pens of foreigners [such as Josiah Gregg and George Kendall], which were invaluable descriptions of New Mexico [notwithstanding their biases and prejudices]." Hispanic New Mexicans, however, "had few outlets for their prose [which] rarely contained analysis or systematic commentary on the larger problems of the province.... Among the few exceptions are two remarkable proposals by Donaciano Vigil, one of New Mexico's leading citizens. ... He hoped they would be brought to the attention of the federal officials in Mexico City."[62]

Weber published the speeches in English and Spanish, shortened the titles to "Arms, Indians, and the Mismanagement of New Mexico," and noted the difficulty of transcribing and translating Donaciano's proposals. He endeavored to remain "as faithful to the original as I could make them, for I sought to retain the structure of [a] mid-nineteenth century New Mexican document." Weber recognized the uniqueness of Donaciano's writing style and sought to "preserve the spirit and flavor of Vigil's prose," even as he critiqued it. Weber's second aim was to achieve "clarity and grace in English," although the two goals proved to be "mutually exclusive." Weber may have been too harsh when he indicated that Donaciano "didn't write clearly or gracefully in Spanish" and that "the writing did not lend itself to translation." Syntax and spelling were "sometimes archaic [or] simply erroneous," and he was frustrated by Donaciano's use of abbreviations: the middle letters of a word were sometimes omitted, and a single line above indicated the omission, as in $\overline{dros}$ (derechos), $gob\overline{n}o$ (gobierno), or $ad\overline{mon}$ (administración). Sometimes he wrote the first part of a word and used two letters slightly above the earlier part to complete the spelling. An example would be $departam^{to}$ or $solam^{te}$. Other challenges were the use of *q* as an ending of a word, as in *porq* (*por que*), or a lack of spacing, as in *porla* (*por la*). Other idiosyncrasies in Donaciano's writing were the interchangeability of certain letters, such as *c* and *s* (as in *cebolla* or *seboya*); *b* and *v* (as in *vado* or *bado*); and *y* and *i* (as in Ignacio or Ygnacio). Finally, there were omissions of silent letters, as in *elado* (*helado*), *ostilizar* (*hostilizar*), or *era* (*hera*).[63] What Weber regarded as Donaciano's poor syntax and spelling, however, might have been a form of shorthand or a purposeful intent to disguise his writing or to shorten the length of his compositions. These forms were used by others in that era, and it is reasonable to assume that most people were able to read them. Donaciano's writing is significant for his conveyance of thoughts and ideas and as a study of the written language in New Mexico in that era.

Weber's obvious admiration and respect for Donaciano were clear when he described the circumstances of his work on the book, which had "been a long time in coming to fruition." Weber traveled to Madrid, Spain, where he spent approximately six months and "worked at the Biblioteca Benjamin Franklin, to polish the transcription and translate into English the frontier Spanish of a one-time subject of Spain's far-flung empire. Donaciano Vigil would have been amazed."[64]

The true essence and pure meaning of Donaciano's words are appreciated by reading them in Spanish as he wrote them, and this is why Weber provided a Spanish transcription. He also provided an English translation that is a true representation of Donaciano's message. The two versions provide clues about his manner of writing (style, phraseology), composition, idiom (choice of words, mode of speech), and artistry, as well as the research that went into their preparation. Just as Weber did in his book, we provide a brief summary of each of the proposals. So that the reader can appreciate Donaciano's own words in context, we recommend a full reading of both speeches in English and Spanish in Weber's book.

Donaciano began his first proposal in a dire tone: "The misfortunes that affect our department have reduced it to a state of such insecurity that it cannot continue in this decadent condition much longer" (Las desgracias que cada dia con mas frecuencia afligen á nuestro departam.to, lo han reducido á un estado tan poco seguro q. yá no podrá seguir mucho tiempo en este estado de decadencia).[65]

Donaciano then offered background information where he compared the period before and after Mexican independence from Spain. Before independence, he pointed out, Spain was able to keep the Indigenous people at bay with the promise of barter, gifts, and other rewards, the "velvet glove," as Weber put it.[66] Small armies of Spanish soldiers were able to launch effective campaigns that enticed the Natives into favorable trade, and the Natives agreed not to raid Spanish settlements. This all changed when Mexico gained its independence and opened the borders to trade with the United States. When Mexico "proclaimed its glorious independence," Donaciano asserted,

> we in New Mexico seconded with such enthusiasm.... We were swept up by ... patriotic discourses.... We expected to enter a new era of happiness, and this word and the word "liberty" were those that were most used and most repeated in those days. We saw everything, then, through rose-colored glasses.[67]

> (Luego q. se proclamó la gloriosa yndepend.ª de la nación Mejicana que el Nuevo Méjico secundó con tanto entuciasmo ... y de los discursos

patrióticas q. circularon entonces entre nosotros nos prometíamos entrar en una era de felicidad, y esta palabra, y la de libertad heran las que tenian mas uso y mayor eco en aquellos tiempos. Todo entonces se nos pintaba con color de rosa.)[68]

Later, however, harassment of American traders by New Mexico officials caused the traders to move outside of New Mexico into American territory, where they built trading posts that dominated the commerce with Indigenous people. The United States became the primary trading partner for the tribes, which were now able to procure guns and other weapons that they used to pillage the New Mexican settlements. This was disastrous for New Mexico. Guns obtained from merchants were used by the Natives to raid New Mexico villages. They carried away livestock (horses, cattle, and sheep), which they used to barter with American merchants, and human captives, whom they sold into slavery. The Natives also used guns to hunt for buffalo, a source of meat and hides for consumption and trade.

Donaciano delivered his first proposal in a speech accompanied by a written document in a meeting on 18 June 1846. He was acting as a suplente and requested that the deputation petition the Mexican Congress to allow guns and munitions to enter New Mexico free of taxation. He argued that increased firepower was vital to New Mexico's defense, and Indigenous people, not the Anglo Americans, were the main threat. He pointed out that relations between New Mexicans and the mobile tribes, such as the Navajos, Utes, and Apaches, had brought "death and destruction," which he attributed to American influence. The trade with Americans had made available better goods at lower prices, but it had shifted the balance of power with the tribes.[69] After New Mexico received word of its "glorious" independence from Spain and "in spirit" from Mexico, the "new era of happiness" was short-lived. New Mexicans were frustrated. They wanted to advance their country, address their "misfortune," and "prove to the nation and the entire world that we, by our own virtues, are worthy in every way of the inheritance of our forefathers."[70]

Persuaded by Donaciano's "solid reasons and justice," the New Mexico deputation followed his advice to send copies of the proposal to the Mexican Congress and to New Mexico's delegate to the congress, Tomás Chávez y Castillo, so he could support and lobby for it. As Weber pointed out, even if the proposal reached Mexico City, it was too late to help the embattled province. Donaciano and his colleagues were not aware of it, but fighting had erupted between the United States and Mexico even as he spoke to his colleagues.[71]

Four days after his speech on arms and munitions, Donaciano returned to the assembly and presented a second proposal. He argued:

> The nation is about to restructure itself.... Therefore I believe ... [it is] an opportune time for this assembly to request that in the future the political and military commands of this department be entrusted to people who are either natives of it, or who have resided among us long enough before their nomination to know our interests and the various needs that arise from our particular situation.[72]

> (Estando para constituirse de Nuevo la nación, creo la ocación oportuna y muy útil al Nuevo Méjico, que V. E. encargue á nuestro representante, que solicite de la autoridad á quien corresponda que enlo futuro los mandos político y militar de este departam.to sean confiados á personas nativas de el ó que hayan recidido entre nosotros el tiempo suficiente anteriormente á su nominación para conocer nuestros intereces y las diferentes necesidades que nos causa lo peculiar de nuestra cituación.)[73]

Donaciano felt that leadership positions should be filled by New Mexicans or those with long residency in the territory. This proposal was self-serving: as a New Mexican and potential office seeker, he stood to benefit by its adoption. However, it is important to note that Donaciano's proposal did not intend to disqualify every non–New Mexican, only those who were not sufficiently experienced by having lived and served in New Mexico and being exposed to its peculiar problems and concerns. Again, he presented arguments based on recent experience where such appointments had led to disaster. He reviewed the records of three previous leaders: Albino Pérez (1835–1837), Mariano Martínez (1844–1845), and General Francisco García Conde (1845), whose performances, in Donaciano's view, had been less than stellar.[74] Governor Pérez had made local leaders feel "snubbed" when he failed to rely on their advice and experience and chose instead to listen to "favorites" who were less knowledgeable. Pérez's campaign against the Navajos had failed because he did not understand Indigenous "psychology" and was outmaneuvered in bargaining with the Natives. Donaciano argued that Pérez had "caused" the 1837 rebellion because he had misread the local sentiments against centralization and a new tax.[75] Donaciano's argument that Pérez was solely to blame contrasted with other interpretations of the rebellion's cause. In particular, some who blamed Manuel Armijo felt that he had helped instigate the revolt by his own power grab. Donaciano, in contrast, sided with Armijo (his mentor) because Armijo had stabilized conditions following the revolt.[76]

Donaciano also focused criticism on Martínez who, like Pérez, had surrounded himself with "sycophants" who did not know how to deal with the Indigenous people and thus blundered into war with the Utes, who had been at peace "since time immemorial." Martínez also squandered department finances, did not pay the troops, and extracted loans from local citizens. He left office as New Mexicans were on the verge of another rebellion.[77]

In the case of García Conde, Donaciano's prejudice against the commanding general of the Fifth Division of the Mexican army may have been professional. The military reorganization that brought García Conde to Santa Fe had subordinated New Mexico to the commanding general in Chihuahua, a position also held by García Conde. Donaciano charged that the general confiscated funds from the treasury, dismissed local treasury officials unfairly, and alienated New Mexico military officers by overextending his authority. Donaciano did not mention García Conde's successful negotiations with the Comanches. Donaciano concluded his second speech by proposing that New Mexico's representative in the congress, Tomás Chávez y Castillo, be advised to seek a measure that would ensure that the chief military and civil offices of New Mexico "always be given to people who have lived long enough among us to know our true interest intimately."[78]

Donaciano's central message in both proposals is a patriot's cry for the very survival of the province. The risk was not from a distant adversary (the United States) threatening to invade the territory, but from an actual enemy (the Indigenous people), who had been slowly and systematically devouring the colony. His speeches were a call to his colleagues, directed through the only representative forum available to them, to enact laws, to take and own leadership for the inevitable struggle, and to inspire their vecinos to take up arms for the defense of their country. He not only was appealing to them as ordinary citizens of the territory, but was appealing to their sense of honor and their humanity as the proud children of a proud people. Donaciano focused on the continuous Native threat to New Mexico rather than the far greater, more powerful, and more consequential threat of imminent invasion by a foreign country. Donaciano may have already foreseen that his *patria* (homeland) would be delivered from the Indigenous threat through absorption by an emerging world power that would incorporate its people into a more powerful nation and resolve the local threat.

It is interesting to speculate what was going through Donaciano's mind, his "breathing thoughts," as he prepared his proposals and equally interesting to speculate on what he hoped to achieve by the "words that burn."[79] Surely, he did not intend to simply restate the well-known truths that New Mexico was short on munitions and needed more and better supplies to carry the war to the Indigenous enemy. He did not say anything new about how the entry of American merchants had complicated matters by making arms available to the Natives, nor were his words about the neglect and mismanagement of New Mexico by Mexico anything novel. It is clear that Donaciano's words were directly intended to inflame New Mexicans' passions about Mexico's maladministration.

In a revealing letter to his mentor, Manuel Armijo, Donaciano expressed frustration at Mexico's "inability to achieve true liberal principles" and even expressed admiration for Texas for having fought a war of independence "to rid herself of an abominable tyranny."[80] It is logical to speculate that by restating well-known truths and showing that they were interconnected, he was proposing a radical departure to approach those problems. He might have reached the conclusion that the plight of New Mexicans, already threatened under Mexico, had become untenable given the American presence. It had become abundantly clear, even to the isolated New Mexicans, that the United States had grand designs on the Southwest, particularly California, and the rumors of an American invasion included New Mexico. Donaciano may have decided that the years of Mexican hegemony over New Mexico were rapidly coming to an end and that a New Mexico under American dominion was an inevitable and perhaps even a desirable outcome.

Thus, the underlying purpose of his speeches may have been to establish a new precedent of open criticism of the Mexican regime, setting an example for his colleagues, some of whom remained loyal to the mother country. This was a risky move on Donaciano's part. His harsh criticism of the Mexican government could jeopardize his relationships with his Mexican military superiors, and he could be stripped of his military rank or, even worse, arrested for sedition. On the other hand, his well-grounded logic, impassioned appeal, and strong rhetoric could encourage his influential colleagues to join the chorus of open criticism of the Mexican government. It could be the beginning of a change in public opinion in favor of an American government.

Padre Antonio José Martínez ultimately reversed his opposition to the Americans and participated in early efforts to secure territorial or statehood status for New Mexico. Padre José Manuel Gallegos would serve terms as New Mexico's delegate to the US Congress. For Donaciano Vigil, those momentous speeches were personally transformative, elevating him to a higher level as a political leader. He would no longer occupy the role of a silent observer, standing on the sidelines as other players determined the outcomes. With the coming of the American occupation and the subsequent vacuum of Hispanic leadership in the new American government, he would be thrust into the political arena, and he would perform admirably.

THE WINDS OF WAR IN NORTH AMERICA

Democrat James K. Polk was elected president of the United States in 1844 after running on a strong expansionist platform and a pledge to support the annexation of the newly independent Republic of Texas. The relative ease with which Texas had secured its independence from Mexico and now sought annexation by the United States made it clear that Mexico's hold on its remaining northern provinces of New Mexico and California was hanging by a thread. In those provinces, Mexico had "virtually lost effective control," and both were ridden by "disaffection and unrest." An independence movement had grown in Texas, and a "peaceful infiltration" by Americans was well advanced. As Otis Singletary wrote, these circumstances "advanced the popularly held belief that eventual possession of the two areas by the United States was inevitable."[1]

Although the previous president, John Tyler, had signed the bill annexing Texas, Mexico vowed war if the United States proceeded with Texas's annexation. Thus, when he assumed office in 1845, Polk inherited the prospect of war and quickly took steps to engage Mexico not only over Texas, but to acquire the expansive New Mexico Territory and California by monetary purchase rather than resorting to military action. The general feeling in Washington was that a "small irregular force could easily overrun New Mexico" since there was no "effective opposition," and California also was "practically abandoned" by Mexico, and its "small scattered population . . . ridden by disaffection and unrest was effectively derelict."[2] To effectuate his plans, Polk strengthened the American naval force under Commodore J. D. Sloat, which was stationed off the California coast, and ordered Sloat to seize San Francisco and other key points. In May 1846, upon news that fighting had broken out along the Rio Grande, Sloat was ordered to capture the Monterey port while awaiting additional vessels to impose a general blockade of the region.[3]

THE AMERICAN MILITARY OCCUPATION OF NEW MEXICO

President Polk's western expansionist agenda was to acquire Texas and California. As the New Mexico Territory, which included all of present-day Arizona up to the California border, was between the two, it had to be included in the strategic land grab. To secure New Mexico and at the same time resolve the New Mexico–Texas border issue, Polk ordered the creation of a detached unit of a volunteer army to march overland to New Mexico. For this task, he called on a career officer, Colonel Stephen Watts Kearny, who had joined the army during the War of 1812 and had spent most of his subsequent duty on the frontier. By 1846, he was commanding the First US Dragoon Regiment at Fort Leavenworth, Kansas. Colonel Kearny's orders were to raise an army of volunteers from Missouri, Kansas, and other western states to join his First Dragoon Regiment and proceed to conquer and pacify the New Mexico Territory. He was to use peaceful means, if possible, but employ force if necessary. The new military contingent was named the Army of the West and was composed of 1,700 troops, including mounted dragoons, infantry foot soldiers, and a supply wagon train. The army was on the road by late June 1846. Just west of Independence, Missouri, it picked up the Santa Fe Trail (see map 1). James Magoffin, a Kentuckian and influential trader on the Santa Fe Trail, traveled ahead with a military escort on a secret mission to augment Kearny's military objective.[4]

The prospect of a peaceful American occupation of New Mexico was seen in the States as a real possibility, and there were credible rumors to support that likelihood. Some rumors speculated about collusion among American and Hispanic New Mexican traders to produce a peaceful outcome. A newspaper in St. Louis, Missouri, reported in 1846 that Governor Manuel Armijo, in a Santa Fe meeting with prominent American traders, had professed friendship and hopes for "peace" between the two countries and had declared that if war was announced "there would be no fighting by the people of New Mexico."[5]

The march of the Army of the West in June and July 1846 followed the traditional route of the Santa Fe Trail and was relatively uneventful aside from the inconveniences of traveling through the arid plains in the summer. Soldiers complained of heat, thirst, dust, fatigue, and the monotony of the daily routine.

FIGURE 4. General Stephen Watts Kearny (c. 1846). Kearny led the Army of the West in the military occupation of New Mexico, oversaw the creation of the Kearny Code in New Mexico, and appointed the first territorial officials under the code. Source: Original daguerreotype engraved by W. P. Welsh for *Graham's Magazine*, Peter A. Juley and Sons, photographer. ZIM, UNM, CSWR, PICT COLLS 000-742-0067.

Still, the soldiers feared the unknown: they were invading an unfamiliar territory defended by an unknown force.[6]

Kearny and his army made the trek from Independence, Missouri, to Bent's Fort in Colorado, which was operated by brothers William and Charles Bent. At Bent's Fort, the army took a brief rest while Kearny finalized plans with Magoffin, who would proceed ahead and apply "tactful persuasion" to convince Armijo to capitulate. Magoffin, accompanied by Colonel Philip St. George Cooke, would deliver a stern warning that military force would be used against any resistance. Both emissaries were to assure the people and officials of New Mexico that they would not be disturbed if they remained peaceably in their homes.[7]

When Magoffin and Cooke arrived in Santa Fe, they were joined by American merchant Henry Connelly, and the group met with Armijo and apparently found him receptive to their offer. No official record was kept of the negotiations, but it appears that during their visit, Armijo agreed to withdraw his troops, even though the group agreed that he would make a show of resistance. Magoffin later submitted a claim to the US government seeking compensation for expenses amounting to $50,000 during the negotiations.[8] The line item of $2,000 for entertaining officials in Santa Fe seemed particularly suspicious, but it was never confirmed that money actually changed hands. If Armijo did settle for $2,000, that had to be the deal of the century, surpassing even President Thomas Jefferson's purchase of the Louisiana Territory.[9] Apparently, the emissaries had a harder time convincing Colonel Diego Archuleta, a more belligerent adversary who had ambitious designs of his own. When Magoffin assured him they were only interested in New Mexico east of the Rio Grande and that perhaps he could emerge as the leader of the western half, this mollified his ambition, at least temporarily.[10]

Following their departure from Bent's Fort, Kearny and his army proceeded west on the mountain route of the Santa Fe Trail through Raton Pass into New Mexico. The Army of the West arrived in Las Vegas, New Mexico, on the evening of 14 August 1846 and camped on a hill along the Gallinas River, just east of the town. Several townsmen approached the camp, some curious and some more enterprising, who sold the soldiers milk, bread, mutton, cream, and cheese. One soldier remembered, "They took care to demand a very high price."[11] On the following day, Kearny and his officers entered the town plaza where the local men had assembled. The women and children hid in the *crestón* (hill) west of town. Kearny climbed a rickety ladder onto the roof of a building (the later Dice Apartments) and spoke to the crowd of 150 men. He proclaimed that he was taking possession of New Mexico on behalf of the United States and that Manuel Armijo was no longer their governor. He offered assurances that "we come among you as friends, not as enemies, as protectors, not as conquerors."[12] Following his explicit orders from President Polk, he made it clear that the American occupation was permanent and that New Mexico and its citizens would be absorbed by the United States, a message he would repeat in San Miguel del Bado and Santa Fe. He then administered the oath of allegiance to the United States to Alcalde Juan de Dios Maes. Kearny left a detachment of troops in Las Vegas, and he and the rest of the army resumed their trip to Santa Fe. Kearny and his troops approached with caution, having heard rumors that 600 Mexican soldiers were awaiting them for battle at El Puertecito (the Little Gate, later known as Kearny Gap) five miles south of Las Vegas (see map 1). However, no one was present, which led one soldier to write in a diary, "We are disappointed in not meeting the enemy today, as all appeared eager for a fray."[13]

THE APPROACH OF KEARNY AND THE ARMY OF THE WEST

When Donaciano Vigil had returned to Santa Fe in the spring of 1846 from his special mission in Chihuahua, Governor Armijo had appointed him secretary to the general staff of the governor and military commander. Donaciano thus participated in the development of the plans for the defense of the territory. He continued in that capacity until the actual deployment of troops at Apache Canyon, at which time he joined the soldiers awaiting the arrival of General Kearny and the Army of the West.

The preparations of the general staff could not have gone much beyond planning a single stopgap defensive measure to halt the American advance at Cañoncito (also known as Apache Canyon). Using military labor to build ramparts and earthworks to fortify the narrow passageway between the mountains was the most efficient use of workers and munitions to stop or stall any military force, and this is what Armijo chose to do. Nevertheless, Armijo seemed more preoccupied with political concerns, such as securing the authorization to force loans from wealthy New Mexicans to pay for the expenses of the army and holding public forums seeking support for the effort. By the summer of 1846, the rumors of a possible invasion by the Americans had morphed into the reality of an impending invasion.

In addition to resuming his military duties, Donaciano also had resumed his duties as suplente vocal in the New Mexico Assembly. Yet even as Kearny's Army of the West was heading toward New Mexico, officials seemed unconcerned. "At first thought, it seems strange that New Mexico was so heedless of the impending conflict, or rather how that conflict was apt to affect her fortunes."[14] Historian Lansing Bloom reflected the American historians' view of how New Mexico in the spring of 1846 seemed oblivious to the looming invasion by the United States. Bloom speculated that perhaps New Mexico felt secure because of the hundreds of miles of prairie that separated New Mexico from the United States, or perhaps New Mexicans felt that any conflict would be confined to Texas or Colorado. Whatever the reasons, some New Mexicans believed that Santa Fe would never be the target of an American invasion. New Mexicans, however, were naïve in not realizing that "California was even more the prize and New Mexico lay in the path overland to California."[15]

On 2 June 1846, Governor Manuel Armijo had installed his household in the Palace of the Governors for what he anticipated would be a five-year residence. On 6 June, he issued an impassioned proclamation to the troops under his command to prepare for war against the United States: "The ambitious government of the United States at the very time it was practicing this hypocritical conduct of dispatching its envoy [John Slidell] to our government, issued orders to its commandants of land and naval forces . . . taking the left margins of the [Rio] Bravo [General Zachary Taylor] and posting its vessels in the port of Veracruz [General Winfield Scott]."[16] He addressed his troops as "my friends" and appealed to them for consistency and endurance as they primed for conflict in the name of the supreme government, as "ye shall make yourselves distinguished in future epochs solely for saving the Fatherland."[17]

On 1 July 1846, Governor Armijo hurriedly convened the assemblymen to inform them of the advancing American army. He had been notified about the progress of Kearny's army by a friend and business partner, Albert Speyer, who had arrived in Santa Fe on 24 June. Speyer had contracted with Armijo to deliver a supply of munitions for the New Mexican militia, but before leaving Missouri, he had heard of Kearny's preparations there and so departed hastily for New Mexico because he feared his shipment of arms would be confiscated.

After Speyer arrived in Santa Fe and delivered the arms to Armijo, the two dissolved their partnership.[18]

The record of the proceedings of the 1 July 1846 meeting clearly reflected the urgency conveyed by Governor Armijo in calling on the assembly for support. The minutes showed that Armijo "informed this Illustrious Corporation of the urgent circumstances which the Department now finds itself placed upon toward which the enemy of the national government is now [advancing]." Without delay, he exhorted the assembly to "present themselves for the discharge of duty entrusted to them ... and decree measures in accord with their prerogatives."[19] The senior vocales were absent, either by choice or by chance, and when they were summoned, they did not show any sense of urgency on the matter. In fact, the assembly continued in subsequent sessions to consider ordinary matters that included how much regular and alternate vocales should be paid and when and how they would be paid.[20]

Finally, in the session of 13 July, Tomás Ortíz, one of the most senior vocales, proposed a resolution for consideration by the assembly that "proper" actions be taken "for the conservation of the national territory whether it be that they tend to securing extraordinary provisions to maintain the forces or that they be of such character as not to allow any other extraordinary resolution."[21] Given that there were no clear guidelines or mandates regarding the extent or nature of the department's and the assembly's powers, it seems that Ortíz's resolution would have been within the scope of the assembly's authority and at the same time provide Governor Armijo with some affirmation of support to act in the best interests of the department. The sad reality is that even on such a seemingly clear, simple, yet significant matter, the assembly was mired in the minutiae of procedural details and could not act: "Deputy Ortíz' resolution did not pass!"[22] Bloom lamented the implications of this failure to act, dismayed that "responsible representatives chosen from among her citizens should have been more concerned about the arrival of the annual United States caravan and the payment of their own salaries than they were to provide adequately for the defense of their country and people against the already declared enemy of their nation."[23] Bloom observed that New Mexico's absorption by the United States would "outweigh the disadvantages.... *La Patria* was more an ideal than a reality—more a sentiment than a fact."[24]

On 9 August, having failed to gain outright support or action from the assembly, Governor Armijo called for a meeting of prominent citizens at the Palace of the Governors to consider his options. Strangely, Armijo was ambivalent at this late stage about how to deal with the upcoming invasion. As governor he had to defend the territory against invasion, and he had set in motion, at least publicly, the chain of events necessary for that, such as his pronouncements to the troops, the assembly, and the public at large. However, the feedback that he received from his officers in the militia, from the assembly, and from the public was divided; some favored resistance, and others advocated peaceful submission.

The 9 August conference at the Palace of the Governors did not resolve matters. The majority of those present preferred peaceful surrender without resistance, but a more vocal minority led by Manuel Chávez, Miguel and Nicolas Pino, and Tomás C. de Baca argued for resistance. The latter prevailed, and they pledged to join with Armijo to prepare the militia for defense of the department.[25] Armijo, displaying his eloquence, issued a final written message to the inhabitants of New Mexico, which affirmed his decision to defend the territory. Armijo exhorted his fellow patriots to defend themselves against the invasion of the American government, and he assured them that he was "ready to sacrifice his life and interest in defense of his beloved country."[26]

On 10 August, the assembly met for its last regular session prior to the American invasion. They discussed a decree that had been presented but tabled in their previous special session. In that session, they had heard communication from Governor Armijo that the invading American forces were proceeding to Santa Fe, and he had begged that the "Exc. Assembly aid him in any way that may be possible and within their powers."[27] On 8 August the president of the assembly, don Felipe Sena, had taken the floor and reported the dismal news from the governor. The circumstances for the department were pressing and calling for action, and he proposed the formation of a committee that "with all due judgement [would] unravel the matter."[28] Assemblyman Donaciano Vigil then took the floor and pointed out that "certainly the straits of the department were exceedingly urgent and for that very reason they should, after discussing the matter, decide in the present session whatever might be best."[29] Donaciano appreciated the urgency in Governor Armijo's plea and at the same time realized that the governor was asking for funds to mobilize and supply the troops in the current crisis. Expressing his own opinion, he urged the assembly to "now occupy itself with requiring the towns to contribute voluntarily according to their due proportion such assistance as they might desire to furnish the government."[30] Assemblyman Antonio Sena objected to Donaciano's and chairman

Felipe Sena's proposals because there was not sufficient time. He felt that the least amount of time required for such actions would be fifteen days, and by then the hostile forces would be in the towns of New Mexico. He suggested that a decree be promulgated to empower the governor with extraordinary authority to take discretionary measures for the sustenance of the forces under his command, which was supported by a majority (Felipe Sena, Santiago Armijo, and Antonio Sena). Donaciano dissented, arguing that the assembly was not empowered to enact such a measure. The final decision was to prepare the decree and present it for discussion and action at the next assembly session.

In the session of 10 August, the assembly took up the matter of issuing a decree. However, the members had received a new urgent message from the governor that Armijo would be marching to meet the invading forces, and "finding himself in extreme necessity . . . [he was making] his last recourse to this assembly so that, utilizing their powers, they may arrange some way of furnishing him no more than 1,000 pesos."[31] Given the exigency reported by the governor, the assembly deferred action on the decree proposed and instead provided for a "forced loan to the amount of 1,000 pesos . . . for said amount the inhabitants of the department lie responsible without exception by reason of person or privileged status [fueros], said amount falling temporarily on five persons of greatest means [and being recognized] . . . as a national debt guaranteed by the general treasury." However, the absence of any signatures attached to the last set of minutes indicated the "abrupt termination of Mexican legislative administration in New Mexico."[32] As the assembly concluded its final actions related to the impending invasion, Governor Armijo continued to seek opinions about the proper course of action while proceeding with the announced and overly delayed plan of preparing himself and the troops for the confrontation at Apache Canyon. The common thread one sees among the governor, the assembly, the militia, and the people of New Mexico at this time was ambivalence and indecision.

When Kearny, having been promoted to brigadier general, and his army arrived at Apache Canyon, the expected site of the highly anticipated battle, they found it abandoned. The ramparts and earthworks provided evidence that an army had recently been stationed there, but now the last possible defensible site had been abandoned. The common feeling among the soldiers was dismay: Apache Canyon was a perfect geographic location to mount a defense, and the Mexican army was not there to defend it. Some American soldiers who had kept diaries or logs of their service expressed their views about the Apache Canyon site, Governor Armijo, and the Mexican army, and their disappointment of being robbed of the opportunity to fight and achieve a great victory on behalf of their country. Marcellus Ball Edwards wrote, "Nature has done more than her portion towards making this an excellent fortification and one day's labor would have secured to them a position from which an army having the strength of theirs quadrupled, could not have dislodged them. We passed through, feeling that the cowardice of these people alone had secured to us an easy passage."[33]

It has not been fully established what exactly transpired between Armijo and his assembled army at Apache Canyon. Eyewitness reports were vague and contradictory in the specific details. Donaciano, usually not at a loss for words, simply wrote, "On the 16th of August, Mr. Armijo declared that without organized troops, he could not resist the invasion of General S. W. Kearny."[34] William Ritch, a territorial secretary and contemporary of Donaciano, wrote perhaps the most accurate and reliable version of what transpired since his account was based on personal interviews with some of the participants.[35]

When Governor Armijo had arrived at the encampment where the earthworks were laid out, artillery was positioned, and several hundred men were in defensive positions, he had already decided against launching a defense and sought some vindication for his decision. There was a large group of private citizens at the site, and when word came of the advancing army, they had urged him to advance with his troops and meet the enemy for battle. However, as soon as the citizens left, he expressed his true intentions. Determined to place his decision to retreat on the shoulders of his troops, he questioned the soldiers' experience and ability to fight a trained army. According to Ritch, Manuel Armijo held several consultations with his officers, repeatedly raising the question of whether they were ready to fight. Finally, some in disgust raised questions about his allegations about the evil intentions of the Americans. Hearing this, he became furious and ordered them to disband the troops and return to their homes. "The officers protested, but he responded with gross abuse, telling them that they were cowards and he would not risk a battle where the discipline and experience of a large portion of the men was only gained in fighting Indians.' He was told that he knew the character and discipline of his men as well before as after ordering them out!'"[36] Armijo selected an escort of regular army dragoons for his escape to Mexico, knowing he would be pursued and arrested by the Americans. Armijo ordered Captain Donaciano Vigil to accompany him in his retreat, at least as far as Socorro, but Donaciano, as Twitchell observed, "peremptorily declined, not choosing to subject himself to the caprice of one who had just proved himself so much of a poltroon, notwithstanding the generally pleasant relations existing between them in the past."[37]

Armijo has been universally vilified by historians as a coward who sought to blame others for his failures and as a traitor to his people in New Mexico, given his final actions on the battlefield and his escape to Mexico. He might have found some sympathy had he remained in New Mexico to answer for his actions in view of the ambivalence and indecision he had encountered among military officers, assembly members, and the people in general in the days before the American occupation. Governor Armijo's actions sealed his fate, however, and he was labeled corrupt, coward, and traitor. He might have been all three, but the circumstances had required that his options be carefully considered. He, perhaps more than any other New Mexican governor, had experienced the frustration of dealing with a Mexican government that had neglected, mismanaged, and exploited his territory. When he faced an advancing foreign army, he was left to fend for himself. He was aware that his forces, notwithstanding their superior numbers, were ill trained, ill equipped, and ill armed to defeat the better-trained and -armed American army. Even if his forces had been victorious at Apache Canyon, they would have most likely suffered many deaths and casualties. And even if they had prevailed in one battle, New Mexico would likely still have lost the war, as it did. Moreover, the prospect of continued subservience to Mexico was dismal at best.

Twitchell blatantly declared that everything that Armijo did in the weeks and days before his capitulation was aimed at justifying his actions and saving face with his superiors in Mexico. Twitchell claimed that Armijo did not resist because of the "lack of proper support by the constituted authorities in Santa Fe, which was his excuse for his cowardly retreat and surrender of his capital. His conduct was a complete exemplification of the fallacy of his favorite saying: 'Vale mas estar tomado por valiente que serlo'" (Better to be thought of as valiant [than] to be it).[38] Ultimately, his escape to Mexico provided him no quarter there—his own dragoon escort reported his cowardly actions—and in New Mexico his own soldiers spread the word of his behavior at Cañoncito.

Writing his autobiography in a third-person narrative, Donaciano described his own actions following Armijo's declaration of retreat: "En este tiempo, Donaciano Vigil como el Gn'ral hizo su manifestación de no resistír y en alguna manera impropia desprecío a sus soldados, él tomo el postidio de abandonar su propiedad que hera el empleo de capitán en la segura confianza que en este país se gosaban libertades." A translation of his words reveals Donaciano's admission that in "some unbecoming manner" he "slighted his soldiers" when he took the "back door" to "neglect duty" as a captain of the militia in the "confidence" that in this country "liberties were valued."[39]

Donaciano's soul-searching observation later in life was indicative of a guilt that perhaps haunted him, but nevertheless he had made the right choice. One does not have to wander very far forward in time to consider the ultimate fate for New Mexico had it remained under Mexico. In all likelihood, the engagement at Apache Canyon would have been a disaster for the Mexican soldiers. While it is true that the Mexican forces greatly outnumbered the Americans, they were comparatively untrained and unfit for battle. Armijo, their own commander, had said as much. The Mexican soldiers were armed with bows and arrows (*arcos y flechas*, in Donaciano's words) while the American soldiers were well equipped for the time with the most modern artillery, including antipersonnel projectiles like canister and grape bombs.[40] The American soldiers were anxious for battle after their long, uneventful trek over the Santa Fe Trail, while the New Mexican soldiers were wary and jittery, especially given their own commander's appraisal of them. If the Mexicans had remained to fight, "it would have been a very bloody day if the undisciplined and unled mob at Apache Pass had tried to resist Kearny's troops.... Thousands of New Mexicans might have been killed."[41]

Donaciano's reference to the fact that "en este pais [the United States] se gozaban libertades" (in this country, liberties were valued) proved to be valid, especially since liberties had proven elusive, as he pointed out, under the Mexican regime after Mexican independence. Further, the "Indian problem," which had more gravely concerned Donaciano in his 18 June 1846 presentation before the New Mexico Assembly, received immediate and forceful attention by General Kearny and his successor, Colonel Alexander W. Doniphan, who quickly marched into Navajo country and arranged for a peace treaty with fourteen Navajo chiefs.[42] General Kearny, Colonel Doniphan, and later Colonel Sterling Price were no doubt chagrined at the fact that American forces had come to New Mexico to fight Mexicans and ended up fighting Natives.

General Kearny's army, having unceremoniously passed through Apache Canyon, reached Santa Fe at six o'clock in the afternoon of 18 August 1846.

FIGURE 5. Kearny expedition postcard (posted 16 October 1946). This (first day of issue) anniversary card of the "acquisition of New Mexico" commemorated the centennial of the Stephen Watts Kearny expedition's arrival in Santa Fe in 1846 and included a postage stamp depicting US soldiers raising the flag over the Palace of the Governors. Source: ZIM, UNM, CSWR, MSS 349 BS, box 1, folder 2v.

FIGURE 6. Palace of the Governors, Santa Fe (ca. 1860–1900). The palace, of adobe construction dating to the seventeenth century, was the seat of government for New Mexico through the Spanish, Mexican, and American regimes for over 300 years. Donaciano spent the greater part of his life working there. Source: ZIM, UNM, CSWR, PICT COLLS 000-742-0649.

Acting Governor Juan Bautista Vigil y Alarid, a cousin of Donaciano, and thirty representatives of the city received the general, his staff, and some senior officers at the Palace of the Governors. Refreshments were served "as the American flag was hoisted over the ancient palace and a salute of thirteen guns from cannon planted on the eminence, afterwards known as Fort Marcy, declared the conquest of New Mexico complete."[43]

The following morning, Kearny addressed those assembled on the Santa Fe Plaza, proclaiming that he had come to take possession of New Mexico with "peaceful intentions and kind feelings and make it part of the United States." His soldiers would take no property without payment, nor would they harm anyone. He assured them that the religious freedoms and property rights of Americans would extend to them. He then absolved them of their citizenship of Mexico: "You are no longer Mexican subjects.... You are now become American citizens subject only to the laws of the United States." Finally, he announced his intent to form a "civil government on a republican basis, similar to those of our own states." He would appoint officers to serve in that government with himself as governor.[44] Clearly, this was Kearny's affirmation of President Polk's orders that New Mexico was now part of the United States.

Following Kearny's speech, Acting Governor Juan Bautista Vigil y Alarid addressed Kearny in a memorable speech on behalf of his fellow New Mexicans.[45] He acknowledged the "wonderful future that awaits us" and expressed allegiance to the established authorities "no matter what our private opinions are." The American forces were stronger and could not be resisted. "To us the power of the Mexican republic is dead. No matter what her condition, she was our mother.... What child does not shed abundant tears at the tomb of his parents? ... Today we belong to a great and powerful nation.... In the name of the entire department, I swear obedience to the Northern Republic and I tender my respect to its laws and authority."[46]

When Colonel John Munroe later became governor of the New Mexico Territory and asked Donaciano Vigil what he thought of the Mexican government, Donaciano responded with a slightly different emphasis than his cousin's: "I felt very much as a son would feel toward a parent, who had given him little or no attention in his youthful days, except as he extracted his hard earnings and left him to shift for himself when in trouble."[47] Donaciano's reaction to his cousin's words might have reflected his own sentiments at the time, and one can assume he felt a sense of pride that they were uttered by a fellow Vigil.

Donaciano's military career had ended unceremoniously on 17 August 1846 when General Kearny dissolved the Mexican army in New Mexico. He had served more than twenty-three years in the Mexican army. Donaciano also lost his position as vocal in the New Mexico Assembly. On 9 May 1870, Donaciano and thirty other *memorialistas* (as they called themselves), including his son Antonio, filed a memorial petition. This was a claim against the Mexican government for wages due to each of the memorialistas for service in the Mexican army. The petition gave their common narrative of the events leading to the deployment of troops and the dissolution of the forces, including the traitorous actions and orders of Governor Armijo, which had led to capitulation despite the objections of senior officers. In July 1870, the Mexican Congress made provision for the payment of this class of claims, but it is unknown if they were ever compensated.[48]

INTRIGUE AND POLITICS OF THE MEXICAN WAR

Having dispatched Stephen W. Kearny to New Mexico in what he anticipated would be a quick invasion, President James K. Polk sent John Slidell on a secret mission to Mexico City to negotiate a resolution to the Texas border dispute, settle $3 million in claims against Mexico, and offer to purchase all of the New Mexico Territory and California. The budget was $30 million for the claims and for the purchase of New Mexico and California. When news arrived in New Mexico of Slidell's overtures, New Mexicans responded not with a sense of Mexican nationalism, but with outrage from a sense of betrayal that Mexican authorities had somehow encouraged the proposal. Some New Mexicans, including Governor Armijo, considered separating from Mexico and forming the independent República Mexicana del Norte. Donaciano was at least sympathetic to the idea, having chided Mexico for imposing duties on the import of munitions to the department from the United States.[49]

Aware of Slidell's intention to attempt a coercive dismemberment of his country, Mexican president José Joaquín de Herrera refused to receive him. When Polk learned of the snub of his emissary, he ordered American troops under Major General Zachary Taylor to occupy the disputed area of Coahuila, Mexico, between the Nueces River and the Rio Grande. The intent was to provoke a Mexican retaliatory attack, which could be used as a justification for war. On 9 May 1846, President Polk began to prepare a message to the US Congress declaring war on Mexico because Mexico had refused to pay US claims and negotiate with Slidell. That same night, he received word that Mexican troops had crossed the Rio Grande on 25 April, moved toward northern and central Mexico, and attacked Taylor's troops, killing or injuring sixteen of them.

Polk quickly revised his message to Congress, which he delivered on 11 May 1846, claiming that Mexico had "invaded our territory and shed American blood on American soil." After hearing Polk's emotional and inflammatory speech, the Congress granted the president his declaration of war against Mexico on 13 May 1846. It is worth noting that the Mexican attack in Coahuila occurred in territory that was and remained part of Mexico after the war. Polk wasted no time in acting on the declaration by ordering General Taylor to proceed with his attack across the Rio Grande toward central Mexico. Major General Winfield Scott was later deployed with another army to sail to the Mexican port of Vera Cruz and proceed to capture the Mexican capital of Mexico City.[50] Following these actions, President Polk proceeded with his underlying objective of carrying the Mexican War to its logical conclusion by engaging Mexico on its own soil. After the Slidell mission stalled, he engaged the deposed president Santa Anna in a scheme to return him to power and deliver the desired territory to the United States. Polk even arranged for Santa Anna to bypass the American naval blockade of Mexico and allegedly delivered a $2 million bribe for his complicity.[51] Instead, Santa Anna reneged on the "shady deal" and arranged with Gómez Farías to have himself appointed as commander of the Mexican army. As Will Fowler observed, Santa Anna's sole concern was "to reorganize an army that could confront General Zachary Taylor's forces in the north ... [and] defend with ardor and enthusiasm the independence of the republic."[52]

When Santa Anna took over the war effort, he was beset by problems because only seven of the nineteen Mexican states sent soldiers, armaments, and money for the military conflict. He was forced to mortgage his own property to finance his army. He and his officers had difficulty training the soldiers. Many of them were conscripts whose loyalty was to local caudillos, and they lacked patriotism to the whole country. Discipline was a constant concern, and desertions were rampant. At the Battle of Buena Vista in February 1847, Santa Anna initially engaged Taylor and the American army, but he was forced to withdraw and restore order in the Mexican capital after an uprising against the government.[53] Still, despite suffering several defeats in continuous battles, he was able to reorganize and reposition his retreating army and prolong the war. Ultimately, the politicians in Mexico City decreed the final outcome as they stripped him of command. He had been reduced to an army of 1,000 while fighting desperately in the southern Mexican town of Huamantla. According to Fowler, again Santa Anna was "blamed for the tragedy" that was the Mexican War, and he became the scapegoat for the loss. Mexican assemblyman Ramón Gamboa concluded that Santa Anna was a "traitor who had purposely lost the war."[54]

In the end, the fatalism that Mexico brought to the war effort was reflected in the words of Mexican president Manuel de la Peña y Peña. He believed that the 1848 Treaty of Guadalupe Hidalgo was a "triumph of sorts," and Mexicans "deserved praise" for having saved half their territory and "not lost it all to the United States."[55]

7

AN AMERICAN POLITICAL LEADER

Preserving a Civil Government amid an Insurrection

In late August 1846, Stephen Watts Kearny settled into his quarters in Santa Fe and commenced the process of governing the newly acquired territory of New Mexico. He ordered the display of the American flag on the plaza and commissioned Captain William Emory, an engineer, to locate a site, draw plans, and begin construction of a defensive fort. Fort Marcy thus was located on the summit of a flat-topped hill, 600 yards north of the Santa Fe Plaza. Kearny then delegated the task of developing a body of laws for the civil government to Colonel Alexander W. Doniphan, a lawyer, who was assisted by another soldier-attorney, William P. Hall. The Kearny Code, as it came to be known, incorporated elements of Spanish, Mexican, New Mexican, American, and Missouri laws. On 7 September 1846, Kearny reported to his superiors in Washington that consolidated opposition to his troops had ceased to exist as "the inhabitants of the country were found to be highly satisfied and contented with the change of government and apparently vied with each other to see who could show us the greatest hospitality and kindness."[1]

On 22 September, Kearny announced the new plan for the civil government of the territory of New Mexico and the first officials he had appointed to fill key positions. Charles Bent was appointed governor; Donaciano Vigil, secretary; Richard Dallam, US marshal; Francis P. Blair, US attorney; Charles Blummer, treasurer; Eugenio Leitensdorfer, auditor; and Joab Houghton, Antonio José Otero, and Charles Beaubien, superior court judges. Two days after appointing these territorial officers, Kearny received general orders to proceed with the bulk of his Army of the West to California, where he was to assume command of the American forces involved in the acquisition of that territory. Colonel Sterling

FIGURE 7. Governor Charles Bent (ca. 1846). Bent was appointed governor of the civil government of New Mexico by General Kearny in September 1846. In January 1847, he went to Taos, his hometown, to quell the insurrection against American rule. He was brutally murdered by the rebels on 19 January 1847. Source: ZIM, UNM, CSWR, PICT COLLS 000-742-0019.

Price was placed in command of the American troops that remained in Santa Fe, and it fell to Price to work with the newly appointed civilian officials.

The selection of Charles Bent as governor was natural. He was an Anglo-American, and this would affirm that Americans were in control. He was from Virginia and a graduate of the US Military Academy at West Point. He had resigned his commission, and he and his younger brother, William, became prominent traders on the Santa Fe Trail in 1838. The Bent brothers formed a partnership with Ceran St. Vrain, another trader, and together they established posts for trade with the Natives. In addition to Bent's Fort in Colorado along the Santa Fe Trail, Charles Bent operated a general mercantile store in Santa Fe while residing in Taos, New Mexico.

A *NUEVOMEXICANO* IN THE FIRST EXECUTIVE CABINET UNDER THE KEARNY CODE

For the position of territorial secretary, essentially equal to a lieutenant governor and second in the line of succession, Kearny selected Donaciano Vigil. Kearny understood the necessity of recruiting able and respected New Mexicans to serve in the new civil government. Their participation would be invaluable in providing a semblance of legitimacy and inclusion in the new government while easing the administrative transition from the previous Mexican government. In selecting Donaciano for the position, Kearny showed insight for someone who had been in New Mexico for just one month. He had consulted with many of the American traders and merchants who came to establish headquarters in Santa Fe, as well as with leading Hispanic citizens. Donaciano had a reputation as honest, fair-minded, prudent, and progressive, and he was chosen, in part, because he had shown a distinct friendliness toward the United States.

Donaciano's intimacy with all aspects of New Mexico society—the people, the culture, the economy, the politics, and the problems—along with his education, bilingual ability, and experience would be invaluable not only in counsel with the governor and military leaders, but as an everyday administrator. His advice would be valuable in matters such as the latent hostility the Americans could expect from disaffected New Mexicans who maintained loyalty to Mexico and would continue to resist the US occupation. Additionally, Donaciano previously had held the similar position of secretary under the Mexican government and was familiar with the issues of landownership, land grants, and land registration, which would continue to be concerns for the new government.

When offered the position, Donaciano was aware of the profound implications of the choice before him. Mexican officials and those who remained loyal to the Mexican government would consider him a betrayer of the Mexican cause. Technically, in Mexico he could be tried as a traitor and possibly hung. Nevertheless, at the risk of his career as an army officer, he had publicly criticized Mexico as a vocal in the assembly. He had felt that the defenseless position of the province, the continuing "Indian threat," the unpreparedness of the military, particularly the lack of munitions and the fact that the Indigenous people were better equipped than the Mexican soldiers, were all critical issues. He had attributed these problems to the inept and corrupt administration under the Mexican government. Now, he felt that these ongoing problems would receive immediate attention under the American government. He had come to appreciate and even laud the "spirit of mercantile capitalism" that Americans had introduced. This spirit had inspired many nuevomexicanos to pursue opportunities as mercantile entrepreneurs and control "various branches of regional trade" throughout the territory.[2]

The United States promised change, progress, trade, commercial and economic development, new technology, a public education system, and the democratic and liberal ideals that were the foundation of a popularly elected government. Donaciano realized that men such as him, native New Mexicans, would have to participate in the new government to ensure that the interests of the Hispanic population were represented, protected, and included in governmental decision-making. He knew the disenchantment and resentment that had arisen when outside officials like Martínez and Pérez were imposed as governors on New Mexicans by the Mexican government. The various events surrounding the 1837 insurrection had shown that Donaciano, as a soldier, was loyal to the government officials (such as Pérez), but at the same time Donaciano was respected and trusted by the rebels, who recruited him as their secretary in the rebel government. That ability to relate to both sides would be crucial in the first months of the American occupation.

At the same time, Donaciano realized that American military officers would be suspicious of New Mexicans because of the differences in culture, language, and religion, so it was essential that he present himself as an example of a native New Mexican who could be respected and trusted and who would be loyal to the new government. Once again, Donaciano was faced with a momentous choice that would affect the future of New Mexico and its people. He rejected the chaos and failure of the Mexican past in favor of the promise of a better future under the US flag. Donaciano swore loyalty to the United States and accepted the position of secretary in the civil government of the territory of New Mexico established under the Kearny Code. Ironically, the Kearny Code is still considered the organic law (the original legal source) of American authority in the state of New Mexico.

REACTIONS TO NEW MEXICO'S INITIAL OCCUPATION BY THE AMERICAN ARMY OF THE WEST

Donaciano's first test of loyalty to the new American government occurred shortly after General Kearny's departure on 24 September 1846, when serious rumors of dissent and possible insurrection began to circulate in Santa Fe. Conditions had deteriorated owing to the conduct of the American troops, especially the undisciplined volunteers. Unlike his predecessor, Colonel Sterling Price was not a strict disciplinarian, and "relaxation and excesses" became more frequent and "good order" less frequent among the soldiers. A letter from Santa Fe published in *Niles' Register* reported that "the soldiers were a degenerated military mob, open violators of law and order and they heaped injury and insult upon the people.... Price's ... inability to control either officers or men had produced among the New Mexicans the strongest feelings of disgust and hatred and ... a desire to rebel existed among the inhabitants."[3] Incipient rebellion had replaced the calm atmosphere that Kearny had experienced in New Mexico. Among Kearny's circle, no one was as keenly aware as Donaciano of the degree and extent of the disaffection among some segments of the New Mexico population regarding the American occupation. As secretary, Donaciano took it upon himself to serve as the eyes and ears of the new administration on such matters. Other Hispanics favorable to the new government saw Donaciano as the one person in whom they could confide. Donaciano felt it was his duty to investigate and uncover plots against the government. William Ritch, a contemporary writer, noted later that Donaciano's "perfect familiarity" with the people and the area "made him of the highest possible advantage in council and to General Kearny and his successors."[4]

Rumors of plots and conspiracies were common in Santa Fe, but given the deteriorating state of affairs, Donaciano sensed something more sinister in the air in the fall and winter of 1846. He sought information on the persistent rumors he heard, and the first credible bit of information came from doña Tules Barcelo, the owner of a saloon and gambling house in Santa Fe. She reported rumors of an impending insurrection to take place in December. Donaciano investigated the matter and uncovered facts indicating that the plot was scheduled for Christmas Eve. The leaders were Tomás Ortíz, Miguel Pino, and Diego Archuleta, and there were at least a dozen other active participants and an untold number of associates in towns such as Santa Cruz, Taos, and Mora. Donaciano informed Price, the new military commander, about the details of the conspiracy. Colonel Price quickly issued orders for the arrest of the conspirators, and the plot was thwarted. The results of Price's investigation, which revealed the magnitude of the plot and the involvement of so many prominent men (including former public officials and militia members), must have seemed overwhelming to Donaciano.

The investigation revealed that Diego Archuleta felt cheated because Magoffin, the American who had negotiated with Armijo on the eve of the military invasion, had promised Archuleta that he could lay claim to all the land in western New Mexico. This promise was not fulfilled. Archuleta and his closest co-conspirator, Tomás Ortíz, a former Santa Fe alcalde, organized a meeting at Ortíz's house on 15 December 1846 that was attended by Juan Felipe Ortíz, a *vicario* (vicar) and the brother of Tomás, Domingo C. de Baca, Miguel E. Pino, Nicolas Pino, Manuel Chávez, Santiago Armijo, Agustín Durán, Pablo Dominquez, José María Sánchez, Antonio María Trujillo, Santiago Martínez, Pascual Martínez, Vicente Martínez, Antonio Ortíz, Facundo Pino, Padre Antonio José Martínez, and José Francisco Leyva of San Miguel. Archuleta presided at the meeting and called for the nomination of Tomás Ortíz as governor and himself as commanding general of the anticipated replacement government to be formed, which was approved by those assembled. They also decided that the participants from Santa Fe, led by Tomás Ortíz, would gather in the parish church on Christmas Eve. Those from outside Santa Fe, led by Archuleta, would arrive in the city and be hidden in private homes. At midnight, the church bell would signal the participants to gather in the Santa Fe Plaza, where they would seize the cannons and aim them at various points in the city. They would also attack the quarters of Colonel Price and his officers and take them as prisoners. Word was sent to other parts of New Mexico to alert other participants in the uprising, who would also take up arms against the Americans.[5]

Colonel Price thwarted the plot by issuing orders for the arrest of the conspirators. Archuleta and Tomás Ortíz escaped, and the uprising was prevented before it even started. Donaciano knew who was involved, where the meetings were being held, and when the uprising would take place.[6]

Donaciano's network of friends and associates did not report another uprising, although he continued to suspect such activity. Responding to the undisciplined conduct of American soldiers, different groups of malcontents began to arm themselves in preparation for such an eventuality. In the first weeks of January 1847, Governor Bent, aware of the discontent following the failed uprising of the previous December, issued a proclamation to New Mexicans calling for restraint. He implored the people "to turn a deaf ear to the false doctrines and to remain quiet, attending to your domestic affairs. . . . By doing so you may enjoy all the prosperity which your best friend wishes you."[7]

At the same time, insurgents in Taos were engaged in rabble-rousing activity, specifically agitating in Taos Pueblo. On 14 January, Governor Bent visited his hometown of Taos, thinking that his presence would calm his friends and neighbors and that he could prevail on the community to resist the malcontents. His friends and allies had sought to discourage him and urged him to wait until a military escort was organized for his protection. As secretary, Donaciano had warned Bent that "his undertaking was rash and begged him not to think of it."[8]

However, Bent ignored all advice and caution and proceeded, oblivious to any threat to his personal safety. He was convinced that he could allay the unrest by appealing in person to people with whom he had lived and worked for years.

On the night of 18 January 1847, "whiskey and wine were flowing.... Under the incendiary persuasions of Pablo Montoya [a local Mexican leader] and Tomásito Romero, an influential Pueblo Indian, the Mexicans and Indians were aroused to a condition of frenzy."[9] The next day, under the leadership of the two rebels, the insurrectionists headed to where the Americans lived and destroyed their homes. Romero led a group to Governor Bent's house and "firing through the door, wounded him in the chin and stomach; the door was next broken down and his body pierced with arrows.... [He was] scalped and killed."[10] Others killed in the Taos attack were Louis Lee, the acting sheriff of Taos; Cornelio Vigil, a prefect and uncle of María Ygnacia Bent; J. W. Leal, the district attorney; Pablo Jaramillo, a brother of María Ygnacia Bent; and Narciso Beaubien, a circuit judge. When word of the insurrection reached Santa Fe on 20 January, Colonel Sterling Price issued orders recalling commanders Major D. B. Edmondson and Captain John Burgwin in Albuquerque, who were to join him with one troop of soldiers and to leave a second troop in Santa Fe under Lieutenant Colonel David Willock to defend the capital.

Buoyed by their success in Taos, the insurrectionists quickly organized themselves into an army, selected leaders, and announced their intention to march to Santa Fe and retake the capital by attacking American military units, wagon trains, and any Americans. It was reported that most towns and villages in the northern part of New Mexico declared their support for the insurrection—except Las Vegas and Tecolote. These two did not join the cause because of the presence of Lieutenant J. R. Hendley, who was leading a detachment of American soldiers.

Following the Battle of Taos and the assassination of Bent, Donaciano, the next highest in civil authority, assumed the role of acting governor at the request of Colonel Price, who formalized the action by securing confirmation from Washington later. Donaciano's first step as acting governor was to issue a series of proclamations to inform the population of the ongoing developments, to allay any fears arising from the insurrection, to calm the residents, to urge adherence to the military authority, and to affirm the determination of the military to quell the uprising and arrest and punish the conspirators.

Colonel Price marched north to suppress the insurrection with five compa-

FIGURE 8. Colonel Sterling Price (ca. 1860). As commander of the Second Regiment of Missouri Cavalry, Price marched to New Mexico with Colonel Alexander Doniphan and joined Kearny's army in Santa Fe. When Kearny departed for California, Price assumed command of the American forces in New Mexico. After Bent was killed, he appointed Donaciano as governor, and they worked together to suppress the insurrection, restore order, and govern under the Kearny Code. Source: ZIM, UNM, CSWR; John H. Vaughan, *History and Government of New Mexico* (State College, NM: Vaughan, 1921), 147.

nies of Missouri Volunteers, Captain William Angney's battalion of infantry, and a company of Santa Fe Volunteers led by Captain Ceran St. Vrain (a partner of Bent in a mercantile business). Two of the soldiers in St. Vrains's company were Manuel Chávez and Nicolas Pino, who had been implicated in the failed Christmas Eve conspiracy. Price's force totaled 353 infantry soldiers and four twelve-pound mountain howitzer cannons. His command included some friends of Governor Bent, and they were determined to avenge Bent's and the others' brutal assassinations.[11]

Belying the long-held assumption that the conquest of New Mexico was carried out without firing a single shot, Colonel Price's army fought a series of battles against largely unorganized but determined insurrectionists trying to dislodge the Americans from New Mexico. Price's troops marched north twenty-five miles to Santa Cruz de la Cañada, where on the afternoon of 24 January they came upon a force of some 1,500 insurrectionists occupying an advantageous position on the heights east of the plaza overlooking the road leading into the village. Price formed his battle lines and deployed his artillery. An effort of the rebels to cut off the supply wagons trailing the main force was nullified, and the train was brought safely into the American position. Price then issued the command to attack. Simultaneously, the artillery opened fire, and several of Price's units under Angney, Lieutenant White, and St. Vrain attacked from different quarters. Within minutes, the insurgents were routed and retreated in different directions so that Price's troops could not pursue them. The American losses were two killed and six wounded while the insurrectionists had thirty-six killed and forty-five wounded.[12]

The next morning, the rebels reappeared on the hills near the town but retreated when the Americans pursued. On 27 January, Colonel Price continued north along the Rio Grande to Los Luceros. He was joined by Captain Burgwin, Lieutenant Wilson with a troop of First Dragoons, and a company of Missouri Volunteers under Lieutenant Boone. This increased Price's force to 479 rank-and-file soldiers. When the Americans reached La Joya, they learned that a party of seventy or eighty insurrectionists had taken defensive positions on the slopes of the mountains on each side of the Rio Grande at Embudo. Since the road to Embudo was not passable for artillery or wagons, Price sent Burgwin and the companies of St. Vrain and White, totaling 180 men, in that direction. Arriving at Embudo, the Americans found nearly 700 rebels positioned on either side of the canyon. Without hesitation, the Americans launched an assault on various sectors despite the difficulty of the terrain. St. Vrain's troops dismounted from their horses and attacked the insurrectionists with great effect. The Americans lost one man and another was severely wounded, both from St. Vrain's company. The rebels lost twenty, and sixty were wounded.[13]

The American forces reunited on 30 January at Las Trampas, thirty-two miles south of Taos, and General Price then directed his combined force toward Taos, where the insurrection had started. The march was hampered by newly fallen snow, two feet deep in places, and some of the men marching on foot suffered from frostbite. Arriving in Taos on 3 February, they learned that 700 insurrectionists were positioned within the fortified walls of Taos Pueblo. Reconnaissance determined that the most vulnerable position in the pueblo, the church in the northwest corner, was perhaps most susceptible to attack. A cross-fire artillery barrage from four howitzers and a six-pound cannon was launched at nine in the morning, aiming at the church. Two hours later, orders were given to storm the church since they had not been able to breach its two-foot-thick walls.

Captain Burgwin advanced on the western side with the dragoons, and Captain Angney attacked through the northern wall with two companies of Second Missouri Volunteers. The insurgents held out initially, pouring fierce fire on the Americans. Burgwin and a small party penetrated a corral in front of the church and tried to force open the door of the church, but the effort drew fire from all sides, and they were forced to retreat carrying their fallen captain, now mortally wounded. Eventually, the Americans created some holes with their axes. The Americans moved the six-pound cannon to within sixty yards of the church and pounded the walls to some effect, whereupon they moved it again to within ten yards and fired three more rounds into the opening. At this, the rebels fled in all directions with the mounted soldiers under Captain St. Vrain pursuing and killing many. The Americans were determined to prevent any counterattack.[14]

The Battle of Taos was costly to both sides, but especially for the insurrectionists who suffered 150 killed and many more wounded. Hispanos and Pueblos comprised the rebellious force, which "mirrored the coalition that had fought in the Rio Arriba rebellion in 1837. Their defeat in the three engagements culminating in Taos would end their resistance altogether."[15] In addition to the losses in battle, many insurrectionists were tried and convicted for their participation in the rebellion. The Americans were victorious in putting down the insurrection. However, their losses at Taos were significant considering that they had been unscathed during the initial occupation of New Mexico.[16]

During this time, there was also other insurrectionist activity. On 20 January 1847, a group of traders returning to Missouri was attacked entering the town of Mora. The party, led by Henry L. Waldo, a well-known trader on the Santa Fe Trail, was detained, all of their supplies were taken, and they were all shot. This raid was attributed to Manuel Cortez. He had a substantial group of followers who evaded the American patrols and continued their raids in northern New Mexico. A final battle at La Cuesta between American forces and 500 insurrectionists led by Cortez resulted in heavy casualities and the capture of fifty rebel prisoners. After this, rebel activity diminished.

In his first proclamation on 22 January, Donaciano had faced the daunting task of informing the people of the demise of the newly appointed governor and that the territory was consumed by insurrection. He had to allay fears, yet be resolute. The approach he took was that of the hombre de bien, decrying chaos and disorder and calling for peace over war, harmony over conflict, and the rule of law over lawlessness. He wrote, "Fellow citizens, your regularly appointed governor ... was the victim of a brutal assassination carried out during a popular insurrection incited by Pablo Montoya and [Manuel] Cortez of Taos." This was Donaciano at his best, an impassioned, logical writer and a sensible leader calling for rationality and calm, while condemning a ruthless mob. He attacked Montoya as a "mischievous fool" and mocked the would-be leader: "Another of his pretended objects is waging war against the foreign government. Why, if he is so full of patriotism, did he not exert himself to lead troops to prevent the entry of American forces in August . . . instead of gutting his insane passions and martial valor by the brutal sacrifice of defenseless victims."[17]

He reminded New Mexicans that Montoya had been one of the leaders of the 1837 rebellion against the government and was notorious for his "insubordination and restlessness." In 1837, "others paid for the execrations and 'this brigand' had been left living on his wits, for he has no home or known property and is engaged in no occupation." Donaciano referred to the rebels as a "gang" composed of insurgent Natives and others "as abandoned and desperate as their rebellious chief." He appealed to New Mexicans for patience in the developing relations with their new country and allegiance to it. He recalled the ambivalence most people had shown prior to the American occupation, including their disaffection with Mexico and the promise of a better future under the United States. He urged them to consider their original collective choice to cast their lot with the US system. "Whether this country has to belong to the government of the United States or return to its native Mexico, is it not a gross absurdity to foment rancorous feelings toward people with whom we are either to compose one family, or to continue our commercial relations? Unquestionably it is."[18]

Donaciano then issued a stern warning that "today or tomorrow, a respectable body of troops" would march to Taos to quell "these disorders"; the government was "determined to pursue energetic measures" until "they are reduced to order," as well as to "care and protect honest and discreet men." He urged his New Mexico compatriots to harken "to the voice of reason, for the sake of common happiness and your own preservation . . . keep yourself quiet and engaged in your private affairs."[19]

Donaciano issued this first general proclamation in a sincere and self-deprecating manner that was to be his trademark. He informed New Mexicans that "neither my qualifications nor the ad-interim character . . . encourage me to continue in so difficult and thorny a post, the duties of which are intended for individuals of greater enterprise or talents, but I protest to you, in the . . . fervor of my heart, that I will devote myself exclusively to endeavor to secure you all [the] prosperity so much desired by your fellow citizen and friend."[20]

In the second proclamation, "Triumph of Principles over Turpitude," Donaciano referred to himself as the "Interim Governor of the Territory of New Mexico" and addressed his words "to the Inhabitants of the Same," phrases he would use consistently in future proclamations, reflecting his need to remind himself and the population of his transitory role in the office of governor. He announced that the gang of Montoya and Cortez in Taos had met their fate at an area close to La Cañada, and order and peace had been restored by government forces. "Their hosts were composed of scoundrels and desperados so that it may be said that the war was one of the rabble against honest and discreet men." Donaciano encouraged New Mexicans to "think only of the security and protection of the law; and uniting with your government will afford it the aid of your intelligence, in order that it may secure to you the prosperity desired by your fellow citizen and friend."[21]

The second general proclamation was followed by a related circular, also written by Donaciano and released on 25 January 1847, titled "Supreme Government of the Territory." This was a summary of interconnected events that had transpired in the territory during the previous ten years, including the most recent conspiracies and insurrections against the government and their leaders.[22] Acting Governor Vigil declared that the conspirators, the "band of murderers and thieves," had met their fate. Diego Archuleta had cowardly retreated, and the others either were killed or would be prosecuted for their participation in the insurrections. Twitchell reported that "the facts as outlined in the proclamations and the logical arguments of Governor Vigil easily had a salubrious effect upon the people of the territory."[23] In March 1847, the "rigorous prosecution of those who had taken up arms against the American authority" was initiated by District Attorney Francis P. Blair in the court of Chief Justice Joab Houghton. A substantial number of those arrested or captured were discharged, however, for want of sufficient evidence to indict them for treason against a government of which, the prosecutor had to agree, "they were not citizens!"[24]

Between August 1846 and January 1847, Donaciano made three of the most consequential and controversial decisions in his life. The decision in August was to lay down his arms and those of his soldiers and not resist the American invasion. The second decision was to accept General Kearny's appointment in September as territorial secretary of New Mexico under the American regime. Third, in January 1847, he assumed the role of acting governor upon the death of Governor Charles Bent. What is important in order to understand Donaciano is that once he had considered all the circumstances and potential consequences, he was resolute in standing by his decision. He never second-guessed himself, never questioned his decision, and never wavered in following through regardless of the obligations, responsibilities, challenges, or consequences. One may ask what the consequences would have been for New Mexico had he not laid down his arms, had he not accepted Kearny's appointment to join the American cause, or had he refused to take the role of acting governor.

THE FORMALIZATION OF THE AMERICAN TERRITORIAL CIVIL GOVERNMENT OF NEW MEXICO

In June 1847 when Washington officials were apprised of the trials for treason of the Taos insurrectionists, they responded by repudiating the Kearny Code. Secretary of War William Marcy wrote to Colonel Sterling Price on 26 June 1847 that "the territory conquered by our arms ... does not become part of the United States ... and the inhabitants of such territory are not ... citizens of the United States."[1] Therefore, the insurgents could be tried by some judicial authority for their crimes but *not* for treason against the United States. Marcy was essentially saying that Stephen W. Kearny, notwithstanding his instructions from President Polk, could not declare New Mexico as part of the United States nor declare New Mexicans as citizens of the United States. Interestingly, Polk would affirm that fact in a message delivered on 24 July 1848.[2]

In New Mexico, Colonel Price and Donaciano Vigil in March 1847 had decided that the Kearny Code was the law, and the territory's government and the officers led by Donaciano would continue to be in charge. There was no other formal government in place and no contrary instruction from Washington. Acting Governor Donaciano must have realized that given the uncertain situation after the assassination of Governor Bent, it was his responsibility to preserve the civil government Kearny had envisioned, and that is what he chose to do.

IMPLEMENTING THE KEARNY CODE

Although Donaciano had been acting governor since the day after the assassination of Charles Bent on 19 January 1847, he continued to have misgivings about his qualifications and even strongly recommended Colonel Ceran St. Vrain for the office. However, Colonel Price, the American commander, issued the order formally appointing Donaciano as acting governor, and this action was confirmed by Washington officials later that year.³ In the aftermath of the Taos insurrection, Price imposed strict martial law, but he realized the necessity of retaining Kearny's "civil government" to act as a buffer against charges of military authoritarianism. By this time, he had come to trust Donaciano, who had remained steadfast in his support of the new order, had proved invaluable in ferreting out conspiracies, and had calmed the majority of the population in the wake of the disorder. This allowed Price to focus on the military mission of suppressing any future insurrections and dealing with recurring problems with the Indigenous people.

As the acting governor of a territory under military occupation with a military commander who was the de facto supreme authority, Donaciano was in somewhat of an untenable position. Using the Kearny Code as a semblance of a constitutional framework, he fashioned a workable government arrangement, exercising civil authority while yielding military control to the military command. This seemed acceptable to a degree to Colonel Price, although they had a rocky relationship at first. Donaciano, never one to mince words, had complained in a letter to US senator Thomas Hart Benton of Missouri about "two ills": the occupying army and its interference in the "business of civil servants," and the failure to "have government workers including myself paid."⁴ Donaciano also complained in a letter to US secretary of state James Buchanan in February 1847 about the boorish conduct of the soldiers, especially the volunteers, and expressed doubt that Price could curtail Navajo raids on settlements and have the Navajos return prisoners, as Kearny had promised. He questioned whether Price could bring about a "lasting submission of the Navajos."⁵

The subordinate position of the governor and other appointees of the civil government became clear to Donaciano at this time. When he wrote to Buchanan, along with expressing complaints about the state of affairs in New Mexico, he submitted a letter of resignation, hoping that Polk would appoint his successor. However, Secretary of War William Marcy wrote to Colonel Price assuring him that as military commander (to whom the civil officer was subordinate), he was empowered to appoint whomever he chose for the office. The method Donaciano used of going around the colonel to his superiors in Washington galled Price to the point where he suspended Donaciano and threatened to remove him from office. Donaciano viewed this as an assault (*atentado*) and expected harsh consequences, although he doubted Price could find someone of his generation (*hombres de mi tiempo*) to replace him. Ultimately, Price affirmed his support of Donaciano and his moving forward with the governmental processes outlined in the Kearny Code, such as the convening of a legislature.[6] Fortunately, the clash between Price and Donaciano did not receive public attention, and Donaciano remained in office. The problem of the volunteers was at least partially resolved when some were mustered out after their enlistment terms ended.

Colonel Price still chafed at the self-expression of local authorities, such as when Donaciano complained to his superiors and when the first territorial legislature created the offices of US attorney and US marshal. When Price reviewed the session's laws, he set aside the provisions calling for those positions in the territory. Price reminded Donaciano and other locals that "the government was essentially military in character."[7]

Another early challenge to Donaciano's standing occurred when a group of his compatriots tried to dislodge him from the governorship by complaining to Price that Donaciano was "disloyal and unpopular." On hearing this, Donaciano again offered his resignation, but Price rebuffed the critics and directed that Donaciano's "acting governor" label be removed; he would continue to hold the offices of both governor and secretary since no one had been appointed to fill the role of secretary when he was elevated to the governorship.[8] In reality, the critics who sought Donaciano's ouster were frustrated that such a respected and popular high-profile Mexican official had embraced the American occupation and had been a barrier to their efforts to dislodge the Americans.

This was a perilous time for Donaciano, as he admitted to several friends at the time and in later years. William Ritch, a friend, confidant, and biographer of Donaciano, wrote of that period, "His subtleness in discovering conspiracies became proverbial and brought down on his devoted head mob violence and a necessity for guarding his movements. For a time, a guard was regularly detailed at his office, and for nearly two years his friends would not permit him to appear on the street without an eye to surroundings."[9]

Having experienced challenging encounters with Price, Donaciano must have been buoyed by the colonel's expression of confidence in keeping him in both offices, removing the "acting" label, and thwarting the efforts of his enemies. Despite his fears, wariness, and self-doubt about his ability to lead New Mexico, "Vigil proved the critical collaborator for the American occupation," Gonzales observed.[10] Donaciano assumed his duties with a new vigor. He assisted a widow in resolving her deceased husband's complicated estate; drafted instructions to the sheriffs who had been appointed by Governor Bent; created the office of county auditor to combat fiscal corruption at the local level; and created a local militia to address a recent resurgence of Comanche raids.[11]

The sheer volume of Donaciano's administrative responsibilities and work, as reflected in his governor's papers, must have been staggering for one person with no staff, clerical help, or budget.[12] Outside of the military expenditures, the US government made no fiscal provision for a civilian government. The civilian officials, including Donaciano, were obliged to rely on any surplus from the meager funds the military commander allocated after his own expenses, which included pay for his soldiers. As part of his duties, Donaciano was required to prepare and distribute proclamations addressed directly to the public. He appointed local officials, such as prefects and constables, wrote letters to other local officials outlining instructions and directives on their duties and responsibilities, and responded to letters of inquiry from such officials or concerned parties about local matters. Most of these letters were composed in his own hand. Donaciano was frustrated in having to rely on and operate through his boss, the military commander. He reached out to US government officials, such as the secretaries of state and war, and even to members of Congress for help in addressing the lack of financial resources. The fact that there was no public bureaucracy in place at the territorial or local level made the job even more complicated. Nevertheless, Donaciano was able to manage pet projects like the soon to be completed Vigil Index of the Spanish/Mexican Archives of New Mexico.

As Donaciano was immersed in the daily governance of the territory, his idealism and progressive ideology began to manifest in his leadership. As Gonzales wrote, Donaciano "spiked the official communication channel with bright and mighty liberalism. He admonished his compatriots to embrace the Kearny Code, as he did, which was equivalent to embracing its principles . . . [of] reciprocal concord and confidence . . . under the aegis of the law and reason."[13]

Gonzales was on target when he wrote that Donaciano was "technically . . . charged with heading up the type of provisional wartime government the U.S. War Department defined as valid for an occupied territory." Nevertheless, Donaciano saw no reason that he could not "fulfill Kearny's declaration of New Mexico as an American territory replete with an understanding of *nuevomexicanos* as effective American citizens. This policy tended to promote politics quite as if New Mexico was already a subset of the United States."[14] The period Gonzales was referring to was before the formal announcement of the Treaty of Guadalupe Hidalgo on 4 July 1848. Thus, Donaciano, according to Gonzales, was formally implementing legal and political principles in New Mexico that would not become effective until July 1848. It is remarkable that in the short span of eighteen months as acting governor and then governor and subordinated to a military commander, Donaciano skillfully constructed an operating territorial government, oversaw the first election and convening of a territorial legislature, and laid a firm foundation for New Mexicans to establish a legitimate territorial government. As Gonzales noted: "Vigil proved the critical collaborator for the remainder of the American occupation.... Vigil reinforced to allies and friends the dawn of a new day of liberal openness in the homeland, conveying in Spanish the incessant tropes of enlightenment, public affairs, public business [*negocios públicos*], and public office [*officio público*]."[15]

Donaciano's colleagues appreciated his leadership. A prominent cleric-politician and former fellow vocal in the New Mexico Assembly, José Manuel Gallegos, "commended the governor for his positive commitment to the new political order and establishing a line of communication with those in political power."[16] Similarly, former governor Francisco Sarracino wrote to Donaciano congratulating him for his philosophy, prudence, and dignity and calling him "the touchstone on which everyone is depending."[17]

Despite the expressions of confidence and support, Donaciano felt somewhat uncomfortable in his elevated role, which he expressed in a letter to a colleague: "If we wish to shape public opinion ... it is necessary to appear without personal aspiration so as not to compromise our work." Determined to remain above the political fray, he added, "As you already know me, when it comes to the public business of my office, I am independent [como ya usted me conoce que en los negociós públicos de mis oficios, soy independiente]."[18] With such convictions, Donaciano proceeded "in discharging the U.S.'s constitutional liberalism and carried out the letter of the Kearny Code as assuredly as its creator would have. Meanwhile, at the time [1847], the war with Mexico continued [with] ... the invasion of Mexico City, [and] the prospects for peace appeared 'gloomier than ever.'"[19]

When Kearny had appointed Donaciano as territorial secretary, Donaciano took responsibility for the official archives and governmental records of New Mexico. The records dated back to the initial Spanish colony and Juan de

Oñate's occupation of New Mexico in 1590 and continued through Mexican control until the American occupation of 1846. Knowing the historical and legal importance of the archives and having become familiar with the records when he worked as military secretary to Governor Armijo, Donaciano took the documents into his custody. He retained them during his first tenure as territorial secretary, then as acting governor, and when he returned to the office of territorial secretary in 1848.[20] In 1849–1850, Donaciano commissioned his son Antonio Basilio and the elderly Domingo Fernández to prepare an index to the archives. The Indice General de Todos los Documentos del Tiempo de los Gobiernos de España y de Méjico hasta el Año de Mil Ochocientos Cuarenta y Seis, known as the Vigil Index, was prepared under Donaciano's oversight.[21] In addition, Donaciano prepared the Register of Land Titles, containing an index of records pertaining to grants of land dating from the Spanish period up to the end of the Mexican administration of the territory. This resource would later prove invaluable for the surveyor general and is still used by land grant historians.

The Kearny Code, adopted for the governance of New Mexico on 22 September 1846, consisted of 115 double-column printed pages, written in English and Spanish. It was based on a combination of Mexican, Texan, and Coahuilan statutes; the Livingston Code of Louisiana; and the Organic Acts of Missouri. It established a workable form of government that conformed to the Northwest Ordinance of 1787, which governed the creation of new territories in the United States. The code also provided for a bill of rights, appointments to civil offices in the territory, and laws for the government of the territory of New Mexico. The code called for an executive branch led by a governor and a secretary, a system that corresponded to the Mexican offices of jefe político and assistant. It called for a legislative branch elected by the citizens of New Mexico that was charged with making laws, not unlike the assembly that existed in New Mexico under the Mexican Constitution of 1824. The code also provided for a judiciary that included three justices, who would preside in individual districts and collectively would form a territorial supreme court, and prefects, who would dispense justice at the local level. Donaciano not only worked doggedly to implement the Kearny Code in New Mexico, but as Gonzales asserted, he invoked the "U.S.'s constitutional liberalism" in carrying out "the letter of the Kearny Code as assuredly as its creator would have."[22] To effectuate the Kearny Code's provision for a legislature, Donaciano issued a call for an election of legislators in 1847 and established the structure for the first popular election since no such structure had existed before in New Mexico. Printed in Spanish by the government press, the proclamation called for twelve to twenty precincts with officials in New Mexico's seven counties, based on size and population.[23]

Donaciano relished every step New Mexico took to legitimize its position within the family of the United States. On 1 July 1847, three days before the celebration of seventy-one years of American independence, Donaciano issued a call for the first elections of New Mexico's territorial assembly under American government. His message informed residents about the importance of voting in any republic, but particularly for the members of the legislative assembly. Donaciano wrote, "My heart rejoices in contemplating that a new era of happiness and good fortune awaits us.... I flatter myself [by] visualizing a happy future and I equally rejoice that for the first time you shall exercise, unfettered, the higher privileges inherent to free citizens [Mi corazón se regocija ... contemplando os ya congregados ... para votar ... los individuos ... que os afianzen vuestra suerte futura ... me lisonjeo de un dichoso porvenir e igualmente me regocijo que por primera vez sin ninguna traba vais a ejercer ... los privilegios inherentes a ciudadanos libres]."[24]

With such phrases as "my heart rejoices" and "a happy future," Donaciano conveyed his excitement and pleasure in seeing all New Mexicans for the first time exercise the suffrage so vital to a republic ("los actos mas importantes ... son los de sufragio"). Finally, he stressed that the spirit of a "republic" was not just a word. Donaciano urged New Mexicans to vote "impartially" for "distinguished, talented, and honorable" men and reject those who might "cause harm" to the territory. He conveyed the message that the manner in which the first election would be conducted, the level of participation, and the candidates elected would send a message to Americans of the time and to future generations of how New Mexicans embraced the most important privilege of US citizenship.[25] Donaciano went beyond his administrative duties. He promoted and extolled an efficacious form of citizenship and a political culture among New Mexicans that would earn them the "veneration of future generations." Impressed by Donaciano, Gonzales wrote that "Vigil transcended Mexico's restricted suffrage and answered the call of Mexico's liberals for popular democracy.... *Hombres de bien* were at one with Vigil's heightened liberalism."[26]

The first election under American control produced a legislature of twenty-one members, seventeen of them Hispanic. For the first legislative session, which convened in December 1847, Governor Vigil delivered a carefully crafted message that outlined an ambitious agenda, but he focused on vitally needed public policy goals. He urged the assembly to consider legislation for "freedom from revolutions and internal dissensions and the security of person and property." He called on the legislature to "limit and define the power of prefects" and hold them to greater financial accountability and for general laws to prevent the defrauding of public revenues. He also urged the assembly to consider legislation to prevent the defrauding of Pueblos.[27]

On religious matters, he urged the legislature to ensure that cemeteries were under local control and open to all, with optional religious ceremonies allowed at burials. Regarding *acequias* (irrigation ditches), he urged the assembly to ensure the equitable distribution of water for irrigation without preference to any group.[28] Donaciano Vigil believed that education was the necessary foundation for democratic government. Given the lack of schools throughout New Mexico in his life and his own experience in education, Governor Vigil urged the legislature to provide for a system of public schools. He showed insight in his philosophy of education and democratic government when he wrote, "It is only through the diffusion of knowledge that a people are enabled to follow the example of those nations whose wise policy shows itself in the higher intelligence and happiness of its people."[29]

The first legislative assembly was successful in enacting several important proposals. The members called for the creation of and appropriated funds for a university, and they passed an act relating to replevin wherein property confiscated by legal authority would be restored to its owner pending the outcome of an action to determine the rights of the affected parties; an act providing for ejectments; and a resolution calling for a convention of delegates to meet in February 1848 in Santa Fe to consider the formal question of the annexation of New Mexico to the United States. The legislative actions were approved by Governor Vigil and by General Price by special orders.[30] The laws passed by the 1847 legislature were ultimately nullified because New Mexico was essentially still part of a foreign country. However, the experience gained in the territory as a popularly elected legislature debated and created public policy was indispensable in the political development that set New Mexico on the road to becoming a viable part of the US political system.

On 23 April 1848, Governor Vigil was surprised to receive a letter from his old boss and mentor, Manuel Armijo. Armijo had returned from his self-imposed exile in Mexico after the notorious outcome at Apache Canyon in August 1846. The ex-governor addressed Donaciano as "my appreciable friend" and said that he had been apprised of the "favorable news" that Donaciano had been selected as "secretary of the government, an honorific destiny that you well deserve." He also acknowledged Donaciano's "good fortune to have been elevated to his new position" as governor and predicted that "it will be followed by even greater positions in the future."[31]

The events of the previous twenty months had vastly altered the circumstances of the two men's lives and that of the New Mexico Territory. The initial letter of reconciliation was followed by an interesting exchange of letters in May 1848. Armijo wrote to Donaciano from Albuquerque three months after the signing of the Treaty of Guadalupe Hidalgo. Armijo addressed Governor Vigil as "my dear friend," acknowledged that New Mexico was now part of the United States, and emphasized that Donaciano could be certain of his friendship. Armijo also reminded Donaciano that certain New Mexicans, such as Diego Archuleta, Tomás Ortíz, and others still loyal to Mexico, along with some of the older clergy now in Mexico were spreading rumors about those who collaborated with and supported the Americans.[32]

Donaciano acknowledged in a letter to Armijo on 21 May 1848 the continued resistance of the clergy "who made war upon me" and abused the powerful privileges bestowed on them by the government by fomenting continued opposition to the new regime. As to the anti-American factions, they had spread false rumors and lies to Governor Bent against Donaciano's appointment, claiming that he was unpopular and would "cause the ruin of this government." When he discovered "the darts of envy" by these enemies, Donaciano had responded by submitting his resignation to Governor Bent and the commandant, who did not accept his resignation and instead supported Donaciano. In what was a remarkably candid, somber, and self-effacing letter to his old mentor and friend, Donaciano laid bare his sentiments about that chaotic period. Donaciano steadfastly stated, "I do not fear my declared enemies because I am not working for self-aggrandizement, but to lift my country out of a shameful [bondage] in which we have been since the independence of Mexico. We were free but the liberty was nominal, we were yet slaves. . . . The holy name of liberty was profaned by those who sought to keep themselves in power." He further stressed, "I am not laboring to keep myself in public positions, these are good for men who have ambitions to fill them." Again expressing his self-doubt, he wrote,

"I am aware of my want of ability and knowledge, I see that I am not capable of advancing the public good, nor desire to promote my own." He lamented:

> I received a very limited education and when I reached the age of discretion, I neglected myself for other things of small amount. If I had conceived that fortune destined me for elevation to high office, I would have applied myself to study and would have been more useful to my country, which has so many needs for its good sons. If New Mexico, should again pertain to old Mexico, I would weep over its misfortune and I would separate myself from it forever.... This is my political faith just as I have declared it and thus conclude and to such I hold.[33]

Notwithstanding his self-deprecating admissions to his longtime mentor and boss, Donaciano performed admirably as governor.

SANTA FE IN 1848: A CITY IN FLUX

Among the problems Governor Vigil faced during the spring of 1848 were the continued troubles caused by the Missouri Volunteers. These troops had rendered invaluable services to General Kearny and Colonel Doniphan in the initial occupation of New Mexico during the Mexican War, defeating the insurrections at Taos, and in several campaigns against the Navajos. However, as an occupying force, they were "overbearing, abusive, and quarrelsome, taking no pains to conceal how much they despised all that was Mexican, and instances of individual insult and outrage were frequent."[34] George F. Ruxton, a British traveler, visited New Mexico at this time and wrote that the appearance of Santa Fe "defies description, and I can compare it to nothing but a dilapidated brick kiln or a prairie dog town. The inhabitants are worthy of their city, as a more miserable, vicious looking population it would be impossible to imagine."[35] His description of the Missouri Volunteers was equally uncomplimentary: "Neither was the town improved, at the time of my visit, by the addition of some three thousand Americans, the dirtiest, rowdiest crew I have ever seen collected together.... Every other house was a grocery as they call a gin or whiskey shop, continually disgorging reeling, drunken men, and everywhere filth and dirt reigned triumphant."[36]

Donaciano faced a dilemma regarding the misconduct of the soldiers in that the troops were under the military commander, who technically was his boss as well. Nor could he appeal to the secretary of war because it would seem as if he were sidestepping the military commander. Governor Vigil had written several letters to Secretary of State James Buchanan seeking his intervention. In his letter of 26 March 1847, he urged that the volunteer force be replaced with regular troops.[37] While Donaciano's letter was not addressed to the person with direct authority over the troops, Secretary of War William Marcy, the letter had an effect. In August and September 1848, two companies of volunteers were withdrawn. At the same time, the force of regular troops was increased. In 1849, the entire number of troops in the territory was 885, including a garrison in El Paso.[38]

Further complicating matters, the Navajo problem reemerged with raids on distant settlements in the northwestern part of the territory. Consequently, Governor Vigil was forced to revisit the issues he had addressed in his "Arms, Indians, and Mismanagement" speeches to the deputation in 1846. This time his appeal was directed to US officials in Washington: "The pacification of the Indians is another necessity of the first order, for as you already know, the principal wealth of this country is the breeding of livestock, and the warfare of the Indians obstructs this almost completely."[39] In 1848, Colonel Edward W. B. Newby, who had temporarily replaced General Price, led a campaign against the Navajos and secured a short-lived treaty with that tribe.[40]

The ratifications of the Treaty of Guadalupe Hidalgo, formalizing the end of the Mexican War and outlining the terms of the agreement between the United States and Mexico, were exchanged on 30 May 1848 and proclaimed in Santa Fe in July of that year. Under the treaty, New Mexico became part of the United States. The southern boundary of the United States and New Mexico was the Rio Grande, the upper Gila River, and a line uniting these rivers just above the latitude of El Paso, Texas.[41]

Despite the adoption of the treaty, the matter of the government of New Mexico, at least until a formal territory was created, remained unresolved, and the effect was that military control under the Kearny Code remained in force. Washington officials formally took the position that the "termination of the war left an existing government, a government *de facto*, in full operation; and this will continue with the presumed consent of the people, until Congress shall provide for them a territorial government."[42] The fact that a former Mexican citizen, Donaciano, was the governor in that de facto government probably contributed to Washington's decision to retain it. Governor Vigil remained in office until 11 October 1848.[43]

Before his replacement as governor, Donaciano was anxious to do what he could to push for progress for New Mexico toward official American status after the Treaty of Guadalupe Hidalgo had formally transferred New Mexico to the United States. Donaciano was in a strategic position to cultivate and steer public opinion among all New Mexicans, especially Hispanics, toward a favorable outcome relative to the consolidation of American government in New Mexico. He doggedly pushed for that official status. Having persuaded the legislature to call for a territorial convention, which would press Washington officials to create the New Mexico Territory (by essentially implementing the preparatory procedures for the process), Donaciano turned his attention to that goal. It was fortuitous that he was not alone. A growing collection of Anglo merchants, former soldiers, and Hispanic New Mexicans were on board with his goals. In a clear effort to advance that cause and the broader visionary spirit of the new "republican mood" inspired by Donaciano's rhetoric, a new newspaper aptly titled the *Republican* began publication in Santa Fe in September 1847. The periodical was put together by Edward T. Davies and George R. Gibson, two experienced newspapermen who had remained in Santa Fe after being mustered out of service with the Missouri Volunteers. Using a printing press borrowed from the army quartermaster general, Oliver Hovey, they offered a bilingual newspaper that would provide news coverage on national and territorial affairs while providing a forum for opinion and public commentary. Its goal was to "serve the communication needs of the public prior to government authorities . . . [and] diffus[e] our laws and institutions throughout the continent."[44] For Donaciano, the weekly newspaper provided a valuable instrument for publicly disseminating his liberal/progressive agenda. He indirectly promoted the newspaper, encouraging friends to pay the nominal annual subscription fee. Donaciano published his proclamations and messages under his own name and also wrote editorials while using a pen name, CEMAPA, to present anonymous viewpoints.[45] The commentaries forcefully promoted the governor's well-known political agenda, including New Mexico's annexation to the United States.

The 1848 annexation convention, as Gonzales called it, evolved into a popular local crusade for annexation of New Mexico, and the new bilingual *El Republicano* (its Spanish title) newspaper was the primary forum for debate on the issue.[46] In a not so subtle fashion, Donaciano became the chief promoter of annexation. The pseudonym CEMAPA was likely an acronym with both an obvious meaning and a hidden hint as to what it stood for. Thus, *ce* could refer to *se*, a reflexive pronoun that can mean "it is said" in Spanish, and *mapa* could refer to "mapping out" in Spanish. Or the pseudonym might possibly have been formed by connecting the first letters of the phrase *ciudadano electoral mexicano avisa por amistad* (Mexican citizen advises for friendship). Another possibility could be *continuando el mensaje avisames por amistad* (continuing our message we advise friendship). The message that the name CEMAPA conveyed was clearly in favor of annexation owing to the obvious realities. New Mexico was already cut off from Mexico due to the American Army of the West's capture of Chihuahua, and a rejection of annexation by the convention might cause the United States to reject New Mexico. CEMAPA argued persuasively, in a manner similar to Donaciano's "Arms, Indians, and Mismanagement" proposals, that rejection of annexation would be a disaster for New Mexico. It would mean the reimposition of the dreaded Mexican centralization policies, including the new national taxes, the appointment of outsiders as governors, the raiding and misappropriation of customs and duties, and the reversal of the positive improvements made in trade, industry, and economic progress.[47]

Donaciano received many letters regarding the future prospects of New Mexico under the United States and responded to them in a manner that expressed his hopes and goals. For example, on 31 August 1848, Donaciano received a letter from the priest José Francisco Leyva of San Miguel del Bado. Leyva, Antonio José Martínez of Taos, Juan Felipe Ortíz of Santa Fe, and José Manuel Gallegos of Albuquerque had been the four most prominent clergymen and politicians in New Mexico. Leyva had served as an interim delegate to the Mexican Congress in 1845 and was an elected member of the assembly in 1846 with Martínez, Gallegos, and Donaciano. Like his colleagues, Leyva had been a vehement opponent of the American occupation, even supporting the 1846–1847 conspiracies and insurrections against American rule. With the signing of the Treaty of Guadalupe Hidalgo, he and his colleagues had accepted the new state of affairs. Obviously concerned about his past differences with Donaciano, he hoped that the governor would "pardon all defects you may discover herein" and "further, the subject . . . [which is] too deep . . . for me to manage."[48] Nevertheless, Leyva wrote that after discussing the subject with Henry Waldo, a prominent lawyer and judge, he had promised to write to the governor "recommending that you procure the election of New Mexico into a state as it is now only a territory, for the many advantages it would gain the government, as such, which it cannot acquire as a territory." Leyva expressed that his opinion regarding the "integrity of the Mexican territory" had not changed, "but it is true that Mexico has lost the [New Mexican] territory," and he now sought "to procure the greatest possible devotion for her, which in my opinion, is to have her on equal footing with the other states of Washington [the United States]."[49] Leyva lamented that he planned to leave "the country" where he had lived for thirty years, but wished New Mexico to have "equal status with other states of North America." He doubted that if he remained he "would be honored with any office" because of his age or be able to "comply with the duties."[50]

Four days later on 4 September 1848, Donaciano wrote back to "my esteemed chaplain." Donaciano acknowledged Leyva's underlying theme of cultural loss due to the separation from the Mexican nation. He understood Leyva's lament of New Mexico's "dismemberment forever." The governor expressed his regret for the loss for various reasons, "such as language, customs, religion, etc. [that] will make our life odious." Donaciano proposed to Leyva that "if you will promise to aid me with your persuasions and counsels among the inhabitants ... I will write to various friends and persons of influence, requesting them to cooperate with their influence and wisdom in order to bring about the change desired." Donaciano felt that a "favorable opportunity" was present "at this time" as a result of the Treaty of Guadalupe Hidalgo, and Donaciano would send a message to the inhabitants "in order to undeceive them as to facts." He expressed the hope that bitterness and resentments would be surrendered "on the altar of concord and unity and only think of what is most conducive to our welfare and aggrandizement awaiting us. These are my wishes and this my political faith under present circumstances.... I may do all on my part that will conduct us to happiness and prosperity."[51]

In every manner conceivable, Donaciano saw himself as the leader in the campaign to secure for New Mexicans the greatest advantage under the US system. He cast his own lot for American territorial status and served as the chief proponent for that transformation. The convention to determine New Mexico's status was originally called to meet in February, but eventually met in Santa Fe in October 1848, the week after Donaciano's replacement as governor. However, Donaciano returned to his former position as territorial secretary, which enabled him to serve as a delegate to that convention. Fully cognizant that the prospects for immediate statehood, as hoped for by Leyva, were remote, he devoted all his energies in the convention to develop a viable plan for a territorial government.

THE ANNEXATION CONVENTION OF 1848

The convention in October 1848 considered the issue of annexation and the form of government preferred by New Mexicans, whether territorial or statehood status. Additionally, since the issue of slavery was at the forefront of US politics, the convention determined whether New Mexico would enter as a free or slave state. At the time, there was considerable debate about the admission of new states into the Union, and southern states were particularly concerned that new states admitted would declare against slavery and thus tip the existing balance of power between free and slave states. General Price prepared an important message for the delegates to consider, cautioning that "seditious and indecorous language against the constituted military or civil authorities, calculated to influence or excite the people against the government . . . will induce me immediately to notice. The utterers of such language will be held responsible and called to strict account."[52]

The convention selected Antonio José Martínez, the influential priest from Taos, as president. The once avowed opponent to the American regime had gone full circle and was now an active participant in the new order. Of the thirteen delegates, ten were Hispanics, illustrating a culture of participation in political affairs that continues to the present. The convention met for four days and reached unanimous consensus on the issues, which were incorporated into a memorial to Congress requesting the "speedy organization by law of a territorial civil government; protesting against claims made by the state of Texas to New Mexico land; and declaring against the introduction or legalization of slavery in the territory." The memorial to Congress was signed in Santa Fe on 14 October 1848 by all thirteen individuals, including Donaciano Vigil, and declared, "We believe our requests to be reasonable and we confidently rely upon Congress to provide New Mexico with laws as liberal as those enjoyed by any of the territories."[53]

Donaciano played a part in the content and wording of the resolution; he was "the controlling spirit."[54] According to William Ritch, "We find the power and influence of Gov. Vigil specially impressed for good. . . . [He insisted on] securing the insertion and adoption of a report declaring distinctly in favor of a territorial civil government . . . and [stated] we do not desire to have domestic slavery within our borders."[55] It was courageous on the part of the delegates to renounce the possibility of slavery in New Mexico since they were aware that in doing so they might be jeopardizing their bid for territorial status. The memorial was dispatched to Senators Thomas Hart Benton of Missouri and John M. Clayton of Delaware. Senator Clayton, a Whig Party member and a strong friend of New Mexico, urged New Mexicans "to meet in convention, provide for a cheap and simple government, and take care of yourselves until Congress can provide for you." In the US Senate, some senators, particularly those from southern states, were "astounded at the insolence of the people of New Mexico."[56] Congressional records of this period show an "almost endless" discussion of the status of New Mexico. While no action was taken at this time by the US Congress relating to the exact form of New Mexico's government, state or territory, the memorial did make a distinct impression on senators who would soon debate the Compromise of 1850.

In 1849, another convention on the statehood and territorial issues was held in Santa Fe. This convention met 24–26 September and consisted of nineteen delegates with Padre Antonio José Martínez again serving as president. One member was former governor Manuel Armijo, who had returned to New Mexico following his self-imposed exile in Mexico. He had been selected from Bernalillo County. This convention included nineteen delegates, thirteen of whom were Hispanic. Although Donaciano was not originally elected as a delegate to this convention, he, Judge Joab Houghton, and Colonel John M. Washington were three of the eight people appointed to a committee to prepare a plan for government to be considered by the delegates. The convention opted for a territorial government and selected Hugh N. Smith, an attorney, as its delegate to Congress with instructions to present the plan before Congress. Colonel Washington, however, acting as governor and military commander, declined to officially recognize the actions of the convention. Nevertheless, Smith proceeded to Washington, but the US House of Representatives declined to admit him as a delegate by a vote of 92–86.[57]

PRESIDENT ZACHARY TAYLOR AND HIS EFFORTS FOR NEW MEXICO STATEHOOD IN 1849–1850

A new form of agitation in favor of a state government emerged in the territory after the arrival in 1849 of James S. Calhoun, an Indian agent appointed by Zachary Taylor. He claimed that the "government in Washington" had given him "secret instructions" to induce New Mexicans to form a state government.[58]

Taylor, born in Virginia and raised in Kentucky, had achieved fame as a war hero for his victories over the Mexican army in the Mexican War. Despite his lack of political experience and a vague ideology, he was elected president under the Whig Party and assumed office in 1849, when the US Congress was embroiled in the battle over sectionalism and slavery. Taylor was a southerner and an enslaver, but he was not a strict advocate for slavery in the new territories being considered for admission: California, New Mexico, and Utah. Rather, he seemed to be more concerned about the bitter sectionalism affecting Congress and the country. He believed that the issue would be resolved if New Mexico would accept statehood by accepting slavery. He instructed Calhoun to do what he could to influence New Mexico to accept slavery as a condition for the "green light" toward statehood. Calhoun made no secret of his instructions. Soon after his arrival, two different groups emerged within the leading political factions in New Mexico. One group was in favor of territorial status, and the other was in favor of statehood. Calhoun, Manuel Álvarez, and Palmer Pillans led the statehood party. Ceran St. Vrain, Judges Beaubien and Houghton, and others, including Donaciano, led the territorial party.

Colonel George A. McCall arrived in 1850 to join the regiment as inspector general in New Mexico. President Taylor had instructed Colonel McCall to work with Calhoun in convincing New Mexicans to pursue statehood. McCall also received a letter from George Crawford, the new secretary of war, reinforcing the president's instructions. Crawford expressed the view that New Mexico had endured a military government due to the failure of Congress to remedy the problem, and the military officers had to perform governance duties that were beyond their spheres of qualification. He did not foresee that the situation would change. But Crawford felt that most people did not believe that New Mexicans were required to wait for the federal government to address their internal governmental issues. Rather, the US Constitution and the Treaty of Guadalupe Hidalgo "guaranteed their admission in the union of our states subject only to the judgement of Congress." Crawford further instructed McCall, "Should the people of New Mexico wish to take any steps toward this object [statehood] ... it will be your duty and the duty of others ... not to thwart, but to advance their wishes."[59]

On his arrival in New Mexico, McCall found the political leaders of the territory divided into the two parties, and he proceeded to join the fray based on the president's and the secretary's instructions. McCall informed the people that there was no likelihood that a territorial government would be formed by Congress and conveyed the determined wish of President Taylor that a state government be formed in order to ensure that the issue of slavery would be resolved. Meanwhile, delegate Hugh N. Smith, who was in Washington to present the memorial for a territorial government, wrote and confirmed the essence of McCall's report that the prospect of a territorial government was dead. At the time these issues were being debated in New Mexico, there was no definitive method for a territory or region to seek statehood. Over time, a process would evolve in which a region would first acquire official territorial status and then, provided it qualified under certain other conditions (e.g., population size), it could apply for statehood after Congress had passed an enabling act. In 1850, no such formal procedure had yet evolved, and new states could be admitted with or without prior formal territorial status.

In advocating statehood for New Mexico, President Taylor did not assume that accepting slavery was a given if New Mexico applied for that status. Rather, he felt that if both California and New Mexico applied for statehood, it would "give Congress an opportunity of avoiding bitter and angry dissensions among the people of the entire country." In other words, Congress could admit states based on their merit alone, not based on issues like slavery. In a direct message to Congress, he stated, "Under the constitution every state has the right of establishing, and from time to time, altering its municipal laws and domestic institutions independently of every other state and of the general government, subject only to the prohibitions and guarantees expressly set forth in the constitution." President Taylor argued that subjects such as slavery should be left exclusively to the respective states and were not designed to become topics of "national agitation."[60]

Another issue reemerged at this time and complicated New Mexico's movement toward statehood: Texas's renewed claim for New Mexico land. President Taylor, siding with New Mexico, argued that if New Mexico had submitted a plan for statehood under the Treaty of Guadalupe Hidalgo and had been admitted as a state, the US courts would have had jurisdiction in resolving boundary issues. Based on this, if New Mexico applied for admission as a state and was then admitted, Texas would have no claim, since the territory in question in eastern New Mexico had not been under Texas jurisdiction during the Mexican period, during the American conquest, or since American occupation.

In his report to New Mexicans on President Taylor's position on statehood,

Colonel McCall offered that argument as another incentive because it would resolve both the long-standing issue of the boundary with Texas and the statehood matter. By this time, the public debate over the issue had become very bitter, spilling to towns and villages throughout the territory and threatening to foment disorder. McCall's delineation of the official position of the government in Washington as favoring statehood seemed to sway the debate in that direction despite the assumption that accepting slavery might be part of the conditions for that outcome. Even the territorial advocates seemed to capitulate in the interest of securing some form of legal status.[61]

Consequently, on 20 April 1850 at a public meeting held in Santa Fe, a resolution was passed, among other declarations, calling for the governor, Colonel John Munroe, to issue a proclamation calling for the people to elect delegates who would meet in a convention on 15 May 1850. This convention elected James H. Quinn as its president, met for ten days, and drafted a proposal for the creation of the state of New Mexico. The proposed constitution was largely the product of Joab Houghton and Murray F. Tuley. Houghton was a lawyer from Virginia who was a judge on the New Mexico Supreme Court, appointed by General Kearny in 1846. Tuley was also a lawyer.[62]

The state constitution adopted by this 1850 convention was modeled after the constitutions of other states recently admitted into the Union and contained a provision prohibiting slavery. Colonel Munroe then issued a proclamation calling for a popular referendum on the proposed constitution and, at the same time if approved, for the election of federal and state officers under the new state government. Munroe made sure his proclamation stated that the constitution and newly elected officers would only be valid upon recognition by the US Congress.

The voters overwhelmingly approved the state constitution in an election held on 20 June 1850. There were only thirty-nine votes cast against it. Henry Connelly was elected governor, and Manuel Álvarez was elected lieutenant governor. William Messervy was elected as a representative to Congress. Governor-elect Connelly was ill and absent, so Lieutenant Governor Álvarez acted promptly to implement the new state government without waiting for Congress to act on the statehood issue. He called the state legislature into session, and among the first actions was the election of two US senators, Francis Cunningham and Richard H. Weightman. In his biography of Donaciano Vigil, Stanley Crocchiola asserted that Donaciano was prominently mentioned as a candidate for the US Senate at that time and would likely have been selected by the Territorial Council, but he declined. Donaciano stated that an "Anglo should hold the office" as it would "thus carry more weight in Washington."⁶³

The action by Lieutenant Governor Álvarez of implementing the state government before securing congressional approval was met with strict opposition from the military commander and governor, Colonel Munroe, who forbade any assumption of power by the officials chosen by the people. As he stated in a letter to the acting governor and the legislature, "The present [military-civil] government shall remain in full force until by the action of Congress another shall be constituted."⁶⁴ Upon receiving this letter, Álvarez forwarded it to the legislature, which was still in session. The legislature adopted a joint resolution that reflected the sentiments of the people of New Mexico in a most vigorous manner: "The people have a clear and sacred right to take any steps to put in operation the state government and . . . this right was superior to and entirely independent of the military government hitherto existing in this territory." The secretary of state delivered copies of the preamble and the joint resolution to the senators and representatives of Congress and to Munroe and Álvarez.⁶⁵

Donaciano once again found himself in a delicate situation. On the one hand, he was supportive of any plan to legally formalize the status of New Mexico in the United States. There was no person more anxious than Donaciano to see New Mexico acquire official status as a state or territory. In that interest, he had participated in the statehood convention, even helping to compose the plan for the state government adopted by the convention. On the other hand, as territorial secretary under the military regime he, like Colonel Munroe, knew that the plan required congressional approval before implementation. Therefore, Acting Governor Álvarez had acted prematurely in implementing statehood. Álvarez had already communicated his directives to the prefects (probate judges) at the county level to implement the statehood provisions, and Donaciano, as territorial secretary, had to intervene to clarify for the prefects the proper course to follow. Accordingly, he sent a directive to the probate judges of all the counties emphasizing that New Mexico must be admitted as a state by the Congress of the United States and cautioning citizens, "You shall therefore unheed the proclamation commands or other acts issued by the hands of said Álvarez, vice-governor, or any other official under the state government, and hold same null and void."⁶⁶

After Colonel Munroe received the joint resolution of the state legislature, he immediately communicated, by swift express across the plains, with his superiors in Washington, explaining the actions he took and seeking confirmation of the validity of his position. Secretary of War C. M. Conrad responded in a manner that must have caused some dismay in the young commander. Conrad informed Munroe that Congress had just "passed a law providing for a territorial government for New Mexico" and that "no necessity seems to exist at present for departure from it." Invoking the constitutional principle of civilian supremacy over the military, he concluded by saying, "You are directed to abstain from further interference in civil or political affairs of that country."[67] Obviously, the commander learned an important lesson, not often appreciated fully by the military establishment, about one of the sacred principles of US constitutionalism. Further, as revealed in Secretary Conrad's message to Colonel Munroe, New Mexicans soon received the welcome news that Congress had officially created the New Mexico Territory as part of the Compromise of 1850.

The role of President Zachary Taylor in the debates leading to New Mexico's admission to the Union has been somewhat clouded with mystery. Since he was a southerner and an enslaver, his motives were suspect when he dispatched two representatives, James S. Calhoun (Indian agent) and Colonel George A. McCall (army inspector general), to advocate among New Mexicans for them to seek immediate statehood. Even though he professed to believe that only by seeking immediate statehood could New Mexicans avoid entanglement in the national debate over sectionalism and slavery, his motives were still questioned. When the attempts for New Mexico's immediate statehood wavered, the newly admitted state of Texas was bolstered by southern segregationists who supported Texas's claim on New Mexican land, since it would mean that part of New Mexico would allow slavery. Texas officials then pressed their contested claim for New Mexico territory east of the Rio Grande (see map 2). Taylor stood fast and opposed Texas's demand.

The Texas claim achieved crisis stage when Texas governor Peter H. Bell sent Robert S. Neighbors as a special agent to Santa Fe to organize eastern New Mexico into six Texas counties. Neighbors was treated with civility, but in May 1848 the *Santa Fe Republican* had pledged resistance to Texas's overture and advised Texas to "send with her civil officers for this country, a large force, in order that they have sufficient bodyguards to escort them back safe. . . . Texas should show some little sense and drop this question and not have it publicly announced that Texas' smartest men were tarred and feathered by attempting to fill the offices assigned them."⁶⁸ When Neighbors returned to Texas and reported back to Bell about New Mexico's "resistance," Bell, who had been elected on a platform calling for "direct action" against New Mexico, fired up Texans into a frenzy, denouncing New Mexico governor John Munroe and President Taylor as insulting the "rights and dignity" of Texans.⁶⁹ Governor Bell sent Taylor an "angry and disrespectful letter" demanding that the president disavow Governor Munroe's efforts to create a new state of New Mexico. At the same time, Bell contacted other southern governors, seeking their support on the matter. On 11 June 1850, the US Senate passed a resolution asking Taylor if he had ordered the US military "to hold possession against the authority of Texas" or in any way to "embarrass or prevent" Texas from exercising "her jurisdiction over that country."⁷⁰ President Taylor responded to the Senate that no such orders had been given and enclosed all correspondence requested. The president, however, added that Robert Neighbors, "styling himself as commissioner of the state of Texas," had gone to Santa Fe to "organize counties under the authority of Texas." While he had no power or wish to interfere in the boundary dispute, he observed that "the possession of the territory into which it appears Mr. Neighbors has gone was actually acquired by the United States from Mexico and has since been held by the United States, and, in my opinion, ought to remain until the question of boundary shall have been determined by some competent authority."⁷¹ President Taylor's response to both the governor of Texas and the US Senate was prompt, stern, and clear.

At the time, Lieutenant Alfred M. Pleasanton was preparing to join his army regiment in New Mexico. President Taylor had a firm message for Pleasanton to take to the governor and military commander, Munroe: "If [you have] not force enough out there to support [you] . . . I will be there myself. . . . I will be there before those people shall go in to that country or have a foot of that territory. The whole business is infamous and must be put down."⁷² It is clear that after months of frustration as he observed the Congress bungle his wise efforts to keep the peace, Old Rough and Ready finally had an issue he could deal with himself. He was the undisputed commander in chief of the American army and navy, and if a military decision should prove to be necessary in New Mexico, he was ready for it.

Ultimately, President Taylor's plan for immediate New Mexico statehood was thwarted even as his companion proposal for immediate California statehood was approved. And then tragedy struck: the president suffered an acute attack of gastroenteritis brought on by severe heat and sun exposure combined with his consumption of raw fruits and vegetables with iced milk. The treatment he was given exacerbated his condition, and within a day he died. Perhaps as a tribute to Taylor's efforts and his popularity, the new president, Millard Fillmore, worked with Congress, led by Stephen Douglas and Henry Clay, to secure passage of the Compromise of 1850. This resolved the main New Mexico issues in congruence with what Taylor had supported. Passage of the compromise in the way he had advocated was his final triumph, and his premature death was a national tragedy. From the standpoint of New Mexicans, we agree with Taylor's biographer's tribute: "In America's pantheon of heroes, Zachary Taylor well-earned the honor and admiration and affection he received during his lifetime and he does not deserve the neglect and misrepresentation he has suffered in the hands of American history. . . . He personified the virtues and ideals most admired by ordinary Americans everywhere."[73]

AT LAST, THE TERRITORY OF NEW MEXICO

The Legal, Political, and Cultural Transformation

In September 1850, the US Congress formally created the New Mexico Territory as part of the Compromise of 1850. The new territorial government for New Mexico was similar to those under which other territories had been created and organized and thus was very similar to the existing Kearny Code. The territorial government went into operation on 31 March 1851. James S. Calhoun was appointed governor by President Millard Fillmore. William S. Allen was appointed territorial secretary, replacing Donaciano Vigil. Grafton Baker was appointed chief justice of the New Mexico Supreme Court, and John S. Watts and Horace Mower were appointed associate justices. Elias P. West was named US attorney, and John G. Jones was appointed US marshal. Governor Calhoun issued a call for elections shortly after his inauguration, and the first territorial assembly under official territorial status met in the Palace of the Governors in June 1851.

No sooner had Calhoun occupied the governorship than he was inundated with problems. The territory's finances were in shambles with no funds to pay for expenses, and the Indigenous people were again raiding outlying homes and villages. The new commander of the Ninth Military Department, Colonel Edwin V. Sumner, reported that the country was "at peace, the Indians generally friendly and the [Navajos and Apaches] have scarcely committed a depredation."[1] Within six weeks of assuming the governorship, Calhoun wrote to his superiors in Washington: "Without a dollar in our territorial treasury, without munitions for war, without authority to call out our militia, without the cooperation of the military authorities of this territory, and with numberless complaints and calls for protection, do you not perceive I must be sadly embarrassed and disquieted?"[2] For Donaciano, the times must have seemed like déja vu all over again.

Although feuding with the governor, Colonel Sumner appeared to make some progress, given his orders to "select new sites for military posts ... [and] to inflict severe punishment upon the hostile Indians." By the end of 1852, Sumner again reported that the "country was ... at peace."[3] However, that assessment was premature as the Indigenous people, particularly the Navajos, continued to be a thorn in the side of the military for another decade. About the same time, Robert Brent, a member of the territorial legislature from Santa Fe, was murdered and scalped by Apaches while traveling through the Jornada del Muerto. A resolution passed by the House of Representatives declared, "Since the entrance of the American army under General Kearny, the territory has been a continual scene of outrage, robbery, and violence carried on by the ... nations by which it is surrounded."[4]

Colonel Sumner was not particularly enthusiastic about the new New Mexico Territory. He issued a recommendation that the government "withdraw all the troops and civil officers ... and let the people elect their own civil officers and conduct their government in their own way under the general supervision of our government." He noted that this would be very satisfying to the people of New Mexico, and "there would be a *pronunciamento* every month or two, but this would be of no consequence, as they are very harmless when confined to Mexicans alone."[5]

Sumner's contempt for New Mexico was outdone by his boss, Secretary of War Charles M. Conrad, who favored a policy of the US government purchasing all of the property in New Mexico held in private ownership and "abandoning all the country to the wild tribes."[6] That irrational view expressed by one of the higher-ranking officials in Washington reflects the deep-seated bias that had taken root there toward New Mexico based largely on reports from military commanders and Anglo-American traders on the Santa Fe Trail.[7] On this occasion, however, New Mexico had a defender in the person of Major R. H. Weightman, New Mexico's territorial delegate to Congress, who sidetracked any serious consideration of Secretary Conrad's suggestions.

The disdain voiced by some American officials toward Hispanics in the territory caused dissension. Article 8 of the Treaty of Guadalupe Hidalgo provided for the rights of former Mexican citizens who chose to remain in the ceded territory. The provision stated that those citizens who chose to remain "where they now reside" would retain their property without being subjected "to any contribution, tax or charge whatever."[8] It further stipulated that those who remained in the ceded territories would either retain the title and rights as Mexican citizens or acquire those of citizens of the United States. However, they were required to make their selection by formal declaration of Mexican or US citizenship within one year after the exchange of ratifications of the treaty (30 May 1848). It further stated that those who remained in the ceded territories after the expiration of that year (by 31 May 1849) without having formally declared their intention to remain citizens of Mexico would automatically become citizens of the United States.[9] To facilitate the process, Colonel Washington, the governor at the time, issued a proclamation informing the public that those who chose to make their election as allowed in the treaty should appear before the prefect in their county on the first day of June and make their election in writing. The clerk in the prefecture office was then required to attach a certificate to the record of names so enrolled and send the record to the territorial secretary. The presumption was that those people who declared US citizenship could remain in the territory, while those who rejected American citizenship could repatriate themselves by moving to Mexican territory. The Mexican government made an appropriation of $200,000 (based on an allowance of $25 per adult and $12 for each child) to assist those individuals. However, as was typical of the Mexican government, only $25,000 was actually made available.[10]

In 1849, Father Ramón Ortíz and Manuel Armendariz were sent from Chihuahua as official commissioners to assist those who wished to repatriate. Father Ortíz was particularly active and passionate about exhorting Mexicans in New Mexico to declare in favor of Mexican citizenship , often making exaggerated claims about the generous royalties and land grants that would be forthcoming to those who chose to repatriate. So persuasive and vehement was Ortíz in his representations that he reported incredible numbers of recruits in some villages and towns. In San Miguel del Bado, the first place he visited, he claimed that 900 or more families had agreed to go, and he estimated as many as 80,000 people would be repatriated.[11] In the meantime, Donaciano Vigil, through his network of friends and associates, received word of Ortíz's exaggerated claims and representations. As later reported by Benjamin Read, "The *cura* [priest] Don Ramón Ortíz came here [New Mexico] as the emissary of the Mexican government, offering the New Mexicans land and all accoutrements necessary for agriculture, transportation for their families and many other conveniences ... [and] already obtained the consent of many families."[12]

Perhaps Donaciano received some surprising numbers about recruitment from the prefects, or perhaps he became concerned when he saw the names of reputable people listed among the repatriates. His own cousin Juan Bautista Vigil y Alarid, the acting governor who had given such an eloquent speech in welcoming General Kearny, was prominently listed as a recruit.[13] In addition, it was reported in a printed transcript of testimony in the court case of *Otero v. Gallegos* that there "are found the names of prominent men who declared their Mexican citizenship, among others, Don Miguel Pino."[14] Donaciano was aware that many people who had originally been enthusiastic about the American occupation had become disillusioned after the continued military presence, the conduct of the soldiers, and the delays in securing official status. However, Donaciano alerted Governor Washington about Ortíz's questionable methods, which caused the governor to complain to Mexican authorities about Ortíz. Through several directives prepared and sent by Secretary Donaciano Vigil, the governor ordered Ortíz to suspend his recruitment visits and leave the country due to rumors that there was the "danger of revolt." On 29 April 1849, Secretary Vigil wrote to Ortíz, "You have overstepped your official duties by advancing your indications thereby producing unrest; I am therefore directing you to suspend your trip returning forthwith to this city."[15]

Ortíz replied on 30 April to Donaciano that he would "obey" the directives, but the "abuses" referenced were "absolutely false," and he did this to ensure that the "good understanding between his [Mexican government] and the United States" may not be altered.[16] In a second letter dated 30 April, he wrote to Secretary Vigil that he had "suspended" his "practice of presenting myself personally in the towns," and he had asked his "commissioners" in the towns he had already visited "to suspend any proceedings on the matter."[17]

On 5 May, in a curt reply to Ortíz's letters, Donaciano wrote: "His Excellency has informed himself of the content of your attentive note ... [that] you have suspended your march ... [and] your deference to the notices sent you. ... Thanking you for your good desires in contributing to the support of the government but ... measures necessary to check the disorder have already been dictated."[18] On 5 May, Ortíz wrote a last letter to Secretary Vigil asking him to inform the governor "that in full accordance with the statement I made ... I have concluded to undertake my journey back to the Republic of Mexico."[19]

Donaciano's concern was that if many New Mexicans, especially prominent people, chose to repatriate, it would be an embarrassment to the United States. In the end, perhaps 3,000 people repatriated to Mexico, and some were prominent people (*hacendados*) who moved back to Mexico with their families and personal property.[20] The actual number of repatriates is unclear because in at least two cases (the Mesilla settlement near Las Cruces and the Refugio settlement near El Paso), the communities were originally made up of repatriates, but when the Gadsden Treaty was finalized, those settlements became US territory, and most of those people became US citizens. The repatriates who relocated to places deeper in Mexico established two settlements: Guadalupe and San Ignacio in the state of Chihuahua, Mexico.[21]

BECOMING AN AMERICAN TERRITORY

Article 9 of the Treaty of Guadalupe Hidalgo assured the former Mexicans that until the time that they were incorporated into the Union of the United States, "they would be maintained and protected in the free enjoyment of their liberty and property, and secure in the free exercise of their religion without restriction." The experience that New Mexicans gained in the relatively short period between 1848 and 1850 in seeking enforcement of article 9 was a lesson not only on US constitutional and republican government, but on the benefits and pitfalls of the political process involved in achieving the rights and privileges associated with American government.

In fact, the Compromise of 1850 served exactly that purpose. The package of bills proposed by Whig senator Henry Clay of Kentucky and advanced by him and Illinois Democratic senator Stephen Douglas had the effect of tempering the sectional conflict that stifled Congress at the time. This was truly a compromise because while each side disliked specific provisions, the consensus was that it was ultimately fair.

For New Mexicans, the most important provision was the one that created the New Mexico Territory. New Mexico would be governed as other territories had been. Utah also became a territory through the Compromise of 1850, and both territories had to decide by popular referendum whether to allow slavery within their borders. New Mexico quickly voted against that. In addition, the state of Texas surrendered its claim to New Mexico territory, as well as claims north of the Missouri Compromise line. It retained the Texas Panhandle, and the federal government assumed Texas's public debt. California was admitted as a free state with its current boundaries. The southern states secured the defeat of the Wilmot Proviso, which outlawed slavery in the new territories. Slave trading (but not slavery) was banned in the District of Columbia, and a stronger "fugitive slave" law was enacted.[22]

The Compromise of 1850 ended a contentious four years of New Mexico's efforts to gain official status in the American family. It is important to consider the geopolitical changes that occurred in New Mexico when it became part of the Mexican nation in 1821 and subsequently with the American occupation in 1846. Profound cultural changes simultaneously occurred due to the opening of trade with the United States through the Santa Fe Trail.

THE DEVELOPMENT OF A "NEW" NEW MEXICAN IDENTITY AND CULTURE

Widespread ambivalence existed among New Mexico's population and leaders regarding resistance to or acceptance of the American occupation. Greg Palmer in his master's thesis, "She Was Our Mother: Manifest Destiny and Misconceptions in New Mexico, 1845–48," offered some insight into the changes that occurred in New Mexico between 1821 and 1846 that contributed to New Mexico's receptiveness to the American occupation. Donaciano's prescient perspective, as reflected in his "Arms, Indians, and Mismanagement" speeches, was similar to Palmer's central themes. Palmer argued that American conceptions of New Mexicans were based on the erroneous assumptions that New Mexicans were eager to become part of the United States, that trade relations had already drawn New Mexico into the American sphere, and that New Mexicans embraced the American idea of manifest destiny. Those misconceptions led to a misreading and misunderstanding of New Mexicans.[23] Instead, Palmer offered the view that New Mexicans were indeed affected by the changes wrought by the Santa Fe Trail, but in a more measured manner. New Mexicans had been so isolated from Mexico that they readily embraced the commerce of the trail because it made available trade products and goods of a higher quality at a cheaper price. New Mexicans came to admire the technology and industry of the Americans that produced these goods. The value of the American commerce also drew New Mexicans into "American trade circles."[24]

However, Palmer offered the perspective that New Mexicans had developed a "regional identity" as nuevomexicanos (a term Palmer said they used) to distinguish themselves from Mexicans or residents of other Mexican territories. According to Palmer, the nuevomexicanos asserted their uniqueness by not "bowing" to the Americans and insisting that the traders speak Spanish and share control of the trade. New Mexicans wanted the American goods, but did not necessarily want the Americans to stay and change their way of life. As the trade relations increased, New Mexicans began to feel greater attachment to the United States and diminished attachment to Mexico. When the American occupation occurred, New Mexicans chose to "become Americans under limited circumstances and choices," in other words, under their own terms. They retained key elements of their culture (language, religion, customs) that distinguished them from other Americans.[25]

Palmer wrote that after New Mexico gained independence from Spain and Mexico, American traders were allowed to conduct business in New Mexico, and the "influence traders had on the economy and the culture of New Mexico [was] immeasurable."[26] The relationships cultivated between New Mexicans and American merchants led to the widespread belief that New Mexicans "had already begun the Americanization process before any troops entered the area."[27] Donaciano's own transformation was an example of that. Palmer reported that Donaciano had acknowledged this influence when he wrote in his proposals that New Mexicans' ability to secure better goods at lower prices encouraged them to enter into American trade circles and move away from Mexican trade. These changes in trading partners led to "a change in economic loyalties."[28] New Mexicans did not "trade their nationality and identity" for money, but their shared economic interests led to cultural changes. The conditions were exacerbated because, as Donaciano also wrote, Mexico's neglect of the northern province was "exploited by the United States."[29] Palmer argued that "as the amount of trade increased between *nuevomexicanos* and the Americans, the culture of the area grew even more distinct and New Mexicans found themselves stuck between the two polarizing and growing nations."[30] The diversity of New Mexico's population also contributed to a unique identity that set it apart from Mexico.

The dominant US idea of manifest destiny convinced most Americans that New Mexicans, like other North Americans, were divinely ordained to become part of that country and nation. "The truth," wrote Palmer, "proved different.... New Mexicans found themselves in a peculiar situation" whereby they simultaneously belonged to two different nations.[31] However, while New Mexicans

FIGURE 9. Arrival of a caravan at Santa Fe (ca. 1840, artist unknown). In 1821, William Becknell initiated the Santa Fe Trail. Wagons laden with manufactured goods stimulated the economy of New Mexico. The commerce and the arrival of Americans triggered social, political, and cultural changes in the territory. Source: Palace of the Governors Photo Archives, NMHM/DCA, negative no. 045011.

"identified closely with their Mexican forefathers and ancestors, they found themselves drawn more and more into an imagined community that the United States began to build in the area."[32] Palmer claimed that history often is portrayed in a way that "makes the events of the past seem inevitable," but that is not always the case. "New Mexicans could have chosen to throw their loyalties behind Mexico or even follow the route of Texas and become an independent nation."[33] Instead, they chose to become Americans under limited circumstances and choices. New Mexicans were keenly aware that what US citizenship would mean was an open question, or as Gonzales observed, "It could [have been] a total farce."[34] Still, New Mexicans figured it out. "Citizenship," said Palmer, "is not the same as nationalism. . . . One may belong and live in a country but their [the people's] self-identification remains with the mother country."[35]

What occurred in New Mexico confirms Palmer's view. By the terms of the

Treaty of Guadalupe Hidalgo, nuevomexicanos comprised the great majority of the population in the vast region acquired by the United States, and most resided in what is present-day New Mexico. Those people were given the right to retain Mexican citizenship or become US citizens. As Gonzales pointed out, many Mexicans did not want to be part of the United States. Two thousand actually declared to retain Mexican citizenship, about 900 of them in the Santa Fe area alone, but they remained in New Mexico. Estimates of those who left for Mexico and remained there vary between 2,000 and 4,000. According to Gonzales, "The larger majority of *nuevomexicanos* became citizens of the United States by default [by remaining in New Mexico] or choice." This last outcome may have occurred at the prompting of Donaciano. As Gonzales also pointed out, he "advised *nuevomexicanos* from atop his liberal soap box on the need to decide their citizenship," while chiding them not to choose "anarchy and oppression [under Mexico] over harmony, equal rights, and peace" under the United States.[36] Thus, even if New Mexicans continued to imagine themselves as part of the Mexican nation, they concluded that it was in their best interest to transition to the new country and nation.[37]

One measure of nationalism is language, both written and oral. The main language in New Mexico remained Spanish, and this pushed New Mexico to build an identity as separate from the other states and people in the area. Many New Mexicans owed their identity to the very things that Americans sought to abolish from their society—mainly Catholicism, the Spanish language, and a mixed culture unique to the area. What many Americans could not or refused to understand about the New Mexican people was why they would choose to identify with Mexico when a much stronger and more powerful nation stood ready to welcome them, even if they would have an inferior socioeconomic status. New Mexicans were not eager to lose social status by becoming Americans.[38] In short, Palmer concluded, "New Mexicans failed to conform to American ideals of race and ethnicity in the nineteenth century. . . . New Mexico remains a land of mystery and its culture is even more diverse than prior to the US-Mexican War."[39]

In echoing Donaciano's speeches regarding the influence of American commercial and trade relations in New Mexico, as well as his claim to Spanish ethnocentrism, Palmer may have understood the unique identity that nuevomexicanos fashioned for themselves in the American milieu and how that identity has served as the foundation for an equally unique New Mexican political culture. It is worth noting that Palmer was not the only non–New Mexican who has viewed the nuevomexicano experience as unique in US history. Different from the Mexican American groups in states such as California and Texas, Hispanics in New Mexico were the majority.

FORESHADOWING A "NEW" NEW MEXICAN POLITICAL CULTURE

The monumental changes that occurred in New Mexico between 1846 and 1850 involved a whirlwind of governmental reform, and Donaciano Vigil was in the thick of it all. Beyond the mechanics of nation building, there was, it seems, a profound effort on the part of Donaciano to alter the mind-set of New Mexicans to advance the idea that a new approach or outlook toward their government was at work. This foreshadowed a new political culture.[40]

In his groundbreaking study, *Política*, Phillip Gonzales provided a long-needed analysis of the early political incorporation of *nuevomexicanos* into the American political system. Gonzales focused on how "*Nuevomexicanos*' political competition was woven into the Democratic and Republican two-party system."[41] This is true. However, in addition to political party competition, other institutions and factors were at play. For one, as Palmer noted, American economic, social, and cultural influences were introduced to Spanish New Mexico by the Santa Fe Trail. These influences created a new and more amenable environment among New Mexicans, who began to welcome American institutions and government as an alternative to the preexisting Mexican affiliation.

Like other informed Mexican citizens, New Mexicans had long admired the US Constitution, and the Mexican Constitution of 1824 adopted many of the elements of its American counterpart. This constitutional arrangement failed in Mexico and its territories because that country lacked a compatible political culture and the belief and support systems that are the foundation of a stable government. Consequently, following the American occupation of 1846, Donaciano was one of those who visualized that this might provide New Mexico a second opportunity to realize the great experiment of 1824. While it would seem presumptuous to assert that Donaciano's views on the US political system included a conception of "American political culture," an idea that did not exist in his day, Donaciano's conception of the American political system went beyond an understanding of its political institutions. He may have sensed that beyond the political institutions, Americans shared a unique view or belief system underlying their view of their own political system, which did not exist among his Mexican counterparts, who did not view their own system in that way. This lack of a faith or belief system may have crippled the Mexican constitutional reforms of 1824. Thus, he may have felt that his compatriots would need to approach the US system in a different way—by embracing the belief system that Americans seemed to share. This could account for the seemingly exaggerated enthusiasm Donaciano expressed to his compatriots in extolling the virtues of the American system. Donaciano understood that New Mexicans needed to adapt their political attitudes and beliefs and embrace elements of American political culture, and he used his position as governor to educate or lobby his fellow New Mexicans about that new political culture.

It is not an overstatement to assert that many New Mexicans were enthusiastic about embracing the American political system, even as others remained loyal to Mexico. As we have shown, significant initiatives were taken by New Mexicans working with Americans in the territory toward the implementation of US constitutional government immediately after the American occupation in 1846 and even before official territorial status was conferred on New Mexico with the Compromise of 1850.

One observer described the cleavage among New Mexicans over retaining allegiance to Mexico or breaking the chain in favor of American annexation as contributing to the emergence of a semblance of a two-party system in New Mexico. Howard Roberts Lamar wrote that "resistance and debate over military rule resulted in the first political parties in American New Mexico."[42] The first manifestation of party factionalism was the conflict between New Mexicans who remained loyal to Mexico, led by Manuel Álvarez and Richard Weightman (the Mexican Party, as they came to be known), and the American Party, led by Joab Houghton, Donaciano Vigil, and Manuel Otero.[43] Later, the factions split into those favoring territorial status for New Mexico and those favoring statehood. Manuel Álvarez was a Mexican Party member who was later a statehood advocate, but other individuals took a different path. Donaciano was an American Party supporter, then a territorial advocate, and still later he participated in the statehood convention. It is clear that Donaciano was supportive of any path to American status provided it followed accepted rules and practices.

Although a Mexican identity seems to have prevailed in Mexico after independence from Spain in 1821, an underlying *hispanidad* (identification with Spanish origins beyond language and surnames) persisted in the "self-imagination" of New Mexicans. Donaciano, for example, in his speech to the departmental assembly in 1846 referred to the "need to preserve the Spanish race."[44] He may have sensed that pride in their Spanish identity could help keep Hispanics unified under American sovereignty.

It is evident in the tone and content of Donaciano's proclamations and pronouncements regarding suffrage, elections, and political participation that he believed that Hispanic New Mexicans would have to adapt and transition to the US system of politics in order to become good citizens and derive maximum benefits from their participation. Several scholars have confirmed that Donaciano was uniquely positioned to help chart this course due to his understanding of that system. Gonzales wrote that the "intellectually gifted, informed, and philosophical Donaciano Vigil" had no formal schooling "but had been taught to read and write by his father.... [He] had the most intimate knowledge of the Spanish and Mexican real property law ... [and] knew more than any other *nuevomexicanos* about American institutions through sheer personal study."[45]

Prior to the American occupation, New Mexico was governed by a Mexican political system that could be described as a parochial political culture. Accordingly, a transformation from that traditional political culture was necessary for New Mexico's former Mexican citizens to adapt to the participant American political culture and system. Even though he had never been a citizen of a republic nor experienced a democratic government, such as that of the United States, nor received formal education on the subject, Donaciano's actions and words revealed a sophisticated level of understanding of the US system and its underlying political culture. Article 8 of the Treaty of Guadalupe Hidalgo had called on New Mexicans to make a choice between continued Mexican citizenship or US citizenship. In September 1848, Donaciano in a newspaper column in the *Republican* had admonished New Mexicans: "I cannot believe that you will hesitate for a moment in making a selection to remain secure under the protection of a grand, powerful and sustainable nation under whose government you shall find peace, harmony, and equal rights or return to the anarchy and oppression of the Mexican republic."[46] His writings on such matters as the importance of informed voting and the role of education in that reflected a fundamental understanding of the type of belief system, broadly conceived by modern political scientists as political culture, that underlies a political system such as exists in the United States.

While Donaciano was informing New Mexicans about the American political structure, he was also in a sense conveying the popular ideals of political culture and the values that support the US political process. His use of words such as "happiness" and "gladdens my heart" clearly expressed his delight and enthusiasm that New Mexicans would embrace the American political system and its political culture. The convening of the first New Mexico legislature in 1847 under the American regime was a significant first step in transitioning into democratic representative government. Ironically, the laws of 1847 enacted by the legislature were declared invalid because New Mexico was still a part of a foreign country. Still, "the significance of the first convocation of New Mexicans was an important step in law making under the new American regime" (de gran importancia real por ser el primer paso dado por los hijos de Nuevo Mexico bajo el Nuevo régimen).[47] Gonzales recognized a special tone in Donaciano's words. In relation to Donaciano's influence on his fellow Hispanic New Mexicans regarding their embracing of liberal democratic theories, Gonzales wrote, "Donaciano Vigil's role glows like a poster child for the liberal theory of modern political diffusion."[48]

Donaciano's performance as governor in the crucial transition period was retrospectively evaluated in several dimensions by Gonzales: "Vigil's idealistic and practical . . . leadership kept a volatile condition of potential ethnoracial" conflict under control during the Taos insurrection. His leadership also demonstrated how "power sharing with the Americans might work." His role in foreshadowing the political culture transition was equally masterful. Donaciano "opened the gates to an experience of participatory dignity for *nuevomexicanos* under immovable American power." Gonzales concluded, "Vigil modeled [a wise approach] for *nuevomexicanos* who intuited a value in being part of the United States" and enjoyed the equality of Americans. His conciliatory language gave New Mexicans "a vision of participatory democracy" far greater than they had known under Mexico and a very real prospect of a republican government, which would give rise to a new American political culture and the "congealing of a new national identification."[49]

Donaciano's messages got through to New Mexicans and were manifested in a letter José Felix Benavidez wrote to the governor. On reading Donaciano's proclamation in the press, Benavidez wrote, "I recognized the liberal principles which adorned it [and] my heart felt a commendable enjoyment and seeing that it discovered that the hero and precursor had planted the sweet and significant honesty in the [home]land."[50] Benavidez proposed a monument to honor Donaciano "so that our successors in the coming centuries could sing the sweet song of hymns that your fine person merits."[51]

POLITICAL SCIENTISTS' PERSPECTIVE ON HISPANIC POLITICS IN NEW MEXICO

Dennis Chávez of New Mexico was the longest-serving and most powerful Hispanic member (as chair of the Senate Public Works Committee) in the US Congress. Easily perturbed over racial slights, he once famously responded to a fellow Democrat, "If they [Hispanics] go to war they're Americans; if they run for office they're Spanish-Americans; but if they're looking for jobs they're damned Mexicans."[52] This is a conviction held by many Hispanics, and that remark from a high-ranking member of the US Senate "is conclusive evidence that the Spanish-American citizenry of New Mexico has long possessed a political power that cannot be ignored."[53]

Political scientist Jack Holmes wrote, "In the case of New Mexico, political institutions of Spanish origin had been functioning for over two hundred years when the United States assumed control of the area in 1846."[54] Those institutions were necessary to "maintain trade routes, ... [protect] from Indian incursions," and provide a system of "administration and justice through appointed *prefects* and *alcaldes*."[55] He also wrote that "the [New Mexican] political order [may be] another example of an acculturating group successfully maintaining a valued identity."[56]

Holmes, whose study of Hispanic politics was exhaustive, devoted an entire chapter, "Political Acculturation of Hispanics in New Mexico," in his book *Politics in New Mexico*. He wrote that a "shrewd knowledge of the mechanics and nuances of politics is not inborn, nor is that knowledge ... a social heritage ... but [it] may be fostered by relevant institutions [over] generations."[57] Holmes provided an excellent example of the transmission of political culture by education. A young man of Taos asked a famed and defrocked politician-priest what kind of government the United States was. Padre Antonio José Martínez replied that it was a republic, and he added that a republic was a "burro on which lawyers jog along better than priests."[58] In New Mexico's case, Holmes argued, scarcely two generations separated the Kearny Code and the 1910 constitution prepared in anticipation of statehood, but "sixty-four years were enough, for the pupils were apt, the tutor proficient ... and the institutions ... had fostered political skills." Holmes asserted that Hispanic power in New Mexico had been "bolstered by the state constitution ... expressed in statutes ... sustained by [party organization] and [maintained] out of conviction and necessity."[59] He also wrote, "Sixty-four years of practice in the ways of *gringo* politics ended in 1910 with the writing of a [New Mexico state] constitution containing extraordinary guarantees of Spanish-American civic and political rights ... [and] the preservation of their traditional way of life and the language of their fathers."[60]

It is not coincidental that the 1910 convention and its unified bloc of Hispanics, who were roughly half of the majority that dominated the proceedings, oversaw the drafting of a constitution that institutionalized unprecedented and unparalleled protections for New Mexico's Hispanic citizens. In the suffrage article, it stated, "The right of any citizen to vote, hold office, or sit upon juries shall never be restricted, abridged, or impaired on account of religion, race, language, or color, or inability to speak, read, or write the English or Spanish language." It mandated in the education article that "the legislature shall provide for the training of teachers in the normal school so that they become proficient in both the English and Spanish languages to qualify them to teach Spanish-speaking pupils." Another section of the same article prohibited segregation in schools by providing that "children of Spanish descent shall never be denied the right and privilege of education and attendance in the public schools ... and they shall never be classed in separate schools." Holmes wrote that such protections "did not occur spontaneously or unheralded in the constitutional convention of 1910.... They are there because Hispanic leaders knew their interests well enough to insist upon their inclusion."[61]

In a work on the Hispanic experience in the United States, *Manifest Destinies: The Making of the Mexican-American Race*, Laura Gómez stressed the "victim mentality"—that Hispanics from the beginning of American conquest were second-class citizens, purposefully subjugated by an oppressive US political and social system. Our perspective is that Hispanic New Mexicans, like Donaciano Vigil, did not operate under that mentality, but purposefully maneuvered to improve their condition in what was a hostile and often discriminatory environment. Hispanic New Mexicans controlled, to the extent that they could, the political environment under which they lived and worked. Even Gómez admitted as much in the postscript to her second edition, where she wrote that "Mexican-Americans [in New Mexico] were the majority of voters and ... office-holders—something unheard of in Arizona, California, and Texas." Gómez concluded, "These outcomes had everything to do with the fact that the vast majority of eligible voters were Mexican-American men."[62] Gómez failed to add another crucial fact not observed in the other states she mentioned. New Mexico's Hispanic men voted, and they voted for Hispanic men who eagerly sought those offices.

In the concluding remarks to his book, Phillip Gonzales echoed our own sentiments about Donaciano and his peers. He referred to them as the "nineteenth century *Nuevomexicano* conquest generation," whose members "fulfilled the range of role possibilities their historical circumstances opened up to them ... [and] constructed the foundation for permanent republican politics in New Mexico. ... *Nuevomexicano* political integration was facilitated and honored by the power-house careers of José Manuel Gallegos, Miguel Antonio Otero, and José Francisco Chavez."[63] From our perspective, we offer in addition the post-statehood political careers of Hispanos Octaviano Larrazolo, Dennis Chávez, and Joseph Montoya, among others.

Erna Fergusson offered a blunt assessment when she wrote that "the United States botched its first opportunity to teach self-government to people [in New Mexico] alien in language and custom." Instead, according to Fergusson, "New Mexico's advance ... from an unkempt, poverty-stricken, and neglected frontier province to a dignified state has been the work of her people without such aid in teaching the new language and customs as the United States gave other non-English-speaking peoples who entered the Union at the end of the century."[64]

DONACIANO: FAMILIAR ROLE, DIFFERENT STAGE

When Donaciano Vigil left the office of territorial secretary in April 1851, it was the end of his permanent active service in the executive branch of New Mexico's government, which began in 1837 when he was territorial secretary under Manuel Armijo and continued under Kearny in 1846. However, this was not the end of his career in government or public office. In his retirement, Donaciano could have chosen to pursue opportunities as a "soldier of fortune," like so many of his Hispanic colleagues had done in their lifetimes and as he was falsely accused of doing by land grant historian critics. Instead he chose the life of a small, common farmer-rancher in Pecos. Still, even that simple idyllic life was interrupted occasionally by the call of public duty, whether it was an isolated event or a prolonged interruption.

In 1851, Grafton Baker was appointed to the joint position of chief justice of the New Mexico Supreme Court and judge in the First Judicial District, and he searched for a suitable location in Santa Fe to conduct the court's work for the district. The most suitable building was the old Castrense, which had always been used as a military chapel by the soldiers of the Santa Fe Presidio. The chapel was located on the south side of the Santa Fe Plaza and was quickly appropriated by the judge. Soon, Donaciano was one of those summoned to serve on jury duty. Donaciano was not by any means a religious zealot. In fact, he often railed against the conservative dogma of the church. But upon taking his seat in the jury box, Donaciano protested that "the court was being held in a place consecrated to sacred objects," and he wished "to be excused from serving in the court where he could not help feeling that he was treading upon the ashes of his ancestors."[65] Judge Baker, having indulged in distilled spirits as he was wont to do, responded with a diatribe against religious interference and a statement that "both the bishop [Jean-Baptiste Lamy] and Father Joséph Machebeaf, the prelate's right-hand man, [be] hanged from the same gibbet."[66]

The next day, widespread indignation over the judge's remarks swept over Santa Fe, and a petition with over a thousand signatures sought justice and a return of the property to the church. Later that day, a mob gathered at the judge's residence. He called for protection from the military, but the soldiers refused to intervene. That evening the judge called the bishop and apologized for his indiscretion, and the following day he turned the chapel over to Bishop Lamy in the presence of the governor and other officials. An alternate location in the Palace of the Governors was found for use as a courtroom.[67]

In the spring of 1852, Governor Calhoun experienced health problems, and on 5 May he left Santa Fe to seek medical attention in the States. En route to Missouri over the Santa Fe Trail, his health worsened, and he died. President Fillmore then appointed William Lane, the former mayor of St. Louis, as governor.[68] When Lane assumed the office, he was confronted by several problems that required immediate attention. An incident had occurred on the night of 3 May 1852 at Vallecitos in Bear Creek, south of Albuquerque, where Natives attacked a sheep-grazing camp belonging to Ramón Martín. The original report received in Santa Fe indicated that Martín and one of his sons had been murdered along with two other boys, and all of Martín's livestock was stolen by the raiding party. Upon further investigation, it was determined that four Natives had attacked the camp, killed Ramón Martín, took five boys captive, and stole some horses and a mule, but the sheep were left in the pen. Three of the boys were soon released, but José Claudio Martín (eight years old), son of Ramón, and José Leonicio Martín (nine years old), a nephew of Ramón, were carried away by the raiding party.

The boys who were released were questioned, and they gave a clear description of the Indigenous people but could not say if they were San Juan Pueblos or Navajos. The investigators examined Martín's body and identified the arrows as being of Navajo origin. The boys who were released offered some insight on the motive for the Navajos' raid on the camp. They said that the Native raiders told the boys that a war captain of the Capote Ute tribe named Tamouche had stolen a paint horse (similar to a pinto) and a mule from the Navajos. If Tamouche would return the animals to the Navajos, the two captive boys and the horses and mules would be returned.[69]

Considering the possibility that this incident could explode into a full-fledged territorial crisis, Governor Lane called on the experienced Donaciano to act as his special agent in the matter. The governor wrote to Donaciano outlining his instructions. Donaciano was to proceed to "Indian country" and seek the murderers of Ramón Martín as well as the fate of the captive boys. He was instructed to recover the boys and all the stolen property, and if the murderers were found, he should demand that the chiefs harboring them surrender them for trial. Donaciano was given the services of Samuel Ellison to act as interpreter.[70] Finally, he was to make it clear to the chiefs that a failure of the Navajo tribe to comply with his demands would be considered a justifiable cause for war. Ellison was provided with a horse and a saddle, two double-barreled shotguns, a Jaeger rifle, and a pistol.[71] When Colonel Sumner was apprised of the instructions given to Donaciano, he was in full accord and added that if the Indigenous people proved to be Navajos, they would be clearly warned that the boys must be returned and the murderers be given up or war against the tribe would commence.

Donaciano initially traveled to Jemez Pueblo, where he was informed that the Navajos he was seeking were part of the band of Chief Águila Negra (Black Eagle), and he could encounter them in the Chuska Valley where the Navajos were gathering.⁷² Indigenous interpreter George C. Carter, a blacksmith who was familiar with "Indian country"; Tosty Hosty, the famous Jemez Pueblo guide; and ten Jemez Pueblo tribesmen were sent to accompany Donaciano. Four days later near a place that Donaciano referred to as Tunicha (Big Water in the Navajo language), Donaciano's party came to a camp with approximately a thousand Navajos. He immediately held a council with Navajo chiefs Cayetano and Águila Negra. The two captive Martín boys were surrendered at once, and three mules were offered as partial payment for the horses and mules taken at Vallecito. When Donaciano learned that the Navajo perpetrators were in the camp, he demanded that they surrender, or war would commence as threatened by Governor Lane and Colonel Sumner. Águila Negra and the other chiefs insisted that they did not have enough force to seize and turn over the accused men. At this point, Jasis (Jesús), the Native accused of the actual murder of Martín, said that he and his companions had not intended to kill Martín, but only to scare him. This admission of guilt was significant, but Jasis insisted that neither he nor his companions should be turned over to *bilagaana* (white men) for punishment. Donaciano, a veteran campaigner, knew not to press his demands, especially when surrounded by a thousand Indigenous people.

Donaciano accomplished his goal of the return of the boys, a partial return of the stolen livestock, an admission of guilt by the chiefs with an implied promise of full compensation for the other livestock, and a specific identification of and admission of guilt by the chief perpetrator of the Martín murder. In spite of these successes, he felt that he was not in a position to forcibly carry out the arrest of the perpetrators and safely walk out of the camp with his party alive. He decided to let Lane and Sumner arrange for repercussions later.

When Donaciano returned to Santa Fe with the Martín boys on 24 May, Governor Lane ordered that the boys be well fed and given new clothes, and in the following days, they were returned to their family. At a later meeting with Lane, Águila Negra promised he would do all in his power to have the murderers brought in, but he feared possible repercussions for himself and the potential for war within the tribe. He asked to be relieved of the US government's demands. Governor Lane replied that Águila Negra's excuses were not acceptable, and if the murderers were not delivered to him by the full moon on 1 July, the Navajo country would be invaded by American soldiers.⁷³ In the first week of June, Colonel Sumner declared that he would carry on a war against the entire Navajo tribe if the Martín murderers were not turned over. But later,

Sumner said that "it would be unjust to hold the whole Navajo tribe responsible for the act of five 'marauding and ungovernable Indians.'"[74]

In the end, despite all the discussion and debate between Governor Lane and Colonel Sumner, the campaign against the Navajo Nation never materialized. On 26 June, mail arriving in Santa Fe from Independence, Missouri, informed Lane that he would be replaced by David Meriwether. On an outgoing stagecoach on the same day, Sumner departed for the United States; he too had been relieved of his command. The plans for the Navajo campaign collapsed.[75]

Later in 1852, it was clear that Donaciano was not done with politics or public service since he was elected as one of four representatives from Santa Fe County to the Second New Mexico Territorial Assembly. The twenty-six-member House of Representatives elected Theodore Wheaton of Taos as speaker and presiding officer. The other chamber in the legislature was the thirteen-member Territorial Council (Senate), which was headed by the president of the council, Father Juan Felipe Ortíz of Santa Fe. The session convened in December 1852.

In 1857, Donaciano again served in the territorial assembly, but this time in the upper body, the Territorial Council, and as a delegate, along with Miguel Sena y Romero, from San Miguel County. By this time, he had moved to Pecos, New Mexico. He was also elected as president of the thirteen-member council that year. He served in 1857 and 1858 in the seventh and eighth legislative sessions, but presided in only the Seventh Territorial Council, which convened in December 1857. By this time, Donaciano was a respected elder political leader in New Mexico, and his fame was recognized throughout the territory. Donaciano was again elected to the Fourteenth Territorial Assembly, serving in the Territorial Council in the 1864 session. He again represented San Miguel County as a resident from Pecos, but this was the final time.

At sixty-two years of age, Donaciano Vigil retired from his last elected public office. His reputation as a legislator was that of a watchdog who kept tabs on legislation and carefully chose the issues he would engage. He was a Democrat in party orientation and a liberal in ideology. He was a staunch advocate of education at all levels and supported the expansion of free public education and the funding to carry such policies through. One of his greatest disappointments must have been the sustained failure of a series of bills aimed at establishing a viable free public school system and colleges in the New Mexico Territory. Most often, the cause was the unwillingness of the population to incur the taxation necessary to support education funding. Finally, he was gratified to see the first permanent public school legislation enacted in 1871 and 1872. Following the enactment of these school laws, he was appointed, at the grand old age of seventy, to be the school commissioner for San Miguel County.

In his biography, Ritch noted that he had questioned an unnamed veteran político in the territory about his view of Donaciano. The político responded, "Oh! He was regarded as a clever old gentleman, was much respected, but rather impracticable. I noticed when he was in the legislature that if there was any matter of special importance up for consideration in the *junta*, . . . the old governor was liable to be counted out." Ritch took that response to be a "higher recommendation in legislative affairs," indicating that Donaciano Vigil was not one to be easily swayed by special interest lobbying or the deal making typical of a legislative body.[76]

10

ASSAULT ON A GIANT, PART I

Donaciano Vigil and Spanish/Mexican/Pueblo Land Grants

Following the creation of the New Mexico Territory under the terms of the Compromise of 1850, one of the first challenges faced by the United States was the enforcement of the article 8 provisions of the Treaty of Guadalupe Hidalgo. These provisions pertained to the property rights of the former Mexican citizens and the Pueblos and the continued efficacy of Spanish and Mexican land grants in the territory.

THE SURVEYOR GENERAL: A DIFFICULT TASK

On 22 July 1854, the US Congress created the office of surveyor general of New Mexico.[1] The surveyor general was directed to locate all records pertaining to land claims, hold hearings regarding them, and then report his findings to Congress, which would make final decisions on the confirmation of the land grants.[2] President Franklin Pierce appointed William Pelham as the first person to occupy that office on 1 August 1854. Pelham's immediate supervisor was John Wilson, the commissioner of the General Land Office, a division of the Department of the Interior under Secretary Robert McClelland. Pelham arrived in Santa Fe about five months later on 28 December 1854 to assume his duties. He quickly realized the nearly impossible task before him: he was a part-time official with a congressional budget that was inadequate. As Victor Westphall concluded, Congress was "derelict" in its handling of the land grant situation in New Mexico because the territory "showed no evidence of such valuable assets as the gold discoveries and seaports of California," and Congress "failed to provide adequate funds and manpower to cope with the problem, and [neglected] to provide some plan for adjudication of the titles."[3]

Pelham was burdened with the enormous responsibility of reviewing, investigating, and recommending to his superiors in the General Land Office and, indirectly, to the US Congress the final adjudication of the major private, community, and pueblo land grants in the territory of New Mexico. The task before Pelham, according to Westphall, was complicated further by his lack of qualifications and experience for the job at hand. Westphall wrote that Pelham "did not speak or read Spanish. He knew nothing of Spanish or Mexican civil law or legal history. . . . Yet his was the thankless task of recommending to Congress either the rejection or confirmation of preexisting claims of land."[4]

Given his lack of experience and preparation for the job, Pelham began looking for help once he arrived in Santa Fe. It is not surprising that Donaciano Vigil was referred to him as one person who could definitely help. Donaciano was experienced as a public official (especially as territorial secretary) under both Mexico and the United States, and he did have expertise in Mexican land law. There were a few other men with similar experience and expertise who could have been consulted—Manuel Armijo, Juan Bautista Vigil y Alarid, and Domingo Fernández, to name a few—but not all were disposed to offer assistance.[5]

By 1855, Donaciano had retired from the militia and the higher-level offices of territorial governor and secretary and was contemplating his retirement from public life altogether and a relocation to Pecos to start, at fifty-three years of age, a completely new chapter in his life as a farmer-rancher. It is logical to assume that having purchased land in eastern Pecos on 26 December 1854, two days before Pelham arrived in Santa Fe to assume his new job, Donaciano was not planning a new career as a speculator in New Mexico land. However, the request to assist an important public official, Surveyor General Pelham, was too great to ignore for one who had dedicated his life to public service. Unfortunately, this last chapter in Donaciano's life would make him vulnerable to charges, valid or not, that would tarnish his life and career.

Despite Pelham's delay in assuming his position as surveyor general, he acted quickly to initiate the land claim and review process. By 18 January 1855, three weeks after arriving in Santa Fe, he had widely distributed a notice that all claimants were to submit their title papers to his office for adjudication. But by the time of his first report, only fifteen claims had been volunteered because Congress had set no terminal date for the submission of claims.[6]

THE END OF PECOS PUEBLO

The book *Four Leagues of Pecos: A Legal History of the Pecos Grant, 1800–1933* was published by the University of New Mexico Press in 1984. The book certainly fits the description provided on the inside flap: "an engrossing account that offers much new and valuable information about the Pecos grant and about the political and economic events in which it is entwined."[7] The study was indeed a very informative and provocative treatise that presented valuable original research on the checkered historical evolution of the grant and its various Indigenous, Hispano, and American owners. As a consequence, some of our background commentary regarding the Pecos Pueblo grant was drawn from it.

Our goal is to fairly examine the particular perspective in *Four Leagues* that the Pecos Pueblos were an aggrieved party and that Donaciano was a primary actor in perpetrating the mischief toward the Pecos people at this critical time. In *Four Leagues of Pecos*, Hall demonstrated how the Pecos were accorded the customary four leagues of land surrounding their pueblo under Spanish land law. He also discussed the evolving Spanish land policies, which were tempered by conflicting legal principles emanating from direct monarchical decrees, monarchical commission decrees, legislative (e.g., cortes) edicts, judicial decisions, and common everyday usage or practice.

One key legal principle in the Pecos Pueblo land situation was whether the Pecos, like other Pueblos, could sell or trade their land. This principle was particularly relevant if one were ascribing a value judgment, such as the "loss of land," to a particular application of a policy. In the case of Pecos Pueblo, there was no single legal principle involved. Whether or not the Pecos Pueblos could sell or trade their land depended on the particular government (Spanish, Mexican, or American) then in power, the particular government policy applicable at the time, and the enforceable or practicable enforcement of the policy in effect. Thus, given the lack of a consistent legal premise in operation through the entire history of the grant, one cannot arrive at a definitive conclusion regarding loss of land based on one policy.

Hall documented what he described as the "assault" on Pecos Pueblo land by a number of Hispano settlers and Anglo-American land speculators in the 1820s and 1830s.[8] In the process, some of the people involved in the ongoing intrigues surrounding the land issue were cast in an unfavorable light, deservedly or not. Hall apparently stood by the legal principle that the Pueblos could not be dispossessed of their land by any means, whether traded or sold, even if that was their own choice. He wrote, "This book deals with the legal history of a particular tract of land owned by a departed people and occupied by a succession of interlopers."[9] However, the use of the word "interloper" is fraught with subjective connotations because the implication is that the land was stolen, taken by force, or otherwise unwillingly alienated. However, what if the land was not taken, but was sold or given in trade? That is exactly what happened. In 1830, the Pecos Pueblos sold a major portion of their best land; in 1838, they completely abandoned their pueblo; and in subsequent years they again sold their interests in the land to willing buyers. Hall wrote that by the 1860s Pecos Pueblos "had sold the entire eighteen thousand acres once to Mexicans and a second time to New Yorkers. Now, in the 1870s and 1880s, they returned occasionally to sell small tracts in the northern portion of the grant for a third time to Hispanic trespassers identified by the Pecos survivors as 'nuestros hermanos!'"[10] Today, there is no physical manifestation of Pecos Pueblos' continued ownership of the land. Even the ruins of the once magnificent Pecos mission church grounds are now the property of the US government through the National Park Service.

In the preface to his book, Hall referred to some of the various people involved in the narrative—Pedro Bautista Pino, Domingo Fernández, Juan Estevan Pino, Preston Beck Jr., Donaciano Vigil, Manuel Varela, John Ward, James Seymour, D. C. Collier, Francis C. Wilson, and John Collier—and mentioned all the claims they made, the battles they fought, the lawsuits they filed, the laws they passed, the victories they won, the losses they suffered, and the friends and enemies they made.[11] Indeed, those were the characters on the stage that was set. What was not mentioned, however, was how some of those principals, as they were called by Hall, were laid bare and suffered from particular portrayals, true or not, of their personal character. One whose reputation suffered was Donaciano.

Two salient themes were present in the pages of *Four Leagues of Pecos*. The first was that nothing that the Pecos Pueblos did that led to the loss of their land was relevant, including the fact that their leaders tried—not once but several times—to sell the land and succeeded in doing so, and the abandonment of the pueblo in 1838. The second was that anyone outside the Pecos Pueblo community who sought to legally acquire the land for homesteading (farming, ranching, building homes or irrigation ditches, etc.), land speculation (purchase and resale), or for its resources (timber, mining, etc.) at any time before or after the Pecos decided to vacate their ownership was cast as an interloper. One does not have to delve deeply into the book to reveal the focus on Donaciano, as most of the narrative of chapter 6, "Donaciano Vigil's Pecos," was devoted to him. Hall wrote:

> Donaciano Vigil's claim to the Los Trigos grant and his presence in Pecos . . . were products of Anglo aggression and Hispanic politics [and he] turned them both to his advantage. . . . Vigil maintained a constant focus on New Mexico land, both for himself and for his friends . . . [and] he contributed significantly to the creation of New Mexico's largest and most controversial land grants. . . . Donaciano Vigil and his less well known friends made the bed that the more famous Santa Fe Ring then lay down in.[12]

Donaciano was depicted in the center of the decisional process that awarded the land grants in the first place. Donaciano served as departmental secretary to Governor Manuel Armijo on two separate occasions (1838 and 1846); both were relatively brief periods of tenure. The focus of his secretarial responsibilities was as a military aide to the military commandant which was, along with government administration, one of the governor's primary duties. Donaciano also served at different times as escribiente (scribe) of the Santa Fe presidial company, which placed him as a subordinate clerk under the governor and military commander. In addition, he occasionally held the title of secretary while serving as a member of the departmental assembly, which sometimes played a role in reviewing and making recommendations on land grant applications. These secretarial positions could have placed Donaciano in a position to record land transactions and maintain land records, but all of that would have been based on the discretion of the assembly acting collectively or of the governor, who was the ultimate authority. The job of secretary did not necessarily carry weight in the proposing or approving of land grants. Nowhere is it documented or confirmed that Donaciano played other than an administrative role in land affairs, or that Donaciano conspired with Armijo or others to create or facilitate illegal land grants.

With a wider lens, David Weber examined the policies of several Mexican governors in allocating large tracts of land. He wrote, "Between 1837 and 1846 Armijo gave away over half of the 31,000,000 acres of land granted by all New

Mexico officials under Spain and Mexico.... Not nearly as reckless as some critics have suggested, Armijo appears to have granted lands to encourage private enterprise to create a barrier against Indians, Texans, and *norte americanos*."[13]

Donaciano's frequent appearances before the surveyor general to testify in regard to land grants and transactions were also questioned by Hall. As a secretary of the territory, soldier, and public official when some of the grants were made and given his familiarity with the archival records, it is not surprising that Donaciano was called to testify regarding his recollections about the circumstances surrounding the grants of land, especially when written records were not always available. The fact that Donaciano affirmed (sometimes with imperfect memory) that grants were made places him as an initiator or decision-maker, and not as a clerk recording the transaction or as an outside observer who may have had some knowledge about the land transactions. It should be remembered that Donaciano was providing testimony at the request of the surveyor general or attorneys, and they were free to accept or reject his opinions or information.

Challenging the charges made against Donaciano requires focusing on the facts. Perhaps the best way to do this is to relate the circumstances under which Donaciano acquired his property in Pecos. If assertions of Donaciano's breadth of influence on land matters are to stand, they must stand in the case where Donaciano actually acquired and used the land and willed it to his family. We briefly describe the history, events, and transactions relating to Pecos lands before and after Donaciano's association with them.

Pecos Pueblo, home of one of the bands of Towas, was one of the oldest Pueblo villages traced to the Anasazi civilization in what is now New Mexico. Known by the Spaniards as Cicuye, it was visited by Francisco Vázquez de Coronado and other Spanish explorers, who described it as one of the largest and most powerful pueblos in the region. The Coronado expedition's chronicler referred to it as "a pueblo of as many as five hundred warriors. It is feared throughout the land."[14] Following Spanish colonization, the Pecos continued to reside on their land without direct interference from the Spanish government.

Under Spanish colonial law (Recopilación de las Leyes de los Reinos de Indias), the Pecos, like other Indigenous tribes, were recognized as legal owners of the land that they had lived on and continuously occupied for centuries. The legal basis of the Pecos Pueblo ultimately was determined to rest on the general grants made to all Indigenous peoples in the New World by the Spanish monarchs through royal cédulas (edicts) and viceroyal and audiencia ordinances incorporated into the Laws of the Indies. This was affirmed when the Cruzate documents were found to be invalid. As detailed in chapter 12, these documents were a series of Pueblo land grants purportedly created by Governor Domingo Jironza Petriz de Cruzate in 1689. Although they were recognized by the New Mexico surveyor general, William Pelham, in 1855 and 1856 and accepted as validation of the core landholdings of nine pueblos by the US Congress in 1858–1860, the documents were later found to be forgeries. Ironically, one of the Cruzate documents was filed with the surveyor general as a claim for Pecos land on 14 September 1855. Pelham filed it along with other evidence in his report of 1856, and a patent was issued to the inhabitants of the pueblo on 1 November 1864.[15] The pueblo had been vacant for twenty-six years at that point. When the remaining Pecos survivors, then residing at Jemez Pueblo, received their patent, they secured the services of John Ward to act as their agent in selling, once again, their interests in the remaining Pecos Pueblo land.[16]

Despite its stellar history, by the end of the eighteenth century Pecos Pueblo had declined drastically in population due to various epidemics (especially smallpox) and frequent harassment and attacks from hostile nomadic tribes, such as the Navajos and Comanches, but particularly from the Plains peoples, as documented by John Kessell.[17] In 1803, only 125 Natives lived in Pecos, and by 1821 its population had diminished to 26 males and 28 females.[18] The decline of the population greatly weakened the Pecos hold on their four leagues, including some prime farmland at a time when the Hispano population was expanding beyond the Rio Grande basin. From the earliest period of colonization, Hispanics were hampered by the fact that Pueblos held much of the most secure arable land along the Rio Grande.

The growing Hispano population crowded presidios and towns such as Santa Fe, and settlers were pressuring the government for grants of tillable land with good sources of water in secure locations in the territory. Settlement of the upper Pecos River land, just below the Pecos Pueblo boundaries, had begun with the establishment of San Miguel del Bado in 1794 and San José del Bado in 1803. Although the northern boundary of the San Miguel de Bado grant in El Gusano was just south of Pecos Pueblo's southwestern league, the pattern of settlement was clearly moving northward toward Pecos Canyon. In 1814, for example, the Spanish governor of New Mexico, on a recommendation from the Santa Fe ayuntamiento, approved a grant of land in a place called Los Trigos, a parcel sandwiched between Pecos Pueblo's southern boundary and San Miguel del Bado's northern boundary. In regard specifically to Pecos Pueblo, it is apparent that some homesteading without legal authority began inside Pecos Pueblo's four leagues even before the first formal request was made in February 1821 by Esteban Baca and thirty other residents from the Santa Fe area. Their petition, however, was not granted.

On 1 September 1823, Domingo Fernández, Rafaél Benavidez, and thirty-one other citizens (including soldiers and former soldiers) petitioned Governor Bartolomé Baca of the Mexican Department of New Mexico for what they called the *sobrantes* (surplus lands) of Pecos Pueblo. The petition, conceived by Fernández, applied a unique approach to Pueblo land. The petitioners did not ask for the whole grant nor question the Pecos ownership of the land; they simply asked for the sobrante within the Pecos Pueblo that the Natives were not utilizing.[19]

The legal basis for the sobrante had been established by the Spanish cortes (legislature) in a progressive law enacted in 1812, but it had been nullified with the return of the monarchy in 1814. The principle was consistent with the Spanish conception of landownership (usufruct), which required that a recipient of a grant of land from the government was required to utilize it. Failure to use it could result in a forfeiture of one's title, and the land would be returned to the state. When Mexico gained its independence from Spain in 1821, the concept of sobrante resurfaced along with other liberal reforms of the late Spanish period.[20]

In addition to the sobrante, the new status of Indigenous people under the Mexican regime had deleterious consequences for Native land rights. The Plan of Iguala guaranteed that Pueblos were full citizens and that all distinctions between them and other Mexican citizens would disappear. Pueblos could now own or sell their land without government protection or regulation. In other words, Indigenous people were no longer wards of the state, and their four leagues were no longer protected from encroachment. In Pecos, the sobrante took on a special meaning because of the continuing decline of the population and the failure of the Pecos to use their *ciénega* (marshland).

Squatters had begun to settle in the rich bottomlands illegally as early as 1821. When Governor Baca received the Fernández-Benavidez petition for sobrante land in Pecos, he directed the alcalde of San Miguel del Bado to investigate the status of Pecos Pueblo lands. The alcalde reported that the ciénega of Pecos was indeed "surplus" land, but the government could not divide it because the Pecos owned the land. The governor then referred the matter to the deputation, the legislative body that was empowered to review land matters. On 12 March 1824, Baca reported to the deputation that the Pecos had complained that they hardly had enough land for their own subsistence and required all of their four leagues. Consequently, the deputation rejected the 1823 Fernández petition.[21]

Meanwhile, other non-Natives appealed to the government for Pecos land. Miguel Rivera, for one, apparently was given an allocation. In May 1824, Diego Padilla was able to secure an allocation of land for himself and five others within the Pecos grant after he convinced the deputation that he had bought the land from the Indigenous people for "six oxen or cows." Padilla apparently moved quickly to settle in Pecos. Others, including some of the Fernández petitioners, had homesteaded in Pecos as they awaited the government's response to their petition. On 1 March 1825, the deputation received four new requests for Pecos land. One was from Miguel Rivera, already living in Pecos, who complained that he had been dispossessed because land previously given to him had been regranted to Padilla. Two others, Rafaél Benavidez and José María Gallegos, who were among the 1823 Fernández petitioners, had homesteaded there and filed separate requests, as did Fernández, who filed a new petition for land. The pressure was clearly building on the deputation to legitimize claims for people who already homesteaded in Pecos and to accommodate the many others who were clamoring for a piece of the action. The deputation succumbed to the pressure.[22]

On 3 March 1825, the deputation created a two-member committee composed of deputies Matias and José Francisco Ortíz to review the Pecos land situation. More specifically, the committee was instructed to apprise the Pecos of the law of 9 November 1812. The government could allocate "surplus Indian land" and "just as their ancient duties ceased, so too their ancient privileges have ended, leaving equal, one to the other, all the additional citizens, who with the Pueblos, form the great Mexican family." The deputation then proceeded to act on the petition submitted on 1 March 1825. It applied the standards of the November 1812 law to Pecos land. First, there would be a *repartición* (repartition) in which the land to remain in Indigenous hands was separated from the sobrante, which would be available for allocation. Second, the sobrante would be allocated to the poorest citizens (*a los vecinos absolutamente desacomodados*). The deputation approved the petitions of the Miguel Rivera party for land next to that claimed by Diego Padilla. It also approved the Rafaél Benavidez group's petition after stipulating that their tract boundaries should be declared so that they could be coordinated with the other allocations.[23]

Historian John Kessell wrote of this tumultuous period that "the real onslaught [in Pecos] began in 1825 [when] Governor Bartolomé Baca and the *diputación provincial* . . . threw open the Pecos League." The "illiterate" Rafaél Benavidez and a group of his companions secured plots of "uncultivated" lands.[24] The boundaries encompassed substantial acreage that stretched as far east as "the little springs" on one side of Rio de la Vaca (Cow Creek), to west of the Pecos River, on the north to the trail from Tecolote, and on the south to the Diego Padilla land. At the same time, Luis Benavidez, a recently retired militia soldier, applied for a "small property in the surplus land . . . of Pecos [to] sow a few maize plants and some wheat" for his large family and gain "relief from so many miseries."[25] Kessell's narrative continued, "With or without grants, they came. Almost overnight dozens of families settled the Cañon de Pecos." Starting with the baptisms in the records of the mission church of two male Roybal infants on 16 April 1825, mention of Hispanos in the Cañon de Pecos became so frequent that Kessell concluded, "This fact was the beginning of the present-day village of Pecos."[26]

Rather than "reviewing" the Pecos land situation, it is apparent that the two-member committee had been directed to implement the deputation's newly adopted position on Pecos land. In addition to apprising the Pecos of the new state of affairs, the committee accomplished the repartición and then proceeded to place the grantees in possession of their tracts. On 19 March 1825, the committee members reported to the deputation that they had made individual allotments of land to ten Indigenous heads of families and to eleven non-Native heads of families (corresponding to the five Rivera and six Benavidez applicants). They also reported that there was still some unused land in Pecos, and they had a list of seventeen individuals requesting the remainder of the sobrante land. The deputation directed the committee members to return to Pecos and allocate the remainder of the land. They also were told to allocate tracts for themselves as payment for their work. The Ortízes returned to Pecos, measured out the unallocated land, and apart from a hundred-yard *abrevadero* (public right-of-way corridor), allocated the remainder of the land to thirty non-Native families.[27] Consequently, by the beginning of the planting season in May 1825, a sizable community of fifty families claimed legal ownership of land in Pecos and began to plant. By the summer of 1826, they had built and were utilizing a new acequia (irrigation ditch) measuring five miles in length and irrigating 8,459 varas of land in Pecos.[28]

Several key points relevant to our study are apparent at this point in the initial settlement of Pecos Pueblo lands. First, nowhere does the name of Donaciano appear, either as a petitioner for land or as a participating public official in the granting or allotment of land. Second, the dispossession of land from Pecos Pueblos was well under way by the mid-1820s by a score of families interested in and determined to secure land in Pecos. Third, Pecos were not entirely oblivious to the developments in their ciénega, which was clearly within their claimed land. One or more Indigenous people were involved in the legitimate sale of land to Diego Padilla for "six oxen or cows." Otherwise, why would he have presented the sale as evidence in his claim for Pecos land, and why would the deputation accept the evidence in granting his claim? Moreover, ten Indigenous people from Pecos Pueblo were among the list of those granted individual tracts by the Ortíz brothers. Thus, whether the Pecos acknowledged the legitimacy of the new land policy or not, their participation in the allocation (which included some of the best land on both sides of the river in the middle of the ciénega) reflected their acceptance of the new state of affairs. Clearly, the Pecos were becoming aware that their continued claim to the entire Pecos Pueblo grant was becoming more tenuous as their numbers declined and as they failed to utilize the most fertile bottomlands of the Pecos ciénega. On the other hand, the non-Natives' complicity in allocating choice land to some of the Pueblos and encouraging them to use the new irrigation ditches reflected their desire to legitimize their own claims by showing that they were living harmoniously with the Indigenous people.

Despite all of that, the Pecos were not going to give up their land without a struggle. On 12 March 1826 in a formal written petition filed by their leader Rafaél Aguilar, the Pecos acknowledged the new state of affairs regarding their land even as they complained to the deputation that some non-Natives had sold their land and others were planting beyond their allotted tracts. This time the Pecos reversed the argument the deputation had used against them. They argued that as Mexican citizens, Indigenous people enjoyed the protection of "all the laws and rights of citizens," and the government could not arbitrarily assert a claim as guardian of the tribe, expropriate their land without their consent, and give it to others. The Indigenous people disputed that there was any sobrante land to give, saying that what land they did not use to plant was used for grazing.[29] The deputation met a week later and directed the governor to inform the non-Native grantees in Pecos that they could not sell or otherwise alienate their land. By this time, it was clear that the deputation was rethinking its earlier position on the allocation of sobrante lands, and the members decided to wait for a formal resolution of the issue by the national government in Mexico, which had received the matter the previous fall.

In October 1826, Governor Francisco Narbona, replying to a request for information from the national government, reported on the state of affairs in Pecos. He said that non-Natives were occupying about 8,400 varas of land on both sides of the Pecos River about a mile and a half from the pueblo itself. The forty-one non-Native families had cleared the tracts that the Indigenous people had abandoned. There were only nine Pecos families left, with a population of less than forty. Narbona's report clearly favored the position taken by the deputation that sobrante land should be allocated to Natives and non-Natives.[30] Still, as Kessell wrote, "a few remaining Indians [at Pecos Pueblo] did not surrender without a fight. When proceedings in their favor were supposedly sent by Governor [Narbona] in 1825 to the Mexican Congress, they tried again the following year. Rafaél Aguilar, Juan Domingo Vigil, and [General] José Manuel Armenta, all Pecos Indians, appealed to the *diputación* to halt the unlawful alienation of their land."[31]

For three years, this confusing set of circumstances continued, with both sides apparently waiting for the final decision of the federal government in Mexico. New non-Native settlers continued to arrive in Pecos and were integrated into the growing farming community. On 1 March 1829, reflecting apparent discord between old and new non-Native settlers in Pecos, a petition signed by thirty-two residents (mostly new ones) protested the behavior of some of the earlier grantees. Some had never broken ground, others had planted one year and then quit, and still others had sold their land. The petitioners requested that the deputation order a redistribution of land to accommodate the new settlers. Eight days later on 9 March, the Pecos, led again by Rafaél Aguilar and now joined by José Cota, seized on the dissension as an opportunity to petition the government again to remove all non-Natives and restore the land to the rightful owners, the people of Pecos Pueblo.

By this time, the membership of the deputation had changed completely; none of the members who had issued the 1825 allocation were now serving. One new member, Juan Estevan Pino, would figure prominently in the future fate of Pecos Pueblo land. Instead of rejecting the new Pecos petition, the deputation decided to reconsider the issue. The members formed a subcommittee made up of Pino and two other deputies. Within a week, the subcommittee issued its report, and on 24 March 1829 the deputation, to everyone's surprise, issued a new order regarding Pecos Pueblo lands. This order, in effect, reversed the previous deputation's actions by acknowledging that the lands claimed by the petitioners belonged to the Pecos Pueblos, and the settlers on the land were to be advised that their right of possession was nullified. It further stated that the ruling only applied to lands that had been expropriated and allocated by the government. It did not apply to lands that Pecos Pueblos may have sold.[32] This was perhaps in reference to the aforementioned purchase of Pecos ciénega land by Diego Padilla from the Indigenous people for "six oxen or cows." The ruling was a victory for Pecos Pueblo. It acknowledged that the Pecos were owners of private property, and the government could no longer take it for lack of use or misuse. However, it also affirmed that some Pecos had individually sold land to non-Natives, such as Padilla, and validated those sales by excluding them from the new decision. The ruling of the deputation, while a defeat for most of the settlers in Pecos, did not result in an immediate exodus of non-Natives since most remained and continued to plant their crops, apparently waiting for the government to enforce the new order. Two or more planting seasons passed.

On 22 September 1830, perhaps as an act of defiance against the non-Native settlers in the Pecos ciénega or in acknowledgment of the inevitable demise of their pueblo, the Indigenous people sold the best part of their land in the ciénega. On that date, José Cota (the same person who had filed the complaint on 9 March 1829), acting as *gobernadorcillo* (little governor) and *en nombre de* (on behalf of) the remainder of the Pecos and in the presence of witnesses Miguel Roibal, deputy justice, and José Ignacio Ortíz, alcalde, contracted by warranty deed to sell to Juan Estevan Pino "todo el terreno conocido con el nombre de ciénega del Pueblo de Pecos" (all that land known by the name of ciénega of the Pecos Pueblo).[33] Cota attested that all the Pecos together (*todos en union*) had agreed to the sale. As payment, Pino would deliver eleven cows with calves (*once bacas paridas*) and three selected bulls (*tres toros escojidos*), which the Pecos could pick from Pino's herd. Cota further affirmed that with such payment, they were comfortable and satisfied (*con cuyo pago quedan conforme y satisfechos*).[34] This statement was perhaps incorporated into the deed to dispel future doubts about the legitimacy of the transaction. It was as if the parties, especially Pino, were aware that later generations might call into question (as they did) the strange trade of land for farm animals. This was further manifested in a subsequent statement in the deed that pointed out that if the grant was of greater value (*si algo mas vale o pueda valer*) than the payment, the excess would be regarded as a donation (*del exceso le hacia gracia y donación*), the contract being irrevocable as in the doctrine of inter vivos. Finally, Cota promised that if any obstacle (*embarazo*) was presented to Pino, the purchaser, in the use of the property, Cota would vigorously defend the legality of the property ownership reflected in the sale. Pino promised that he would fence the land and place his animals (*bueyes y bestias*) inside the fence during the growing season so that they would not harm the Indigenous people's crops.[35]

It is clear from the wording of the warranty deed and the various officials who witnessed and attested to the signatures that Pino was taking great care to assure present and future doubters of the validity and legality of the land sale. One salient fact to be emphasized is that Pino, the purchaser of the Pecos Pueblo land, was also the dominant leader of the deputation at this time. He was one of the three members who had reviewed the validity of non-Native claims and reversed the previous cessions to non-Natives. At that particular time in New Mexico, the deputation was the ultimate authority regarding land grant issues; even the governor deferred to its authority. Given Pino's status, no one in New Mexico could question the validity of the sale. Nevertheless, historians have suggested that the Indigenous people acted under duress. Hall stated, "Hispanic *Pecoseños*, according to the Indians, killed the Pueblo's few remaining animals and poisoned water holes between 1830 and 1840. Life became increasingly isolated and intolerable for the Indians."[36] But none of the various complaints filed by the Pecos about non-Natives settling in Pecos and their planting mentioned such harassment between 1830 and 1840. Moreover, it is unlikely that the Mexican governor and the members of the deputation in Santa Fe, who had proven to be quite sensitive to Indigenous people's property rights, would have tolerated such crimes against the Indigenous people and continued harassment by non-Native trespassers on Indigenous land.

Hall acknowledged the significance of the Pino-Cota transaction: "A private real estate deal signaled the end of Pecos pueblo.... In the process of winning the battle against expropriation of its unused communal lands, it lost the war to maintain its own land base. Pecos pueblo surrendered when it sold its most valuable asset to Juan Estevan Pino."[37] Yet, having written about the "end" of Pecos Pueblo in a transaction that occurred in 1830 between the Pecos leader José Cota and Pino, Hall asserted that Donaciano, who bought his first land in

Pecos from Preston Beck in 1854, was directly connected to the Pecos Pueblos. He wrote, "In developing his claim to the Pecos pueblo grant, Donaciano Vigil demonstrated how that organization [the Santa Fe Ring] worked to acquire interests in New Mexico land, even Pueblo lands."[38] However, Donaciano's purchase of the former Pecos Pueblo land was separated in time (1854 versus 1830), person (Beck versus Pino), and place (Vigil bought a portion of the eastern half of the entire tract Beck had secured from Manuel Pino). It is worth restating that Donaciano did not buy land in Pecos from the Pecos; he bought it from Preston Beck, who had foreclosed on it because of a loan to Manuel Pino, who had inherited it from his father, Juan Estevan Pino, who had bought it from the Pecos people in 1830.

Why did the Pecos concede to sell the ciénega after fighting for six years to keep it? More than likely, the 1830 sale was a final act of desperation by tribal leaders to give their people one last chance of survival in their Pecos land. Certainly, the three bulls and eleven cows with calves were sufficient to jump-start a small herd of cattle. Also noteworthy is that the Indigenous people had long since abandoned their ciénega and had previously shown a willingness to sell part of it, even trading land for livestock from Padilla. Perhaps their dismay at seeing their land allocated by the government in Santa Fe was not based so much on the utility of the land to them as the fact that they were not being compensated for it. It is obvious that they did not wait very long (less than two years) before they found a buyer and sold the Pecos ciénega.

Whatever the reasons, the 1830s proved no better for the Pecos than the prior decade had been. Survival at the pueblo became more untenable for the beleaguered tribe, and finally, in 1838, the dozen or so survivors packed up their personal belongings and sacred objects and abandoned the pueblo, moving to the home of their Towa language cousins at Jemez Pueblo.[39]

Between 1830 and 1840, the Hispano settlement of the ciénega of Pecos continued to evolve and assume the appearance and character of a typical Hispano land-based farming and ranching community of that era. Pino had established his cattle and sheep ranching headquarters on his acquired Pecos land. By 1834, the community was large enough that they built their first church, and in 1837, the bishop of Durango, Mexico, granted a license establishing the parish of Saint Anthony.[40] Saint Anthony's parish records began to document the births and marriages of the growing small Hispanic community and the interlocking of different families in kinship and social relationships.

In 1839, Juan Estevan Pino, the first Pecos patriarch, died, and his vast landholdings and estate were divided among his heirs. His oldest son, Justo Pastor, secured land lying north of the ciénega of Pecos, and Manuel Doroteo secured the portion of land that Juan Estevan had bought from the Indigenous people in the ciénega of Pecos. In the decade of the 1840s, the fortunes of Juan Estevan's sons diminished. Neither had inherited their father's astuteness as a land speculator, merchant, or stockman. Perhaps management of the various enterprises proved difficult at a time of economic uncertainty. Whatever the reason, by the early 1850s both sons were so financially strapped that they were forced to sell or borrow heavily, using their Pecos and other lands as collateral in order to stay afloat. Justo Pastor Pino was the first to sell. On 2 January 1851, he sold his land north of Pecos to Alejandro Valle for 5,275 pesos (about $1,200). Interestingly, Donaciano appeared as a witness and recorder of the deed, his first indirect contact to land in Pecos.[41]

On 18 April 1851, Donaciano was replaced as territorial secretary. For the second time since he had enlisted as a soldier with the Santa Fe presidio company in May 1821, Donaciano found himself without a job. Not one to dwell on personal misfortune, Donaciano set out in search of new opportunities. On 16 August 1851, Donaciano applied for and was granted a dram shop license that entitled him to "sell liquors [at] his stand or shop in the city of Santa Fe in less quantities than one quart."[42] For that privilege, Donaciano paid $45.50 in territorial and county taxes and $13 to the city of Santa Fe.

In 1852, Donaciano was elected to the House of Representatives of the Second New Mexico Territorial Assembly, which met in December. Because of his experience in both military and civilian affairs, Donaciano frequently undertook various assignments for the government and testified in various forums on land and other issues. For example, on 30 March 1853, he was appointed as treasurer (*colector de la renta de Bayles*) for Santa Fe County by probate judge Tomás Ortíz.[43] Donaciano's establishment of a tavern in Santa Fe, his time in the legislature, and his continued service to the territory are all indicative of his intent to settle into a normal civilian life with his family in Santa Fe.

Manuel Doroteo Pino, the second son of Juan Estevan Pino, had been managing his share of his father's land and cattle business from his headquarters in Pecos. Short of cash and facing litigation over another property (the Ojo de las Gallinas grant) claimed by his father, he was forced to mortgage his properties to raise cash. Manuel had inherited the land in the Pecos ciénega that his father had bought from the Pecos people. On 14 June 1853, Manuel and his wife, Josefa Ortíz, borrowed $2,460 from Preston Beck at a rate of 12 percent interest and pledged his land as collateral for the loan. In addition to the Pecos property, Manuel also pledged half of the Ojo de las Gallinas grant.

The Pecos property is described in the deed as being "situated in the 'Cañada de Pecos' and lying on both sides of the Pecos River [and] bounded on the north by the properties of Manuel Varela and Blas Ortega, on the east by public lands, on the south by the lands of Pablo Moya, Manuel Baca, and Vicente Quintana, and on the west by public lands, containing about three hundred acres of land and heretofore known as the ranch of Manuel Pino at Pecos."[44] Of interest in the deed is that the amount of land conveyed, 300 acres, is considerably larger than the amount that would be sold to Donaciano (74 varas wide, or 50 acres) later. Two adjoining property owners named in this deed, Pablo Moya and Vicente Quintana, later appear as sellers of land to Donaciano or his family. After Pino and his wife failed to pay the note, Hugh N. Smith, acting as Preston Beck's trustee, initiated foreclosure proceedings on 29 August 1854. In accordance with the mortgage agreement, a foreclosure sale was held, and Beck purchased the two properties for $3,000. On 12 December 1854, Smith executed a deed transfer as trustee for Preston Beck.[45]

Beck's interest in acquiring the Pecos land was simple: he was an investor and land speculator. He was one of several American and European investors, stockmen, merchants, bankers, miners, and lawyers who appeared in New Mexico in the middle of the nineteenth century and become involved in landowning and land speculation. Following New Mexico's annexation by the United States, it was inevitable that New Mexico would be inundated by such adventurers seeking to capitalize on the cheap land and related opportunities. Beck, Andrés Dold, William and Charles Bent, and Ceran St. Vrain were later followed by Thomas B. Catron, Stephen B. Elkins, Frank Springer, and others who became prominent land speculators in New Mexico. Using personal fortunes or wealth acquired from mercantile businesses, stock raising, or similar pursuits, they speculated in land. It is, however, important to distinguish such wealthy speculators, whose sole pursuit was to acquire land for its possible resale value, from Donaciano Vigil, Manuel Varela, and others in Pecos who had a genuine interest in farming or ranching on the land.

Preston Beck was the prototype of the Anglo-American speculator. Starting as a Missouri trader on the Santa Fe Trail, by the 1850s he was a partner in a

Santa Fe mercantile store. Soon he was a well-known banker (moneylender), financer of various enterprises, and land speculator. Beck would have probably become more notorious in New Mexico had he not been killed in a knife duel in 1858. His opponent, John Gorman, also died from injuries sustained in the duel.[46] Before his death, Beck had been involved in a number of New Mexico land transactions, including the mortgage loan to Manuel Doroteo Pino.

On 26 December 1854, just four months after completing the foreclosure proceeding on the two properties secured from Pino, Preston Beck did what every speculator does: he began to subdivide and sell his newly acquired properties. On that date, he sold to Donaciano "a certain piece or parcel of land lying and being situate[d] ... on the east bank of the Pecos River ... bounded and described as follows—north by lands of Blas Ortega, south by the lands of Vicente Quintana, east by public lands and west by the old channel of the Pecos River."[47] The deed pointed out that an "island" lying between the two channels of the Pecos was included in the transfer, but the property of Juan Valencia of some "75 varas" and located within the tract of land being conveyed was excepted from the sale. The deed further described the property sold to Donaciano as "being that part of the same lying on the east bank of the Pecos River heretofore known as the Rancho of Manuel D. Pino."[48]

The deed clearly declared that the sale was made "in consideration of the sum of one thousand five hundred dollars to me paid by Donaciano Vigil."[49] How did Donaciano amass what was, at the time, a considerable amount of money for the land purchase? Donaciano operated a dram shop, so he could have used profits from the business. He may have simply sold the liquor establishment since he moved to Pecos early the following year. He also was earning pay for his service in the legislature, and he surely had saved some money. Thus, taken at face value, the deal was a simple real estate transaction in which the legal owner, Preston Beck, reaped a profit by selling for $1,500 approximately one-sixth of the Pecos portion of the properties he had secured from Manuel D. Pino for a $2,460 loan plus the $540 purchase price ($3,000 total) in the foreclosure auction. Hall, however, saw a more sinister aspect to the transaction, depicting this acquisition as not born from an innocent good faith "as non-Indian interests in Pueblo land were said to be elsewhere.... The Pecos Pueblo grant land came to Donaciano Vigil from legal and financial dealings supposedly characteristic only of much more sophisticated environments than mid-nineteenth century New Mexico."[50]

It is clear that Donaciano came upon this property, the main Pecos property that passed to his heirs, in an entirely legitimate manner. It is likely that Donaciano took up residence in Pecos, as Crocchiola said, in the spring of 1855. It is possible that at first Donaciano remained in Pecos only temporarily during the growing season. However, by 1860, as reflected in the Census for that year, he and all his family, including his eldest son, Antonio Basilio, who was married to María de la Luz Rolenes and had one son, Bartolomé, were listed as residents and neighbors in Pecos.[51]

However, old habits die hard, and even as Donaciano was embarking on a new career as a farmer-rancher in Pecos, the pull of public life continued to beckon. In 1857, he was elected to the Seventh New Mexico Territorial Assembly. This time he was representing San Miguel County and serving in the upper chamber, the Territorial Council (Senate), and as president of that body. To make a transition from serving in the lower house as a representative from one county, and then move to another county and be elected to the higher body and serve as its presiding officer—all within a period of four years—shows the honor he was accorded as an elder statesman.[52]

11

ASSAULT ON A GIANT, PART II
The Los Trigos Land Grant

An excerpt from Donaciano's last will and testament opened chapter 6 of *Four Leagues of Pecos*, "Donaciano Vigil's Pecos." Donaciano introduced the will this way: "Declaro tener dos ranchos de terreno . . . uno en el lugar que llaman El Gusano y el otro en Pecos donde resido" (I declare that I have two ranches of land . . . one in the place called El Gusano and the other in Pecos where I reside).[1] Hall made two references in his book identifying the Gusano ranch as the same Los Trigos land that Donaciano had claimed in an application to the surveyor general on 17 July 1855. Hall wrote, "By May 1877 his [Donaciano's] estate had increased tremendously. It had come to include the Los Trigos grant just south of the Pecos Pueblo grant."[2] He also wrote that "Vigil . . . attempted to solidify his own claims . . . in Pecos and El Gusano [Los Trigos]."[3] It is clear from these two passages that Hall considered the El Gusano ranch to be the same as the Los Trigos claim.

Hall wrote in regard to Los Trigos that two aspects of that grant related to "Donaciano Vigil's land ventures." First, although no one could definitively locate where the boundary was, it was agreed that the southern boundary of the Pecos Pueblo grant was also the northern boundary of Los Trigos; the two grants adjoined each other. The other aspect was that Donaciano was filing a "technical" claim squarely against a "growing community's more intensive use of it."[4] Hugh N. Smith, who had been Preston Beck's counsel in the Pecos ciénega loan and the foreclosure against Manuel Pino, was Donaciano's attorney in filing a claim for Los Trigos. The claim identified "Donaciano Vigil, a citizen of the United States and resident of the territory of New Mexico[,] and the 'legal' representatives" of Francisco Trujillo, Diego Padilla, and Bartolomé Márquez as claimants for the Los Trigos land grant.[5] In other words, Donaciano was acting for himself and for the legal representatives of the original grantees—Trujillo,

Padilla, and Márquez—who had received the grant of land from Spanish government officials in Santa Fe in 1814. In a subsequent reference to the grant, Hall stated categorically that "Donaciano Vigil's application for the Los Trigos grant came to the surveyor general as a *private claim* from one individual, rather than as an application for land belonging to a community.... Vigil claimed the entire Los Trigos grant as his private property."[6] This seems to contradict the wording of the claim. If it was a private individual claim, why was the phrase "and the legal representatives of" Trujillo, Padilla, and Márquez added?

The Los Trigos land grant application prepared by Smith for Donaciano was indeed a private claim. However, it is important to note that there was no formal distinction made between types of grants under Spanish/Mexican law. American land grant historians have developed the terms "community" land grant and "private" land grant to distinguish between the two forms. The US General Accounting Office report on the subject of community land grants said, "We found that the term is frequently used to refer to grants that set aside some land for general communal use (*ejido*) or for specific purposes including hunting (*caza*), pasture (*pastos*), wood gathering (*leña*), or watering (*abrevederos*)."[7]

Under the General Accounting Office's universally adopted definition, the original Los Trigos grant was *not* a community land grant because it did not incorporate the key provision calling for "general communal use (*ejido*)." Although the grant was for grazing and identified three recipients, it was a private grant. This is why Smith in drafting Donaciano's claim retained the private claim designation even though it implied that there could conceivably be multiple valid claimants who could prove descent or legal standing through one or more of the original grantees. There seems to have been no intent in Smith's claim on behalf of his client to assert that the grant was Donaciano's private property. Rather, the words indicated that Donaciano was filing the claim as a private claim for himself and the legal representatives of the original grantees of the Los Trigos grant.

The original 1814 grantees had faced constant pressure in holding on to the land due to continual harassment and raids by Indigenous people. Domingo Fernández, who gave testimony on the Los Trigos grant before the surveyor general, affirmed that the three grantees had settled on the land and built at least one house, they worked the land, and the Apaches had been a constant threat. At one time, the Apaches had even killed an Indigenous boy who worked for the grantees as a shepherd. The three grantees had not abandoned their land.[8]

Domingo Fernández authenticated the 1814 Los Trigos grant to Trujillo, Padilla, and Márquez, saying he knew they had received it. He had stopped and slept there sometime in 1822 on a return trip from San Miguel del Bado. He said there was a small house built by one of the original grantees, which was used by shepherds who watched over the flocks of sheep. There was also a plot of cultivated land about 200 varas in length. In response to questions, he testified that the area was very "dangerous" to live in because of the "troublesome Indians" who frequented the region. He offered the opinion that despite the dangers the grant was never abandoned. Of the three grantees, one was very old (Márquez), one was blind, and the other was still in possession at the time.[9]

Despite the seemingly valuable information Fernández provided, Hall suggested that Donaciano brought him to testify in exchange for Donaciano's testimony regarding Fernández's interest in another claim (San Cristóbal).[10] Hall's suspicion of a sinister motive in the testimony of Fernández and Vigil seems unjustified since both had been directly involved in maintaining land records at various times during the Spanish/Mexican period. In the Preston Beck case, Fernández testified that he had been directly involved in maintaining land records in the archives between 1825 and 1846. In similar testimony, Donaciano stated his involvement with recording and maintaining land records at different times in his career. Since both were often asked to attest to their acquaintance with the principles involved in various grants, as well as their familiarity with the signatures of the government officials and the nature of the grants themselves, it is logical that the surveyor general sought their experience and testimony.

Even though Fernández's testimony was that the grant had never been abandoned by the original grantees, which supported Donaciano's view, some argued otherwise. A group of squatters had settled on the grant and claimed that it had been abandoned when they arrived there in 1842. This group, headed by Rafaél Gonzales, filed a counterclaim to that of Donaciano. They also claimed that in the same year the alcalde of San Miguel del Bado, Manuel Baca, had allocated the land to them after giving public notice of his intent to do so.[11] Hall wrote in support of these claimants that "Donaciano Vigil's brother Gregorio, the *alcalde* of San Miguel del Bado after Baca also approved the [Baca] distribution. . . . In other words, various Mexican officials had confirmed the possession of Gonzales and the twenty-four others then living on the grant. Donaciano could not now claim it as his own."[12] Hall identified Baca as the alcalde, as did the Gonzales counterclaim. Actually, according to the surveyor general's record, Baca had been deputized by Santiago Ulibarri, the probate judge, to distribute the lands. Gregorio Vigil had served as alcalde, but he was not Donaciano's half brother, Gregorio Trujillo, who sometimes used the Vigil surname; he was a cousin.

The essence of the claims before the surveyor general was thus as follows. Donaciano's argument was that the 1814 grant was still valid and that he, acting for himself and the legal representatives of the original grantees, was entitled to the land, and no one else could claim the right to it or be at variance with it. The Gonzales group disagreed, arguing that the original members had abandoned the grant, that the 1814 grant had been for grazing only and limited to the plots the original grantees had occupied, and that later settlers could take possession of unoccupied parts of the grant, which is what the Gonzales group had done. Finally, as Hall noted regarding Donaciano, "The man who according to all reports was more informed about American custom than any other native New Mexicans produced no written evidence before the surveyor general to support his personal claim to the Los Trigos grant."[13]

To counter Domingo Fernández's testimony in support of Donaciano's claim, the Gonzales group presented several of their own witnesses, including Rafaél Vigil. It was not stated that he was related to Donaciano, but he was an uncle of Rafaél Gonzales and a first cousin of Matias Alarid, another of the Gonzales group. Rafaél Vigil testified that he had been to the Los Trigos area four or five times, and he had seen the house and the "three valleys in cultivation in 1816" that Fernández mentioned. He also said that three people had been killed in the area—an unnamed Indigenous boy, a man identified only as Villanueva, and an unnamed French man. Villanueva and the French man were killed at Cañon de los Soldados. Rafaél Vigil offered the opinion that the grant had been abandoned in 1818, and original grantee Márquez had remained one more year. This contradicted Fernández's testimony. Manuel Baca testified that he had been deputized by don Santiago Ulibarri to distribute the lands at Los Trigos, which he did in 1842. Antonio Nieto, the clerk to Ulibarri, confirmed that Ulibarri had deputized Baca for the distribution.[14] It is interesting that Ulibarri, a substantial landowner in the region and a land speculator in his own right, escaped attention in this matter.

Notwithstanding their argument that they had resided in the area since 1842 and the impressive list of witnesses who affirmed their presence there, the Gonzales group failed to prove that they had proper authority to occupy the grant. They could not produce land grant documents from provincial-level officials authorizing the grant, and the ayuntamiento-level officials that allowed the distribution did not have the authority to grant land. Moreover, since they were essentially claiming a private land grant, there was no basis for them to claim status as new colonists on a community land grant. The private Los Trigos grant did not allow for new colonists. As Hall pointed out, the Gonzales group had no more standing than Donaciano had. Ultimately, the surveyor general recommended and Congress approved on 21 June 1860 that the Los Trigos grant belonged to the "legal representative[s] of the original grantees, Francisco Trujillo, Diego Padilla, and Bartolomé Márquez."[15]

Although Donaciano presented no documents to the surveyor general regarding his own connection to Los Trigos, he had acquired properties in Gusano and had various connections to the original claimants. Donaciano was a personal friend of Diego Padilla who, along with Teodocio Quintana, had served as witness for his marriage to María del Refugio Sánchez in Santa Fe on 10 October 1825.[16] It is possible that Donaciano filed his claim to protect the interests of Padilla's family. Donaciano also had connections to the family of Francisco Trujillo, another original grantee at Los Trigos. Trujillo's daughter Tomasa Trujillo was married on 1 February 1843 to Thomas Rowland (aka Tomás Rolenes), a merchant in San Miguel del Bado. Rolenes's daughter María de la Luz was married to Donaciano's eldest son, Antonio Basilio, on 1 October 1848. Since Donaciano was a soldier assigned to San Miguel, he likely was a friend of Francisco Trujillo and his heirs.

Donaciano's half brother, Gregorio Trujillo, was the first son of his mother, Antonia Andrea Martínez, and her first husband, Juan Francisco Trujillo. Gregorio was born about 1778. Shortly after, Juan Trujillo died, Antonia married Juan Cristóbal Vigil, and they had six children: Ana María, Juana María, Paula, María Ygnes, Donaciano, and Juan Bautista. Apparently, Donaciano maintained a very close relationship with his half brother, who was about twenty-four years older. For example, Gregorio, then seventy-two years old, was listed as a member of Donaciano's household in the 1850 Census for Santa Fe,[17] and he sometimes used the Vigil surname. This could be why he was mistaken as Donaciano's full brother. Juan Trujillo, Gregorio's father, may have been related to Francisco Trujillo (the Los Trigos grantee) since Gregorio had pursued an interest in Los Trigos land.

Gregorio Trujillo purchased several properties in his lifetime. Among these was a ranch in El Gusano in San Miguel County that he acquired in 1843. In that year, Trujillo purchased a parcel of land from Rafaél Perfecto Benavidez, acting on behalf of his brothers Patricio, Juan, and Ramon Benavidez, joint owners of the parcel in Gusano. Trujillo, then living in Santa Fe, was represented by Gregorio Vigil in the proceeding, which occurred before Juan María Diego Ulibarri justice of the peace of the First Demarcation. The parcel consisted of ninety-five varas of land and a house with nine vigas (beams). Rafaél Benavidez had previously sold to the same Gregorio Trujillo land in the same *ancon* (core), which had belonged to his late father. That land consisted of 109 varas of land and a house with one room and five vigas.[18] Both parcels later passed to Donaciano when his half brother's age and ill health led him to grant power to Donaciano over his personal affairs. Donaciano also administered Trujillo's estate when he died on 23 March 1853.

In 1854, Donaciano purchased another parcel of land in Gusano from José F. Sena and his wife, Luciana Rodríguez. The parcel was known as Rancho del Gusano en el Ancon and had been owned by their uncle, the deceased Francisco Trujillo (one of the original grantees of Los Trigos). The property consisted of ten varas of land and was bounded on the north and south by the Pecos River, on the east by the land of Celso Benavidez, and on the west by land already owned by Donaciano. Donaciano bought the small property for five pesos. The transaction took place before Vicente López, justice of the peace of the Fifth Demarcation (Santa Fe), who affirmed that Sena and Rodríguez had appeared before him on 12 April 1854 to validate the transaction.[19]

Donaciano acquired still another property in Gusano from José Ulibarri, who had purchased it from Jesús García and his wife (her name is unknown). García had inherited the property from his deceased grandmother Juliana Olguin in 1845. The property, located at Punto del Gusano, measured 51 varas wide in the north and 50 varas in the south and was 154 varas long. It was bordered on the north by the Pecos River, on the south and west by the lands of the deceased doña Lucia Trujillo, and on the east by the lands of Francisco Sena of Santa Fe. The first sale of the property between Ulibarri and the Garcías had not been properly documented. Thus, Jesús García and his wife appeared before Alcalde Miguel Sena y Romero in 1854 to affirm the sale to Ulibarri. Following that proceeding, apparently on the same day, Ulibarri in turn transferred the property to Donaciano, who was acting with power of attorney for Gregorio Trujillo, for thirty-eight pesos in silver. This proceeding also took place before

Alcalde Miguel Sena y Romero in San Miguel del Bado.[20] Consequently, by 1854, a year before he filed his claim for Los Trigos, Donaciano had acquired four adjacent properties in different purchases from three separate parties, and all of them constituted Donaciano's ranch in Gusano.

Around 1842 or 1843, Donaciano had prepared a will while he was living in Santa Fe, which was much shorter than his second will. He mentioned his house and property in Santa Fe and that he and his wife, María, had "ten children five of whom had died in infancy." He also wrote, "I have 195 varas of land which I got by inheritance and purchase from my two brothers."[21] Some of the land mentioned in this will was apparently acquired from his half brother, Gregorio Trujillo Vigil. It is not clear what property he had acquired from his brother, Juan Bautista Vigil. The first will confirms Donaciano's prior landownership.

As evidenced by all of these purchases and associations, Donaciano did own land in Gusano, presumably in the Los Trigos claim he filed for in 1855. From the names of some of the people who transferred land to Donaciano and others mentioned, it appears that they were heirs of the original three grantees. Thus, Donaciano could have been counted among the class of heirs he represented in his claim for Los Trigos in 1855. That Donaciano owned land in Gusano is therefore established. The question that remains is whether Gusano and the property Donaciano owned there was within the boundaries of the Los Trigos grant.

In the 1870s, the question of the exact boundaries of the grant were still contested, and a survey prepared by Sawyer and McElroy, deputy surveyor generals, referred to as the Los Trigos or Donaciano Vigil survey, was under review in the boundary discussions. That survey was not authenticated. However, in testimony heard on 8 March 1882 before Surveyor General Henry M. Atkinson, Pedro Duran, a ninety-four-year-old resident of San Miguel, testified that the western boundary of the San Miguel del Bado grant was at Gusano.[22] Another witness testified about a pointed hill, an arroyo, and a cañoncito referred to as Gusano, which were commonly regarded as the western boundary of the San Miguel del Bado grant. It has generally been understood that the Los Trigos grant was situated between the San Miguel del Bado grant and the Pecos Pueblo grant. If so, the western boundary of the San Miguel del Bado grant at Gusano would also have been the common eastern boundary of Los Trigos, and thus Gusano, it would seem, would have been within the Los Trigos grant.[23] Why Donaciano did not present this information to support his claim is unclear. Perhaps the documentary evidence was not available to him at the time.

On 18 January 1883, Antonio Basilio and Epitacio Vigil, as heirs of Donaciano, sold two tracts of land in Gusano to Manuel García for seventy pesos apiece. The documents describing these two sales are essentially conjoined with the documentary evidence pertaining to Donaciano's earlier acquisitions of land in Gusano from his half brother's estate, from Sena, and from Ulibarri. All of the acquisitions were presented for *protocolación* (filing) on 30 December 1887 and registered on 13 January 1888 at the San Miguel County Clerk's Office, so they could have been held until that time of recording by Donaciano's sons.[24] It is important to note that in the period in question, 1840–1880, it would have taken several days to travel from place to place, and people could not readily travel to the county seat to file property documents. Often they postponed such errands to coincide with other business or simply neglected to file documents in a timely manner. Regardless of the timing of the recording of the transaction, the 1887 sale by Donaciano's sons was of what remained of the ranch in Gusano, which Donaciano mentioned in his will. Clearly, it was incorrect to state that Donaciano was referring to the Los Trigos grant in his will when he referred to his rancho in Gusano.

Acting as agent for the legal representatives of the Los Trigos claim, Donaciano did make a transfer of land in the Los Trigos grant to Anne Carolyn Houghton "in consideration of the services rendered by Joab Houghton as attorney in obtaining confirmation of the said grant." The transfer was for land 440 yards from north to south and extending from the ridge of the mesa on the west to the Pecos River on the east.[25] Other than this questionable transfer, which he had promised to Joab Houghton as a standard payment in land for services rendered, it appears that Donaciano did not personally ever occupy, sell, or claim any of the Los Trigos grant other than the acquisitions at Gusano already mentioned. The Los Trigos grant was ultimately adjudicated by the surveyor general as belonging to the "legal representatives of the original grantees," but not to Donaciano. Perhaps that surveyor general left the door open for Donaciano to validate his connection to the grant, since the open-ended result apparently led a later surveyor general to order a survey of the grant. A map produced in December 1860 was titled "Donaciano Vigil or Los Trigos Grant." This survey led to further hearings before Surveyor General George Julian in January 1888, during which several witnesses referred to the Gusano hill, Gusano arroyo, and Gusano cañoncito, all of which were placed at the commonly shared eastern boundary of the Los Trigos grant and the western boundary of the San Miguel de Bado grant that adjoined it.[26] This survey was questioned and ultimately not validated. Interestingly, that map shows the words "Arroyo Guzano" just below the boundary line separating the two grants. Whether the Gusano referred to in the map was the location of Donaciano's ranch and whether the ranch was within the Los Trigos grant were apparently never determined.

One thing is true: Donaciano did not benefit from the claim (in Spanish, *no lo logro*). In the 1860s–1880s, land speculators secured deeds from the presumptive heirs of the Los Trigos grantees and sold the land to the Atchison, Topeka and Santa Fe Railroad, among other buyers. The Los Trigos debacle ended badly for Donaciano, who clearly had botched whatever aspirations he had for the grant. Hall described the outcome, "Donaciano Vigil had tried to grab it all for himself and had lost it for everyone connected with it."[27] Hall's assertion is open to debate, however. As a citizen who owned land either within or adjacent to Los Trigos, Donaciano was within his rights to file a claim for it, given the uncertain boundaries of the grant. He had not "lost it for everyone" since the surveyor general probably would not have validated the original grantees' claim. Whatever caused Donaciano to file the claim for Los Trigos and then abandon it completely after his partial victory, we will never know, as Donaciano carried that story to his grave.

THE SIGNIFICANCE OF DONACIANO VIGIL'S WILL

Using Donaciano's will for an evaluation of his economic status is interesting, but it is not easy to judge a Hispanic person's wealth in nineteenth-century New Mexico. It was common in the wills of that era for the testator, regardless of wealth, to list every item owned—from a valuable house and property to minor pieces of clothing, such as a shirt, or a tool, as Donaciano did.[28] We cannot assert, as Hall did, that Donaciano's wealth had increased "tremendously," given that we do not actually know what his wealth was before he left Santa Fe, excluding the Gusano property. In his description of Donaciano's last will, Hall did not see the discrepancy between his own characterization of Donaciano and the words in Donaciano's will. Donaciano's description of his life possessions is hardly what one would expect from a wealthy person, but instead he lists the remnants of a modest estate left by an ordinary medium-level farmer and rancher in New Mexico in the last quarter of the nineteenth century. However, Hall wrote, "Yet about his most valued possessions, the land, he spoke only vaguely: I declare to have two ranches . . . one in the place called El Gusano and the other in Pecos where I reside."[29]

Donaciano's "vague" reference to the land was not a deception, but a real expression of its value. The fifty acres of land he had purchased in Pecos from Beck, along with the subsequent acreage he had purchased from Quintana and Moya, had been reduced to almost nothing since he had deeded it piece by piece, a few acres at a time, to his sons and daughters at various stages. Donaciano's reference to his "rancho" in Gusano was to property he had acquired there and not to the Los Trigos grant, as stated before. Every indication in the disposition of the Los Trigos grant is that Donaciano did not pursue his personal claim after the surveyor general recommended that it be accorded to the "legal representatives of Francisco Trujillo, Diego Padilla, and Bartolomé Márquez."[30] At the time he wrote his will, Donaciano was not the wealthy *patrón* of a vast estate living in an ostentatious hacienda and *estancia* that encompassed many acres of land and thousands of cattle and sheep herded by untold numbers of vaqueros and peones. The practical reality of Donaciano's wealth, contrary to Hall's assumption, was reflected in the detailed list of tools and equipment named in his will.

Allusions to Donaciano's "constant focus on New Mexico land" and his role in "the creation of New Mexico's largest and most controversial land grants under the regime of the Mexican Governor Armijo and . . . the preservation of those claims . . . under the Kearny Code . . . [and] their approval by the surveyor general and confirmation by the Congress of the United States" are overstatements. Targeting Donaciano regarding the "creation" of the "largest and most controversial land grants" and referring to his "preservation of these sometimes fantastic claims to land" are overreach.[31] It is an exaggeration to directly link Donaciano to securing the congressional confirmation of any land grants. It is inconceivable that a former enemy, a Mexican official in New Mexico, could have had any role in securing the confirmation of land grants by the US Congress. It must be understood that in the brief periods he served as secretary of the territory under the Mexican or American regimes, it was Donaciano's duty to create and maintain records of government actions, and in New Mexico making and keeping records of land transactions was his primary responsibility. In most cases, the territorial secretary was not directly involved in decisions to grant land; the power to do so was vested in the governor, who often consulted a territorial legislative body, a municipal council, or a local alcalde. Given the chaotic state of affairs regarding New Mexico land, it is appropriate to consider how much worse conditions would have been had no records been created or preserved. All indications are that Donaciano did a credible job of preserving the archival documents.[32]

Donaciano's responsibility for providing information and his testifying before the surveyor general are also subject to a different interpretation. The records suggest that Surveyor General William Pelham regarded Donaciano's knowledge and testimony as valuable resources in helping him perform his difficult job. In his biography of Donaciano, Crocchiola wrote that Donaciano served as the "engrossing clerk" in 1854–1855, during which time he made "a complete study of the land grants" (the Vigil Register of Land Titles). It was on the basis of that study and his "testimony before the commissioner [surveyor general] that the Pueblos were permitted to retain their land."[33] Hall challenged that statement when he wrote that "Donaciano had almost nothing to do with the 1856 confirmation of eighteen grants to pueblos."[34] Yet in another passage, Hall wrote, "In other instances Vigil supplied the surveyor general with all the information available to that American official concerning the history of New Mexico and the applicable laws of the antecedent sovereigns."[35] Later Hall admitted that "in a minor way, Donaciano did substantiate the story that the Pueblos had themselves told Pelham."[36] Their land claim stemmed directly from the king. In fact, Donaciano's direct assertion of that truth was repeated in his affidavit of 1856 and his testimony of 20 August 1855 regarding the Preston Beck Jr. grant.[37] These statements carried significant weight. Hall reported that in supporting documents the surveyor general included Donaciano's sworn statement: "the Pueblos were entitled to four square leagues, with or without documents."[38]

Donaciano's information and testimony regarding the Pueblo land grants as flowing directly from edicts and decrees from the Spanish monarchy helped shape Pelham's prompt and successful recommendations to his superiors, which resulted in most of the Pueblo tribes receiving US government patents for their lands. This is why when Pelham submitted his second report on the Pueblo land grants in 1856, he arranged for Donaciano's controversial affidavit, which affirmed that the Pueblo grants came directly from the Spanish monarchs. When the Cruzate grants were declared spurious, it was that legal basis that sustained the validity of the confirmed patent the Pueblos had received.

Donaciano's retirement to Pecos was a very real undertaking for his wife, four of their sons, and their families. The land that Donaciano had acquired had few homes fit for habitation. Some of the land was marsh in need of drainage and flood control. The construction of acequias would provide for irrigation, and the valuable and rich bottomland would become suitable for the cultivation of subsistence crops. The land would sustain his large extended family and the families of Varelas, Riveras, Valencias, Roybales, Quintanas, and many others in the close-knit Hispanic community of Pecos. Even as Donaciano was supervising the enormous task of relocation to Pecos, he faithfully fulfilled his civic duty and continued to testify before the surveyor general, ensuring that the interests of both Hispanic and Pueblo vecinos of New Mexico would be represented and protected. Providing testimony required frequent long trips to Santa Fe on horseback, by burro, or by wagon, making for a greater sacrifice on Donaciano's part.

12

ASSAULT ON A GIANT, PART III
The Cruzate Land Grants

Several other writers have also offered interpretations of Donaciano Vigil's involvement with the Pueblo land grants in New Mexico. The critiques of Donaciano's alleged role in the historically controversial Cruzate grants are found in scholarly historical works: a PhD dissertation from the University of New Mexico, an article in the *New Mexico Historical Review* on the same subject by the same author, and a book featuring several land grant scholars, one of whom is a former New Mexico state historian. In this chapter we explore plausible alternative explanations of the events analyzed by those writers.

SANDRA MATHEWS-LAMB AND THE NINETEENTH-CENTURY CRUZATE GRANTS

In the 1990s, Sandra K. Mathews-Lamb, a graduate student searching for a PhD dissertation topic, settled on the intriguing subject of the Cruzate land grants, which she later referred to as "the greatest land grant mystery in New Mexico history" and a topic of interest for some land grant historians. She said, "Scholars, such as Myra Ellen Jenkins, G. Emlen Hall, and Victor Westphall have mentioned the 'spurious Cruzate grants' without explaining their origins."[1] Focusing her inquiry on why "so many scholars" had declared the Cruzate grants to be fraudulent but had not identified who wrote them and why, she set out to, in her words, "place the grants in historical perspective." In other words, her goal was to determine their source.

Mathews-Lamb noted that the grant documents were all of similar format and originated in the headquarters of Domingo Jironza Petriz de Cruzate near present-day El Paso, Texas. Cruzate had been appointed governor of the Mexican province of New Mexico in 1689 following the Pueblo Revolt of 1680, during which the Spaniards were expelled from New Mexico. As governor, Cruzate was ordered to restore Spanish control of the New Mexico Territory for Spain. Cruzate launched several military campaigns to recapture New Mexico. In one encounter, his forces captured a Zia war captain named Bartolomé de Ojeda, who was brought to El Paso for interrogation. Ojeda was literate in Spanish. Mathews-Lamb observed, "Ojeda's testimony served as the basis for Cruzate's claim to knowledge and recognition for recording of pueblo boundaries."[2] Governor Cruzate recorded Ojeda's testimony and allegedly drafted land grant documents for the various Pueblo tribes in New Mexico affirming their ownership of their land, which became known as the Cruzate grants.

Mathews-Lamb examined the "logistics" of the Cruzate documents. If indeed the tale were true, and "if Cruzate had penned these documents, witnessed purportedly by Secretary of Government and War, Pedro Ladrón de Guevara, and even some by Ojeda himself, the next step [as governor] would have been to deliver the documents to New Mexico's Pueblos."[3] This, according to Mathews-Lamb, did not happen since "from their purported creation in 1689, these grants disappeared from oral, written, and legal history until the mid-nineteenth century when they surfaced for the first time as corroborated documentary record in the 1850s in Santa Fe."[4] In a footnote, Mathews-Lamb speculated that a logical recipient of the documents would have been Diego de Vargas, Cruzate's successor as governor, who reconquered New Mexico for Spain in 1692. However, Vargas neither received nor enforced the documents, which suggests they might not have existed in the official archives of the New Mexico Territory. According to Mathews-Lamb, "Cruzate's personal papers have not yet been found. Some scholars have privately expressed their belief that once discovered, this archive will contain the original Cruzate grants."[5]

Donaciano Vigil entered Mathews-Lamb's narrative as purportedly the person who made "the first official mention of the grants as 'Cruzate grants.'"[6] Mathews-Lamb erroneously suggested that a direct quote referenced Donaciano's testimony. In fact, her quote is from Hall's commentary on Donaciano's testimony: "When pressed, however, he [Donaciano Vigil] admitted he had only seen Sandia Pueblo's 1748 grant [and] 'none of the earlier Cruzate grants.'"[7] The use of the quote from Hall's book is quite revealing of Mathews-Lamb's perspective when one compares it to the actual record of the testimony that Donaciano gave before the surveyor general on 20 August 1855.[8] There are, as Hall pointed out, two versions of the testimony, the Spanish version, which is likely the official one, and the English translation.⁹ Donaciano responded to questions in Spanish in a calm, candid, matter-of-fact manner and was not "pressed" or forced to "admit" anything. Nor were there contradictions, as Hall implied, and Donaciano never used the word "Cruzate" in either the Spanish or the English version of his testimony. He answered questions regarding the manner in which grants of land were made by authorities in New Mexico and was then asked questions regarding Pueblo land grants.¹⁰

What Mathews-Lamb claimed was the first reference to the Cruzate grants in 1855 was actually Hall's characterization of the Cruzate grants and not Donaciano's own words. Why did Mathews-Lamb rely on Hall's rendition of Donaciano's testimony rather than locate the quote from his testimony before the surveyor general to underscore her point in footnote 12? In footnote 11, she had referred directly to Donaciano's later testimony before the surveyor general on 21 June 1856. To bolster her suggestion that the 1855 testimony was the first "official mention" of "Cruzate grants"—and that Donaciano had coined the phrase—Mathews-Lamb rebuked Donaciano for not using the more correct name "Jironza grants, knowing that the patrilineal name would be the first of the surnames, not the final."¹¹ Historical evidence has confirmed that Governor Cruzate was known by that surname, and historians as early as Twitchell in his *Spanish Archives of New Mexico* used that name in referring to the former governor.¹² The tendency of Mathews-Lamb to slant her research toward a preconceived target (notably, Donaciano) was apparent in her narrative, and her influence was pronounced on later critics of Donaciano, who used her work as a foundation for their study.

MYSTERIES SURROUNDING THE DONACIANO VIGIL AFFIDAVIT OF 1856

Mathews-Lamb pointed out that "by 1856, Vigil had already served as the secretary and recorder of public documents for the Territory of New Mexico and therefore had intimate knowledge of New Mexico's land titles and grant boundaries."¹³ Mathews-Lamb quoted from the affidavit that Donaciano gave to the surveyor general on 21 June 1856, in which Donaciano stated that Indigenous land was granted by the Spanish government in the late seventeenth century and that "from time immemorial they have continued in the pacific and quiet enjoyment of the lands they occupy without any question being raised as to their legal rights."[14] Donaciano's reference to the "close of the seventeenth century" might have suggested to Mathews-Lamb, as it had to Hall and other critics, that Donaciano was referring to the Cruzate grants that dated to 1689.

The affidavit where Donaciano allegedly gave testimony is of interest for the reason it was given, for what Donaciano allegedly said, and for the form it took. Hall, who was Mathews-Lamb's source on the matter, indicated that Donaciano provided the affidavit to accommodate Surveyor General William Pelham, who was about to submit his second report on Pueblo grants to his superiors in Washington. In his first report of September 1855, Pelham had submitted paperwork supporting his recommendations to the commissioner of the General Land Office, and thus to Congress, that five pueblos be granted patents for their land. Included were the Cruzate grant documents for the five pueblos, testimonies of Pueblo *caciques* (chiefs) and elders, and his own comments related to Spanish land law. In his second report in September 1856, Pelham recommended patents for ten additional Pueblo tribes. He again reproduced the Cruzate documents and translations for the tribes that had the documents and provided the sworn testimonies of caciques and elders. Hall stated, "For those five Pueblos that could not produce one [Cruzate grant], Pelham included the sworn statement of the *cacique* . . . a war captain . . . to the effect that the Pueblos possessed grant documents, but had lost them, [and the affidavit where] . . . Donaciano Vigil swore again that all recognized that the Pueblos were entitled to four square leagues, with or without documents."[15]

This affidavit is an important document in the surveyor general's records because it was used by Donaciano's critics to underscore basic contradictions in his testimony before the surveyor general, but the document is itself suspect for several reasons. Why would Donaciano provide that affidavit on that subject at that time? He had no personal stake in the land of the Pueblo tribes then under consideration. On the one hand, it repeated what he had said before, but on the other, it contradicted his prior testimony that he had not seen individual grants to the Pueblos in the archives. The affidavit repeated the contradiction: Donaciano said the "lands held" by the four tribes were "by virtue" of grants made by Spanish authorities "toward the close of the seventeenth century," and at the same time, they had held those lands "free from time immemorial." It appears the surveyor general was using Donaciano's words to confirm two conflicting perspectives on Pueblos' titles to their land. It is apparent that Donaciano gave the 21 June 1856 affidavit not of his own initiative, but to accommodate Pelham's

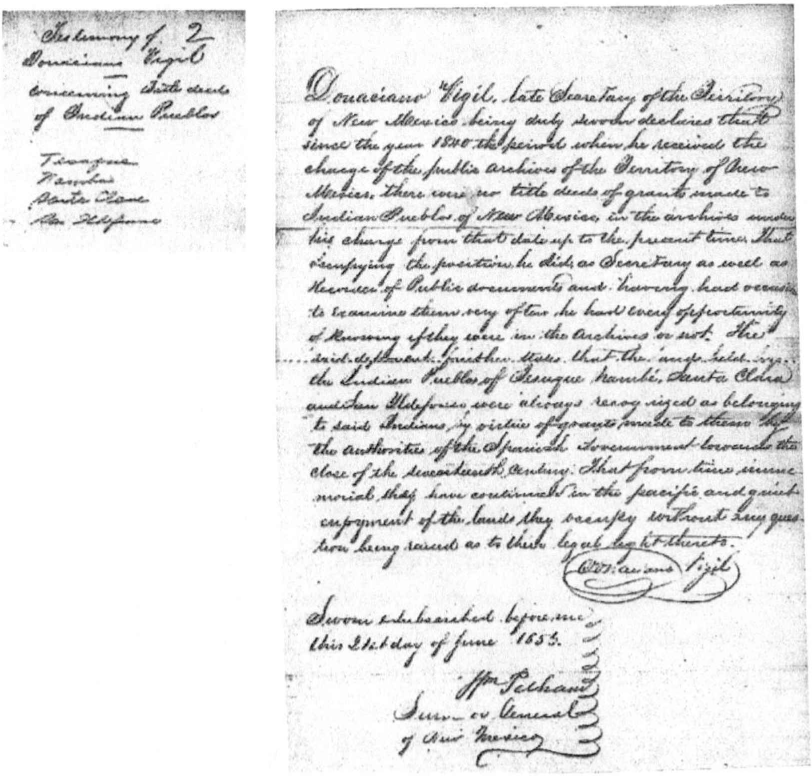

FIGURE 10. Donaciano Vigil affidavit (21 June 1856). Microfiche tag reads: "GENERAL DOCUMENT (ORIGINAL) REFERRING TO NUMEROUS PUEBLOS, SEPT. 20, 1689." Source: Pueblos General Documents, roll 7, frames 7–8 (microfilm produced by UNM Library, 1955–1957), Surveyor General of New Mexico Records, University of New Mexico/Center for Southwest Research, and Donnelly Library, Special Collections, New Mexico Highlands University.

need for testimony that would support and vouch for his recommendations for confirmation of those Pueblos that did not have their own documents.

Several factors in relation to the timing and placement of the affidavit confirm that view. The affidavit produced on 21 June 1856 was within a week of the testimony given to the surveyor general by various officials of the tribes of Tesuque (14 June 1856) and Santa Clara and San Ildefonso (16 June 1856). There were also extraneous notations added to the document after it was produced that seemingly sought to guide the interpretation of it in a specific direction. Those notations are here identified as "added." The typed (added) notation of the affidavit, made presumably by the surveyor general or a staffer, referred to

"General Document (Original) Referring to Numerous Pueblos, 20 September 1689," indicating an effort to connect the affidavit to the dates of the Cruzate documents. The title (added) of the affidavit was "Testimony of Donaciano Vigil Concerning Title Deeds of Indian Pueblos" and, as this was not specific enough, underneath in different penmanship (added) was written "Tesuque, Nambé, Santa Clara, and San Ildefonso." Donaciano's affidavit, it seems based on the cursive handwriting, was written out by Pelham himself and confirmed by him with his signature and date.

The order in which the documents appeared in the surveyor general's record is also informative. The first five of the ten tribes that were included in the 1856 report all had Cruzate documents. In their case, the Cruzate document in its original Spanish form appeared first, followed by an English translation and then the testimony of tribal officials. However, in the case of the tribes that lacked Cruzate documents, the testimony of tribal officials and Donaciano's affidavit were presented by the surveyor general to support his recommendation for those tribes. All of these documents appeared in the same archive.[16]

The document labeled "affidavit" appeared more like a surveyor general's document than a personal affidavit. In addition to the added title and different handwriting, the surveyor general in the document referred to Donaciano as a "deposant,"[17] as if he were giving testimony. As implied in the title, however, there was no question-and-answer format, which was Donaciano's customary manner of testifying and was the form of testimony for tribal leaders. There was also no first-person narrative, nothing that reflected Donaciano's own words in his own affidavit. The document was worded as if narrated by a third party—perhaps the surveyor general himself. A portion of the affidavit stated, "Since the year 1840 . . . there were no title deeds of grants made to Indian Pueblos of New Mexico, in the archives under his charge. . . . The said deposant further states that the lands held were always recognized as belonging to said Indians."[18]

It appears that in 1856, Surveyor General Pelham felt pressured to submit recommendations for the approval of land grants for the remaining Pueblo tribes that had not been submitted in his 1855 report. Moreover, he was convinced that the Cruzate land grant documents were the most compelling proof of the validity of those grants. The Cruzate grants' spurious nature would not be suspected until two decades later. In Pelham's mind, the written Cruzate documents were more compelling than oral testimony from whatever source. So, lacking a written Cruzate document for the five tribes he was submitting in 1856, he needed some form of corroboration that such documents for those tribes had existed, which accounts for the wording in Donaciano's affidavit.

It is plausible that given the needs of the surveyor general at that point in time, Pelham either drafted the affidavit or guided the wording to secure the content needed to support the recommendations he was making regarding the five pueblos that had no documents to support their claims. For his part, Donaciano affirmed the position he had previously stated. The Pueblos' claims to land were derived from the king through decrees or edicts, and the Indigenous people had held their land from time immemorial. The only difference was the reference to the four tribes that derived their claims from "authorities of the Spanish government toward the close of the seventeenth century."[19] For Pelham, that reference to the "close of the seventeenth century" may have been purposely intended to date the grants to the same period as the Cruzate grants. For Donaciano, the phrase could not have held particular significance since all grants were derived from the Spanish monarchical authority. Moreover, there was at least one legitimate (non-Cruzate) grant made by Spanish authorities to an individual pueblo, the Sandia Pueblo grant of 1748, and Donaciano had declared in his Preston Beck grant testimony that the Sandia Pueblo grant was in the archives. Donaciano may have also perceived the "close of the seventeenth century" as referring to that period when Spanish control was restored in New Mexico.

Donaciano continually argued before the surveyor general and territorial courts that Indigenous rights were patrimonial; their titles to their land dated to the period of the Spanish conquest and were based on grants made by the Spanish monarchs to all Indigenous peoples and enforced through royal ordinances. Technically, it could be argued that Spanish dominion over New Mexico dated from Juan de Oñate's expedition and first permanent colonization of New Mexico in 1598. However, the Pueblo Revolt of 1680 had resulted in the expulsion of the Spaniards, and Spanish control was not restored until Diego de Vargas's reconquest in 1692.

The only official record of the affidavit was in English; there was no Spanish version. Even though the document was signed by Donaciano, its legitimacy is therefore still suspect because of the lack of a Spanish version. It has been debated whether Donaciano could speak, read, and write English; however, what is certain is that he preferred to communicate in Spanish. Donaciano wrote hundreds of letters (both official and personal), directives, speeches, notes, proclamations, essays, and other documents. While many of these were translated into English, there was always an original in Spanish. That the affidavit was written in English and that Pelham attested to Donaciano's signature strongly suggest that he, not Donaciano, authored the document. Pelham labeled Donaciano's statement as testimony, which accounts for the title later attached to it. It was also later characterized as an affidavit by Ralph Emerson Twitchell, a lawyer:

> This affidavit is of importance (historically) for several reasons: Vigil was a very sagacious man; he was well read; took a pronounced interest in these state papers. If anyone knew anything about them at that time he did. When the office of surveyor-general was created in 1854, Vigil assisted in going over all of the old archives which had been in his sole possession, for the purpose of delivering to the surveyor-general those which were deemed of importance in the administration of the affairs of his office, which was done. It was many years later when the archives not so turned over to the surveyor-general were supposed to have been burned and sold by Governor Pyle. I do not believe that any were so burned or lost that were of consequence; many were stolen and carried off after Pyle's time—that is certain.[20]

In her interpretation of Donaciano's affidavit, which she accepted at face value, Mathews-Lamb took a cue from Hall, who had first pointed out the supposed contradiction in Donaciano's testimony. Hall had written in his 1984 book, *Four Leagues of Pecos: A Legal History of the Pecos Grant, 1800–1933*, that when Donaciano was asked if he had at any time seen any of the Pueblo land grant documents, he replied that he had, and they were signed by the king. However, Donaciano Vigil stated that he had only seen the "1746 [sic] grant to Sandia Pueblo.... Of course, stated Vigil, one could find the Pueblo grants in the archives, where they were supposed to be. By June 1856, Vigil would say he had never seen a Spanish grant to a Pueblo and that he knew of none in the archives he had been in charge of since 1840."[21] Mathews-Lamb's conclusion on the same quote was that "taken with a statement he made ten months prior, Vigil's testimony has served to confuse historians rather than to clarify."[22]

Both Hall and Mathews-Lamb concluded that Donaciano's contradictory statements reflected a motive to deceive the surveyor general. Mathews-Lamb wrote, "Having done an extensive index of the archives for Governor Mariano

Martínez, Secretary Vigil should have known that the documents were not in the archives. In 1846, the first year of American rule, Vigil completed an inventory of the documents in his custody. He did not mention any grants issued by Cruzate."[23]

THE VIGIL INDEX TO THE SPANISH AND MEXICAN ARCHIVES

While it is true that Donaciano was familiar with the Spanish and Mexican Archives and was in charge of the archives on at least two occasions, Mathews-Lamb's assertion that Donaciano produced an index or inventory of the archives requires elaboration. Mathews-Lamb referred to "an extensive index of the archives for Governor Mariano Martínez" and to "an inventory ... of documents in his custody," which Donaciano compiled "in the first year of American rule."[24]

In 1846, after General Kearny occupied New Mexico and established a civil government to administer the territory, he appointed Donaciano as territorial secretary. According to Daniel Tyler, "Kearny had given no instructions regarding the [New Mexico territorial] archives.... The appointment [of Vigil] was a good one, at least in the sense that Vigil had worked with the archives as military secretary to Governor Manuel Armijo. With dispatch he took the documents into his custody [and] during the next few years, the archives remained in the Governor's Palace in Santa Fe."[25]

Apparently, Donaciano began to create a chronological listing of the documents, which continued over the next few years as he occupied the offices of territorial secretary, then governor, and then secretary again. In 1849, he commissioned his son Antonio Basilio and Domingo Fernández to complete the work. In an affidavit given in 1892, Antonio said, "During the years of 1849 and 1850, my father ... who was then Territorial Secretary of New Mexico ... employed Domingo Fernández and me to organize and prepare an index for the documents in the said archives and under his order and direction we organized and prepared the above index."[26] It is true that Donaciano should have had a general knowledge of what was in the archives, but he would not necessarily have had the detailed knowledge of the people who produced the index. Mathews-Lamb was unwilling to consider the possibility that Donaciano might not have memorized the index, which contained several hundred entries on a wide range of matters. Based on her erroneous assumption that Donaciano personally produced the Vigil Index in 1846, she drew certain conclusions she attributed to Donaciano. She wrote, "He did not mention any grants issued by Cruzate and in fact recorded only one document existing in the archives penned by Cruzate.... Furthermore, only one document existed in the archives dated 1689."[27] Neither of those two documents, according to Mathews-Lamb, related to Pueblo grants. Her own research of the Vigil Index showed that there were no entries for the year 1689 pertaining to the capture of Ojeda, his testimony to Cruzate, or Cruzate's drafting of the grants. Still, she focused on the contradictions in Donaciano's testimony, failing to consider that the absence of the Cruzate grants from the index confirmed Donaciano's testimony that Indigenous grants (except for Sandia) were not in the archives at the time they were in his custody.[28]

Donaciano has been characterized as an adversary to Pueblo land rights. In fact, he was the first to point out and ultimately prevail upon the surveyor general to recognize that the Pueblo land grants came directly from the king of Spain through decrees or as edicts from special commissions or legislative bodies that dealt with such matters. These were subsequently incorporated into the Laws of the Indies. The Pueblos did not receive separate land grants made by Spanish officials in New Mexico, as was the case with private or community land grants made to Hispano vecinos. Mathews-Lamb conceded that "Pelham [the surveyor general] believed Vigil's statement. Vigil further stated that although the original documents [of Pueblo land grants] did not exist physically, the lands specified by the Pueblo Indians were legitimate by customary law."[29] Thus, Mathews-Lamb affirmed that when Cruzate land grant documents were found to be spurious, the only remaining source of validity of the Pueblo grants was the Spanish edicts and decrees found in the Laws of the Indies. Donaciano continually argued before the surveyor general that they were the ultimate authoritative sources for Pueblo land.

Mathews-Lamb appeared to be ambivalent about Donaciano and pointed out that "Vigil's language skills, and experience as Governor Armijo's territorial secretary won Vigil the office under Kearny.... According to one historian, Donaciano was 'highly regarded at the time as a scrupulous archivist and public servant.'"[30] This statement was reportedly made by historian Ward Allen Minge to Richard Hughes, who today is a lawyer for Santo Domingo Pueblo. Hughes offered his personal perception of Donaciano's scruples by informing Mathews-Lamb that his review of Santa Ana Pueblo land grant records showed that Indigenous people from that pueblo brought documents to Donaciano to be registered in 1848 and again in 1852 to be recopied. Donaciano was "careful about indicating on other recopied grants that they were copies of originals."[31]

That Donaciano was scrupulous, meticulous, and responsible in his handling of the Spanish and Mexican Archives is stressed by those who have examined the archives. Most historians, like Daniel Tyler, give him credit for ensuring their preservation when other officials were less conscientious about them. Tyler wrote about the neglect of the archives and how on one occasion Governor William Pile directed that the documents be removed from an area he would be occupying: "Several wagonloads were dumped into the streets, where they were picked up by Elauterio Barela, a wood hauler from Cieneguita. Several years after Pile's departure when the newspapers blasted Pile for his vandalism of the archives, Barela brought back some of the documents. In 1886, he turned over the remainder to territorial librarian Samuel Ellison."[32]

THE CRUZATE LAND GRANT DOCUMENTS DECLARED TO BE SPURIOUS

Mathews-Lamb revisited the theme that the Cruzate documents were declared fake as a result of William Tipton's revelations in an 1893 lawsuit filed by the Laguna Pueblos to confirm their grant. Tipton, a government translator and handwriting expert who had worked for the surveyor general, declared the Laguna grant to be "spurious." The ramifications of Tipton's declaring "the grants as fake ... no doubt sent chills down the spines of Pueblo leaders across New Mexico," according to Mathews-Lamb, since they had no other formal documents to prove ownership of their land.[33]

It is worth noting that Tipton's determination regarding the Cruzate grants foreshadowed other historians by only a few years. In his classic work *History of Arizona and New Mexico* (1889), Hubert Howe Bancroft expressed suspicions regarding the source of the Cruzate grants: "I confess that these doc. are very mysterious to me; and I cannot imagine why the gov. on such occasion at El Paso, on the testimony of a captive that the rebels were disposed to submit, should have troubled himself to fix the town limits."[34] Moreover, Twitchell in his work *The Spanish Archives of New Mexico*, published in 1914, agreed that the grants made in 1689 were spurious and that Congress was aware of this when the grants were confirmed.[35] It is noteworthy that Twitchell, perhaps the first non-Hispanic expert on the Spanish Archives of New Mexico, was not as quick to accuse Donaciano of complicity in the creation of the Cruzate documents as some modern historians have been, nor did his wariness of the Cruzate documents dissuade Twitchell from penning a biography of Donaciano (see the introduction to this book).

However, despite Tipton's revelations, according to Mathews-Lamb, the Pueblos did not lose their land: "Even though the court now recognized the grants as fraudulent, by removing these documents as the legal basis for the Pueblo grants, the royal ordinances [Laws of the Indies] . . . became the fundamental basis for the Pueblo grants of New Mexico."[36] This observation was consistent with Hall's interpretation of Donaciano's statements before the surveyor general regarding Pueblo land grants. Hall said, "Donaciano Vigil, an influential and knowledgeable native Hispano . . . swore in June 1856 that he had studied and been in charge of all land documents under both Mexican and early American sovereignty. In his years of work, he had never seen 'title deeds of grants made to Indian Pueblos of New Mexico there.'"[37] Later, according to Hall, when several pueblos were trying to prove their claims of landownership and could not produce any documents, "Donaciano Vigil swore again that all recognized that the pueblos were entitled to four square leagues, with or without documents. Finally, Pelham added to his [second] report [to the General Land Office] what little he knew of Spanish and Mexican law, to support the pueblos' claims."[38]

THE MARIANO PAPER MYSTERY

Mathews-Lamb next turned her attention to the paper that was used in the drafting of the Cruzate grants and stated, "The author of the Cruzate grants utilized 'MARIANO' watermarked paper."[39] She pointed out that this was significant because other documents with that watermark are dated no earlier than 1839, and the author of the Cruzate grants used only the side of the seventeen-by-fourteen-inch paper with the Mariano mark. Without factual documentation of the overall number of literate people in New Mexico or the number who may have written personal or official correspondence and the type of paper they used, she made this observation: "Most interesting is the revelation that few authors penned either personal or official correspondence between the years 1835 and 1846 using the same brand of watermarked paper. Arguably, the only individuals who did included Hispano *ricos*, government officials, and American traders."⁴⁰ Although Mathews-Lamb perceived this to be a small amount of users, it conceivably could have been quite a large group of people in New Mexico between 1835 and 1846 who wrote on this paper. According to Mathews-Lamb, "The most prolific users [of Mariano paper], ironically, were Manuel Armijo (and his family) and Francisco Sarracino during the 1840s.... The most interesting example of MARIANO paper usage was a letter written by Francisco Sarracino, a close associate of Governor Manuel Armijo and Donaciano. Writing to Donaciano, he complained about the defamation of his character by the commandant of Albuquerque."⁴¹

What is interesting to us is her effort to link Donaciano to the paper used in a letter written *to him*. Mathews-Lamb stressed that actually "very few New Mexicans utilized MARIANO watermarked paper." So few, in fact, that she named them and the year they used it: "Manuel Armijo y Mestas in 1843, Francisco Sarracino in 1850, and New Mexican Surveyor General John A. Clark as late as 1862."⁴² Mathews-Lamb further reported that "MARIANO paper surfaced most during the mid-1840s, employed by such authors as Albino Montoya ... Jose Francisco Sarracino, Jose Antonio Chávez, and Manuel Armijo—the latter having prepared the majority of those documents—*all friends or associates* of [Donaciano] Vigil."⁴³ Clearly, Mathews-Lamb tried to link the Mariano paper to Donaciano, but the best she could do was make a link to his associates. Despite this, Mathews-Lamb's closing comments on the Mariano paper was telling: "With the lack of widespread usage of this paper in New Mexico, one might argue that the Armijo family's access to it implicated them."⁴⁴

In sum, Mathews-Lamb uncovered only two Mariano documents with Donaciano's signature, and both were land title documents signed by both Donaciano and Manuel Armijo, whom she had already identified as the most frequent user of Mariano paper. She also referred to two letters on Mariano paper sent *to* Donaciano from Francisco Sarracino and Jose Antonio Chávez. We can logically assume that Donaciano did not supply the paper for letters sent to him. Mathews-Lamb's effort to uncover the source of the Cruzate documents by tracing them to the users of the Mariano paper was exhaustive. As she pointed out in a footnote, "I examined every document located in private collections dated between 1825 and 1870 in the New Mexico State Records Center and Archives and the University of New Mexico Center for Southwest Research during the years 1994 to 1996."⁴⁵

Having failed to find a direct link between Donaciano and the Mariano paper, she resorted to an indirect allusion to the "associates of Donaciano Vigil." Still, she felt compelled to explain her use of the term. She wrote, "The term 'close associates' in this reference includes confidants of Donaciano Vigil from whom Donaciano Vigil received many letters (as evident in his collection in Santa Fe)."[46] There is a Spanish proverb that says, "Dime con quién andas y te diré quien eres" (Tell me who you walk with, and I will tell you who you are). Apparently, Mathews-Lamb subscribed to that message, which implies guilt by association and does not suffice in a court of law. In fact, Mathews-Lamb's research on the Mariano paper served more to exclude rather than implicate Donaciano as a frequent user of Mariano paper.

The allusion she made to Donaciano's associates had a more nefarious suggestion when she referred to the influence they had. Mathews-Lamb, who embraced Hall's characterization of Donaciano, wrote, "Perhaps his earlier association with Manuel Armijo, who granted immense tracts of land during the 1840's encouraged others to foster a relationship with Vigil. His familiarity with the archives and ability to acquire grants made Vigil a powerful ally.... Vigil and Fernández stand out among Hispanic speculators in the Mexican era."[47] Mathews-Lamb seemed to believe that Donaciano was guilty of using Mariano paper because a few of his associates used it.

THE DE LA O CONSPIRACY

The next piece of the Cruzate grant's puzzle explored by Mathews-Lamb involved a Mexican man named Victor de la O and a court case filed against him and others by Acoma Pueblo in Socorro County in 1854. Apparently, de la O had been trafficking in Cruzate Pueblo land grant documents and had entered into an agreement with the residents of Acoma Pueblo to sell them their specific document for the price of $600. Acoma Pueblo brought suit against de la O, charging him with extortion for trying to sell them a document that was legally theirs. After district judge Kirby Benedict ruled in favor of the tribe, de la O appealed to the New Mexico Supreme Court. The case was continued until 1857 when Judge Benedict, now serving as a supreme court justice, upheld his earlier decision, ruling that "we are satisfied that it [the Cruzate grant] is the property of the Pueblo, and that Delo [sic] has no right to withhold it from them, the possession. That he has no lien upon the thing ... in relation to their title."[48]

Once again, Mathews-Lamb seized an opportunity to link Donaciano to this twist in the Cruzate grants drama. After having stressed incorrectly that Donaciano was the first to use the phrase "Cruzate grants" in his 1855 testimony before the surveyor general, she reported that "many others knew of the trade in Pueblo titles."[49] In a letter dated 21 June 1856 from Surveyor General William Pelham to New Mexico Indian agent A. G. Mayers, Pelham related that "certain Pueblo grants were in the possession of a Mexican residing in Socorro." Pelham said that the information came from ex-governor Donaciano Vigil "who cannot state the name of the person in whose possession they are, but . . . the information can be obtained from an Indian of the Pueblo of Santo Domingo, named Juan Esteban," who had said that "the grants of Santo Domingo, Sandia, and Jemez were obtained by the same person."[50] Pelham further pointed out that "the acquisition of the grants is of utmost importance to the Indians and to the government" and asked Mayers to investigate the matter and to "obtain any such grants the person may have in his possession."[51]

At that time, Pelham had no reason to doubt the validity of what were essentially the Cruzate grants. Like Pelham, Donaciano had no reason to suspect that the documents in question were not legitimate, even if, as he said more than once, he had not seen a specific Pueblo grant other than Sandia's. If Donaciano had a hand in drafting the Cruzate grants, as his critics have stated, why would he even remotely play a role in reporting any information to the surveyor general? Logic would have dictated that he maintain distance from any association with the documents, but that is not what Donaciano did. He reported the information to the official directly concerned with them. If we know anything about Donaciano, it's that he had a keen investigative mentality to ferret out conspiracies, and he was not shy about reporting to the proper authorities. That was the case when he reported to Colonel Sterling Price regarding the 1846 Christmas Eve insurrection plot against the Americans. In this case, he probably heard from Juan Esteban about a person who was in possession of "certain pueblo grant documents" and that the same person had provided the documents for Santo Domingo, Sandia, and Jemez. Donaciano knew that such documents were of great interest to the surveyor general and true to form, he told Pelham about them and referred him to the person who could provide more information.

Pelham's letter said that Donaciano "cannot state the name of the person in whose possession they are."[52] We cannot say why Donaciano did not reveal the name of the person. He may not have known. He may have considered the information to be secondhand and was unwilling to implicate a person on that kind of information. He may simply have deferred to the surveyor general to conduct his own investigation and obtain the information firsthand. It certainly does not follow that by not providing the name of the person in possession of the documents, Donaciano was "withholding information," as Mathews-Lamb stated.[53] It is also worth considering that another person may have chosen not to get involved as Donaciano did.

In continuing her narrative, Mathews-Lamb was still focused on Donaciano. She speculated on who might have informed him, even after she suggested that it probably was Juan Esteban (the Santo Domingo individual), Armijo, or Francisco Sarracino. He could have heard about it from a court case, *Acoma Pueblo v. Victor de la O*.[54] If all the people Mathews-Lamb suggested could have informed Donaciano about the man in possession of the Pueblo grants, it multiplies exponentially the number of people who in one way or another knew about the story. Moreover, since there was a court case litigated by Acoma Pueblo on the matter, it is likely that such information was widely known in New Mexico. Why was the fact that Donaciano informed the surveyor general in 1856 a revelation? Why was he seen as withholding information from the surveyor general?

The only definitive conclusion Mathews-Lamb offered regarding the Cruzate grants was that they were not produced in the seventeenth century. She wrote, "The author has contended that someone created the Cruzate grant documents during the nineteenth and not the seventeenth century. So much specific historical detail is included in the text of the Cruzate grants that the authors must have had access to books and documents relatively easy to find in the territorial archives."[55] While Donaciano was one of those individuals who had the knowledge and access to the archives, Mathews-Lamb did not indict him based on what he knew and when he knew it. She correctly rejected the temptation to declare an unproven conclusion based on circumstantial evidence and admitted that "while my efforts to discover the true origin of the Cruzate grants have failed temporarily, I have nonetheless come closer than anyone."[56] Later writers, relying mainly on her research, were not so reluctant to draw the wrong conclusions.

THREE LAND GRANT HISTORIANS AND
THE CRUZATE LAND GRANTS

In 2014, a book titled *Four Square Leagues: Pueblo Indian Land in New Mexico* revisited the topic of the Cruzate land grants in the chapter "The Surveyor General and the Cruzate Grants." The authors began by stating, "The core landholdings of nine New Mexico pueblos ... are based on documents dated 20 or 25 September 1689, purporting to be grants to those pueblos from Governor Domingo Jironza Petriz de Cruzate (1689–1691). Congress confirmed most of these grants in 1858, so they are conclusively presumed to be valid from a legal standpoint."[57] This view was consistent with Mathews-Lamb's conclusion in her dissertation. However, the authors also made the following assertion: "Yet *all* scholars of New Mexico history who have studied the Cruzate grants believe them to be fraudulent."[58] Ebright, Hendricks, and Hughes offered no evidence for this all-inclusive statement, but it was a contradiction of Mathews-Lamb, who was careful to assert that such scholars as Charles R. Cutter of Purdue University disagreed that the Cruzate documents were forgeries.[59] The authors of *Four Square Leagues* asserted, "This chapter provides an overview of the evidence that has been proffered to show that these documents are not authentic, including the facts that the paper used was not produced until the 1840s and was certainly not used in 1689 and that some of the language in two of the Cruzate documents came from a book published in 1832."[60]

Ebright, Hendricks, and Hughes relied on and reiterated much of what Mathews-Lamb presented in her research, but where she declined to draw definitive conclusions, they were prone to do exactly that, even as they presented the same incomplete and contradictory evidence. For example, they maintained, "That the documents are not authentic 1689 documents is beyond dispute, but the possibility that these documents were somehow derived from authentic originals that are now lost cannot be entirely ruled out."[61] The authors reiterated the basic questions Mathews-Lamb raised: "Who created the existing documents, and when, and with what motive are questions that remain unanswered."[62] This was basically where Mathews-Lamb left off, but the authors also made the following statement: "there are clues in the documents recorded as to who might be involved, but the *evidence is scant and entirely circumstantial*, and the origin of the Cruzate documents remains one of the most extraordinary mysteries of New Mexico history."[63]

SURVEYOR GENERAL WILLIAM PELHAM'S COMPETENCE

In the course of the Cruzate chapter, Ebright, Hendricks, and Hughes repeated the extraordinary story that surrounds the Cruzate documents and even embellished those circumstances. For example, they exaggerated William Pelham's status as a hapless, incompetent public servant in a situation that was way over his head. This opinion of Pelham suggested that his ignorance and lack of qualifications for the job made him susceptible to the influence of unscrupulous individuals who manipulated him and the office. They failed to mention that few Americans at the time would have been ideally qualified for the extraordinary task of New Mexico's surveyor general. Given the conditions, Pelham tackled the job responsibly and conscientiously.

Historian Victor Westphall provided perhaps the most thorough and objective analysis of the work and accomplishments of Pelham as surveyor general of New Mexico, devoting an entire chapter to that subject in his classic work *Mercedes Reales: Hispano Land Grants of the Upper Rio Grande Region*. That chapter was aptly titled "Implementation: Impossible Task of the Surveyor General." Pelham, according to Westphall, was appointed surveyor general by President Franklin Pierce on 1 August 1854, but it was five months before he arrived in Santa Fe on 25 December to assume his duties. His superior in Washington, DC, was John Wilson, commissioner of the General Land Office, who served under Robert McClelland, US secretary of the interior. Westphall conceded that Pelham encountered a formidable task as surveyor general: "William Pelham served as surveyor general from 1854 to 1868. While he evidently possessed a high order of integrity, intelligence, and common sense, he was ill-prepared in certain regards to perform the difficult and specialized tasks related to his office."[64] Nevertheless, Pelham rose to the occasion, learned quickly, and adapted to the tremendous challenges, both administrative and cultural, that he encountered because "his was the thankless job of recommending to Congress either the rejection or confirmation of preexisting claims of land."[65] It is clear that Westphall admired the work and accomplishments of Pelham. Notwithstanding the enormity of the task before him and the unwillingness of his superiors to provide sufficient financial help and other resources, Pelham addressed his job with professional diligence, impartial determination, and boundless energy. Pelham was given a budget of $3,000 a year for "office rent, books, stationery, and incidental expenses," which was meager even for those times.⁶⁶ He struggled to find the necessities, such as chairs, tables, and a carpet for the dirt floor in the modest adobe home he rented, with an eye to maintaining "appearances."⁶⁷

It is interesting from Pelham's perspective, as reflected in a letter to his boss, John Wilson, that "his duties in connection with Spanish and Mexican land grants were of a minor but important character."⁶⁸ This was true since seven of the eight sections outlining the duties for the office dealt with the "public domain," including such matters as land surveys, donations to settlers, school and university allotments, and preemption. Only section 8 dealt with "land claims originating before the Treaty of Guadalupe Hidalgo of 1848."⁶⁹

Westphall cited a particularly vexing regulation that required the original title papers of the Pueblos to be sent to Washington for examination. Pelham realized that this rule was problematic for the Indigenous people, who were reluctant to release custody of their titles lest unscrupulous law officials destroy their only evidence of ownership of their land. Instead, he secured approval from his superiors to allow him to submit a certified copy and retain the original papers in the land office in Santa Fe. This process assured the Pueblos that their documents were safe and well protected and encouraged their confidence while they waited patiently for the "patenting of their lands."⁷⁰

Pelham, according to Westphall, "always careful and thorough in his instructions, was particularly so regarding . . . surveys of Pueblo Indian land."⁷¹ Following the issuance of a patent, a formal survey of each grant was carried out. Pelham was also mindful of the complexity of Spanish/Mexican and Pueblo relationships, particularly in cases where the two sides occupied adjoining land. Where water flowed through the grant areas, mainly from the Rio Grande, "other citizens of the territory would have to submit to any impositions when the Indians might choose to subject them, or else do without water to irrigate their crops."⁷² Pelham cited decrees and regulations indicating that all the watering places, pastures, and timberlands were required to be free and common to all. This was the well-known and clearly expressed policy of Spain as well as Mexico. These grants did not show on their face any authority from the sovereign to the granting officer to concede water running through Indigenous lands, nor were the Natives given unrestricted water privileges to the exclusion of their Spanish neighbors. All were entitled to use from a Pueblo river the water they needed for domestic purposes. It was the duty of the United States to follow the clear policy set forth by Spain and Mexico.⁷³

Pelham, according to Westphall, "submitted five annual reports to the General Land Office in Washington, each of which dealt seriously with the inadequacy of the system for adjudicating Spanish and Mexican land grants and as the years passed, successive reports became increasingly insistent that remedial action be taken."[74] According to Westphall, Pelham's instructions from his superiors made it clear that a very important part of his duty "was to report on all pueblos in the territory, showing the extent, number of inhabitants, and locality of each, and the nature of their title to the land. He was further instructed to collect data from authentic sources relative to these pueblos so that he could fully inform Congress about them, thus enabling it to legislate in such a manner as to do justice to all concerned."[75]

Pelham's first report was dated 30 September 1855, only nine months after he assumed office, yet he was already able to see clearly the fundamental weaknesses of the system and to suggest logical remedies.[76] In that first report, Pelham expressed concern about the ongoing "alienation" of Pueblo land that was taking place "because of the laxity in enforcement on the part of careless and corrupt officials whose duty it was to administer the law."[77] In a rare personal comment, Pelham injected an opinion to Washington officials when he submitted his second recommendation on claims in 1856: "The Pueblo Indians are constantly encroached upon by Mexican citizens . . . and in many instances the Indians are despoiled of their best lands; I therefore respectfully recommend that these claims be confirmed by Congress as speedily as possible, and that their boundaries be permanently fixed."[78] Westphall was careful to point out that "this is not to say that there was not considerable alienation of Pueblo Indian lands under Mexico. . . . One must be careful not to view these petty transgressions as any evidence of legal change."[79]

In compliance with his instructions and concerns, Pelham made a thorough investigation of the lands of the Pueblo people, identifying twenty pueblos in all with a population of some 8,000. Of the seventeen Pueblo claims (San Cristóbal was extinct, and Pecos was listed as active, even though it had been vacated in 1838) that were approved and filed by Pelham in 1855 and 1856 and ultimately confirmed by Congress, all but one (Acoma) were surveyed in 1859.[80]

In the report of September 1855 to his superiors in the General Land Office in Washington, DC, Surveyor General Pelham stated that "the grants made by the government of Spain to the pueblos of Silla [sic], Santa Ana, San Juan, Jemez, and Pecos have been filed, examined, and approved by this office."[81] Pelham also submitted the populations of each pueblo and the Cruzate documents to support his recommendations for approval by Congress of the grants.

In his next report of 30 September 1856, Pelham submitted recommendations for ten additional pueblos. In this case, five of the pueblos had Cruzate documents, which the pueblos provided, and Pelham submitted copies and a translation of each. For the remaining five pueblos that did not provide a document, Pelham submitted sworn statements of the cacique (tribal leader) and war captain attesting to the fact that the tribe had once possessed documents but had lost them. It is apparent that Pelham was aware of a potential problem with the authentication of those grants due to the lack of direct supporting documents for those remaining tribes. Accordingly, he sought a sworn statement from the one person who had consistently testified that the pueblos were entitled to their four square leagues by virtue of royal decrees from the Spanish monarchs. Donaciano's sworn affidavit of 21 June 1856 was apparently arranged by the surveyor general and submitted with his report of 30 September 1856.

All the Pueblo grants Pelham recommended were approved by Congress, and the tribes were given patents. Ironically, some of the pueblos that submitted Cruzate claims were given grants based on that paperwork. Pelham, Hall pointed out, added into the reports accompanying his recommendations "what little he knew of Spanish and Mexican law, to support the pueblos' claims.... Pelham referred to a royal decree of the Spanish crown dated October 15, 1713."[82] Pelham also embraced Donaciano's sworn statement that "all recognized that the pueblos were entitled to four square leagues, with or without documents."[83] Hall concluded, "Such ambiguities did not concern Pelham.... The 1689 documents confirmed the Pueblo testimony of 1855. The 1713 decree seemed to support both. Why should Pelham, with a year's experience in New Mexico, a year of constant affirmation by the Pueblos themselves that the Cruzate documents measured their claim to land, doubt the validity of the documents?"[84] A living testament to the work of Pelham is that, notwithstanding the difficult situation, he secured confirmation of legal titles for the Pueblos of New Mexico to the land they had held for centuries and continue to hold to this day.

REVISITING THE MARIANO PAPER

Ebright, Hendricks, and Hughes in *Four Square Leagues* also examined the handwriting controversy associated with the Cruzate documents and generally affirmed the conclusions of Will Tipton, the government translator and handwriting expert who declared the Cruzate documents to be "spurious." Mathews-Lamb wrote in a footnote that "while Donaciano Vigil, Domingo Fernández and Manuel Armijo all had access to these records, the documents are not in their handwriting. This does not preclude their participation in their creation, however."[85] Ebright, Hendricks, and Hughes concurred with Mathews-Lamb's conclusion regarding the signatures of some of the principal Spanish officials associated with the Cruzate documents. They stated that "the signatures unquestionably reflect an effort to forge the signatures and *rubricas* of the persons whose names are affixed to the documents."[86]

They found, however, that the paper used in the documents was a more significant issue because the Cruzate grants submitted to the surveyor general "were written on paper that bear the watermark 'MARIANO' in block letters on the first sheet, and a flowery letter 'M' on the facing folios. Although the origin of the watermark has yet to be identified, it appears to date these documents to the 1840s."[87] The discussion of the Mariano paper presented Ebright, Hendricks, and Hughes with the opportunity to implicate Donaciano in the Cruzate documents imbroglio. Despite their earlier admonition that the "evidence is scant and entirely circumstantial," they offered definitive conclusions. It appears that these authors tried to use Mathews-Lamb's PhD dissertation research to indict Donaciano. One only needs to compare what she said with what they claimed she said to see the contrast.

As stated above, although she presented substantial research on the issue of the Mariano paper and the Cruzate documents, Mathews-Lamb never definitively identified Donaciano as a user of that paper or as the author of the documents. Her exact words: "The most prolific users, ironically, were Manuel Armijo (and his family) and Francisco Sarracino during the 1840s."[88] Ebright, Hendricks, and Hughes, however, wrote, "Mathews-Lamb . . . examined hundreds of nineteenth century documents from New Mexico and found that 'MARIANO' marked paper was apparently scarce in New Mexico but that it was occasionally used by Donaciano Vigil, Manuel Armijo y Mestas (nephew of Governor Manuel Armijo), Francisco Sarracino . . . and a few others."[89] In an endnote, they were even more explicit in misquoting Mathews-Lamb: "According to Mathews-Lamb, Donaciano and Manuel Armijo were among the few people in New Mexico who utilized paper bearing the MARIANO watermark on which the Cruzate grants are written."[90] Mathews-Lamb's research verified that Donaciano was not a frequent user of Mariano paper and that his "associates" were occasional users, so it is telling that Ebright, Hendricks, and Hughes listed Donaciano first among the users of the paper.

It is clear that Ebright, Hendricks, and Hughes's main target was Donaciano: "He surely exaggerated somewhat in his 1856 affidavit; he *might* have known of the 1748 grant to Sandia by Governor Joaquín Codallos y Rabal, the 1763 grant to Santa Clara for the Cañada de Santa Clara, the 1770 grant to Santo Domingo and San Felipe.... Vigil's indisputable point was ... that the Cruzate documents were not previously part of the official archives of the territory."[91]

BLAMING THE MESSENGER

Ebright, Hendricks, and Hughes also addressed Mathews-Lamb's discussion of the de la O case. It is worth recalling that Mathews-Lamb examined the story because she saw a potential linkage to Donaciano. He was the messenger who first relayed the information to the surveyor general about a Mexican man (de la O) residing in Socorro, New Mexico, who was in possession of "certain Pueblo grants." The grants for Santo Domingo, Sandia, and Jemez had been obtained from the same person.[92] Again Ebright, Hendricks, and Hughes seized the opportunity to contribute their own speculation, which implicated Donaciano in a conspiracy with de la O and others.

After retelling the de la O narrative in their own words, the authors questioned de la O's story and the resultant chain of events, including the documentary evidence. They clearly rejected the story as a viable explanation of the source of the Cruzate documents, which was ostensibly their main purpose in that chapter. It seems to us that the de la O story was, in fact, the most plausible explanation offered as to the origin and distribution of the Cruzate land grant documents. If the details and facts of the de la O narrative and the documented *Acoma v. de la O* court case records are reviewed carefully, the story certainly seems more plausible than the alternative contained in the documents themselves about the captive Ojeda relaying the information on the Pueblo grants to Governor Cruzate, who then inexplicably drafted the Cruzate documents.

These are the facts of the de la O story: Victor de la O claimed that his father, Gregorio, a soldier in the Mexican army, was a well-educated, literate man who had many books, manuscripts, and documents. As the only child, Victor inherited the collection when his father died. Victor moved to Socorro in 1833. In 1836, his wife joined him, bringing the remaining documents with her. Victor, being illiterate, did not realize the value of the documents. He sought the assistance of Vicente Aviluead, who apprised him of their potential value to the Pueblos. Together with Aviluead and Ramon Sánchez, he marketed some of the documents to the Pueblo tribes of Santo Domingo, Sandia, Jemez, and, through Armijo, Laguna. Victor admitted that he had other similar documents in his possession and intended to market them to the remaining Pueblo tribes. He offered one to Acoma tribal leaders, and they tendered a deposit of $8 with a promise to pay $600 on his delivery of their document. However, the Acoma tribal leaders instead hired attorney Spruce Baird, who charged Victor with illegally securing the Acoma land grant document and extorting $600 for its return. Victor, confident that the documents were his by inheritance and possession, hired attorney John Watts to defend him against the charges. Watts responded to the charges against his client and as a result, Aviluead and Sánchez were excused from the case. Watts also pressed Victor's case that the documents were his valid property. Judge Kirby Benedict ruled on the face of the document, which showed a grant of land to Acoma Pueblo that validated their ownership of the document. Thus, de la O had no right or lien to withhold the title from Acoma Pueblo to their property. Although Judge Benedict rejected his story and his claim to ownership, Victor persisted by appealing Benedict's decision to the New Mexico Supreme Court, only to have Benedict now sitting as a supreme court justice. Justice Benedict again ruled against him.

This story was a plausible explanation of the Cruzate documents' origin, including when and how they may have been prepared, brought to New Mexico, and then marketed and distributed. Gregorio de la O (Victor's father) possibly prepared them; Victor's wife brought the documents to New Mexico in 1836; and Victor, with the help of Aviluead and Sánchez, marketed and sold some to at least four tribes, leading up to the 1854 Acoma court case. Further, de la O admitted that those already marketed had been in his possession along with the Acoma document, and others were still in his possession. The court case contained the fully documented evidence of how and why the case arose, the parties and lawyers involved, and its ultimate resolution by Judge Benedict.

In closing their narrative, Ebright, Hendricks, and Hughes largely dismissed Victor de la O's story as fiction (his "account as to the document's origin . . . [was] apparently not truthful"), but then asserted that his "account cannot simply be dismissed," since he had several Cruzate documents in his possession, and "De la O clearly believed that the documents were authentic and important."⁹³ Ultimately they dismissed the de la O story and again reverted to their focus on Donaciano. They speculated, "De la O's apparent connections with persons who are known to have utilized paper bearing the 'MARIANO' watermark raises the intriguing possibility that he was involved with General Armijo's nephew, Francisco Sarracino and/or Donaciano Vigil in the creation of the documents, who perhaps worked from original documents that were in De la O's collection."⁹⁴ Comfortable with that speculation, they were confident in affirming, "It also appears that he [Donaciano] was the person who informed Pelham that De la O was peddling land grant documents."⁹⁵ In essence, they blamed the messenger.

Their speculation on the authorship of the Cruzate grants became even more suspect when they wrote, "One can only wonder at the extraordinary peculiarity of how its authors designed this enterprise, seen in its totality. Had someone of this period set out to fabricate old Spanish grants, it is most difficult to imagine that such a person would have gone about it in the way the creators of the Cruzate documents did; rather, such a person would have no doubt produced more conventional looking grant documents."⁹⁶ Ironically, the person most responsible for outlining this "conventional" method of land grants to the surveyor general was none other than Donaciano Vigil. That is another exculpatory argument that Donaciano had no part in the drafting of the Cruzate documents.

OVER THE TOP: THE *FOUR SQUARE LEAGUES* AUTHORS CHARGED VIGIL WITH "COLLUSION"

Having strayed well beyond Mathews-Lamb's findings in their previous summaries of her research, Ebright, Hendricks, and Hughes delved into unbridled speculation in their conclusions on the Cruzate matter. They wrote, "In short, while there seems to be little doubt that the Cruzate documents are not authentic seventeenth century documents and in fact were probably written in the mid-nineteenth century, why they were created at all, and by whom, remains a mystery."⁹⁷ Apparently, it was not such a great mystery to these authors, for they next wrote: "The account of Victor de la O as to the [Cruzate] documents' origin, although apparently not truthful in and of itself . . . together with the evidence as to other use of paper bearing the 'MARIANO' watermark, are highly suggestive of the possibility that Donaciano Vigil or Manuel Armijo's nephew and de la O *colluded in the creation of the documents*."[98] If that quote were not enough, the next passage made it clear that Ebright, Hendricks, and Hughes were targeting Donaciano in their damning commentary: "[Donaciano] was the person who informed Pelham that de la O was peddling grant documents, but this makes the affidavit Vigil gave Pelham, insisting that no grants were ever in the archives extremely puzzling: if he went to the extraordinary effort to produce the Cruzate grants . . . passing the documents off as genuine, why would he then seek to impeach them?"[99] In considering their own question, Ebright, Hendricks, and Hughes failed to consider the possibility that Donaciano may not have been involved in the writing of the Cruzate grants.

In examining possible motives for such an undertaking, Ebright, Hendricks, and Hughes alleged that all Hispano citizens were involved. They wrote: "That Donaciano Vigil, or any other Hispano citizen [of that time period] in New Mexico, would go out of his way to assist the pueblos in asserting claims to land seems incredible. . . . The former Mexican citizens of the territory were far more interested in taking pueblo land than they were in helping the pueblos hold onto it and Vigil was never known as a friend of the pueblos."[100] Obviously, not all Hispanics were involved in "taking pueblo land." Victor Westphall wrote more objectively that there were genuine attempts to support the Indigenous people in their relationship with the Spaniards: "The regulations for their benefit were recognized as minimal rights; they were acknowledged to own all the land actually occupied and cultivated. . . . While not always successful, the intent of Spanish law and administration was to protect the Indians in their personal and communal land-water rights."[101] Charles Lummis wrote on the same subject: "The most ethnologic effect of the coming of Spain, was to make the Pueblo from a sedentary to a fixed Indian. . . . To each of his communities was given a generous grant of land, and upon that grant he must stay. . . . The Pueblo is an Indian who lives not upon a reservation but upon a United States patent."[102] It is interesting that Lummis, who spent a lifetime living with, interacting with, studying, and researching New Mexico's Pueblos, had a far greater appreciation of the influence of the Spaniards in ensuring the survival and preservation of Pueblo lands and culture than some modern writers.

Ebright, Hendricks, and Hughes, the authors of *Four Square Leagues*, offered a related motive for the complicity of Donaciano and "Hispano citizens" in allegedly producing the Cruzate documents. "Some historians," they said, "have suggested that, to the contrary, the grants were intended to limit Pueblo land claims under the U.S. regime, not to substantiate their claims."[103] The statement of these authors that "Vigil was never known as a friend of the pueblos" was a contradiction of the facts. Both Westphall and Hall recognized his important role in informing Surveyor General Pelham on Spanish and Mexican land grants and law, particularly Pueblo rights under the Laws of the Indies and royal edicts that acknowledged the Pueblos' "league" of land. Hall also noted that Donaciano's role with the surveyor general "did not stop there. Between 1854 and 1857 he testified personally so frequently that it is difficult to believe, as his only biographer states, that Vigil retired from public life with his 1854 Pecos land purchase and became just another farmer."[104]

Donaciano's critics faulted him for his role in recording and maintaining the records of land grants and transactions and for subsequently testifying before the surveyor general as to their authenticity. The fact of the matter is that this was his job. When he served as territorial secretary for New Mexico, one of his primary duties was to maintain the records of government actions and to make and keep records of government land grants. When it became necessary to preserve the records of land transactions in the chaotic period following the American occupation, Donaciano, as Daniel Tyler pointed out, "took the documents into his custody."[105] In his testimony before the surveyor general, Donaciano performed a valuable service in helping Pelham sort through the maze of Spanish law, archival, and land grant records, thus helping him to do his job, particularly in relation to preserving Pueblo lands. For his part, Surveyor General Pelham never registered a complaint about Donaciano, his lapse of memory, or any contradictions or confusion. On the contrary, it seems, the surveyor general came to trust and respect Donaciano's word and willingness to help in resolving the quagmire of land grant issues in New Mexico, considered by many an enormous and impossible task.

We do not contest the conclusion that the notorious Cruzate documents may be forgeries; that historical mystery is beyond the scope of this book. Sandra Mathews-Lamb, whose research was the first basis for the allegations regarding Donaciano and the Cruzate grants, was quite circumspect, never categorically stating that Donaciano was responsible for creating the documents. However, the conclusion that Ebright, Hendricks, and Hughes made that "Donaciano Vigil . . . colluded in the creation of the [Cruzate] documents" was not justified based on their research.[106] Despite their statement that "evidence is scant and entirely circumstantial and the origin of the Cruzate documents remains one of the most extraordinary mysteries of New Mexico history," those writers made a definitive charge that Donaciano was complicit in their creation.

The key word Ebright, Hendricks, and Hughes used was "colluded." According to *Merriam-Webster's Collegiate Dictionary*, collusion is broadly defined as a "secret agreement or cooperation esp. for an illegal or deceitful purpose."[107] The authors referred to the fact that the "Cruzate documents are not authentic seventeenth century documents and in fact were probably created in the mid-nineteenth century."[108] This may be true, but they did not prove who authored the documents. In the chapter "The Surveyor General and the Cruzate Grants," based on circumstantial evidence, Ebright, Hendricks, and Hughes speculated that Donaciano colluded in the production of the Cruzate documents. However, their research failed to prove that Donaciano participated in the creation of the Cruzate documents.

It appears that these critics of Donaciano failed to confirm his complicity in relation to the Cruzate documents and resorted to implying that since he possessed unique and exclusive knowledge related to Spanish and Mexican law, land grants, and New Mexico history, he was linked, by default, to the Cruzate grants. His knowledge was thus the yoke Ebright, Hendricks, and Hughes used to implicate Donaciano. We do not, in the United States, charge and convict people for what they know; we prosecute them for their actual violation of the law. Collusion implies conspiracy, which is, rightly, one of the most difficult crimes to prosecute, often requiring incontrovertible evidence to prove the crime occurred. This is why we may never know who authored the Cruzate documents. Circumstantial evidence is the only evidence available in this case. However, speculation based on circumstantial evidence is not acceptable, and this is what Ebright, Hendricks, and Hughes offered—their speculation. If they misinterpreted the evidence, they needlessly tarnished the record and legacy of one of New Mexico's most important Hispanic political leaders. If there is no other compelling message we convey in this book, it is clear that it would have been completely out of character for Donaciano Vigil to have been part of the Cruzate grant conspiracy.

In a review of the book *Four Square Leagues*, Richard Flint wrote in regard to Ebright, Hendricks, and Hughes's discussion of the Cruzate grants: "Even so who the makers of the nineteenth century partial copies were and why the copies were made remain, despite Ebright, Hendricks, and Hughes'... research, a confounding mystery of New Mexico and southwestern history."[109] In other words, Flint was not convinced they solved the mystery of the Cruzate documents. We agree, and we reiterate that the person they accused of collusion was not involved.

The disposition of the archives following Donaciano's tenure is of interest given that all his critics referred to his role as custodian of the archives in the period 1846–1850. Daniel Tyler shed light on the matter when he wrote that the Vigil Index was an important document because it revealed the extent of Donaciano's inventory before the land records were segregated by the surveyor general. Tyler wrote, "In 1850 New Mexico became a territory, but the documents were neglected. During the next decade, they were shunted back and forth between the librarian and the territorial secretary while the Palace underwent various stages of remodeling."[110] In her classic *New Mexico: A Pageant of Three Peoples*, Erna Fergusson also commented about the condition of the archives: "Irreplaceable papers blew about Santa Fe's dusty streets or were used to wrap meat or chewing tobacco.... Don Donaciano Vigil, custodian of land records, managed to salvage enough to make property records fairly complete."[111] Despite Donaciano's efforts to organize and preserve the archives, five years later they were neglected and in disarray.

CONCLUSION

The conventional wisdom in New Mexico historical scholarship has been that nuevomexicanos were inactive bystanders in the most significant political events of the transitional period from Spanish to Mexican to American rule in New Mexico. The reality, as scholarship such as Phillip Gonzales's *Política* has shown, is that not only were they active players, they profoundly influenced the subsequent political development and political culture in the Land of Enchantment toward the robust political activity manifested today. Our book not only confirms this perspective, but has underscored how, when, and why one of those previously neglected actors, Donaciano Vigil, played an active role as a soldier, statesman, and governor in the development of New Mexico's unique political development and political culture. This conclusion focuses on the last chapter of Donaciano's life as he joined the ranks of typical New Mexicans as a farmer-rancher in the quintessential Hispanic village of Pecos.

DONACIANO IN PECOS

In 1850, Donaciano at forty-eight years of age could justifiably be proud of what he had contributed to the development of New Mexico during what was arguably the most eventful period in the territory's history. New Mexico had evolved from an isolated, neglected, sparsely populated province of New Spain, to a bustling, expanding, troubled region in the newly independent nation of Mexico, and then to the newest territory of the rapidly expanding, progressive, and acquisitive United States. Donaciano was in the thick of all these developments as a soldier and officer in the New Mexico militia, as a clerk and military secretary to the governor, and as a vocal (assemblyman) in the New Mexico Assembly, all under Mexico. Then after the American occupation, he was a prominent figure, serving as secretary and governor in the nascent New Mexico Territory of the United States.

Throughout his life, Donaciano extracted a meager living for himself and his large family on the scant and undependable wages paid to soldiers and politicians in the Mexican regimes and later as a US territorial official. He associated with the enterprising ricos of the territory, many of whom had already amassed fortunes as merchants, cattle and sheep barons, and landowners since the opening of the Santa Fe Trail. At the same time, he learned the ways of the *extranjeros*, the Anglo-American, French, and German entrepreneurs who moved into the province. In particular, he witnessed the shrewd manipulations of opportunistic lawyers, who took advantage of the confused state of affairs in landownership, the new governmental system, and the newly introduced US legal system to acquire vast amounts of land and wealth through land speculation.

During his time as a soldier, Donaciano traversed much of the territory of New Mexico on campaigns against the Indigenous people, military escort service, or other patrols, so he was familiar with many streams and valleys that had the potential for settlement. During his service in San Miguel del Bado, he frequently visited and became particularly fond of the land east of Santa Fe known as Cañon de Pecos, where the Pecos River cascades wildly out of the Sangre de Cristo Mountains into a lush green valley. He must have contemplated its potential for a farming and ranching community. Spring runoff fed the rich bottomland where acequias could channel water to irrigated land (regadillos), any form of crop could be grown, and the river provided a constant source of pure, clean water for animals and domestic use. The rolling hills above the valley afforded a natural year-round pasture for grazing livestock and could be used for dry land farming (temporales). The piñon, juniper (*sabino*), and ponderosa pine (*pinabete*) promised an abundant source of timber for construction and firewood to sustain a small community. In addition to his familiarity with the terrain, Donaciano was undoubtedly aware of the decline of Pecos Pueblo, its diminished Native population, and their precarious hold on their land.

In December 1854 Donaciano was apprised that Preston Beck had acquired two separate parcels of land in Pecos and in the Hacienda de San Juan Bautista del Ojito del Rio Gallinas, lying farther east on the Pecos River. The acquisition carried out by attorney Hugh N. Smith in a trusteeship arrangement with Beck, as stated above, was for some of the choicest land in the Pecos ciénega on both sides of the Pecos River. The land had been acquired by Juan Estevan Pino from the Pecos Pueblo in 1830, and there Pino established the headquarters of his sprawling ranch. The elder Pino died in 1839, and his son Manuel Doroteo, who inherited the Pecos property, fell on hard times and used the land as collateral on a loan from Beck. He eventually lost the property. Hugh Smith was a friend of Donaciano. He knew of Donaciano's plans to move to the country and surely informed him that Beck's intent was to sell. When Smith informed Donaciano that this land was available, he must have seen it as a miracle, a dream come true, a sign from providence that it was his destiny to spend the remainder of his life there. He jumped at the chance, despite the $1,500 price tag.

On 26 December 1854, Beck sold Donaciano a parcel of land on the east side of the Pecos River. In the twilight of his life, Donaciano decided to settle down and devote the remainder of his life to working the land. As Father Stanley Crocchiola put it, "Here [in Pecos] the politician gave way to the family man, the provider, the builder, the citizen, the friend. Most of his time from 1855 to 1877 was spent in Pecos and Gusano."[1] As always, Donaciano's move to Pecos was a family affair, including his wife, María Refugio Sánchez, and their children. His eldest son, Antonio Basilio; Antonio's wife, María de la Luz Rowland; and their son, Bartolomé, also would join them in the move to Pecos.

The parcel that Donaciano bought from Beck amounted to about 50 acres, which was one-sixth of the 300 acres on both sides of the Pecos River that Beck had secured from Manuel Pino.[2] It is clear that Beck made a handsome profit in selling one-sixth of the land in Pecos for $1,500, which was exactly half of the total price he paid for all his Pecos property and the parcel at the Ojito del Rio Gallinas site. For Beck, this was part of his role as a land speculator, buying and selling land for profit. For Donaciano, it was the purchase of a lifetime. He had never paid more for any property, and it became the greatest part of the humble estate he left to his large family. It certainly seems unlikely that Donaciano was involved in some kind of conspiracy when he secured the land in Pecos.

By the time Donaciano arrived in Pecos in 1855, there was already a sizable presence of non-Native Hispanic residents in the ciénega, and the pueblo had been abandoned for almost two decades. Hall wrote, "Even as new actors, Anglo land speculators ... became claimants to Pecos land ... [and] shared a common dislike for those Hispanic settlers who were prospering and increasing in the richest part of Pecos pueblo lands, indifferent to patent recognition."[3] John Grenier, a new agent working for the Indian agency in New Mexico, prepared a report on the northern pueblos and wrote about Pecos. According to Hall, "There is no suggestion here of restoring Pecos lands to their Indian owners, no mention of the Hispanic settlers living on the Pecos grant lands, let alone of ejecting them from their home. Instead, Grenier simply drew on the popular press of the day for his report. Pecos Pueblo lands had already passed into the special world of myth."[4] All this makes it abundantly clear that by the time Donaciano arrived, the Pecos Pueblos were in the rearview mirror in the minds of Hispanic *pecoseños*, and he would join that mind-set.

Donaciano readily adapted to the life of a farmer in Pecos, and soon he and his sons had much of their newly acquired land under cultivation. As an acknowledged leader of the community, manifested by his prompt election to the Territorial Council, it fell to Donaciano and a few other pioneers, such as Manuel Varela, Miguel Rivera, and Clemente Valencia, to establish land use patterns and traditions that would govern the small agricultural community. In Pecos, as in other rural New Mexico villages, the land tenure system combined elements of both private and community landownership. Thus, individuals privately owned their own land, which was often fenced off. At the same time, all the members of the community shared usage of common land called *ejido*, which included land for the pasturage of animals and as a source of lumber for construction purposes and firewood.[5] This land was in the foothills surrounding the village of Pecos and was still technically owned by the Pecos Pueblos. This would remain so until 1929–1933 when the Pueblo Lands Board directed a survey of that foothill land lying between the private properties of the village and Pecos Pueblo's eastern boundary (essentially the Santa Fe National Forest). The resultant strips were deeded to each private property holder whose property bounded the pueblo land, and the survivors of Pecos Pueblo were compensated for that final extinguishment of their title to Pecos area land. Thus, many Pecos residents, including Donaciano's direct heirs, found themselves owning strips of additional acreage between the village and the US Forest Service boundary.[6]

Many, including my grandparents, farmed the area referred to as temporales (unirrigated farmland), which was watered only by spring and summer rainstorms.[7] In addition to the planting and harvesting of crops, Donaciano had a "small herd of sheep" and "a certain number of cattle . . . a mare with calf, three burros, and three little pigs," as he mentioned in his will.[8]

In conjunction with the planting, another task was the improvement, extension, and maintenance of the community irrigation ditch (*acequia de la communidad*), parts of which had been constructed by the Indigenous people and earlier Hispanic settlers of Pecos. The rich bottomland between the irrigation ditch and the river was referred to as regadillos (irrigated land) and was used for growing wheat, corn, beans, peas, and chiles. Owners fenced their regadillo during the growing season from May to October, and the fences were removed in the fall so that the community's livestock could graze on the *rastrojos* (remains or stubs) of the harvested crops.[9] In addition to sharing their private land for common pasture in this way, each family would help others in the planting and harvesting of crops. A select portion of the irrigated land near the placita was set aside for arboleras (orchards) of apple, peach, pear, and plum trees. A narrow strip of land above the acequia was referred to as *el mancomún*, or land owned by the united community that was available for public roads or rights-of-way.[10] Included in the unique jargon of the Pecos village was the term *la otra banda*, which was used by locals to refer to the community on the opposite bank of the river. For residents of eastern Pecos, la otra banda was western Pecos and vice versa. Eventually, the forested foothills above the Pecos Valley were cleared and became temporales where the farmers could plant beans and corn.[11] In time, Donaciano and his sons were planting, harvesting, drying, and packing many food plants (corn, chilis, beans, lettuce, squash, peas, beets, onions, tomatoes, carrots, and radishes) and fruits (apples, pears, peaches, plums, apricots, and cherries) grown in arboleras set aside from the other crops. Donaciano sought to innovate with new seeds and tree cuttings that would work in the high elevation and short growing season of the Pecos Valley.

Along the hills and above the river placita were *las eras* (common corrals) used by all the farmers to thresh their wheat. At a slow gait in a circular path on the flat, hard surface of the corral, a horse tethered to a pole in the center would crush the wheat plants, and the breeze would complete the work of separating the wheat from the chaff.[12] Anxious to utilize new technology, Donaciano built a *molino* (gristmill) for grinding corn and threshing wheat. Local artisans and laborers, including his son Desiderio (a blacksmith), used local building materials to construct a fully functional molino. Soon, several of his sons and, later, grandsons were grinding corn and threshing wheat for most of the Pecos community. To power the wooden wheels of the molino, Donaciano built a smaller ditch (*acequia del molino*), which was later used to power saws in a lumber mill that Donaciano and his sons constructed below the molino. Small gardens were irrigated by the water from the smaller ditch, which then wound its way back to the river.[13]

Of all of Donaciano's many innovations in Pecos, none had a more direct and overwhelming impact than the molino. B. A. Reuter wrote about the mill and Donaciano, and what both meant to the Pecos community. Reuter was a resident of Pecos and a writer for the Works Progress Administration Writers Project, and he prepared a number of articles on the Pecos area after interviewing old-timers in the 1930s. Several of those articles focused on Donaciano. In an effort to ascertain the date of the construction of the mill, Reuter reported that Teodocio Ortíz recalled that when he was seven years old in 1862, the mill was referred to as the "old mill." Reuter speculated that Donaciano might have acquired the property earlier than 1855 and built the mill before he moved to Pecos; in 1939, he said the mill was over 100 years old. We know that Donaciano acquired the property in 1854 and moved there in 1855, so the mill must have been built after 1855. Therefore, it could not have been 100 years old in 1939 when Reuter wrote the article.[14]

Reuter said that there were four mills in the Pecos area at that time, and they differed only in the size of the grinding stone and minor features of construction. The four mills were the Vigil mill in eastern Pecos; the mill at the Valley Ranch (a dude ranch), above and north of Pecos; the mill on the ranch of José Varela, not far from the Pecos Catholic church; and the mill on the property owned by Reuter, which was in the gorge below the village of Pecos. "The Vigil mill is said to have had the largest millstone and produced the best flour."[15]

The Vigil mill was adjacent to the Pecos River on a sharp curve where the river turns, heading southward after flowing in an easterly direction in the northern part of the ciénega of the Pecos village. Reuter described the mill as being about a half mile north of the Harrison Country Store in Pecos. The Adelo family later acquired the Harrison Country Store, which continues to operate as the Adelo Town and Country Store in the same location, the crossroads of New Mexico State Roads 63 and 50. The Vigil mill, according to Reuter, was like "all early mills of this section with the simplest type of water driven machinery for the reduction of grain into flour. The entire affair could be built with native materials, excepting the small iron plate and short piece of iron or steel shaft for connecting the upper mill rock to the wooden propeller."[16]

The operation of the molino was basic. At some point above the mill, a small dam on the edge of the river diverted water through a sluice gate into a small ditch (acequia del molino). This conveyed the water at sufficient speed to generate enough energy, perhaps two to five horsepower, after it was transferred from the ditch through a wood trough. The water struck the blades of a turbine-like propeller, which continuously rotated and in the process transferred power through a system of levers and axles that lifted, turned, and maneuvered the large circular grinding stone. The large grinding stone was positioned above a similar stone below. The wheat or corn was placed between the stones, and the rotation of the stones broke down the kernels of grain and produced wheat or corn flour.

The mechanism was located inside a millhouse, which made it possible to operate the mill continuously in any kind of weather. While the Vigil mill was not of the most modern design available in that period, it was functional enough to serve the needs of the community. "Some of the older folks, who can still remember when the mill was an important instrument of service to the community, speak regretfully of the decline in the mill's ability to produce. It once ground many sacks of meal a day that now takes the greater part of a day to grind as much as a hundred pounds."[17] At the peak of the mill's history, it was also used to power a mill to cut lumber from pine, piñon, juniper, and cedar trees harvested in the nearby forests.

For his story, Reuter interviewed José Asisclo Vigil, who was the regular operator of the mill at the time. José Asisclo was my grandfather, one of Donaciano's grandsons, and the second-youngest son of Donaciano's eldest son, Antonio Basilio. Reuter was not impressed by José Asisclo and his generation of Donaciano's descendants, whom he described in this way: "The sons of Gov. Vigil were all men of outstanding ability, but for various causes the bloodstream has weakened, for the living descendants of this great man show little of his powerful physique and mental qualities. They are mostly gentle folk, honest and well-mannered but are lacking in force of character and ability."[18] Reuter wondered "whether this weakening of the mental and physical fiber" was due to "marriage" or "some unknown biological cause," but he was certain that "it [the regression] is positive with all the descendants of Gov. Vigil in this section."[19]

I never knew my grandfather because he died in 1941, the same year I was born. Nevertheless, I was impressed a few years ago when scavenging through my father's records in search of old property deeds. I found an old log kept by my grandfather, a ledger from the Gross, Kelly and Company Mercantile and Lumber store at Decatur, New Mexico. The ledger was used by the company to record deliveries of lumber and other hardware purchased from Gross, Kelly and Company and delivered through private contractors to various locations in the Decatur service area. José Asisclo was a private freight contractor (*fletero*), who hired himself and his horse and wagon for such deliveries. The logbook had been discarded, and somehow José Asisclo gained possession of it. He recycled it, using the blank back pages as his personal diary. He carefully emulated his grandfather Donaciano's penchant for recording important family events (like the Donaciano *cuaderno*). In Spanish, José Asisclo noted the names, birth dates, and *padrinos* of all his children and grandchildren.[20]

In addition, José Asisclo kept personal financial records. For example, on 17 February 1934, he purchased a plot of land from Florencio Martínez. Below the name of Martínez, which was written on the dotted line as the "freighter" for that particular delivery, José Asisclo wrote the following note: "me entrego 450 pieces de terreno en los temporales" (sold me 450 feet of land in the dry farmland). Just below were written the names of Cesario Esquibel and Genovebo Vigil (José Asisclo's son), who were listed as witnesses.[21] On the blank back of the book, José Asisclo recorded his *abonos* (payments) to Martínez for the temporal land.

This record kept by José Asisclo Vigil, the grandson of Donaciano, demonstrated two facts. First, contentions that Donaciano was a wealthy patrician-style property owner with vast landholdings, immense herds of livestock, and capital wealth are not valid. Sixty-two years after his death, his descendants were living a modest existence as small farmers and day laborers. Though they owned small plots of land, they were generally cash poor, and while they were always in the market to buy additional plots of land, they did so at great sacrifice. An example is José Asisclo's purchase of land from Florencio Martínez for about $25. The monthly installment payments ranged from $2 to $9 in cash. Other payments took the form of labor, such as *moliendo mais* (grinding corn) for a fee of thirty-five cents, or a special order of blue corn for *nixtamal* for fifty cents, or selling *oja* (cigarette leaf) for $3.40. Second, contrary to Reuter's observations, José Asisclo was an astute, capable, conscientious, and hard-working man who could read and write, maintain his financial accounts, and effectively provide for his large family by farming his land, operating the gristmill for profit, and hiring himself and his horse and wagon to deliver goods for Gross, Kelly and Company.

Shortly after settling in Pecos, Donaciano had an opportunity to expand his landholdings. On 28 January 1857, Donaciano purchased a strip of land belonging to Juan Valencia for $204. This land was within the boundaries of Donaciano's own property and had been exempted from his purchase from Beck in 1854. The property measured 154 varas and was bounded on the north and south by Donaciano's property, on the west by the Pecos River, and on the east by the hills.[22] The property contained a house and unified Donaciano's land on the east side of the Pecos River.

In September 1864, Donaciano bought additional property from Pablo Moya for the price of $150. This property was divided into two portions. One portion measured 200 varas long from north to south, seventy-one varas wide on the north end, and thirty-one and a half varas wide on the south side. This land contained a grove of plum trees. Most of this property was surrounded on the north, south, and east by the property of Manuel Varela. The other portion was 150 varas long from north to south and contained three rooms of a partially constructed house. This property was bounded on the north by property of Manuel Varela, on the west by the irrigation ditch, on the south by land owned by Jesús María Baca, and on the east by Donaciano's land.[23] This purchase expanded Donaciano's holdings north and west of his prior property holdings.

Another purchase was made by Antonio Basilio Vigil, Donaciano's eldest son. He purchased a strip of land measuring 235.5 varas from north to south from Vicente Quintana for the price of $135. This purchase extended the Vigil holdings farther southward. The warranty deed conveying this property identified it as the same property purchased by Vicente's father, Mariano Quintana, from *los naturales del Pueblo de Pecos* (the Natives of Pecos Pueblo). This deed suggests that the Pecos probably sold some of their property in individual transactions not previously known about. This marked the second time the Vigils purchased land previously sold by the Pecos.[24] Overall, the relatively small purchases made by Donaciano and his family after 1855 affirm his economic status as typical of a small- to medium-level farmer-rancher in his era.

Thus, by the mid-1850s, the land and the people that would comprise the village community of Pecos were joined. In the following decades, the community evolved, tempered by the common social, cultural, and religious values of New Mexican rural Hispanic society and the day-to-day experiences of the people. Donaciano, like Juan Estevan Pino before him, became a permanent and contributing member, a central figure in the evolution and development of the community. Not only through his knowledge and wisdom, but also by his example of integrity, ingenuity, diligence, and steadfastness, Donaciano helped shape the character of the community of Pecos.

On 26–28 March 1862, Donaciano was a close witness to the Civil War battle at Glorieta Pass, which was fought within ten miles of his home in Pecos. Sixteen years before, he had been poised as a Mexican soldier and officer to fight General Kearny's American army in defense of his home and of Mexico. Now in the same location, he observed his adopted country's devastating Civil War played out almost in his backyard. As a Union man, he must have been pleased that two of his sons, Desiderio and Epitacio, served as Union soldiers. Whether he contemplated the irony of history, we will never know.

As opportunities presented themselves to secure more property adjoining his own, Donaciano did so legitimately. His growing numbers of relatives and neighbors toiled to extract a living from the land. Donaciano's life was hardly that of a genteel patrician overlooking a vast estate. Instead, it was a simple communal existence where Donaciano led by example a large, extended family and shared in the everyday rigors with his friends and neighbors to harvest crops and tend to the livestock.

Donaciano and his sons certainly honored the biblical dictum to "go forth and multiply," as manifested by the censuses of Pecos, which recorded a rapidly burgeoning family. Four of Donaciano's five surviving sons—Antonio Basilio, Ermenejildo, Desiderio, and Epitacio—settled in Pecos; only Epifanio remained in Santa Fe.[25] Of the five sons, Antonio had the largest family with ten children (seven boys and three girls). In all, Donaciano had fifteen grandchildren, twelve boys and three girls, who lived to adulthood. In addition to Vigil, other surnames linked to the family are Quintana, Armijo, Valencia, Segura, Rivera, López, Ortega, Varela, and Roybal, among others. The names of these people, all direct descendants, dot the records of births, marriages, and deaths in St. Anthony's parish and the graves at the village cemetery on the westside hills. The San Miguel County Courthouse contains the legal records of the multiple real estate transactions.

It is unknown if Donaciano was a member of a prominent literary and mutual aid society known locally as La Literaria, which thrived in Pecos with headquarters in a stone building along New Mexico State Road 63. This organization brought men together to discuss, debate, and share ideas on classic and contemporary literary works and to present dramatic plays for the community, such as *Los Pastores*, a popular Christmas folk drama. In the 1860s, he applied for membership in the Historical Society of New Mexico, although it is unknown if he became a member. Donaciano was not a member of the local chapter of La Sociedad de Nuestro Padre Jesús Nazareño (Society of

Our Father Jesus of Nazareth), known as the Penitente Brothers, which is still active in Pecos. However, some of his direct descendants were among the founders and members of this religious brotherhood. In fact, the children of Toribio Vigil, the only son of Desiderio Vigil, donated and deeded to the society the property where the morada is located.[26] Another deed records a donation of land to the Pecos School District in eastern Pecos by José Asisclo Vigil, a grandson of Donaciano.[27]

Since he was larger than life during his lifetime, it is not surprising that Donaciano became the stuff of legends after he died. Many of these stories, albeit unbelievable and probably untrue, persist in Pecos lore, and some were retold by his biographer Crocchiola. One legend suggests that Donaciano owned slaves, whom he referred to as peones (workers), and that he had "reclaimed" them, as was his custom, from the Indigenous people who had captured them. When Donaciano moved to Pecos, it is said, he had twenty-one such peones whom he educated and trained as carpenters, shepherds, and planters. These laborers built his houses and molinos, planted and harvested his crops, and tended his herds of sheep and cattle. Donaciano, of course, provided food, clothing, and shelter to his peones. Every Saturday, Donaciano hosted a matanza with a cow or calf slaughtered and barbecued in a large outdoor *horno* (oven), and he invited all his workers to share in the feast.[28]

Another legend suggests that when Abraham Lincoln became president, Donaciano wrote to him inquiring about what to do with his peones. Lincoln replied that since, in essence, they were enslaved, he should give them their freedom, and if he continued to employ them, their wages should be appropriate. Donaciano wrote a second letter to the president, asking if fifty cents a day was sufficient since he provided for all their needs. The president replied that seventy-five cents would be more appropriate. Donaciano complied with the president's suggestion and subsequently gave each worker a small plot of land where they could build a home and plant a small garden to provide for their families.[29] This beneficent gesture, according to this story, accounted for the other families that lived in Pecos. No doubt, direct descendants of Donaciano delighted in these tales since they portrayed their patriarch as a benevolent patrón and themselves as a form of privileged elite.

Another story recounted the legendary strength of Donaciano, who was described as a towering figure. On one occasion, Donaciano was trying to corral a yearling steer for butchering. The elusive steer would have none of it, and Donaciano had to chase after him. By the time he was able to corral him, Donaciano was so angered that he struck the animal with a mighty blow on the head, which killed it. On a later occasion, Donaciano again lost his temper and struck one of his peones, Rafaél Gonzales, so hard that the poor man was bedridden for days. Later, Gonzales filed a suit against Donaciano, and the judge fined Donaciano five dollars. When he went to pay the fine, Donaciano gave the judge ten dollars because he intended to strike the man again for suing him. The judge warned Donaciano that if he could kill a steer with one blow, he could kill Gonzales, and he would be in a lot more trouble.[30] It is unknown if the incident helped to quell Donaciano's temper.

Another story relates the legendary cleverness of Donaciano. An old man owned a fifty-dollar gold coin that he proudly showed to his friends. One day it was missing, and since the neighborhood only consisted of four families, he naturally suspected all of them. Uncertain about what to do, he went to Donaciano for advice. Donaciano told him to spread a rumor that he intended to start a small banking enterprise. For every coin a person gave to him, he would give two of equal amount. Soon after the rumor circulated, the coin and the suspect appeared, and the old man got his coin back.[31]

Donaciano spent the remainder of his existence living, as one reviewer of this manuscript suggested, "a bucolic life," wandering through the village of Pecos on his trusted burro and visiting with his extended family, neighbors, and friends. His primary occupations were supervising the clearing of fields; draining marshes; renovating homes; building corrals, stables, and fences for his animals; and planting and harvesting subsistence crops for his family and alfalfa and hay for his livestock. Occasionally, the persistent call to public service required trips to Santa Fe to attend a legislative session, provide testimony, or lobby for a favorite policy. On such trips, he rode a sturdy horse until arthritic aches and pains forced him to traverse the approximately twenty miles of rough, winding dirt roads on a horse-drawn wagon. Still, it seemed that in his mid-fifties in the prime of his life, he had walked away from what could have been a fortune for the taking. In contrast to some of his contemporaries, he chose not to become a powerful politician or a wealthy entrepreneur. Surely, he could have sought economic power in mercantile operations or in large-scale ranching and farming, such as the Romeros of Las Vegas, the Pereas of Bernalillo, and the Pinos of Santa Fe, or he could have been a powerful politician, such as the Oteros of Las Vegas, the Lunas of Los Lunas, or José Manuel Gallegos,

TABLE 1. Donaciano Vigil's *Cuaderno*

Maurilio E. Vigil located a cuaderno that was written by Donaciano Vigil or dictated by him. The cuaderno is in the William G. Ritch Collection at the Huntington Library in San Marino, California. Ritch was secretary of the territory of New Mexico from 1873 to 1885 and a friend of Donaciano. The Center for Southwest Research at UNM offers an online digital copy of the Ritch Collection (WGR R2-D69). Interestingly, the cuaderno shows that all of Donaciano's sons (except for Antonio) had the first name José and his daughters had the first name María. Donaciano introduced the cuaderno as follows:

Cuaderno en que constan los días en que han nacido mis hijos con expresión de los Padrinos de Bautismo y Padres que los bautisaron. Abuelos paternos Juan Cristóbal Vigil y Antonia Andrea Martínez, Abuelos maternos Diego Antonio Sánchez y María Manuela Gallegos.

[Table listing the birth dates of all my children along with their baptismal godparents and priests who baptized them. Paternal grandparents Juan Cristóbal Vigil and Antonia Andrea Martínez, maternal grandparents Diego Antonio Sánchez and María Manuela Gallegos.]

NAME	BIRTH DATE	GODPARENTS	PRIEST	CHURCH
Antonio Basilio Vigil	13 June 1827	don Francisco Narbona and wife	Fernando Ortiz	Castrense
José Desiderio Vigil	23 May 1828	don Agustin Duran and Rosario Ortiz	Fernando Ortiz	Castrense
José Mateo Vigil	21 September 1829	don José Abreu and Joséfa Baca	Juan Felipe Ortiz	Castrense
María Salomé Vigil	22 October 1830	don Santiago Abreu and Joséfa Baca	Fernando Ortiz	Castrense
María Guadalupe Vigil	12 December 1831	Captain Blas de Hinojos and doña Jesús Trujillo	Juan Felipe Ortiz	Castrense
José Epifanio Vigil	7 April 1832 [1833?]	don Jesús Maria Alarid and Joséfa Sánchez	Juan Felipe Ortiz	Santa Fe Curato
José Ermenejildo Vigil	13 April 1834	don Francisco Sarracino and Gertrudes Telles	Juan Felipe Ortiz	Santa Fe Curato
José Epitacio Vigil	13 May 1837	don Tomás Valencia and Joséfa Vigil	José Francisco Leyva	*parroquia* church
José Amador Vigil	1 March 1838 (died 1 March 1840)	Sergeant Tomás Martínez and Maria Antonia Tenorio	José Francisco Leyva	*parroquia* church
José Tomás Vigil	18 September 1840 (died 28 December 1840, buried in Castrense Cemetery)	Alférez Antonio Sena and Refugio Ortiz Vicario	Juan Felipe Ortiz	*parroquia* church

TABLE 1. *continued*

The cuaderno notes that Donaciano's father, Juan Cristóbal, died on 21 September 1832 in Santa Fe and was buried in the Castrense Cemetery; his brother Juan died on 7 August 1838 and was buried in the Guadalupe Cemetery; his mother, Antonia Andrea Martínez, died on 24 January 1839 and was buried in the Guadalupe Cemetery; his half brother, Gregorio Trujillo, seventy-five years old, died on 23 March 1853 and was buried in the Parrish Cemetery; his wife, María del Refugio Sánchez, died on 13 May 1861 and was buried in the Pecos Chapel. Finally, there is a note dated 28 March 1882 by Epifanio Vigil stating that his father, Donaciano, died on 11 August 1877 in Epifanio's house in Santa Fe and was buried in the Nuestra Señora del Rosario Cemetery on 13 August. Epifanio then added his signature stating that the cuaderno was a true copy of the family record of Donaciano then in his possession.

SOURCE: Donaciano Vigil, Cuaderno, Vigil Family Papers, William G. Ritch Collection, Huntington Library, San Marino, CA, HL R 2, D.93 (1823–1877); ZIM, CSWR Digital WGR R2-D69.

the multiple-term New Mexico territorial delegate to Congress. Perhaps as an innately humble man, Donaciano was uncomfortable with the high profile of public life, into which he had been thrust and then eagerly sought refuge from. With his move to Pecos, Donaciano happily spent the last two decades of his life in relative comfort.

Other than the land he left to his heirs, he left little capital and few other assets. Hall summarized the modern presence of Donaciano's heirs: "Pecos, still huddled on both sides of the Pecos River in the Pueblo grant's northern reaches, today reflects the intricate heritage of Donaciano Vigil bequeathed on it. More than ninety percent of the 600 Spanish-Americans living and farming there trace their lineage directly to Donaciano Vigil and the tract he acquired in 1854."[32] In the last analysis, even Hall admitted, "Yet, beneath it all, Donaciano Vigil remained true to the rich culture from which he had come. He publicly espoused the liberal ideas of his times.... This other side of Donaciano Vigil was also reflected in his interest in land in the way he used Pecos Pueblo land, not in the means by which he acquired it."[33]

DEATH AND ACCLAIM

In early August 1877, Donaciano suffered from a stomach ailment that had plagued him in his later years. Usually he was able to persevere until the pain subsided, but this time a recurrence of a perennial asthmatic condition also bothered him. There were no physicians in Pecos, so he rode to Santa Fe to seek medical care and stayed with his son Epifanio. On the "morning of Saturday August 11, shortly before seven he was seized with an attack of wheezing and whistling in an effort to catch his breath. A half hour later, he was dead. The doctors said it was a case of hernia and asthma."[34]

In life, Donaciano had always sought a humble place, notwithstanding the lofty heights he had achieved in public life. However, in death, "the honors he eluded in life, found him [as] the whole country acclaimed him as a man of high repute and esteem."[35] Word of his death spread quickly and as far as Santa Cruz and Taos.

The territorial governor, Samuel B. Axtell, issued a proclamation calling for a large public meeting, and "no one was prepared for the throng that assembled."[36] Stephen B. Elkins, New Mexico's territorial delegate to Congress, drew up resolutions that appealed to the legislature and New Mexicans:

> Whereas the people of New Mexico, being desirous of recording the high appreciation of the great worth of Donaciano Vigil, as a citizen and official, and bearing testimony to his many virtues therefore be it resolved that the people of New Mexico have received with deepest regret the sad intelligence of the death of Governor Donaciano Vigil, who for more than fifty years, was a distinguished and worthy citizen of that Territory; that it is with sorrow we part with the deceased, distinguished for his administrative ability, his perfect integrity; just in the exercise of his prerogatives, when governor of this Territory; respected by all, beloved for his kindness of heart, his memory will continue green with his friends, and the people, as one who was the type of a perfect gentleman; that while we bow our heads in humble submission to the unerring will of Providence in severing a tie so closely welded by long years of intimacy with the deceased in a frontier Territory, so incident with danger and severe trials during many years of his life, we tender our sincere sympathy and condolences to his family, assuring them that the entire community shares with them in their great loss; that a copy of these resolutions, with the proceedings of the meeting, be furnished the family of the deceased, and published in all the papers of the Territory.[37]

On 13 August 1877, the *Santa Fe Weekly New Mexican* reported the funeral events with the editor adding:

FIGURE 11. Donaciano Vigil bronze bust by Signe Bergman (2006). This bust was unveiled in a ceremony on 9 September 2006 at the Palace of the Governors where the Vigil committee presented it to the "people of New Mexico" and the New Mexico History Museum on behalf of the Donaciano Vigil family. Source: Photo by Alberta M. Vigil, Maurilio E. Vigil Collection.

National flags were at half-mast at military headquarters, Col. Sol Spiegelberg's and other places in Santa Fe in honor of ex-governor Donaciano Vigil, deceased, the second governor of the Territory of New Mexico, who had always been a staunch friend of the American population, as well as his own race. He died poor to purse, but then this did not prevent our citizens showing every mark of esteem for his many virtues and distinguishing traits of character while occupying offices of trust and honor among his people.[38]

The funeral, according to Twitchell, was "by far the largest and most distinguished gathering ever witnessed in New Mexico."[39]

A BELATED MEMORIAL

On 9 September 2006, a group of Donaciano's descendants led by Bill Vigil from Fresno, California; Ray and Virgil Vigil from Santa Fe; and Maurilio Vigil presented a bronze bust of Donaciano Vigil to the New Mexico History Museum (symbolically representing the people of New Mexico) on behalf of the extended Donaciano Vigil family. The bust was created by painter-sculptor Signe Bergman and crafted at Santa Fe Bronze. It is the only memorial that exists to honor the public life, career, and service of Donaciano Vigil.

NOTES

INTRODUCTION

1. Tate, *Guadalupe Hidalgo Treaty of Peace*. Bill Tate is an artist, writer, and gallery owner in Tijeras, NM.
2. Ibid., 1.
3. Ibid., 3.
4. Ritch, "Governor Donaciano Vigil," 1.
5. Donaciano Vigil, "Message to the First New Mexico Legislative Assembly," Santa Fe, 1847, Notes and Speeches, box 7, folder 208, Donaciano Vigil Collection, 1961-002, New Mexico State Records Center and Archives, Santa Fe. Speech translated from Spanish to English by Ralph Emerson Twitchell in *Leading Facts of New Mexico History*, 2:265n190. See also Twitchell, *History of the Military Occupation*, 220–21.
6. Twitchell, *Leading Facts*, 264n189.

CHAPTER ONE

1. Weber, *Arms, Indians, and the Mismanagement of New Mexico*, 7–8.
2. Malthus, *Rise and Fall of the Spanish Empire*, 7–16.
3. Ibid.
4. Faya Díaz, *Nobleza en la Asturias*, 93. According to the *Vox Diccionario Español-Inglés* (1972), in a mayorazgo an owner declared his estate to be entailed, that is, designated to be permanent in nature. Once established, it passed to the firstborn son of each new generation by the rule of primogeniture.
5. Faya Díaz, "Noblesa y Mundo Rural," 455–56. "La constitucion de Mayorazgos sobre el patrimonio rústico heredado y las estrategias matrimoniales nos ayudan a explicar el engrandecimiento de algunas casas a lo largo del tiempo." For a discussion of the use of the mayorazgo and marriage among various families (Arguelles, De la Rua, Valdes) to advance economic and political power in Oviedo and Asturias, see Rivero, *Oviedo y El Principado de Asturias*, 155–62.
6. Perrigo, *American Southwest*, 20–21.
7. Faya Díaz, *Nobleza en la Asturias*, 15–20.
8. Faya Díaz, "Noblesa y Mundo Rural," 453, quoting Jovellanos, *Cartas*, 145.
9. Faya Díaz, "Noblesa y Mundo Rural," 455–65.
10. Faya Díaz, *Nobleza en la Asturias*, 16.
11. Ibid., 15.

12. Esparza, *Gran Aventura*.
13. Cañellas Secades, *Libro de Oviedo*.
14. Cuesta, *Libro de Siero*. Also see Alonzo Cabeza, *Páginas de la Historia*.
15. Díaz Álvarez, *Ascenso de una Casa Asturiana*, 48–49.
16. María Angeles Faya Díaz, prologue, in Díaz Álvarez, *Ascenso de una Casa Asturiana*, 19–21.
17. Faya Díaz, *Nobleza en la Asturias*, 15.
18. Ibid., 16.
19. O'Hara, "Juan Rodriguez de Fonseca," 131–50.
20. Rodriguez, Rodriguez, and Villar, *Casa de Contratación*, 149–51. See also Cavendish, "Casa de Contratación," 57.
21. Vigil, "The Word and the Name," 12. It is of interest that this first Vigil in New Spain is from Siero, as is our later principal figure, Juan Montes Vigil II. Rodrigo preceded the latter by almost a century. Might Rodrigo be related to Juan Montes II? Michael Vigil, our source for this information, does not cite his source or elaborate further on Rodrigo.
22. Contratación no. 5536, book 5, folio 349, Pasajeros a Indias, Archivo General de Indias, Seville, Spain.
23. The records of Juan Montes Vigil are conjoined with those of Jacinto de Olmos in the Casa de Contratación archive because Vigil sought to travel as a criado (servant) to Olmos. Contratación no. 5323, ramo 28, pertains to Olmos, and no. 5328, ramo 29 to Montes Vigil. The Juan Montes document (Contratación 5328, ramo 29) is a remarkable story that tells much about the Spanish background of the Montes Vigil family that would settle in New Mexico. The document was presented by Juan Montes Vigil II to the Casa de Contratación as part of his application for a royal license to travel to the Indies. The document was initially prepared by Bartolomé de Vigil, regidor of the village of Siero, on behalf of his nephew Juan Montes Vigil II. In it, Bartolomé presents his own and other people's testimony describing the origin and parentage of Juan Montes II. Subsequent parts of folio 29 were added by Juan II as part of the application.
24. Vigil, Contratación no. 5328, ramo 29.
25. Ibid.
26. Olmos, Contratación no. 5323, ramo 28.
27. García, *Sevilla y las Flotas de Indias*, 41–44, 133.
28. Olmos, Contratación no. 5323. Olmos may have missed the fleet to the mainland and sought passage to New Spain rather than wait another year. The circumstances surrounding the travel to New Spain by Olmos and his servant Juan II helps explain why Vigil ended up in New Spain rather than in Peru, as originally intended in his license application. Whether Olmos and Juan II ever traveled to Peru and how or why Juan II took up residence in New Spain are both unknown.
29. Olmos, Contratación no. 5323, ramo 28.
30. Vigil, Contratación no. 5328, ramo 29.
31. Ibid. "Digo que el dicho mi menor pretende pasar a la Indias en Nuevo España y otras provincias de su majestad y para que en las partes donde estuviere conste de que es

hijo dalgo notario de solar conocido de armas poner y pintar por ser desciendente por linea recta e lejítima de la casa y solar de Vigil que es de las calidades veteridas e una de las antiguas e principales de este consejo e principado."

32. Ibid.

33. Ibid.

34. Ibid.

35. Hendricks and Colligan, "Beyond Origins of New Mexico Families," 1. Colligan in researching the archive in Zacatecas, Mexico, located two wills of Juan Montes Vigil (Juan Montes III), who was the son of Juan Montes II and Catalina Herrera de Cantillana, both deceased and natives of the kingdom of Castile.

36. Miller, "Descendants of Lucas and Ysabel de Vigil."

37. Rick Hendricks and John Colligan, researchers; Charles Martínez y Vigil and José Antonio Esquibel, translators, "The 1st Will of Juan Montes Vigil" and "The 2nd Will of Juan Montes Vigil," Archivo Historico del Estado de Zacatecas, Zacatecas, Mexico.

38. Vigil, *Early Roads*, 12–13.

39. Martínez, *Some Descendants of Domingo Montes Vigil*, xii–xiv.

40. Ibid., xvi.

41. Ibid., xvi. The connection of this two-year-old orphan, Carlos Vigil, to Juan Montes III is a mystery. It is not likely that he was another son, since Juan Montes III was willing to acknowledge Francisco Montes as his hijo natural. Especially intriguing is the identity of Francisco's mother and the circumstances that caused Juan Montes III to embrace Francisco as his hijo natural.

42. Ibid.

43. Ibid.

44. Martínez, "Notes on the Montes Vigil Family," 45, as well as other personal records of Juan Montes Vigil III.

45. Martínez, *Some Descendants of Domingo Montes Vigil*, xvi.

46. Ibid.

47. Meyer and Sherman, *Course of Mexican History*, 208–11.

48. Martínez, *Some Descendants of Domingo Montes Vigil*, xvi.

49. Colligan, *Juan Paez Hurtado Expedition*, 39–40. Colligan's spelling Anciso varies from our spelling, which is Ancizo.

50. Ibid., 65.

CHAPTER TWO

1. Colligan, *Juan Paez Hurtado Expedition*, ix.

2. Ibid., 13.

3. Ibid., 5.

4. Ibid., 14.

5. Ibid.

6. Ibid., 15.

7. Ibid., 16.

8. Strout, "Resettlement of Santa Fe," 267.
9. Colligan, *Juan Paez Hurtado Expedition*, 64–65.
10. Ibid.
11. Ibid., 17.
12. Ibid.
13. Ibid., 18.
14. Ibid.
15. Martínez, *Some Descendants of Domingo Montes Vigil*, x–xi.
16. Ibid.
17. Vigil, *Early Roads*, 26.
18. Chapman, "New Mexico Generations," 41–69.
19. Vigil, *Early Roads*, 28.
20. Ibid.
21. Ibid., 37.
22. Ibid., 38.
23. Genealogical Society of America, *Nuestras Raices*, 85.
24. Rosina Lasalle, "Vigil Family Memory Book," call no. LCSW 929.2 L348, New Mexico State Library, Santa Fe.
25. Chapman, "New Mexico Generations," 44.
26. Vigil, *Early Roads*, 38.
27. Ibid.
28. Ibid. This author incorrectly wrote that Manuel Montes Vigil's son Juan Luis Vigil and Ynes López were the parents of Donaciano Vigil.
29. Ibid. In an anomaly of sorts, I discovered in genealogical research that Elena Vigil's husband, Diego Gonzales II, was the fifth-tier great-grandfather of Alberta Gonzales, my wife. Thus, both I and my wife are direct genealogical descendants of Francisco Montes Vigil.
30. Lasalle, "Vigil Family Memory Book."
31. Herrera, *Juan Bautista de Anza*, 126–29.
32. Ibid., 95–110.
33. Lasalle, "Vigil Family Memory Book."
34. Julian Josue Vigil, in Taos Census of 1790, New Mexico State Records Center and Archives, Santa Fe.
35. Vigil, *Early Roads*, 52.
36. Ibid. The middle name of this son has been alternately spelled as Cristóval or Cristóbal. Since a birth record has not been found, we use the *b* spelling to distinguish the son from his father of the same name. We refer to him as Juan Cristóbal, which also helps to distinguish him from his father.
37. Ibid.
38. Virginia Olmstead, "Spanish Enlistment Papers of New Mexico, 1732–1820" (Juan Cristóbal Vigil), film 56946, frame 896, New Mexico State Records Center and Archives, Santa Fe.
39. The birth dates of the children were derived from roster of the Santa Fe Presidial

Company listing Juan Cristóval [Cristóbal] Vigil and his dependents, reel 221, frames 515 and 516, Spanish Archives of New Mexico, New Mexico State Records Center and Archives, Santa Fe.

40. Will of Juan Cristóbal Vigil, 31 May 1832, folder 314, and Will of Antonia Andrea Martínez, 27 May 1834, folder 316, both in box 7, Donaciano Vigil Collection, 1961-003, New Mexico State Records Center and Archives, Santa Fe.

41. Sze, *Within Adobe Walls*, xvi–xvii. This book incorporates the journals kept by Charlotte White, who purchased the Vigil property in 1958. The house and property underwent a massive restoration project to preserve the house.

42. Loomis, *Old Santa Fe Today*, 16.
43. Sze, *Within Adobe Walls*, xvi.
44. Ibid.
45. Olmstead, "Spanish Enlistment Papers of New Mexico."
46. Jenkins, "Donaciano Vigil House," 2.
47. Lasalle, "Vigil Family Memory Book."

CHAPTER THREE

1. Coan, *History of New Mexico*, 281.
2. Francis, "Donaciano Vigil," 4.
3. Coan, *History of New Mexico*, 281.
4. Ibid.
5. Francis, "Donaciano Vigil," 6.
6. Ibid., 4–6.
7. Fergusson, *New Mexico*, 190.
8. Ibid., 7.
9. Bloom, "People of New Mexico," 34–35.
10. Tyler, *Sources for New Mexican History*, 8.
11. Bloom, "Barreiro's Ojeada sobre Nuevo Méjico" (April 1928), 73.
12. Ibid., 78.
13. Ibid., 78–79, 92–93.
14. Ibid., 84–85.
15. Ibid., 85.
16. Ibid., 94–95; Bloom, "Barreiro's Ojeada sobre Nuevo Méjico" (July 1928), 150–57.
17. Bloom, "Barreiro's Ojeada sobre Nuevo Méjico" (July 1928), 150–51.
18. Ibid., 145–48, 165–66.
19. Ibid.
20. Ibid.
21. As quoted in Weber, *Mexican Frontier*, 240.
22. Pino, *Exposición*, 43.
23. Ibid., 44.
24. Ibid., 45.
25. Coan, *History of New Mexico*, 280–81.

26. Francis, "Donaciano Vigil," 8.

27. Donaciano Vigil, "Short Personal Autobiography," n.d., Spanish version and English translation, Biographical and Autobiographical Notes, box 7, folder 308, Donaciano Vigil Collection, 1961-003, New Mexico State Records Center and Archives, Santa Fe.

28. Ibid.

29. Vigil, *Early Roads*, 52.

30. Ibid.

31. Twitchell, *History of the Military Occupation*, 208.

32. Ibid.

CHAPTER FOUR

1. The Santa Fe presidio consisted of a military force alternately referred to as a militia or a garrison of regular army soldiers. Those serving in Santa Fe were career soldiers enlisted in the Mexican army for ten or more years, but the force resembled a militia (such as today's National Guard) in that the members did not live and work permanently in a separate military *cuartel* (fort). Instead, the Santa Fe garrison was more like a military headquarters where command offices, military supplies, and meeting facilities were located (in the Palace of the Governors). Soldiers generally lived in their own homes with or without family. They attended to their military duties in the garrison headquarters and were often deployed for days, weeks, or months in military operations. Proposals to establish a separate garrison by some military leaders, such as Governor Juan Bautista de Anza, Fernando de la Concha, and José Antonio Viscarra, were generally unsuccessful.

2. Bloom, "Texan Crisis," 267.

3. Crocchiola, *Giant in Lilliput*, 1.

4. Ibid.

5. Ibid.

6. Archive of the Archdiocese of Santa Fe, reel 31, frame 307, 10 October 1825; Ritch, "Governor Donaciano Vigil," 1.

7. Twitchell, *Leading Facts*, 2:41.

8. Ibid.

9. Ibid.

10. Ibid., 41–42.

11. Torrez, "Presidio of Santa Fe," 187–88.

12. Ibid., 190–91.

13. Ibid., 188.

14. Tyler, "New Mexico in the 1820s," 185.

15. Torrez, "Presidio of Santa Fe," 191.

16. Ibid., 190–91.

17. Ibid., 192.

18. Ibid., 193.

19. Torrez, "Presidio of Santa Fe," 193.

20. Torrez, "New Mexico's Navajo Wars," 201.

21. Will of Antonia Andrea Martínez, 27 May 1834, box 7, folder 316, Donaciano Vigil Collection, 1961-003, New Mexico State Records Center and Archives, Santa Fe.

22. First Will of Donaciano Vigil, ca. 1842, box 7, folder 319, Donaciano Vigil Collection, 1961-0003, New Mexico State Records Center and Archives, Santa Fe. It should be noted that Donaciano's brother Juan died on 7 August 1838, before their mother's death. Donaciano's half brother, Gregorio Trujillo, continued to reside with Donaciano's family until his death on 23 March 1853, as noted in the 1850 US Census for Santa Fe. Also see Sze, *Within Adobe Walls*, xvii.

23. Tyler, "New Mexico in the 1820s," 188.

24. Ibid.

25. Ibid.

26. Torrez, "New Mexico's Navajo Wars," 196–97.

27. Tyler, "New Mexico in the 1820s," 189.

28. Ibid., 199.

29. Donaciano Vigil dram license, in Business Papers, Licences, and Receipts, 1845–1875, box 7, folder 320, Donaciano Vigil Collection, 1961-003, New Mexico State Records Center and Archives, Santa Fe.

30. Torrez, "Presidio of Santa Fe," 196.

31. Tyler, "New Mexico in the 1820s," 199.

32. Torrez, "Presidio of Santa Fe," 196.

33. Twitchell, *Leading Facts*, 42.

34. Salazar, "Military Career of Donaciano Vigil," 1–2.

35. Twitchell, *Leading Facts*, 43.

36. Weber, *Arms, Indians, and the Mismanagement of New Mexico*, 7.

37. Brooks, *Captives and Cousins*, 363.

38. Tyler, "New Mexico in the 1820s," 199n84; Fondo de Gratificacion, 12 August 1829, in Donaciano Vigil, Records of Military Career, Offices Held, and Company/Military Records, Filiaciones, 36:884, Mexican Archives of New Mexico, New Mexico State Records Center and Archives, Santa Fe.

39. Salazar, "Military Career of Donaciano Vigil," 2.

40. Twitchell, *Leading Facts*, 22–23.

41. Cooke, *Scenes and Adventures in the Army*, 84–88.

42. Twitchell, *Leading Facts*, 23–24.

43. Ibid., 23–24.

44. Donaciano Vigil, "Personal Account of Expedition That Escorted an American Commercial Caravan to the Arkansas River," addressed to Capitan Permanente del Bado, Departamento de Nuevo Méjico, 31 May 1844, Biographical and Autobiographical Notes, box 7, folder 208, Donaciano Vigil Collection, 1961-003, New Mexico State Records Center and Archives, Santa Fe.

45. Salazar, "Military Career of Donaciano Vigil," 2–3.

46. Vigil, Records of Military Career, 36:884.

47. There are several different spellings of this family's name in the archival records: Rowland, Roland, and Rolenes. We use the spelling Rolenes for Tomás and for María

de la Luz. Antonio Basilio later served as the administrator of his father-in-law's estate after the latter was stabbed to death following a robbery in his store at San Miguel.

48. Twitchell, *Leading Facts*, 44.
49. Salazar, "Military Career of Donaciano Vigil," 3.
50. Twitchell, *Leading Facts*, 44.
51. Gregg, *Commerce of the Prairies*, 1:289.
52. Salazar, "Military Career of Donaciano Vigil," 3.
53. "Vigil Quarrels with Capt. Cavallero for Which He Was Placed under Arrest," as told to and recorded by Epifanio Vigil in an interview with Juana Prado, 30 March 1878, Donaciano Vigil Papers [R 1, 1873], New Mexico State Records Center and Archives, Santa Fe.
54. Twitchell, *Leading Facts*, 58.
55. Lecompte, *Rebellion in Rio Arriba*, 16–20, 172–74.
56. Ibid., 31–35.
57. Ibid.
58. Wroth, "1837 Rebellion in Rio Arriba."
59. Ten sworn statements from participants and witnesses of Sergeant Donaciano Vigil's conduct during the battle against rebel forces in the rebellion of 1837 are in possession of the author.
60. Gonzales, *Política*, 54–56; Donaciano Vigil, "La Convencion."
61. Lecompte, *Rebellion in Rio Arriba*, 44–47, 50–53.
62. Ibid., 43.
63. Ibid., 50–53.
64. Twitchell, *Leading Facts*, 64.
65. Lecompte, *Rebellion in Rio Arriba*, 54–55.
66. Ibid., 55–56.
67. Ibid.
68. Ibid., 64–65.
69. Ibid., 70–71.
70. Ibid., 73.
71. Ibid.
72. Twitchell, *Leading Facts*, 65–66n48; Lecompte, *Rebellion in Rio Arriba*, 48.
73. Twitchell, *History of the Military Occupation*, 213.
74. Reséndez, *Changing National Identities*, 170–72, 175–80, 183–90, 195–96.
75. Salazar, "Military Career of Donaciano Vigil," 2.
76. Ibid., 6.
77. Ibid., 7.
78. President Anastasio Bustamante Commission of Donaciano Vigil as Teniente of the Company of Bado, 17 August 1841, box 2, folder 83, Donaciano Vigil Collection, 1961-003, New Mexico State Records Center and Archives, Santa Fe.
79. Webb, *Handbook of Texas*, 1:729.
80. Frantz, *Texas*, 80–82.
81. John Rowland was likely the brother of Thomas Rowland (aka Tomás Rolenes).

Both had French Canadian origins and had lived in Pennsylvania before moving west to Missouri and then to New Mexico in the 1820s. Both were described as fur trappers and merchants. Tomás Rolenes was the father of María de la Luz Rolenes, who married Antonio Basilio Vigil, Donaciano's son, in October 1848. Chávez, *Origins of New Mexico Families*, 355.

82. Webb, *Handbook of Texas*, 1:729.
83. Ibid. Also see Perrigo, *American Southwest*, 112, 152–53.
84. Perrigo, *American Southwest*, 112.
85. Frantz, *Texas*, 81.
86. Webb, *Handbook of Texas*, 1:729.
87. Ibid.
88. Ibid.
89. Ibid.
90. Ibid.
91. Kendall, *Narrative of the Texan–Santa Fe Expedition*, 16. The weapons the Mexican soldiers carried are indicative of the primitive state of munitions they used, even when meeting soldiers outfitted with much better weapons.
92. Ibid. Gregorio Vigil was a cousin of Donaciano Vigil, and they had been close during his service in the Bado company.
93. Kendall, *Narrative of the Texan–Santa Fe Expedition*, 16, as quoted in Twitchell, *Leading Facts*, 78.
94. Twitchell, *Leading Facts*, 78n55.
95. Ibid., 81–82.
96. Webb, *Handboook of Texas*, 1:729.
97. Torrez, "Governor Armijo's Medal of Honor," 6. See also Salazar, "Military Career of Donaciano Vigil," 6; Crocchiola, *Giant in Lillput*, 76–81.
98. Salazar, "Military Career of Donaciano Vigil," 6–7.
99. "Donaciano Vigil, "Short Personal Autobiography," n.d., Spanish version and English translation, Biographical and Autobiographical Notes, box 7, folder 308, Donaciano Vigil Collection, 1961-003, New Mexico State Records Center and Archives, Santa Fe.

CHAPTER FIVE

1. Bloom, "Beginnings of Representative Government," 76.
2. Ibid., 74.
3. Ibid., 78.
4. Ibid.
5. Fowler, *Santa Anna*, 5.
6. Ibid., 21.
7. Ibid.
8. Ibid., 128.
9. Donaciano Vigil, "Notes on the History of New Mexico, 1821–51," ca. 1851, Notes and Speeches, box 7, folder 309, Donaciano Vigil Collection, 1961-003, New Mexico State Records Center and Archives, Santa Fe, NM.

10. Weber, *Mexican Frontier*, 32.
11. Fowler, *Santa Anna*, 143, 158–61, 258.
12. Ibid., 365.
13. Weber, *Mexican Frontier*, 22.
14. Ibid., 22–32.
15. Ibid., 22.
16. As quoted ibid., 28.
17. Ibid., 33.
18. Donaciano Vigil, "Notes on the History of New Mexico, 1621–1851," ca. 1851, 2, Notes and Speeches, box 7, folder 309, Donaciano Vigil Collection, 1961-003, New Mexico State Records Center and Archives, Santa Fe.
19. Gonzales, *Política*, 45.
20. Ibid., 45–46.
21. Ibid., 56.
22. Bloom, "Six Months," 251–52.
23. Bloom, "Beginnings of Representative Government," 78.
24. Weber, *Mexican Frontier*, 27–41.
25. Fowler, *Santa Anna*, 214, 244, 377–82.
26. Alamán, *Historia de Mexico*, 28, as quoted in Krauze, *Mexico*, 135.
27. Weber, *Mexican Frontier*, 32.
28. Minge, "Frontier Problems," 154.
29. Ibid., 155.
30. Ibid., 167.
31. Ibid.
32. Ibid.
33. Ibid., 154–56.
34. Weber, *Mexican Frontier*, 271.
35. As quoted in Krauze, *Mexico*, 137.
36. Minge, "Frontier Problems," 158–59.
37. Ibid., 155.
38. Bloom, "Constitutional Government Reestablished," 167.
39. Ibid., 167–69.
40. Ibid., 168.
41. Weber, *Mexican Frontier*, 271.
42. Chavez, *But Time and Chance*, 68.
43. Bloom and Donnelly, "The Mexican Interlude," 187–88.
44. Weber, *Mexican Frontier*, 271.
45. Bloom, "Constitutional Government Reestablished," 166–68.
46. Ibid.
47. Ibid., 166.
48. Ibid.
49. Ibid., 167.
50. Ibid.

51. Weber, *Mexican Frontier*, 230.
52. Ibid. See also Bloom and Donnelly, *New Mexico History and Civics*, 185.
53. Oczon, "Bilingual and Spanish Language Newspapers," 45–46; Bloom and Donnelly, *New Mexico History and Civics*, 185.
54. Oczon, "Bilingual and Spanish Language Newspapers," 45. Oczon incorrectly wrote that *La Verdad* operated from 1842 to 1845. The correct dates are 1844–1845. See Weber, *Mexican Frontier*, 230–31.
55. Oczon, "Bilingual and Spanish Language Newspapers," 46.
56. Ibid.
57. Gonzales, *Política*, 164–67.
58. Bloom, "Third and Last Chance for Armijo," 252.
59. McClure, "Mexican New Mexico," 105–6.
60. Gray, *Selected Poems*, 1.
61. Weber, *Arms, Indians, and the Mismanagement of New Mexico*, 1, 9, 17, 29.
62. Ibid., ix–x.
63. Ibid., xviii–xix.
64. Ibid., xx.
65. Direct quotes of Donaciano's proposals in both Spanish and English are reprinted here by permission of Texas Western Press. Donaciano Vigil, "Vigil on Arms, Munitions, Trade, North Americans, and Barbaric Indians" (18 June 1846) and "Vigil Opina sobre Armas, Municiones, Comercio, Norteamericanos, y Indios Bárbaros," both in Weber, *Arms, Indians, and the Mismanagement of New Mexico*.
66. Weber, *Mexican Frontier*, 105.
67. Vigil, "Vigil on Arms, Munitions, Trade," 3.
68. Vigil, "Vigil Opina sobre Armas, Municiones, Comercio," 11.
69. Ibid., x–xii.
70. Ibid., 20–21.
71. Ibid., xii.
72. "Vigil on the Maladministration of New Mexico under Governors Pérez and Martínez and under Commanding General García Conde" (22 June 1846), in Weber, *Arms, Indians, and the Mismanagement of New Mexico*, 17.
73. "Vigil Opina sobre la Maladministración de Nuevo México bajo los Gobernadores Pérez y Martínez y bajo el Comandante General García Conde" (22 June 1846), in Weber, *Arms, Indians, and the Mismanagement of New Mexico*, 29.
74. Weber *Arms, Indians, and the Mismanagement of New Mexico*, xiii–xiv.
75. Ibid., 20–21.
76. Ibid., xiv.
77. Ibid.
78. Ibid., xv.
79. Gray, *Poetry of Thomas Gray*, 1.
80. Gonzales, *Política*, 78.

CHAPTER SIX

1. Singletary, *Mexican War*, 56.
2. Ibid.
3. Ibid.
4. Ball, "Stephen W. Kearny," 55.
5. As quoted in Gonzales, *Política*, 78.
6. Perrigo, *American Southwest*, 163–65.
7. Twitchell, *Leading Facts*, 206.
8. Perrigo, *American Southwest*, 164.
9. Vigil, "New Mexico Sold for $2,000," 5.
10. Perrigo, *American Southwest*, 164.
11. Perrigo, *Gateway to Glorieta*, 12.
12. Ibid., 13.
13. Ibid.
14. Bloom, "Closing Months," 351–52.
15. Ibid.
16. Ibid., 352–53.
17. Ibid., 353.
18. Perrigo, *American Southwest*, 163–64.
19. Bloom, "Closing Months," 356–58.
20. Ibid., 354–56.
21. Ibid., 357.
22. Ibid., 357–58.
23. Ibid., 359.
24. Ibid., 360.
25. Ibid., 362–63.
26. Ibid., 363.
27. Ibid., 361–62.
28. Ibid., 362.
29. Ibid.
30. Ibid., 362–63.
31. Ibid., 364.
32. Ibid., 364–65.
33. Johnston, Edwards, and Ferguson, *Marching with the Army of the West*, 158–59.
34. Donaciano Vigil, "Short Personal Autobiography," n.d. This was written by his own hand in Spanish and translated by Maurilio Vigil, 4 January 2017. Biographical and Autobiographical Notes, box 7, folder 308, Donaciano Vigil Collection, 1961-003, New Mexico State Records Center and Archives, Santa Fe.
35. Ritch, "Governor Donaciano Vigil."
36. Ibid.
37. Twitchell, *History of the Military Occupation*, 215.
38. Twitchell, *Leading Facts*, 67n49.

39. The original Spanish version, which I verifiedto be the true penmanship, syntax, and signature of Donaciano Vigil, is found in the Donaciano Vigil Papers, New Mexico State Records Center and Archives, Santa Fe. Also in the papers is an anonymously typed English translation of the original. Interestingly, that translation does not convey Donaciano's admission of neglecting his duty as a captain. That translation makes him seem entirely virtuous in his actions. Note the following passage in the anonymous translation: "made his declaration of non-resistance, and in a fashion, somewhat irregular, dispersed his soldiers. He decided to resign his post, that is, his appointment as captain in the firm assurance that in this country liberties would be enjoyed."

40. Kraemer, "Donaciano Vigil," 12–14.

41. Ibid.

42. Twitchell, *Leading Facts*, 217–18.

43. Ibid., 209.

44. Ibid., 209–10n146.

45. Vigil y Alarid became acting governor because Governor Armijo had appointed him secretary and lieutenant governor in the days before the invasion. When Armijo fled the territory, Vigil assumed the role of acting governor.

46. Twitchell, *Leading Facts*, 210–11.

47. Kraemer, "Donaciano Vigil," 7.

48. Memorial of Donaciano Vigil et al., 9 May 1970, no. 207, Twitchell Collection, Spanish, Mexican, and American Manuscripts and Autographs, New Mexico State Records Center and Archives, Santa Fe.

49. Weber, *Mexican Frontier*, 272.

50. Perrigo, *American Southwest*, 160–61.

51. Fowler, *Santa Anna*, 146.

52. Ibid., 258.

53. Ibid., 262.

54. As quoted ibid., 279.

55. As quoted ibid., 156.

CHAPTER SEVEN

1. Twitchell, *Leading Facts*, 212–14. See also Loomis, "New Mexico and the Sectional Controversy," 206–9.

2. Gonzales, *Política*, 72.

3. As quoted in Twitchell, *Leading Facts*, 230n166.

4. Ritch, "Governor Donaciano Vigil," 1. This material was adopted as a Senate resolution in the 11 August 1877 session of the New Mexico Territorial Legislature, and it was later printed as a eulogy in the *Santa Fe Weekly New Mexican*.

5. Twitchell, *Leading Facts*, 232–33n168.

6. Ibid.

7. Twitchell, *Leading Facts*, 233–34n169.

8. Twitchell, *History of the Military Occupation*, 218.

9. Twitchell, *Leading Facts*, 234n170.
10. Ibid., 234–35.
11. Ibid., 237–39.
12. Ibid., 239–40.
13. Ibid., 240.
14. Ibid., 241–42.
15. Needham, *Acoma's Lincoln Cane*, 1.
16. Twitchell, *Leading Facts*, 241–43.
17. Ibid., 248–49.
18. Ibid., 249n177.
19. Ibid., 248–49n177.
20. Ibid.
21. Ibid., 248–50.
22. Ibid., 250–51.
23. Ibid., 251.
24. Ibid.

CHAPTER EIGHT

1. Gonzales, *Política*, 136.
2. Ibid., 880n243.
3. Ritch, "Governor Donaciano Vigil," 1; Twitchell, *Leading Facts*, 263–64; Headquarters Ninth Military Department, Santa Fe, 17 December 1847, General Order no. 10, "Declaring That Lieutenant Governor Donaciano Vigil Is Hereby Appointed Civil Governor of the Territory of New Mexico. By Order of Brig. Gen. S. Price, W. E. Prince, A. D. C. & A. A. Adj.'t. Gen.," New Mexico State Records Center and Archives, Santa Fe.
4. Gonzales, *Política*, 142.
5. Ibid., 142–43.
6. Larson, *New Mexico's Quest for Statehood*, 8–9.
7. Ibid., 154.
8. Twitchell, *Leading Facts*, 264; Gonzales, *Política*, 142–44; Vigil to Armijo, 21 May 1848, document 124, William G. Ritch Collection, Huntington Library, San Marino, CA.
9. Ritch, "Governor Donaciano Vigil," 1.
10. Gonzales, *Política*, 139.
11. Ibid., 140.
12. Donaciano Vigil's governor's papers are found in several archives and locations. The governor's main records are located in New Mexico Governors under United States Military Occupation, Donaciano Vigil (Civil), 1847–1848, New Mexico State Records Center and Archives, Santa Fe; the Ritch Collection, Huntington Library, San Marino, CA; and the Southwest Collection at the University of New Mexico Center for Southwest Research. Smaller troves are found at many other public and private collections, libraries, and archives.
13. Gonzales, *Política*, 140.

14. Ibid.
15. Ibid., 140–42.
16. Ibid., 143.
17. Ibid.
18. Letter to Antonio Otero, n.d., quoted ibid.
19. Ibid., 144.
20. Tyler, *Sources for New Mexican History*, 11–12.
21. "The General Index of All the [Governmental] Documents Dating from the Governments of Spain and Mexico up to the Year of 1846," Antonio Basilio Vigil, sworn affidavit regarding his role in the preparation of the Vigil Index, Santa Fe County, NM, 12 October 1892, Matias Dominquez, notary public, New Mexico State Records Center and Archives, Santa Fe.
22. Launius, *Alexander William Doniphan*, 115; Gonzales, *Política*, 144.
23. "Early Printing in New Mexico," 389–92.
24. Donaciano Vigil, "Gobernador Interino del Territorio de Nuevo Méjico, A los Habitantes del Mismo" [Interim Governor of the Territory of New Mexico, to the Inhabitants of the Same], 1 July 1847, Notes and Speeches, box 7, folder 309, Donaciano Vigil Collection, 1961-003, New Mexico State Records Center and Archives, Santa Fe.
25. Ritch, "Governor Donaciano Vigil," 1.
26. Gonzales, *Política*, 145.
27. Ritch, "Governor Donaciano Vigil," 1.
28. Ibid.
29. Twitchell, *Leading Facts*, 264–65n189.
30. Ibid., 264.
31. Letter from Manuel Armijo to Donaciano Vigil, 23 April 1848, William G. Ritch Collection, printed by permission of the Huntington Library, San Marino, CA.
32. Letter of Manuel Armijo to Donaciano Vigil, 18 May 1848, document 25, William G. Ritch Collection, printed by permission of the Huntington Library, San Marino, CA.
33. Letter of Donaciano Vigil to Manuel Armijo, 21 May 1848, document 324, William G. Ritch Collection, printed by permission of the Huntington Library, San Marino, CA.
34. Bancroft, *History of Arizona and New Mexico*, 431.
35. Ruxton, *Adventures*, 189.
36. Ibid.
37. Kraemer, "Donaciano Vigil," 20.
38. Twitchell, *Leading Facts*, 263.
39. Kraemer, "Donaciano Vigil," 20–21.
40. Twitchell, *Leading Facts*, 263.
41. Ibid., 265.
42. Ibid., 265–66n191.
43. Ibid., 266.
44. Gonzales, *Política*, 147.
45. Ibid., 164–67.
46. Ibid., 161, 167.

47. Ibid., 164–67.
48. Letter from José Francisco Leyva to Donaciano Vigil, 31 August 1848, document 47, 1, William G. Ritch Collection, Huntington Library, San Marino, CA.
49. Ibid., 2.
50. Ibid.
51. Letter from Governor Donaciano Vigil to José Francisco Leyva, Santa Fe, 4 September 1848, document 24, William G. Ritch Collection, Huntington Library, San Marino, CA.
52. Twitchell, *Leading Facts*, 266n191.
53. Ibid., 267–68n192. The memorial to Congress was signed by Antonio J. Martínez, Francisco Sarracino, Santiago Archuleta, Gregorio Vigil, José Pley, Elias P. West, Juan Perea, James Quinn, Ramón Luna, Manuel A. Otero, Antonio Sais, Charles Beaubien, and Donaciano Vigil.
54. Ritch, "Governor Donaciano Vigil," 1.
55. Ibid.
56. Ibid.
57. Twitchell, *Leading Facts*, 268–70n194.
58. Ibid., 270–71.
59. Ibid., 270–71n195.
60. Bauer, *Zachary Taylor*, 241, 292–95.
61. Twitchell, *Leading Facts*, 271.
62. Ibid., 270–71.
63. Crocchiola, *Giant in Lilliput*, 164–65. See also Stegmaier, *Texas, New Mexico and the Compromise of 1850*, 130.
64. Twitchell, *History of the Military Occupation*, 190.
65. Twitchell, *Leading Facts*, 275–76n200.
66. Crocchiola, *Giant in Lilliput*, 164–65.
67. Twitchell, *History of the Military Occupation*, 191–92; Twitchell, *Leading Facts*, 277n201.
68. Smith, *President Zachary Taylor*, 246.
69. Ibid.
70. Ibid., 247.
71. Ibid.
72. Ibid., 247–48.
73. Ibid., 257.

CHAPTER NINE

1. Twitchell, *Leading Facts*, 285–89.
2. Ibid., 284.
3. Ibid., 285.
4. Ibid., 292.
5. Ibid., 288.

6. Ibid.
7. One such influential book was Gregg, *Commerce of the Prairies*.
8. Tate, *Guadalupe Hidalgo Treaty of Peace*, 12.
9. Ibid.
10. Bancroft, *History of Arizona and New Mexico*, 472–73n51.
11. Ibid., 472.
12. Read, *Illustrated History of New Mexico*, 456.
13. Samuel Sisneros, "Juan Bautista Vigil y Alarid (1792–1866)," Office of the State Historian of New Mexico, http://newmexicohistory.org/filedetails.php?fileID=729.
14. Twitchell, *Leading Facts*, 291n215.
15. Read, *Illustrated History of New Mexico*, 456.
16. Ibid., 456–57.
17. Ibid., 457–58.
18. Ibid., 458.
19. Ibid., 459.
20. Want, "Crumbling Adobes of Chamberino," 286–87.
21. Sisneros, "Juan Bautista Vigil y Alarid," 6.
22. Perrigo, *American Southwest*, 200.
23. Palmer, "She Was Our Mother," 2.
24. Ibid., 15–17.
25. Ibid., 16, 19–20.
26. Ibid., 14.
27. Ibid., 15.
28. Ibid., 16.
29. Ibid.
30. Ibid., 20.
31. Ibid., 22.
32. Ibid., 23.
33. Ibid., 24.
34. Gonzales, *Política*, 177.
35. Palmer, "She Was Our Mother," 25.
36. Gonzales, *Política*, 176–77.
37. Palmer, "She Was Our Mother," 24–25.
38. Ibid., 44.
39. Ibid., 43.
40. Political culture is defined as the "set of attitudes, beliefs, and sentiments that give order and meaning to a political process and which provide the underlying assumptions and rules that govern behavior in the political system." Morlino, Berg-Schlosser, and Badie, *Political Science*, 66–67; Almond and Verba, *Civic Culture*.
41. Gonzales, *Política*, dust jacket.
42. Lamar, *Far Southwest*, 61.
43. Gonzales, *Política*, 204–5, 213–14, 217–18. Hispanidad manifested in racial/cultural pride is characteristic of nuevomexicanos. In his introduction to *Política*, Gonzales related

a story about Lieutenant Colonel George A. McCall, who returned to New Mexico after a "brief sojourn" in Washington in 1849. McCall spoke about all the "rage engrossing the attention of all classes of people" over the "remarkable fact of politics." The twin seeds of American politics and Hispanic racial/cultural pride created a hybridized "distinct political culture among *nuevomexicanos*." Gonzales, *Política*, 1, 23.

44. Ibid., 1, 23.
45. Ibid., 60–61.
46. Donaciano Vigil, "El Gobernador al Pueblo del Territorio," *Republicano*, 23 September 1848, 1. "Yo no puedo creer que ustedes se detengan un momento en hacer su elección, sea para quedar seguros bajo la proteccion de una granda, poderosa, y sustenible nación bajo cuyo Gobierno ustedes hallaran páz, armonia y iguales derechos o volver a la anarchía y oppression de la república Mexicana."
47. Gonzales, *Política*, 169.
48. Ibid., 169–70.
49. Ibid. The "normative core of this mindset," according to Gonzales, was that someday "*nuevomexicanos* would resemble the typical Anglo, English-dominant, educated citizen attuned to the U.S. nationality." It was as if Donaciano hoped that "*nuevomexicanos* would follow [his] lead [in] finding the assimilation view of American belonging compatible with their collective identity."
50. Ibid. "Reconoci los principios liberales de que se halla adornado. Entonces sintio mi corazón un plausible gozo viendo que se descubria en el pais que habitó el héroe y precursor de la dulce y apreioable honiestidad."
51. Ibid.
52. Holmes, *Politics in New Mexico*, 17.
53. Ibid.
54. Ibid., 18.
55. Ibid.
56. Ibid., 17.
57. Ibid., 29.
58. Ibid., 29. A variation of the quote is as follows: "The American government resembles a burro; but on this burro lawyers will ride, not priests." Smith, *New Mexico State Constitution*, xxi.
59. Holmes, *Politics in New Mexico*, 19.
60. Ibid., 50–51.
61. Ibid.
62. Gómez, *Manifest Destinies*, 174.
63. Gonzales, *Política*, 802.
64. Fergusson, *New Mexico*, 263.
65. Ritch, "Governor Donaciano Vigil," 1.
66. Poldervaart, *Black Robed Justice*, 39.
67. Ibid.
68. McNitt, *Navajo Wars*, 21.
69. Ibid., 218–20.

70. Crocchiola, *Giant in Lilliput*, 170.
71. McNitt, *Navajo Wars*, 221.
72. Ibid.
73. Ibid., 223.
74. Ibid., 225.
75. Ibid., 227.
76. Ritch, "Governor Donaciano Vigil," 1.

CHAPTER TEN

1. Westphall, *Mercedes Reales*, 85–87.
2. Ibid., 87.
3. Ibid.
4. Ibid., 88.
5. The list of people who were educated and fluent in Spanish and knowledgeable about Spanish/Mexican land laws and procedures for land grants was extensive. It included many who served in government positions, such as governor, territorial secretary, assembly members, local ayuntamientos, alcaldes, as well as many educated and wealthy citizens involved in large- or medium-scale ranching or farming operations and entrepreneurial pursuits. Such private people dealt in an economy where land was a marketable commodity used to obtain credit, loans, and other forms of wealth.
6. Westphall, *Mercedes Reales*, 88.
7. In his narrative, Hall refers to the "assault" on Pecos Pueblo land. Hall, *Four Leagues of Pecos*, 33. In a related article, "Giant before the Surveyor General," Hall echoed Crocchiola's biographical book on Donaciano, *Giant in Lilliput*. Thus we title the three chapters discussing the various critiques of Donaciano with the phrase "assault on a giant."
8. Hall, *Four Leagues of Pecos*, 33.
9. Ibid., xviii.
10. Ibid., xv.
11. Ibid., xix.
12. Ibid., 147–48.
13. Weber, *Mexican Frontier*, 190–91.
14. Kessell, *Kiva, Cross, and Crown*, 10.
15. Hall, *Four Leagues of Pecos*, 80–81, 88.
16. Ibid., 93.
17. Kessell, *Kiva, Cross, and Crown*, 450–55.
18. Ibid., 491–92.
19. Hall, *Four Leagues of Pecos*, 36–37.
20. Ibid., 16–17.
21. Ibid., 32–40.
22. Ibid., 39–44.
23. Ibid., 40–44.
24. Kessell, *Kiva, Cross, and Crown*, 445.

25. Ibid. See also Luis Benavidez, Santa Fe, 8 March 1825, I, no. 135; Rafaél Benavidez et al., Santa Fe, 3 March 1825, I, no. 135, both in Spanish Archives of New Mexico, New Mexico State Records Center and Archives, Santa Fe.

26. Kessell, *Kiva, Cross, and Crown*, 445.

27. Hall, *Four Leagues of Pecos*, 46–47.

28. Ibid., 40.

29. Ibid., 49–50.

30. Ibid., 50–53.

31. Kessell, *Kiva, Cross, and Crown*, 455.

32. Hall, *Four Leagues of Pecos*, 55–57.

33. José Cota to Juan Estevan Pino, warranty deed, dated 22 September 1830, recorded 29 May 1896, Deed Book 46:474, San Miguel County Clerk's Office.

34. Ibid.

35. Ibid.

36. Hall, *Four Leagues of Pecos*, 60.

37. Ibid., 59.

38. Ibid., 147.

39. Kessell, *Kiva, Cross, and Crown*, 56.

40. Hall, *Four Leagues of Pecos*, 61–62.

41. Justo Pastor Pino and Gertrudes Rascón (his wife) to Alejandro Valle, warranty deed, dated 2 January 1851, box 7, folder 337, Donaciano Vigil Collection, 1961-003, New Mexico State Records Center and Archives, Santa Fe.

42. Crocchiola, *Giant in Lilliput*, 170.

43. Donaciano Vigil, Appointment as Treasurer and Collector by Tomás Ortíz, Probate Judge, 30 March 1853, box 7, folder 337, Donaciano Vigil Collection, 1961-003, New Mexico State Records Center and Archives, Santa Fe.

44. Manuel Doroteo Pino and Josefa Ortíz, mortgage deed, dated 14 June 1853, recorded in Mortgage Documents, 9 December 1853, 64, 65, 67, San Miguel County Probate Court.

45. Hugh N. Smith to Preston Beck, Deed of Trust, dated 30 September 1854, recorded 12 December 1854, Deed Book 3:81, San Miguel County Clerk's Office.

46. Hall, *Four Leagues of Pecos*, 151–52.

47. Preston Beck to Donaciano Vigil, warranty deed, dated 26 December 1854, recorded 21 July 1887, Deed Book 33:36, San Miguel County Clerk's Office.

48. Ibid.

49. Ibid.

50. Hall, *Four Leagues of Pecos*, 153.

51. New Mexico Territorial Census, 1860, San Miguel County, Pecos, frame 34.

52. *The New Mexico Blue Book, 1882* (rpt., Albuquerque: University of New Mexico Press, 1968), 102, 105.

CHAPTER ELEVEN

1. Hall, *Four Leagues of Pecos*, 143.
2. Ibid., 144.
3. Ibid., 144, 147.
4. Ibid., 160.
5. Ibid.
6. Ibid.
7. US General Accounting Office, "Report to Congressional Registers," 7.
8. Hall, *Four Leagues of Pecos*, 163.
9. Domingo Fernández, "Testimony before the Surveyor General," ser. I, Land Grant Records, SG-8, roll 3, frame 310, Spanish Archives of New Mexico.
10. Hall, *Four Leagues of Pecos*, 162.
11. Manuel Baca and Antonio Nieto, "Testimony before the Surveyor General," ser. I, Land Grant Records, SG-8, roll 3, frame 310, Spanish Archives of New Mexico.
12. Hall, *Four Leagues of Pecos*, 163.
13. Hall, *Four Leagues of Pecos*, 164.
14. Baca and Nieto, "Testimony before the Surveyor General."
15. "Los Trigos Grant," 8, Surveyor General of New Mexico Records, New Mexico State Records Center and Archives, Santa Fe.
16. Marriage certificate of Donaciano Vigil and María del Refugio Sánchez, 10 October 1825, Castrense Chapel, Vigil Family Private Papers, box 7, folder 337, Donaciano Vigil Collection, 1961-003, New Mexico State Records Center and Archives, Santa Fe.
17. US Census Record for New Mexico, 1850, Santa Fe County, Donaciano Vigil household.
18. Transaction for sale of land in Gusano between Rafaél Benavidez and Gregorio Trujillo before Juan María Ulibarri, justice of the peace of the First Demarcation, 1843, New Mexico State Records Center and Archives, Santa Fe.
19. José Sena and wife (Luciana Rodríguez) to Donaciano Vigil, warranty deed, dated 12 April 1854, Deed Book 35:150, San Miguel County Clerk's Office.
20. José Ulibarri to Donaciano Vigil as trustee for Gregorio Trujillo, warranty deed, n.d., Deed Book 35:151–52, San Miguel County Clerk's Office.
21. Donaciano Vigil, First Will, Santa Fe, 1842 or 1843, box 7, folder 337, Donaciano Vigil Collection, 1961-003, New Mexico State Records Center and Archives, Santa Fe.
22. In the records of this testimony, the place was often spelled Guzano. To minimize confusion, we use the spelling Gusano except in direct quotations.
23. Bowden, "Private Land Claims in the Southwest." A segment of Bowden's six-volume thesis was published by the New Mexico Land Grant Council in 2018. One of the forty-four land grants discussed is the Los Trigos grant (46–48).
24. Antonio Basilio Vigil and Epitacio Vigil to Manuel García, warranty deed, n.d., Deed Book 35:151–52, San Miguel County Clerk's Office. The last transactions are located in the same deed books as the earlier deeds, which suggests that the earlier deeds were not *protocolados* (filed for recording) at the time of sale and were recorded at a later date.

25. Donaciano Vigil to Anne Carolyn Houghton, warranty deed, n.d., Donaciano Vigil acting as agent for the legal representatives of the original grantees to the Los Trigos grant, Deed Book 9:92–93, San Miguel County Clerk's Office.

26. Private Land Claims, "Donaciano Vigil or Los Trigos Grant," 165–66. See also Plat of Donaciano Vigil or Los Trigos Grant, 20 April 1970, book 2, plat 196 (7732), San Miguel County Clerk's Office. In the original documents, the name of the place was often spelled Guzano.

27. Hall, *Four Leagues of Pecos*, 165.

28. Vigil, "Early Spanish Wills," 24.

29. Hall, *Four Leagues of Pecos*, 143–46.

30. Ibid., 165.

31. Ibid., 147.

32. Tyler, *Sources for New Mexican History*, 11–12.

33. Crocchiola, *Giant in Lilliput*, 187.

34. Hall, *Four Leagues of Pecos*, 156–57.

35. Ibid., 157.

36. Ibid.

37. Donaciano Vigil, affidavit, 21 June 1856, Pueblos General Documents, roll 7, frames 7–8, and testimony of Donaciano Vigil, 20 August 1855, roll 12, frame 43, Preston Beck Grant, both in Surveyor General of New Mexico Records, New Mexico State Records Center and Archives, Santa Fe.

38. Hall, *Four Leagues of Pecos*, 82.

CHAPTER TWELVE

1. Mathews-Lamb, "Nineteenth-Century Cruzate Grants," 78.

2. Ibid., 79–81.

3. Ibid., 81.

4. Ibid., 82.

5. Ibid., 82n9. Mathews-Lamb pointed out that historian Charles Cutter had argued that the "Cruzate grants could in fact be 'poorly prepared' copies of originals yet to be found [and that] the documents are probably copies of genuine seventeenth century documents." Mathews-Lamb, "Nineteenth-Century Cruzate Grants," 100–102, referring to Cutter, "'Spurious' Seventeenth Century Pueblo Grants"; see also 100–101nn70–72.

6. Mathews-Lamb, "Nineteenth-Century Cruzate Grants," 83n12.

7. Ibid., quoting Hall, *Four Leagues of Pecos*, 157. In note 13, Mathews-Lamb provided the correct citation from the microfilm record. The problem is that the record does not include Donaciano's use of the words "Cruzate grants."

8. Testimony of Donaciano Vigil, 20 August 1855, Preston Beck Jr. Grant, roll 12, frame 43, Surveyor General of New Mexico Records, New Mexico State Records Center and Archives, Santa Fe.

9. Hall, *Four Leagues of Pecos*, 327n47.

10. Testimony of Donaciano Vigil, 20 August 1855. An excerpt:

QUESTION: Have you not seen in the archives of this territory grants approved by the Kings or Queens of Spain?
ANSWER: Only the one made to Oñate who held certain prerogatives and special orders afterwards authorizing the governor to make the grants of land.
QUESTION: Was it not customary to obtain the approval of the Superior government to grants made by the government after the declaration of independence under the Mexican government?
ANSWER: It was not.
QUESTION: Have you not seen in the archives some [grants] that were approved by the Spanish government during the time you held office?
ANSWER: I have not, nor have any been forwarded for approval.
QUESTION: Have you seen any ... grants made to the Pueblo Indians?
ANSWER: I have.
QUESTION: By whom were they signed?
ANSWER: By the King.
QUESTION: How many of the grants made to the Pueblo Indians have you seen?
ANSWER: That of Sandia.
QUESTION: Do you know where the special order is giving authority to the governors to grant lands? And by whom was it given?
ANSWER: They should be in the archives. It was given by the King.
QUESTION: Was the order in manuscript or was it ever published?
ANSWER: I do not remember, but I have seen a copy made by the government in the possession of Don Alejandro.

Reexamined by counsel for Beck:
QUESTION: Have you ever seen any other grants made by the King or the Superior government to private individuals besides the one referred to?
ANSWER: I have not.

11. Mathews-Lamb, "Nineteenth-Century Cruzate Grants," 83n12.
12. Twitchell, *Spanish Archives*, 1:377–80.
13. Mathews-Lamb, "Nineteenth-Century Cruzate Grants," 82.
14. Ibid., 83. It is worth noting that the surveyor general did not refer to Donaciano's words on 21 June 1856 as an "affidavit." Ralph E. Twitchell, an attorney and historian who wrote *The Spanish Archives of New Mexico*, was perhaps the first to refer to it that way. The surveyor general likely saw it as "testimony" since he used the word "testator" in the document, and he or someone in his office later applied the title "Testimony of Donaciano Vigil." As we suggest, it was neither testimony nor an affidavit.
15. Hall, *Four Leagues of Pecos*, 82. According to John Kessell, "Spaniards ... applied the title *cacique* to whomever they perceived as the paramount leader. In New Mexico they used the term interchangeably with governor.... Pueblo Indians came to regard *caciques* as chiefs who served for life or at the pleasure of elders and maintained [the] traditional harmony and well-being of the pueblos." Kessell, *Pueblos, Spaniards, and the Kingdom of New Mexico*, 70–71.

16. Donaciano Vigil, affidavit, 21 June 1856, Pueblos General Documents, roll 7, frames 7, 8, SGNM. Microfilm produced by UNM Library, 1955–1957, UNM Library/CSWR, and New Mexico Highlands University Donnelly Library.

17. Ibid., frames 7–8.

18. Ibid.

19. Ibid.

20. Twitchell, *Spanish Archives of New Mexico*, 1:456.

21. Hall, *Four Leagues of Pecos*, 157.

22. Mathews-Lamb, "Nineteenth-Century Cruzate Grants," 83.

23. Ibid., 83–84.

24. Ibid.

25. Tyler, *Sources for New Mexican History*, 11–12.

26. Antonio B. Vigil, sworn affidavit regarding preparation of Vigil Index, Santa Fe County, NM, 12 October 1892, Matias Dominquez, notary public, New Mexico State Records Center and Archives, Santa Fe.

27. Mathews-Lamb, "Nineteenth-Century Cruzate Grants," 84.

28. See Vigil Index, entry no. 720, Spanish Archives of New Mexico: "Peticion del padre Fray Juan Melchero marcada con el numero setecientos veinte." This entry refers to Juan Miguel Melchor's petition to New Mexico governor Joaquín Codallos y Rabal requesting permission for the resettlement of Sandia Pueblo. The petition was approved, leading to the restoration of the Sandia Pueblo grant.

29. Mathews-Lamb, "Nineteenth-Century Cruzate Grants," 85. This view was affirmed by Westphall in *Mercedes Reales*, 109. Westphall wrote, "By removal of the Cruzate document for the Pueblo grants as the foundation for the Pueblo grants, earlier royal *cédulas*, together with vice regal and *audiencia* ordinances passed for the benefit of the Indians, became the fundamental basis for the grants."

30. Mathews-Lamb, "Nineteenth-Century Cruzate Grants," 86.

31. Ibid., 92n42.

32. Tyler, *Sources for New Mexican History*, 12–13.

33. Mathews-Lamb, "Nineteenth-Century Cruzate Grants," 95.

34. Bancroft, *History of Arizona and New Mexico*, 195n35.

35. Twitchell, *Spanish Archives*, 1:477–78.

36. Mathews-Lamb, "Nineteenth-Century Cruzate Grants," 95, quoting Brayer, *Pueblo Indian Land Grants*, 15.

37. Hall, *Four Leagues of Pecos*, 81.

38. Ibid., 82.

39. Mathews-Lamb, "Nineteenth-Century Cruzate Grants," 96.

40. Ibid., 97.

41. Ibid., 98–99.

42. Ibid., 98n62.

43. Ibid., 99.

44. Ibid., 100.

45. Ibid., 100n69.

46. Ibid., 86.
47. Ibid., 86, 89.
48. Ibid., 107–8.
49. Ibid., 104.
50. Letter from Surveyor General William Pelham to Indian agent A. G. Mayers, Santa Fe, 21 June 1856, roll 56, frame 1, Surveyor General of New Mexico Records, New Mexico State Records Center and Archives, Santa Fe, quoted in Mathews-Lamb, "Nineteenth-Century Cruzate Grants," 104.
51. Letter from Pelham to Mayers.
52. Mathews-Lamb, "Nineteenth-Century Cruzate Grants," 104.
53. Ibid., 104–5.
54. Ibid., 104.
55. Ibid., 127.
56. Ibid., 184.
57. Ebright, Hendricks, and Hughes, *Four Square Leagues*, 205.
58. Ibid., emphasis added.
59. Mathews-Lamb, "Nineteenth-Century Cruzate Grants," 100, citing Cutter, "'Spurious' Seventeenth-Century Pueblo Grants," 9.
60. Ebright, Hendricks, and Hughes, *Four Square Leagues*, 205.
61. Ibid.
62. Ibid.
63. Ibid., 206, emphasis added.
64. Westphall, *Mercedes Reales*, 88.
65. Ibid., 113.
66. Westphall, *Public Domain*, 4.
67. Ibid.
68. Ibid., 3.
69. Ibid., 4.
70. Ibid., 115.
71. Ibid., 115–16.
72. Ibid., 117–18.
73. Ibid., 118.
74. Ibid., 88.
75. Ibid., 113.
76. Ibid., 88.
77. Ibid., 112.
78. Hall, *Four Leagues of Pecos*, 83.
79. Westphall, *Public Domain*, 111–12.
80. Ibid., 115.
81. Hall, *Four Leagues of Pecos*, 80–81.
82. Ibid., 80–82.
83. Ibid., 82.
84. Ibid.

85. Mathews-Lamb, "Nineteenth-Century Cruzate Grants," 127n67.
86. Ebright, Hendricks, and Hughes, *Four Square Leagues*, 222.
87. Ibid., 221.
88. Mathews-Lamb, "Nineteenth-Century Cruzate Grants," 98.
89. Ebright, Hendricks, and Hughes, *Four Square Leagues*, 221.
90. Ibid., 397n129.
91. Ibid., 223.
92. Mathews-Lamb, "Nineteenth-Century Cruzate Grants," 104.
93. Ebright, Hendricks, and Hughes, *Four Square Leagues*, 232.
94. Ibid.
95. Ibid.
96. Ibid., 233–34.
97. Ibid., 232.
98. Ibid., emphasis added.
99. Ibid., 232–33.
100. Ibid., 233.
101. Westphall, *Public Domain*, 109.
102. Lummis, *Land of Poco Tiempo*, 27–30.
103. Ebright, Hendricks, and Hughes, *Four Square Leagues*, 233.
104. Hall, *Four Leagues of Pecos*, 154–55.
105. Tyler, *Sources for New Mexican History*, 11.
106. Ebright, Hendricks, and Hughes, *Four Square Leagues*, 232.
107. *Merriam-Webster's Collegiate Dictionary*, 10th ed. (1997), s.v. "collusion."
108. Ebright, Hendricks, and Hughes, *Four Square Leagues*, 233.
109. Flint, "Review of *Four Square Leagues*," 429–30.
110. Tyler, *Sources for New Mexican History*, 12.
111. Fergusson, *New Mexico*, 203.

CONCLUSION

1. Crocchiola, *Giant in Lilliput*, 177.
2. Preston Beck to Donaciano Vigil, warranty deed, dated 26 December 1854, recorded 21 July 1887, Deed Book 33:36, San Miguel County Clerk's Office.
3. Hall, *Four Leagues of Pecos*, 68.
4. Ibid., 75–76.
5. Van Ness and Van Ness, *Spanish and Mexican Lands Grants*, 8–9. Although Pecos village was not a community land grant, as many other communities in New Mexico were, the land tenure system that evolved in Pecos resembled that of the community land grants.
6. Hall, *Four Leagues of Pecos*, 263–68. The US Forest Service created the Santa Fe National Forest in 1915. The eastern boundary of the old Pecos Pueblo grant effectively became the western boundary and the dividing line between private land and the Santa Fe National Forest.

7. Personal observation and discussions with Melecio Vigil, my father, who was a great-grandson of Donaciano and a resident of Pecos from 1899 to 1939.

8. Donaciano Vigil, Last Will and Testament, and Works Progress Administration translation, 14 May 1877, box 7, folder 324, Donaciano Vigil Collection, New Mexico State Records Center and Archives, Santa Fe.

9. My personal observations and discussions with my father, Melecio Vigil. My father was a resident of Pecos, and he frequently used the same terminology and participated in the common agricultural practices involving regadillos and rastrojos.

10. Ibid.

11. Ibid.

12. Ibid.

13. B. A. Reuter, "Flour Mill Erected by Gov. Vigil and Other Mills of Pecos District," Works Progress Administration Writers Project, 28 July 1939 (an interview of José A. Vigil, my grandfather, a grandson of Donaciano Vigil and in 1939 the operator of the mill).

14. Ibid., 2.

15. Ibid.

16. Ibid., 4.

17. Ibid., 4–8.

18. Ibid., 8.

19. Ibid.

20. José Asisclo Vigil, 17 February 1934, personal logbook, Pecos, NM, in possession of author.

21. Ibid.

22. Juan Valencia et al. to Donaciano Vigil, warranty deed, dated 28 January 1857, recorded 20 July 1887, Deed Book 33:35, San Miguel County Clerk's Office.

23. Pablo Moya to Donaciano Vigil, warranty deed, dated 8 September 1864, recorded 5 August 1874, Deed Book 8:182, San Miguel County Clerk's Office.

24. Vicente Quintana y Velarde and Marina Ortega (his wife) to Antonio Vigil, warranty deed, dated 1 April 1870, recorded 20 July 1887, Deed Book 33:38, San Miguel County Clerk's Office.

25. Territorial Censuses of 1860, 1870, 1880, 1890, and 1900 for Pecos, San Miguel County.

26. Estate of Desiderio Vigil to Sociedad de Nuestro Padre Jesús Nazareño, warranty deed, dated 24 February 1934, Deed Book 145:595, San Miguel County Clerk.

27. José A. Vigil to Pecos Board of Education, warranty deed, dated 16 April 1914, Deed Book 128:168–69, San Miguel City Clerk.

28. Crocchiola, *Giant in Lilliput*, 188.

29. Ibid., 189.

30. Ibid.

31. Ibid.

32. Hall, "Giant before the Surveyor General," 65.

33. Hall, *Four Leagues of Pecos*, 148.

34. Crocchiola, *Giant in Lilliput*, 202.
35. Ibid., 201.
36. Ibid., 202.
37. Ibid., 202–3.
38. Ibid., 203.
39. Twitchell, *History of the Military Occupation*, 226.

BIBLIOGRAPHY

BOOKS

Alamán, Lucas. *Historia de Mexico (1848–52)*. Vol. 5. Mexico: N.p., 1940.

Almond, Gabriel, and Sidney Verba. *The Civic Culture: Political Attitudes and Democracy in Five Nations*. New York: Sage, 1963.

Alonzo Cabeza, María Dolores. *Páginas de la Historia de Siero*. Oviedo, Spain: Foncalada, 1992.

Aviles, Tirso de. *Armas y Linaje de Asturias y Antiguedades del Principado*. Edited by José M. Gómez-Tabariera. Oviedo, Spain: Gea, 1991.

Bancroft, Hubert Howe. *History of Arizona and New Mexico, 1530–1888*, vol. 17 of *The Works of Hubert Howe Bancroft*. San Francisco, CA: History Company, 1889.

Barreiro, Antonio. *Ojeada sobre Nuevo Mexico*. Edited by Lansing Bloom. 1832; rpt., Santa Fe, NM: El Palacio Press, 1927.

Bauer, Jack. *Zachary Taylor: Soldier, Planter, Statesman of the Old Southwest*. Baton Rouge: Louisiana State University Press, 1993.

Beck, Warren A., and Ynez D. Haase. *Historical Atlas of New Mexico*. Norman: University of Oklahoma Press, 1969.

Bloom, Lansing, and Thomas C. Donnelly. *New Mexico History and Civics*. Albuquerque: University of New Mexico Press, 1933.

Bolton, Herbert E. *Coronado: Knight of the Pueblos and Plains*. Albuquerque: University of New Mexico Press, 1949.

Brayer, Herbert. *Pueblo Indian Land Grants of the Rio Abajo*. New York: Arno, 1979.

Brooks, James F. *Captives and Cousins: Slavery, Kinship, and Community in the Southwest Borderlands*. Chapel Hill: University of North Carolina Press, 2002.

Cañellas Secades, F. *El Libro de Oviedo: Guia de la Ciudad y Su Consejo*. Oviedo, Spain, 1887.

Chávez, Fray Angélico. *But Time and Chance: The Story of Padre Martínez of Taos, 1793–1867*. Santa Fe, NM: Sunstone, 1984.

———. *Origins of New Mexico Families: A Genealogy of the Spanish Colonial Period*. Santa Fe: Museum of New Mexico Press, 1992.

Christensen, Carol, and Thomas Christensen. *The U.S.-Mexican War, 1846–48*. San Francisco, CA: Bay Books, 1998.

Coan, Charles. *A History of New Mexico*. New York: American Historical Society, 1925.

Colligan, John B. *The Juan Paez Hurtado Expedition of 1695: Fraud in Recruiting Colonists for New Mexico*. Albuquerque: University of New Mexico Press, 1995.

Cooke, Philip St. George. *The Conquest of New Mexico and California in 1846–48*. Albuquerque, NM: Horn and Wallace, 1964.

———. *Scenes and Adventures in the Army; or, Romance of Military Life*. Philadelphia, PA: Lindsey and Blakiston, 1859.

Crocchiola, Stanley. *Giant in Lilliput: The Story of Donaciano Vigil*. Pampa, TX: Pampa Print Shop, 1963.

Cuesta, Gáspar Fernandez. *El Libro de Siero*. Oviedo, Spain: Patronato de Cultura de Siero, 2002.

Díaz Álvarez, Juan. *Ascenso de una Casa Asturiana: Los Vigil de Quiñones, Marqueses de Santa Cruz de Marcenado*. Oviedo, Spain: Real Instituto de Estudios Asturianos, 2006.

Dorgan Meketa, Jacqueline. *Legacy of Honor: The Life of Rafaél Chacon, a Nineteenth-Century New Mexican*. Las Cruces, NM: Yucca Tree Press, 2000.

Duff Gordon, Lady Lucie. *The Story of Assisi*. London: J. M. Dent, 1900.

Ebright, Malcolm, Rick Hendricks, and Richard Hughes. *Four Square Leagues: Pueblo Indian Land in New Mexico*. Albuquerque: University of New Mexico Press, 2014.

Esparza, José Javier. *La Gran Aventura del Reino de Asturias: Asi Empezo la Reconquista*. Madrid, Spain: La Estera de Los Libros, 2009.

Faya Díaz, María Angeles. *La Nobleza en la Asturias del Antiguo Regimen*. Oviedo, Spain: KRK Ediciones, 2004.

Fergusson, Erna. *New Mexico: A Pageant of Three Peoples*. New York: Knopf, 1951.

Fernandez, Luis Suarez. *Los Reyes Católicos: La Conquista del Trono: Trastamara y Los Reyes Católicos*. Madrid, Spain: Gredos, 1989.

Fowler, Will. *Santa Anna of Mexico*. Lincoln: University of Nebraska Press, 2007.

Frantz, Joe B. *Texas: A Bicentennial History*. New York: Norton, 1976.

García, María del Carmen Mena. *Sevilla y las Flotas de Indias: La Gran Armada de Castilla del Oro, 1513–1514*. Seville, Spain: Universidad de Sevilla, 1998.

Gómez, Laura. *Manifest Destinies: The Making of the Mexican-American Race*. 2nd ed. New York: New York University Press, 1968.

Gonzales, Phillip B. *Política: Nuevomexicanos and American Political Incorporation, 1821–1910*. Lincoln: University of Nebraska Press, 2016.

Grant, Ulysses S. *Personal Memoirs of U. S. Grant*. New York: Charles L. Webster, 1885–1886.

Gray, Thomas. *The Poetry of Thomas Gray: Poetry Is Thoughts That Breathe and Words That Burn*. N.p.: Portable Poetry, 2014.

———. *Selected Poems*. Oxford: Carcanet Press, 1981.

Gregg, Andrew K. *New Mexico in the Nineteenth Century: A Pictorial History*. Albuquerque: University of New Mexico Press, 1968.

Gregg, Josiah. *Commerce of the Prairies*. New York: Henry G. Langley, 1844.

Gustafson, Sarah. *Pecos National Historical Park*. Tucson, AZ: Southwest Parks and Monuments Association, 1997.

Hall, G. Emlen. *Four Leagues of Pecos: A Legal History of the Pecos Grant, 1800–1933*. Albuquerque: University of New Mexico Press, 1984.

———. "Giant before the Surveyor General: The Land Career of Donaciano Vigil." In *Spanish and Mexican Land Grants in New Mexico and Colorado*, ed. John R. Van Ness and Christine Van Ness. Manhattan, KS: Sunflower University Press, 1980, 64–73.

Herrera, Carlos R. *Juan Bautista de Anza: The King's Governor in New Mexico.* Norman: University of Oklahoma Press, 2015.
Holmes, Jack E. *Politics in New Mexico.* Albuquerque: University of New Mexico Press, 1967.
Huddle, F. P. *Admission of the New States: Editorial Research Reports.* Washington, DC: CQ Press, 2017.
Johnston, Abraham, Marcellus B. Edwards, and Philip G. Ferguson. *Marching with the Army of the West.* Edited by Ralph P. Bieber. Glendale, CA: Arthur H. Clark, 1936.
Jovellanos, G. M. *Cartas del Viaje de Asturias.* Edited by J. M. Caso. Salinas: KRK Ediciones, 1981.
Kendall, George W. *Narrative of the Texan–Santa Fe Expedition.* New York, 1844.
Kessell, John. *Kiva, Cross, and Crown: The Pecos Indians and New Mexico, 1540–1840.* Albuquerque: University of New Mexico Press, 1987.
———. *Pueblos, Spaniards, and the Kingdom of New Mexico.* Norman: University of Oklahoma Press, 2008.
Krauze, Enrique. *Mexico: A Biography of Power.* New York: HarperCollins, 1997.
Lamar, Howard Roberts. *The Far Southwest: A Territorial History.* Albuquerque: University of New Mexico Press, 2000.
Larson, Robert. *New Mexico's Quest for Statehood, 1846–1912.* Albuquerque: University of New Mexico Press, 1968.
Launius, Roger P. *Alexander William Doniphan: Portrait of a Missouri Moderate.* Columbia: University of Missouri Press, 1997.
Lecompte, Janet. *Rebellion in Rio Arriba.* Albuquerque: University of New Mexico Press, 1986.
Lieutenant Emory Reports: A Reprint of Lieutenant W. H. Emory's Notes of a Military Reconnaissance. Albuquerque: University of New Mexico Press, 1958.
Loomis, Sylvia Glidden. *Old Santa Fe Today.* Santa Fe, NM: Historic Santa Fe Foundation and the School of American Research, 1966.
Lummis, Charles. *The Land of Poco Tiempo.* Albuquerque: University of New Mexico Press, 1973.
Malthus, William S. *The Rise and Fall of the Spanish Empire.* New York: Palgrave Macmillan, 2009.
Martínez, María C. *Some Descendants of Domingo Montes Vigil.* San Pablo, CO: N.p., 1999.
McCormac, Eugene Irving. *James K. Polk: A Political Biography.* Berkeley: University of California Press, 1922.
McNitt, Frank. *Navajo Wars: Military Campaigns, Slave Raids, and Reprisals.* Albuquerque: University of New Mexico Press, 1990.
Meyer, Michael, and William Sherman. *The Course of Mexican History.* New York: Oxford University Press, 1983.
Morlino, Leonardo, Dirk Berg-Schlosser, and Bertrand Badie. *Political Science: A Global Perspective.* London: Sage, 2017.
Needham, Katie. *Acoma's Lincoln Cane.* Washington, DC: Lincoln Cottage, 2009.

Perrigo, Lynn I. *The American Southwest: Its People and Cultures.* Chicago, IL: Holt, Rinehart, and Winston, 1971.

———. *Gateway to Glorieta: A History of Las Vegas, New Mexico.* Santa Fe, NM: Sunstone, 2010.

Poldervaart, Arie W. *Black Robed Justice.* Santa Fe, NM: Santa Fe Historical Society Publications in History, 1948.

Read, Benjamin. *Illustrated History of New Mexico.* Santa Fe: New Mexican Printing Press, 1912.

Reséndez, Andrés. *Changing National Identities at the Frontier, 1800–1850.* Cambridge: Cambridge University Press, 2005.

Rivero, Margarita Cuartas. *Oviedo y el Principado de Asturias A Fines de la Edad Media.* Oviedo, Spain: Instituto de Estudios Asturiaros, 1983.

Rives, George Lockhart. *The United States and Mexico.* New York: Scribner's Sons, 1918.

Rodriguez, Antonio Acosta, Adolfo Gonzales Rodriguez, and Enriqueta Vila Villar. *La Casa de Contratación y la Navegación entre Espana y las Indias.* Seville, Spain: Universidad de Sevilla, 2003.

Ruxton, George. *Adventures in Mexico and the Rocky Mountains.* London: John Murray, 1847.

Singletary, Otis. *The Mexican War.* Chicago, IL: University of Chicago Press, 1960.

Smith, Chuck. *The New Mexico State Constitution: A Reference Guide* Westport, CT: Greenwood, 1996.

Smith, Elbert B. *President Zachary Taylor: The Hero President.* New York: Nova Science, 2011.

Stegmaier, Mark J. *Texas, New Mexico and the Compromise of 1850: Boundary Dispute and Sectional Crisis.* Kent, OH: Kent State University Press, 1996.

Stevens Fithian, Donald. *Origins of Instability in Early Republican Mexico.* Durham, NC: Duke University Press, 1991.

Sze, Corinne P. *Within Adobe Walls: A Santa Fe Journal.* Santa Fe, NM: Historic Santa Fe Foundation, 2001.

Tate, Bill. *Guadalupe Hidalgo Treaty of Peace, 1848, and the Gadsden Treaty with Mexico, 1853.* Truchas, NM: Tate Gallery, 1967.

Twitchell, Ralph Emerson. *The History of the Military Occupation of New Mexico by the Government of the United States.* Denver, CO: Smith-Brooks, 1909.

———. *The Leading Facts of New Mexico History.* Vol. 2. Cedar Rapids, IA: Torch Press, 1912.

———. *The Spanish Archives of New Mexico.* 1914. Rpt., Santa Fe, NM: Sunstone, 2008.

Tyler, Daniel. *Sources for New Mexican History, 1821–1848.* Santa Fe: Museum of New Mexico Press, 1984.

Van Ness, John R., and Christine Van Ness, eds. *Spanish and Mexican Land Grants in New Mexico and Colorado.* Manhattan, KS: Sunflower University Press, 1980.

Vigil, Maurilio. *The Hispanics of New Mexico: Essays on History and Culture.* Bristol, IN: Wyndham Hall, 1985.

Vigil, Philip Arnold. *Early Roads to the Sangre de Cristo Mountains: A Historical Journey of the Vigil Family from Spain to the American Southwest*. Cheyenne, WY: Las Placitas, 2010.

Webb, James Josiah. *Adventures in the Santa Fe Trade, 1844–1847*. Edited by Ralph P. Bieber. Lincoln: University of Nebraska Press, 1995.

Webb, Walter Prescott, ed. *The Handbook of Texas*. 2 vols. Austin: Texas State Historical Association, 1952.

Weber, David, ed. and trans. *Arms, Indians, and the Mismanagement of New Mexico by Donaciano Vigil, 1846*. El Paso: Texas Western Press, 1986.

———. *The Mexican Frontier, 1821–1846: The American Southwest under Mexico*. Albuquerque: University of New Mexico Press, 1982.

———. *Myth and History of the Hispanic Southwest*. Albuquerque: University of New Mexico Press, 1987.

Westphall, Victor. *Mercedes Reales: Hispanic Land Grants of the Upper Rio Grande Region*. Albuquerque: University of New Mexico Press, 1983.

———. *The Public Domain in New Mexico, 1854–1891*. Albuquerque: University of New Mexico Press, 1965.

ALL OTHER SOURCES

Allison, W. H. H. "Santa Fe in 1846." *Old Santa Fe: A Magazine of History, Archaeology, Genealogy and Biography* 2, no. 4 (April 1915): 392–96.

Ball, Durwood. "Stephen W. Kearny." In *Soldiers West: Biographies from the Military Frontier*, ed. Paul Andrew Hutton and Durwood Ball. Norman: University of Oklahoma Press, 2009.

Bloom, Lansing. "Barreiro's Ojeada sobre Nuevo Méjico." *New Mexico Historical Review* 3, no. 1 (April 1928): 73–96.

———. "Barreiro's Ojeada sobre Nuevo Méjico." *New Mexico Historical Review* 3, no. 2 (July 1928): 145–78.

———. "Beginnings of Representative Government in New Mexico." *El Palacio* 12, no. 6 (16 March 1922): 74–78.

———. "The Closing Months of Mexican Administration." *Old Santa Fe: A Magazine of History, Archaeology, Genealogy and Biography* 2, no. 4 (April 1915): 351–65.

———. "Constitutional Government Reestablished." *Old Santa Fe: A Magazine of History, Archaeology, Genealogy and Biography* 2, no. 2 (October 1914): 157–69.

———. "A Glimpse of New Mexico in 1820." *New Mexico Historical Review* 3, no. 4 (April 1928): 145–78.

———. "New Mexico as a Department, 1837–1846." *Old Santa Fe: A Magazine of History, Archaeology, Genealogy and Biography* 2, no. 3 (January 1915): 221–77.

———. "The People of New Mexico." *Old Santa Fe: A Magazine of History, Archaeology, Genealogy and Biography* 1, no. 1 (July 1913): 23–35.

———. "Six Months under the Senior Deputy." *Old Santa Fe: A Magazine of History, Archaeology, Genealogy and Biography* 2, no. 3 (January 1915): 235-87.

———. "The Texan Crisis in the United States and in Mexico." *Old Santa Fe: A Magazine of History, Archaeology, Genealogy and Biography* 2, no. 3 (January 1915): 263–77.

———. "A Third and Last Chance for Manuel Armijo." *Old Santa Fe: A Magazine of History, Archaeology, Genealogy and Biography* 2, no. 3 (January 1915): 249–62.

Bloom, Lansing, and Thomas C. Donnelly. "The Mexican Interlude." In *New Mexico History and Civics*, 187–88. Albuquerque: University of New Mexico Press, 1933.

Bowden, J. J. "Private Land Claims in the Southwest." Master's of law thesis, Southern Methodist University, 1969.

Cavendish, Richard. "The Casa de Contratación." *History Today* 53, no. 1 (January 2015): 23-38.

Chapman, Charles C. "New Mexico Generations: Genealogies of the Candido Barela, Vigil, Jaramillo, and Related Families." Unpublished paper, 1994, in New Mexico State Library, Santa Fe.

Cutter, Charles. "The 'Spurious' Seventeenth Century Pueblo Grants of New Mexico: A Closer Look." N.d. Unpublished manuscript in possession of Sandra K. Mathews-Lamb.

"Early Printing in New Mexico." *New Mexico Historical Review* 4, no. 4 (October 1929): 389–92.

Faya Díaz, María Angeles. "Gobierno Municipal y Venta de Oficios en la Asturias de los Siglos XVI y XVII." *Hispania* 63, no. 213 (2003): 75–136.

———. "Noblesa y Mundo Rural del Oriente de Asturias en la Edad Moderna." In *El Mundo Rural en la Espana Moderna*, ed. Francisco José Aranda Pérez. Cuenca, Spain: Ediciones de la Universidad de Castilla La Mancha, 2004, 2:453–65.

Flint, Richard. "Review of *Four Square Leagues: Pueblo Indian Land in New Mexico*." *Southwestern Historical Quarterly* 118, no. 4 (April 2015): 429–30.

Francis, Helen M. "Donaciano Vigil: His Life and Times." Unpublished paper presented to Nanette M. Ashby, New Mexico Western College, Silver City, NM, 1962.

Genealogical Society of Hispanic America. *Nuestra Raices* 14, no. 3 (Fall 2002).

Hendricks, Rick, and John R. Colligan. "Beyond Origins of New Mexico Families." *Herencia* 4, no. 2 (April 1996): 1–6.

Horsman, Reginald. "The Northwest Ordinance and the Shaping of an Expanding Republic." *Wisconsin Magazine of History* 73, no. 1 (Fall 1989): 21–32.

Jenkins, Myra Ellen. "The Donaciano Vigil House." *Bulletin of the Historic Santa Fe Foundation* 12, no. 3 (December 1980): 1–9.

Kraemer, Paul M. "Donaciano Vigil: The Gifted Giant—but Was He a Traitor?" In *Sunshine and Shadows in New Mexico's Past*, ed. Richard Melzer. Los Ranchos, NM: Rio Grande Books, 2011, 5–28.

Loomis, Morton Ganaway. "New Mexico and the Sectional Controversy, 1846–1861." *New Mexico Historical Review* 18, no. 3 (July 1943): 205–15.

Martínez, Robert D. "Notes on the Montes Vigil Family of Zacatecas." *Herencia* 12, no. 4 (October 2004): 43–47.

Mathews-Lamb, Sandra K. "Designing and Mischievous Individuals: The Cruzate Grants and the Office of the Surveyor General." *New Mexico Historical Review* 71, no. 4 (October 1996): 341–59.

———. "The Nineteenth-Century Cruzate Grants: Pueblos, Peddlers and the Great Confidence Scam?" PhD diss., University of New Mexico, 1998.

McClure, Charles Robert. "Mexican New Mexico: 1837–1846." Master's thesis, University of Oklahoma, 1971.

Miller, LaDeane. "Descendants of Lucas and Ysabel de Vigil." April 2002. lmiller@cox.net.

Minge, Ward Allen. "Frontier Problems in New Mexico Preceding the Mexican War, 1840–1846." PhD diss., University of New Mexico, 1984.

Oczon, Annabelle. "Bilingual and Spanish Language Newspapers in Territorial New Mexico." *New Mexico Historical Review* 54, no. 1 (January 1979): 45–52.

O'Hara, John F. "Juan Rodriguez de Fonseca: First President of the Indies, 1493–1523." *Catholic Historical Review* 3, no. 2 (July 1971): 131–50.

Palmer, Greg Merrill. "She Was Our Mother: Manifest Destiny and Misconceptions in New Mexico, 1845–48." Master's thesis, University of Utah, Logan, 2014.

Pavone, Tommaso. "Political Culture and Democratic Homeostasis: A Critical Review of Gabriel Almond and Sidney Verba's *The Civic Culture*." Princeton Scholar Paper, 7 April 2014, Princeton University. Unpublished paper in possession of author.

Pino, Pedro Bautista. *The Exposición of Don Bautista Pino, 1812* (1812). In *Three New Mexico Chronicles*, ed. and trans. H. Bailey Carroll and J. Villasana Haggard. Albuquerque, NM: Quivira Society, 1942.

Ritch, William B. "Governor Donaciano Vigil: Biographical Sketch." *Santa Fe Weekly New Mexican*, 28 August 1877.

Salazar, J. Richard. "The Military Career of Donaciano Vigil." Guadalupita, NM: Center for Land Grant Studies, 1974.

"Society Minutes, 1859–1863: Applications for Membership [New Mexico Historical Society] from the Following Persons, viz, Donaciano Vigil . . ." *New Mexico Historical Review* 18, no. 3 (July 1943): 286.

Soto, Miguel. "The Monarchist Conspiracy and the Mexican War." In *Essays on the Mexican War*, ed. Wayne Cutter. College Station: Texas A&M Press, 1986, 66–84.

Strout, Clevy L. "The Resettlement of Santa Fe, 1695: The Newly Found Muster Roll of 1695." *New Mexico Historical Review* 53, no. 3 (July 1978): 263–71.

Torrez, Robert J. "Donaciano Vigil: Traitor or Hero?," *Round the Roundhouse* (Newsletter of New Mexico State Employees Association) 19, no. 3 (2007).

———. "Governor Armijo's Medal of Honor." *Round the Roundhouse* (Newsletter of New Mexico State Employees Association) 13, no. 10 (2001): 6.

———. "New Mexico's Navajo Wars." In *Sunshine and Shadows in New Mexico's Past*, vol. 18, ed. Richard Melzer. Los Ranchos, NM: Rio Grande Books, 2010.

———. "The Presidio of Santa Fe." In *Sunshine and Shadows in New Mexico's Past*, vol. 18, ed. Richard Melzer. Los Ranchos, NM: Rio Grande Books, 2010.

Tyler, Daniel. "New Mexico in the 1820s: The First Administration of Manuel Armijo." PhD diss., University of New Mexico, 1970.

US General Accounting Office. "Report to Congressional Registers: Treaty of Guadalupe Hidalgo: Definition and List of Community Land Grants in New Mexico." Washington, DC: General Accounting Office, September 2001.

Vigil, Donaciano. "La Convencion." *Republicano*, 29 January 1848.

Vigil, Maurilio. "Early Spanish Wills: An Art unto Themselves." *Herencia* 31 (Fall 2001): 24.

———. "New Mexico Sold for $2,000." *Santa Fe Reporter*, July 1987.

Vigil, Michael. "Donde Esta la Casa de Vigil." Montville, NJ: Vigil Genealogy Club, 1997.

———. "Vigil: The Word and the Name, AD 100 to Present." Montville, NJ: Vigil Genealogy Club, 1998.

Want, Marguerite Taylor. "The Crumbling Adobes of Chamberino." *New Mexico Historical Review* 39, no. 3 (July 1964): 286–87.

Wroth, William A. "1837 Rebellion in Rio Arriba." Office of the New Mexico State Historian. Newmexicohistory.org.

Yohalem, Jeffrey. "New Mexico: The Cinderella of American Statehood." Yale University, 18 March 2005. Unpublished paper in possession of author.

INDEX

Page numbers in *italic* text indicate illustrations.

Abreu, Ramón, 61, 89–91
acclaim, of Donaciano, 249–51
acequias, 139
Acoma Pueblo, 220
Acoma Pueblo v Victor de la O, 222, 229
Adelo family, 241
adobe houses, in Santa Fe, 38
affidavit of 1856, 209–15, *211*; Pelham on, 214; Twitchell on, 214
Águila Negra (Navajo chief), 172–73
Aguilar, Rafaél, 186, 187
Alamán, Lucas, 84
Alameda grant, 29–30
Alarid, José, 54
Alarid, Matias, 198
Albuquerque, 41–42; population of, 39
alférez, 34–35
Alfonso X (King of Spain), 11
Allen, William S., 155
almude, 49
Álvarez, Manuel, 148, 150–51, 165
American Party, 165
Anasazi, 181
Angney, William, 126, *127*
annexation convention of 1848, 143–44; Martínez, A. J., in, 146–47; Vigil, Donaciano, in, 146–47
Antoine Leroux grant, 35
Anza, Juan Bautista de, 35
Apache Canyon, 106; Armijo, M., at, 111–12; confrontation at, 110–11; Kearny at, 110–11; Vigil, Donaciano, at, 111–12
Apaches, 56, 196–97

Aragon, 8, 12
arbolera, 37, 240
Archivo General de Indias, xiv, 14
Archuleta, Diego, 105, 123, 130
Arguelles, Catalina de, 18
Arista, Mariano, 53, 66
Armendariz, Manuel, 157
Armenta, José Manuel, 187
Armijo, José, 54
Armijo, Manuel, 47, 53, 64, 65, 68, 71–73, 75, 85, 88, 90, 99, 103, 177, 180, 228; at Apache Canyon, 111–12; Magoffin and Cooke negotiations with, 105; Mariano paper used by, 219; as New Mexico governor, 86, 92; Twitchell on, 112; on US government, 107–8; Vigil, Donaciano, and, 112–13, 139–40; vilification of, 112
Arms, Indians, and the Mismanagement of New Mexico (Weber), 4, 94
"Arms, Indians, and Mismanagement" speech, 95, 142, 160
Army of the West, 104, 106–16, 119; reactions to, 122–31; on Santa Fe Trail, 103–5
Ascenso de una Casa Asturiana (Díaz Álvarez), 12–13
asesor, 41
Asturias, 12; customs of, 11
audiencia, 25–26, 44, 181
Aviluead, Vicente, 230
Axtell, Samuel B, 250
ayuntamiento, 81

Baca, Bartolomé, 48, 50, 183–84
Baca, Jesús María, 89, 244
Baca, Manuel, 192, 197, 198
Baca, Tomás C. de, 109
Baird, Spruce, 230
Baker, Grafton, 171
Bancroft, Hubert Howe, 217
Barcelo, Tules, 123
Barela, Elauterio, 217
Barreiro, Antonio, 41–43, 89–90, 91
Bases Orgánicas, 84, 86
Battle of Buena Vista, Santa Anna at, 117
Battle of La Cuesta, 128
Battle of Palo Alto, 53
Battle of Pojoaque, 66–67
Battle of Taos, 124–28
Bautista de Anza, Juan, 35–36
Bay of Biscay, 11
Beaubien, Charles, 119, 148
Beaubien, Narciso, 125
Beck, Preston, 190, 195, 197, 205, 213, 237; as land speculator, 238; Pecos Pueblo lands of, 192–93
Beckell, William, 162
Bell, Peter H., 152; Taylor and, 153
Benavidez, Celso, 200
Benavidez, José Felix, 167
Benavidez, Luis, 185
Benavidez, Rafaél, 183–84, 200, 273n18
Benedict, Kirby, 220, 230
Bent, Charles, 4, 105, 119, 120, 124, 140, 192; assassination of, 125, 130; as New Mexico governor, 120
Bent, María Ygnacia, 125
Bent, William, 105, 120, 192
Benton, Thomas Hart, 133, 147
Bent's Fort, 105
Bergman, Signe, 251, 251
Biblioteca Benjamin Franklin, 95
Bill of Rights, 1
birth, of Donaciano Vigil, 2–3
Blair, Francis P., 119, 130

Bloom, Lansing, 41; on government of Mexico, 76–77; on New Mexico, 77, 107–8
Blummer, Charles, 119
Bocanegra, José María, 79
Boudreau, Helene, xv
Bravo, Nicolás, 84
Brenham, Richard, 71
Brent, Robert, 156
Brooks, James, 56
Buchanan, James, 133, 142
Burgwin, John, 125, 127
bust, of Donaciano Vigil, 251
Bustamante, Anastasio, 69

Caballero, Esquipula, 60–61, 68
Caballero, José, 50, 64
cabo, 50, 54
caciques, 210
Cádiz, 43–44
Calhoun, James S., 147, 152; death of, 171–72; as New Mexico Territorial governor, 155–56
California, 107, 116; statehood of, 153–54
Calvo, José, 66
Canalizo, Valentín, 84, 87
Cañoncito, 106, 112
Cañon de Pecos, 185, 237
cantón, 61–65
Capote Ute, 172
Carter, George C., 173
Casa de Contratación, 14–17, 254n23
Castile, 8, 12
Castillo, Antonia de, 33
Catholicism, 44, 163
Catron, Thomas B., 192
caudillo, 25, 117
Cayetano (Navajo chief), 173
cédula real, 14, 16, 18–19
CEMAPA, 143–44
Chapel of Our Lady of Guadalupe, 37–38
Chapman, Charles C., 33
Charlemagne, xv

Chávez, Dennis, 168, 170
Chavez, José Francisco, 170
Chávez, Manuel, 109, 126
Chávez, Mariano, 85–86, 87, 93
Chávez y Castillo, José, 88, 91–92
Chávez y Castillo, Tomás, 97
Chihuahua, 44, 53, 75, 157
childhood, of Donaciano Vigil, 2–3, 39–45
Cicuye, 181
ciénega, 190–91
citizenship: Mexican, 156–57, 159, 163, 166; nationalism and, 162–63; US, 138, 157, 162, 166
Civil War, 244–45
Clark, John A., 219
Clay, Henry, 154, 159
Clayton, John M., 147
Coahuila, 116
Codallos y Rabal, Joaquín, 229
Collier, D. C., 179
Collier, John, 179
Colligan, John B., 25, 29
collusion, charges of, 231–35
colonization: of New Mexico, 7–8; of New World, 8–9; of US, 8–12
Columbus, Christopher, 8, 13
Comanches, 35–36, 43, 56, 135, 182
comandante, 48, 52, 56–59, 67, 75–76, 86–87, 94
Compromise of 1850, 155, 159, 176
Concha, Fernando de la, 49
Connelly, Henry, 105
Conrad, C. M., 152, 156
Constitution, US, 1, 80; Mexican Constitution of 1824 and, 164
Cooke, Philip St. George, 57; Armijo, M., negotiations with, 105
Cooke, William, 71
Coronado, Francisco Vázquez de, 181
cortes, 43–44, 80, 183
Cortés, Hernan, 14–15
Cortez, Manuel, 128

Cota, José, 187; on Pecos Pueblo land grants, 188–89
Cote, Pedro, 17
Council of Siero, 17
Crawford, George, 148
El Crepúsculo de la Libertad, 89, 91
criado, 16–17, 56
Crocchiola, Stanley, xiii, 33, 46, 150–51, 194, 205, 238, 246
Cruzate, Domingo Jironza Petriz de, 24–25, 182, 207–8, 223
Cruzate documents, 182, 227; Bancroft on, 217; Mariano paper, 218–20; in de la O conspiracy, 220–22, 230–31; Pelham on, 212–13; spurious, 217–18; Tipton on, 217; Twitchell on, 217–18
Cruzate land grants, 5, 205–6; affidavit and, 209–15; first references to, 208–9; Flint on, 234–35; land grant historians on, 223; Mathews-Lamb on, 207–9, 222; Vigil, Donaciano, mentioning, 208–9
cuaderno, 248–49
cuartel, 49–50
Cuerno Verde, 35
La Cuesta, 128
culture, New Mexican, 160–64, 166
Cunningham, Francis, 150
cura, 92
Cutter, Charles R., 223, 274n5

Dallam, Richard, 119
Davies, Edward T., 91, 143
death, of Donaciano Vigil, 249–51
defrauding, of Indigenous people, 139
Democratic Party, 174
departmental secretary, 180
deposants, 212
Díaz Álvarez, Juan, 12
Díaz Caballero, Nicolás, 20
Dios Maes, Juan de, 106
District of Columbia, 160
Dold, Andrés, 192

Donaciano Vigil Collection, 69
Donaciano Vigil House, 38, 52
Donaciano Vigil Papers, 265n39
Doniphan, Alexander W., 113, 141
Douglas, Stephen, 154, 159
dram shop, 191
Dryden, William G., 69
Durango, 26

Ebright, Malcolm, et. al., 223; on Mariano paper, 227–29; on de la O conspiracy, 229–31; on Vigil, Donaciano, 231–35
Edmondson, D. B., 125
education: Vigil, Donaciano, championing, 174–75; of Vigil, Donaciano, 44–45
Edwards, Marcellus Ball, 111
ejido, 239
Elkins, Stephen B., 192, 250
Ellison, Samuel, 217
Embudo, 127
Emory, William, 119
las eras, 240
escribiente, 56–57, 180
Escudo de Honor, 4, 74
españoles, 22
Esquibel, Cesario, 243
Esquibel, Juan José, 61, 65
Esteban, Juan, 221–22
Eugenio, Juan, 27
Exposición (Pino, P.), 43

Farfán, Fray Francisco, 25
Faya Díaz, María Angeles, 9–10, 12–13, 16, 17
feligresia, 12, 15, 19
Ferdinand II, 8
Fergusson, Erna, 170, 235
Fernández, Domingo, 137, 177, 179, 183, 196–97, 228; Hall, G. E., on, 197–98; Los Trigos land grant and, 197
fiesta de huevos pintos, 11
Fillmore, Millard, 154, 155, 171

First US Dragoon Regiment, 103
Flint, Richard, on Cruzate land grants, 234–35
flota, 16
Fort Marcy, 115, 119
Four Leagues of Pecos (Hall, G. E.), 178, 195, 214
Four Square Leagues (Ebright, Hendricks, and Hughes), 223, 227–28
Fowler, Will, 79, 117
Frantz, Joe, 69
Fray Angelico Chavez library, xiv

Gadsden Treaty, 159
Gallegos, José Manuel, 47, 101, 136, 144, 170
Gallegos, José María, 184
Gallegos, Maria Manuela, 47, 248
Gallinas River, 105
Gamboa, Ramón, 118
García, Jesús, 200
García, Manuel, 17
García, Vicente, 51
García Conde, Francisco, Vigil, Donaciano, on, 98–99
genealogy, 8
General Accounting Office, US, 196
General Land Office, 210, 224; Pelham reporting to, 226
genízaros, 56
Giant in Lilliput (Crocchiola), xiii, 33
Gibson, George R., 91, 143
Gijón, 11
Gila River, 142
Glorieta Pass, 245
Gómez, Laura, 169–70
Gómez Farías, Valentín, 78–79, 117
Gonzales, Diego, II, 256n29
Gonzales, José, 62, 67
Gonzales, Phillip B., 2, 236, 269n43; Donaciano fulfilling Kearny's declaration of New Mexico as American territory, 135–37; Donaciano's mighty liberalism,

135, 167; hombre de bien, 63; on New Mexico, 170; on nuevomexicano incorporation, 164; on Vigil, Donaciano, as collaborator for American incorporation, 134–36, 138, 166
Gonzales, Rafaél, 197, 247
Gonzales Bas, Juan, 30
Gonzales group, 198–99
Gorman, John, 193
governor, Donaciano Vigil as, 125–26, 129–30, 132; agenda of, 139; discomfort in role of and expressions of confidence in, 136; influence of, 143–44; leadership of, 136; on religion, 139; replacement of, 142–43; resignation attempt of, 133–34; self-doubt of, 140–41
Gray, Thomas, 93
Gregg, Josiah, 59, 90–91
Grenier, John, 238
Gross, Kelly and Company Mercantile and Lumber Store, 242–43
Guadalajara, 44
Guadalupe, 159
Guadalupe Hidalgo Treaty of Peace, 1848, and the Gadsden Treaty with New Mexico, 1853 (Tate), 1
El Gusano, 182, 199, 203–4, 273n22

Habsburg monarchs, 10
Hacienda de San Juan Bautista del Ojito del Rio Gallinas, 237–38
Hall, G. Emlen, 205; end of Pecos Pueblo, 178–94; on Fernández, 197–98; on interloper's encroachment on Pecos Pueblo lands, 178–79, 183–89; on Vigil, Donaciano, 180–81, 214, 218; on Vigil, Donaciano, depicted for focus on and creator of largest land grants, 180–81, 204; on Vigil, Donaciano, last will and wealth, 195, 203–5; on Vigil, Donaciano, and Los Trigos grant, 195–98; on Vigil, Donaciano, and surveyor general, 181, 204–5

Hall, William P., 119
Harrison Country Store, 241
Hendley, J. R., 125
Hendricks, Rick, et. al., 218, 223; on Mariano paper, 227–29; on de la O conspiracy, 229–31; on Vigil, Donaciano, 231–35; on Vigil, *herencia*, 2
Hernandez, María, 15
Hernandez, Tomás, 20
Herrera, José Joaquín de, 84; Slidell and, 116–17
Herrera Cantillana, María de, 20–21
Herrera de Cantillana, Catalina, xv, 19
hijo dalgo, 17
hijo natural, 20–21
Hinojos, Blas de, 58
Hispanic population, in New Mexico, 1–2, 168–69
Hispaniola, 16
historic trails, New Mexico, 28
History of Arizona and New Mexico (Bancroft), 217
Holmes, Jack, 168–69
hombre de bien, 63, 138
Houghton, Anne Carolyn, 202
Houghton, Joab, 119, 130, 147, 150, 165
House of Representatives, 147
Hovey, Oliver, 91, 143
Huamantla, 118
huerta, 37, 54
Hughes, Richard, et. al., 216, 223; on Mariano paper, 227–29; on de la O conspiracy, 229–31; on Vigil, Donaciano, 231–35

Iberian Peninsula, 9
identity: Mexican, 165–66; of New Mexico, 160–64, 166; of nuevomexicanos, 160–61, 270n49; Spanish, 165–66
immigration, from Spain, 9–11, 13

Indigenous people, 33; economy of, 56; land rights of, 183; Los Trigos land grant and, 196–97; in New Mexico, 39–40, 48, 56; Pecos Pueblo land grants and, 186, 188; status of, 183; Sumner on, 156; Vigil, Donaciano, negotiating with, 172–73; Vigil, Donaciano, on, 97; Westphall on, 232

Insurrection of 1837, 67–68

inválido, 8, 50, 54

irrigation ditches, 239–40

Isabella II, 8

Iturbide (Emperor), 80

Jaramillo, Pablo, 125

Jasco, Tomás, 54

Jasis, 173

jefe político, 48, 76, 81, 137

Jefferson, Thomas, 78, 105

Jemez Pueblo, 172, 190, 229–30

Jenkins, Myra Ellen, 207

Jiménez de Ancizo, María, xv, 21–24, 29–30; family of, 23, 27, 30–32

Jones, John G., 155

Jovellanos, Gáspar Melchor, 10

Juez, 66

Julian, George, 202

junta electoral, 82

junta popular, 63

Justiniani, Cayetano, 66

Kearny, Stephen Watts, 4, 103, 104, 123, 130; at Apache Canyon, 110–11; expedition postcard, 114; on New Mexican government, 119–20; in New Mexico, 106–16; in Santa Fe, 119

Kearny Code, 4, 104, 126, 169, 204; executive cabinet under, 120–22; implementation of, 132–41; introduction of, 119; Vigil, Donaciano, on, 121–22, 132–33, 135–37

Kearny Gap, 106

Kendall, George W., 72, 73

Kessell, John, 182, 275n15; on Pecos Pueblo land grants, 185, 187

Ladrón de Guevara, Pedro, 208

Laguna Colorada, 72

Lamar, Howard Roberts, 165

Lamar, Mirabeau B., 69, 73

Lamy, Jean-Baptiste, 171

land grants: General Accounting Office on, 196; laws for, 271n5; Los Trigos, 5, 180, 182–83, 195–96; Pelham approving, 212; Sandia Pueblo, 208, 213, 214, 221; Vigil, Donaciano, on, 180–81, 204–5; Weber on, 180–81. *See also* Cruzate land grant; Pecos Pueblo land grant

land rights, of Indigenous people, 183

Lane, William: as governor, 171; on Navajos, 173–74

language, nationalism and, 163

Larrazolo, Octaviano, 170

last will and testament, 195, 203–6; properties listed in, 203–4

Laws of the Indies, 181–82, 218

leadership, 167

The Leading Facts of New Mexican History (Twitchell), 6

Leal, J. W., 125

Lee, Louis, 125

legends, about Donaciano Vigil, 246–47

Leitensdorfer, Eugenio, 119

letrados, 68

Lewis, William G., 72, 74

Leyva, José Francisco, on statehood of New Mexico, 144

Library of Congress, xiii

Lincoln, Abraham, 246

La Literaria, 245

Livingston Code, 137

Llano Estacado, 71–72, 74

López, Ynes, 32, 256n28

Los Trigos land grant, 5, 182–83; Fernández and, 197; Gonzales group

and, 198–99; Indigenous people and, 196–97; Smith and, 195–96; Trujillo, G., and, 197–200; Vigil, Donaciano, and, 180, 195–99, 202, 204
Luján, Antonia Nicolasa, 32
Lummis, Charles, 232
Luna, Juana de, 36

Machebeaf, Joséph, 171
Magoffin, James, 103, 123; Armijo, M., negotiations with, 105
mancomún, 240
Manifest Destinies (Gómez), 169–70
manifest destiny, 161–62
Manrique, José, 43
Marcy, William, 132, 133, 142
Mariano paper, 232; Armijo, M., using, 219; Ebright, Hendricks, and Hughes on, 227–29; Mathews-Lamb on, 218–20
Market House of Seville, 14
marquesado, 9, 13
Márquez, Bartolomé, 195, 197, 199
Márquez, María Estela, 32
Martín, José Claudio, 172
Martín, José Leonicio, 172
Martin, Ramón, 171–72
Martín, Sebastian, 31
Martínez, Antonio José, 47, 91, 101, 144, 168–69; in annexation convention of 1848, 146
Martínez, Felix, 30
Martínez, Florencio, 243
Martínez, María, 21–22
Martínez, Mariano, 89–90, 92; as New Mexico governor, 86–88; Vigil, Donaciano, on, 98–99
Martínez, Román, 52
matanza, 11, 246
Mathews-Lamb, Sandra, 233, 274n5; on Cruzate land grants, 207–9, 222; on Mariano paper, 218–20; on de la O conspiracy, 220–22; on Vigil,

Donaciano, 208–9, 214–15, 228; on Vigil Index, 216
Mayers, A. G., 221
mayorazgos, 9, 10, 12–13, 253n4
McCall, George A., 148–49, 150, 152, 270n43
McClure, Charles Robert, 93
McLeod, Hugh, 71–72
Medina, María Teodora, 34
memorial, 251
memorialistas, 116
mercantile capitalism, 121
Mercedes Real (Westphall), 224
Meriweather, David, 174
Mescalero Apaches, 43
Messervy, William, 150
mestizos, 21–22
Mexican Constitution of 1824, 80, 137; US Constitution and, 164
Mexican Party, 165
Mexican War, 116–18
Mexico, 7; Bloom on government of, 76–77; centralization of power in, 77–81; citizenship, 156–57, 159, 163, 166; government of, 79–80; identity of, 165–66; independence of, 43, 113; land law, 177; New Mexico under control of, 80, 113, 166; politics of, 79; Polk on, 116–17; repatriation to, 159; US relations with, 116–17; Vigil, Donaciano, as traitor to, 121; Vigil, Donaciano, on, 100–101
Mexico City, 116
military service, 46–75, 237
Miller, LaDeane, 15
mills, 240–42
Minge, Ward Allen, 216
Miranda, Guadalupe, 42
Missouri Cavalry, 126
Missouri Compromise, 159
Missouri Volunteers, 126, 127, 141, 143
Mogollón, Juan Ignacio, 30
molino, 240–42
Montoya, Albino, 219

Montoya, Antonio Abad, 62, 65–66
Montoya, Joseph, 170
Montoya, Pablo, 64, 125, 130; Vigil, Donaciano, on, 128–29
morada, 38, 246
morcilla, 11
Moya, Pablo, 192, 244
mulatto, 21–22
Muñoz, Pedro, 66
Munroe, John, 115, 150

Naranjo, José, 30
Narbona, Francisco, 187
nationalism: citizenship and, 162–63; language and, 163
National Park Service, 179
Navajos, 43, 51, 56, 68, 113, 172, 182; conflict with, 55, 58–60; Donaciano, Vigil, on, 133; Lane on, 173–74; Vigil, Donaciano, negotiating with, 172–73
Navarre, 8
Navarro, José Antonio, 71
Neighbors, Robert S., 152, 153
Newby, Edward W. B., 142
New Mexico, 141; *alcaldías*, 82–83; American military occupation of, 103–6; annexation convention, 143–44; archives and governmental records of, 136–37; Armijo, M., as governor of, 86, 92; Bent, C., as governor of, 120; Bloom on, 77, 107–8; colonization of, 7–8; constitution of, 1–2; as *diputación territorial*, 83–84; Donaciano, V., as governor, 4–5; economy of, 42, 160–61, 162; education in, 42; executive Cabinet under Kearny Code, 120–22; Gonzales, P. B., on political culture of, 170; government of, 77; Hispanic population in, 1–2, 168–69; Hispano involvement in, xiii–xiv–; historic trails, 28; identity and culture of, 160–64, 166; Indigenous people in, 39–40, 48, 56; Kearny in, 106–16; Kearny on government of, 119–20; land speculation in, 192; legislative assembly of, 138–39; Leyva on, 144–45; Martínez, Mariano, as governor of, 86–88; Mexican control of, 80, 113, 166; military budget in, 50–51; military salaries in, 49–50; party factionalism in, 165; political culture of, 164–68; political scientist perspective on, 168–70; population of, 39, 41–42; postcard of anniversary of acquisition of, 114; *prefecturas*, 82–83; reactions to initial occupation of, 122–31; self-government of, 170; slavery and, 152, 159–60; under Spanish rule, 7, 39–41; state constitution, 150–51; statehood of, 144–45; suffrage in, 138; surveyor general of, 176–77; Taylor and statehood of, 147–54; Texas and, 68–75, 149, 152–53; United States and, 100, 121–22, 138; US annexation of, 115; US invasion of, 106–16; Vigil, Donaciano, as advocate for, 94–101; Vigil, Donaciano, on identity of, 165–66; Vigil family in, 31–34
New Mexico (Fergusson), 170, 235
New Mexico Assembly (*diputación*), 4, 50, 77, 116, 185, 187; first stage of, 82–84; as forum for dissent, 85–86; Vigil, Donaciano, in, 83, 236
New Mexico Constitution (1910), 169
New Mexico Highlands University, xiii, xiv
New Mexico Historical Review, 207
New Mexico militia, 3, 4, 29, 32–37, 47
New Mexico State Records Center and Archives, xiv, xvi, 219
New Mexico Supreme Court, 150, 155, 171, 220, 230
New Mexico Territory, 1–5, 13, 102–3, 115–16, 119, 122, 129, 137, 140, 143, 174, 176, 236; Calhoun as governor of, 155–56; formal creation of, 152, 155; government of, 159–60

New Spain, 7–11. 14–19, 21–25, 34–41, 49. See also Mexico
New World: colonization of, 7–9; Spain in, 7–10, 13–18, 22, 29
Nicolasa (slave), 20–21
Nieto, Antonio, 198
Niles' Register, 122
Nueva Galicia, 19–20, 25
Nueva Vizcaya, 25
nuevomexicanos: Gonzales, P. B., on incorporation of, 164; identity of, 121, 135, 160–61, 167, 236, 269n43, 270n49

obituary, of Donaciano Vigil, 250–51
de la O conspiracy: Cruzate documents in, 230–31; Ebright, Hendricks, and Hughes on, 229–31; Mathews-Lamb on, 220–22
Oczon, Annabelle M., 91
Ojeada sobre Nuevo Mexico (Barreiro), 41–42, 91
Ojeda, Bartolomé de, 208, 216, 229
Ojo Caliente, 35
Ojo de las Gallinas grant, 191–92
Olguin, Juliana, 200
Olmos, Jacinto de, 16, 17, 18, 254n23, 254n28
Oñate, Juan de, 24, 213
Order of the Crown of Charlemagne, xv
Organic Acts of Missouri, 137
oro comun, 26
Ortega, Blas, 192, 193
Ortega, Melquiades Antonio, 80
Ortíz, Josefa, 192
Ortíz, José Francisco, 184, 186
Ortíz, José Ignacio, 188
Ortíz, Juan Felipe, 123–24, 144, 174
Ortíz, Matias, 184, 186
Ortíz, Ramón, 157; on Vigil, Donaciano, 158–59
Ortíz, Teodocio, 241
Ortíz, Tomás, 89, 92, 108, 123–24, 140, 191
Otermín, Antonio de, 24

Otero, Antonio José, 119
Otero, Manuel, 165
Otero v. Gallegos, 158
la otra banda, 240

Padilla, Diego, 47, 184, 186, 190, 195, 197, 199; during Pecos Pueblo land grants, 188
Padilla, Luis de, 17
Paez Hurtado, Juan, 22–23, 25–26, 31, 46
Palace of the Governors, 42, 50, 60, 67, 82, 93, 107, 109, 114, 115, 155, 171; Vigil, Donaciano, bust, 251
Palmer, Greg, 160, 162–63, 164
Paredes, Mariano, 84
Parral, 26, 162
pasajeros a Indias, 14–15
Los Pastores, 25, 27, 245
patrón, 204, 246
Los Patrones (Vigil, M. E.), xiii
Pecos, 5; common land in, 239; innovations in, 240–41; molino in, 240–42; public roads in, 240; Vigil, Donaciano, in, 236–49; Vigil family in, 51, 171, 174, 177, 245
Pecos Canyon, 182
Pecos Pueblo land grant, 213; attacks on, 178–79; Beck and, 192–93; ciénega in, 190–91; Cota on, 188–89; Hall, G. E., on, 178–94; Indigenous people and, 186, 188; Kessell on, 185, 187; Padilla, D., during, 188; Pino, J. F., during, 187–89, 191–92; repartitions in, 184; resistance to, 186–87; review of, 184–85; sobrante lands, 183–85; Vigil, Donaciano, and, 186, 189–90, 193, 204–5, 216
Pedro Policarpio Montes Vigil (aka Pedro Montes Vigil de Santillana), 23, 27, 32, 34
Pelham, William, 176–77, 182, 205, 233; on affidavit of 1856, 214; competence of, 221, 224–27; on Cruzate documents, 212–13; General Land Office reports,

Pelham, William (*continued*)
226; land grants approved by, 212; on Pueblo land grants, 210, 216, 218, 226–27; Pueblos defended by, 226; Westphall on, 224–25, 231, 232, 233
Peña y Peña, Manuel de la, 118
peninsulares, 13, 21–22
Penitente Brothers, 246
peones, 39, 204, 246–47
Pérez, Albino, 47, 50, 59–63, 67, 76, 78, 81, 83; Vigil, Donaciano, on, 98–99, 122
Peru, 16–17, 19
Philip V (King), 29–30
Pierce, Franklin, 176, 224
Pile, William, 217
Pillans, Palmer, 148
Pino, Juan Estevan, 64, 179, 237, 244; death of, 191; during Pecos Pueblo land grants, 187–89, 191–92
Pino, Justo Pastor, 191
Pino, Manuel Doroteo, 191, 193, 195, 237
Pino, Miguel, 109, 123, 158
Pino, Nicolas, 109, 126
Pino, Pedro, 43–44, 179
piracy, 16
placita, 38, 240
Plan de Tomé, 63–64
Plan of Cuernavaca, 79
Plan of Iguala, 183
Pleasanton, Alfred M., 153
La Pola, 11–12
Politica (Gonzales, P. B.), 2, 162, 163, 164, 166, 167, 236, 269n43
"Political Acculturation of Hispanics in New Mexico," 168
political culture: defining, 269n40; of New Mexico, 164–68
Politics in New Mexico (Holmes), 168–69
Polk, James K., 102, 106, 115, 132; on Mexico, 115–17
postcard, New Mexico acquisition, 114
Price, Sterling, 4, 113, 119–20, 122, 123, 124, 126, 132, 139, 221; in Battle of Taos, 125–28; Donaciano, Vigil, and, 133–34; in Santa Fe, 119–20; in Taos, 127–28, 146
printing press, 90–91
pronunciamento, 85, 86, 156
property law, 166
Provincias Internas del Oriente, 80
public roads, 240
Pueblo land grants, xiv, 5, 182, 205, 207, 209, 216, 218, 225; Pelham on, 210, 226–27; Vigil, Donaciano, on, 210–11. *See also* land grants; Pecos Pueblo land grant
Pueblo Lands Board, 239
Pueblo Revolt, 24, 29, 207–8, 213
Pueblos, 33, 88, 211–13, 218, 232; Pelham defending, 224–27
El Puertecito, 106
Punto del Gusano, 200

querencia, 2
Quinn, James H., 150
Quintana, Mariano, 244
Quintana, Teodocio, 47, 199
Quintana, Vicente, 192, 193, 244
quinterna, 83

Rancho of Manuel D. Pino, 193
Rascón, Juan Rafaél, 42
rastrojo, 240
Raton Pass, 105
Read, Benjamin, 157
Real Alencaster, Joaquín del, 39–40
Recopilación de las Leyes de los Reinos de Indias, 181
regadillos, 37, 237, 239–40
regidor, 17
Register of Land Titles, 137, 205
reglamentos of 1729, 49
reglamentos of 1796, 49
religious matters, 139
remonta, 75
repartición, 184–85

República Mexicana del Norte, 116
El Republicano, 63, 143–44, 166
Republic of Texas, 69, 102
Reséndez, Andrés, 67–68
retirement, of Donaciano Vigil, 170, 174–75, 177, 205–6
Reuter, B. A., 240–42
los reyes católicos, 8, 12
Ribera, 72
ricos, 33, 39–40, 45, 47, 67, 68, 219, 237
Riley, Bennet, 57
Rio Abajo, 62, 63, 64, 83
Rio Arriba Rebellion, 3, 60–67, 78
Rio de la Vaca, 185
Rio Grande, 83, 92, 142, 152, 182, 225
Ritch, William, 111, 175; on Vigil, Donaciano, 123, 134, 146–47
Rivera, Miguel, 184, 239
Rodriguez de Fonseca, Juan, 13
Roibal, Miguel, 188
Rolenes, Tomás, 58, 259n47
Romero, Antonio, 31
Romero, Juan Antonio, 27
Romero, Martín, 31
Romero, Tomásito, 125
Rowland, John, 69, 260n81
Rubi, José Pedro, 39
Ruxton, George F., 141

Saint Anthony parish, 190
Salazar, Antonio de, 20
Salazar, Damasio, 73
Salazar, Pascuala, 32, 34
Sánchez, Manuela, 33
Sánchez, Ramón, 54, 230
San Cristóbal, 197, 226
Sandia, 64, 229–30
Sandia Pueblo grant, 208, 213, 214, 221, 229, 230
San Ignacio, 159
San Ildefonso, 211
San José del Bado, 182
San Martíno, 12

San Miguel County, 174–75, 194, 200, 202
San Miguel del Bado, 53, 58, 68–69, 71, 73, 74, 75, 106, 157, 182–83, 197, 199, 201, 237; land grant, 203
Santa Anna, Antonio López de, 4, 59, 61, 67, 74–75, 81; at Battle of Buena Vista, 117–18; birth of, 78; as military leader, 77–79; as president, 79–80, 84–88
Santa Clara, 211
Santa Cruz de la Cañada, 27, 30, 39, 41–42, 66, 124, 126
Santa Fe, 37, 41–42, 81, 107–8, 112; caravan arrival at, 162; in 1848, 141–45; Kearny in, 119; Palace of the Governors, 114, 115; population of, 39; soldiers in, 141–42; Sterling Price in, 119–20; uprising conspiracies in, 123–24; Vigil, F. M., in, 27–31
Santa Fe National Forest, 239
Santa Fe Pioneers, 69, 71, 72, 74
Santa Fe Plaza, 37, 49, 50, 115, 119, 124
Santa Fe Railroad, 203
Santa Fe Republican, 91, 152
Santa Fe Ring, 180, 190
Santa Fe River, 34, 37, 44
Santa Fe Trail, 41, 57, 78, 89, 156, 160, 162, 164, 237; Army of the West on, 42, 69, 103–5
Santa Fe Weekly New Mexican, 2, 250–51
Santa Rita del Cobre, 40
Santo Domingo, 61, 62, 216, 221, 229–30
Sarracino, Francisco, 61–62, 136, 219, 222, 228, 231
Second New Mexico Territorial Assembly, 174; Vigil, Donaciano, in, 191
self-government, 170
Sena, Antonio, 92, 109–10
Sena, Felipe, 62, 87, 92, 109–10
Sena, Francisco, 200
Senate Public Works Committee, 168
Sena y Romero, Miguel, 174, 200–201
Seventh Territorial Council, 174
Seville, 14, 16–17

Seymour, James, 179
"She Was Our Mother" (Palmer), 115, 160
Siero, 11–15, 18, 19
Siete Leyes, 79, 86
Silva, José, 53, 69
Singletary, Otis, 102
slavery, 21, 56, 85, 97, 246; New Mexico and, 146, 150, 152, 159–60; in new territories, 159–60; Taylor on, 148–49
Slidell, John, 107; Herrera, J., and, 116
Sloat, J. D, 102
Smith, Hugh N., 147, 149, 192; Los Trigos land grants and, 195–96; Vigil, Donaciano, and, 196, 237–38
sobrante lands, 183–85, 187
La Sociedad de Nuestro Padre Jesús Nazareño, 245–46
Spain: American colonies and, 7–12; colonial law, 181; fleets of, 16; migration from, 9–11, 13; New Mexico under rule of, 7, 39–41; in New World, 9–10; nobility of, 9; unification of, 8–9
Spanish and Mexican Archives, 215–17; assembly of, 217
Spanish Archives of New Mexico (Twitchell), 209, 217–18, 275n14
Spanish colonial architecture, 38
Spanish identity, 165–66
speeches, of Donaciano Vigil, 94–100; "Arms, Indians, and Mismanagement," 95, 142, 160
Speyer, Albert, 107
Springer, Frank, 192
squatters, 183–84, 197
Strout, Clevy L., 26
St. Vrain, Ceran, 120, 126, 127, 128, 132–33, 148, 192
Sumner, Edwin V., 155–56, 172, 173; on Indigenous people, 156
suplente, 75, 82, 83
"Supreme Government of the Territory" proclamation, 130
Tamouche, 172

Taos, 41, 64, 68, 74; Battle of, 124–28; insurrection, 124–25, 132–33, 167; population of, 39; Price in, 127–28
Taos Census, 36
Tapia, María, 32
Tate, Bill, 1
Taylor, Zachary, 107, 116–17; Bell and, 153; death of, 154; New Mexico statehood and, 147–54; as president, 148; on Texas, 149
temporales, 47, 237, 239–40, 243
teniente, 35
Teodoro de Croix, 35
Territorial Council, 151, 174, 194, 239
territorial secretary, 5, 111, 120, 130, 136–37, 145, 151, 155, 170–71, 177, 191
Tesuque, 211
Texan-Santa Fe expedition, 4, 69, 70, 73–74
Texas: annexation of, by US, 92; land claims of, 152–53, 159–60; New Mexico and, 68–75, 149, 152–53; Taylor on, 149. *See also* Republic of Texas
Texas land claim, 70
Texas State Historical Association, 72
Thomas, George, 71
tierra firme, 16
Tipton, William, 217, 228
Tornel, José María, 79
Torrez, Robert, 49, 51
Tosty Hosty, 173
Towas, 181, 190
Las Trampas, 127
Treaty of Guadalupe Hidalgo, 1, 118, 140, 162–63, 225; Article 8, 156, 166, 176; Article 9, 159; formal denouncement of, 136; ratification of, 142–45, 148, 149
"Triumph of Principles over Turpitude" proclamation, 129–30
Trujillo, Francisco, 195, 197, 199
Trujillo, Gregorio, 37, 249, 273n18; Los Trigos land grant and, 197–200; properties of, 199–200

Trujillo, Juana, 32
Trujillo, Juan Francisco, 37, 199
Trujillo, Lucia, 200
Trujillo, Mateo, 32
Tuley, Murray F., 150
Tunicha, 173
Twitchell, Ralph Emerson, 6, 45, 47–48, 55, 57, 73, 209, 275n14; on Armijo, M., 112; on Cruzate documents, 217–18; on Donaciano affidavit of 1856, 214; on Vigil, Donaciano, 130
Tyler, Daniel, 215, 233; on Vigil, Donaciano, 217; on Vigil Index, 235
Tyler, John, 102

Ulibarri, José, 200
Ulibarri, Juan María, 273n18
Ulibarri, Santiago, 198
United States (US): Armijo, M., on, 107–8; citizenship, 138, 157, 162, 166; Mexico relations with, 116–17; military occupation of New Mexico by, 103–6; New Mexico and, 100, 121–22, 138, 160–61; New Mexico annexation by, 115; New Mexico invaded by, 106–16; New Mexico reactions to initial occupation by, 122–31; political institutions of, 164–65, 166–67; Spain and colonies of, 8–12; Texas annexed by, 92; trade with, 160–61; Vigil, Donaciano, on invasion by, 109–10; Vigil, Donaciano, on political system of, 164–65; Vigil, Donaciano, swearing loyalty to, 122
Utah, 159
Utes, 43, 56

Valencia, Clemente, 239
Valencia, Juan, 243–44
Valencia, Tomás, 60
Valle, Alejandro, 191
Valley Ranch, 241
Van Ness, George, 71
vaquero, 11, 204

Varas, 185, 187, 192–93, 197, 200–201, 243–44
Varela, José, 241
Varela, Manuel, 179, 192, 239
Vargas, Diego de, 213
Vargas Zapata y Luján Ponce de León y Contreras, Diego de, 25–27
vecinos, 19, 53, 61, 85, 99, 206, 216
Velasco, Cristóbal de, 25
Vera Cruz, 16
La Verdad, 89–94
Vigil, Amador, 248
Vigil, Ana María, 37, 51, 199
Vigil, Antonia Andrea Martínez, 37, 38, 199, 249; death of, 51
Vigil, Antonio Basilio, 53, 58, 137, 194, 202, 238; land purchases of, 244; on Vigil Index, 215
Vigil, Bartolomé, 17–18
Vigil, Bill, 251
Vigil, Carlos, 20–21, 255n41
Vigil, Cornelio, 125
Vigil, Desiderio, 245, 246, 248
Vigil, Domingo Montes, 27 32–33
Vigil, Donaciano, 203. *See also specific topics*
Vigil, Elena Montes, 30, 256n29
Vigil, Epifanio, 245, 248, 249, 250
Vigil, Epitacio, 202, 245, 248
Vigil, Ermenegildo aka Ermenejildo, 245, 248
Vigil, Francisco de, 15, 18
Vigil, Francisco Montes, xv, 20–23, 24, 26, 255n41; in Santa Fe, 27–31
Vigil, Genovebo, 243
Vigil, Gertrudes Montes, 30, 34
Vigil, Gregorio, 73, 74, 200
Vigil, Isabel de, 15
Vigil, José Amador, 248
Vigil, José Asisclo, 242–43, 246
Vigil, José Mateo, 248
Vigil, Juan, 15
Vigil, Juana María, 37, 51, 199

Vigil, Juan Carlos Montes, 23, 27, 32
Vigil, Juan Cristóbal Montes, II, 36–38, 45, 52, 54, 76, 199, 249, 256n36; death of, 51
Vigil, Juan Cristóval Montes, I, 34–36
Vigil, Juan Domingo, 187
Vigil, Juan Luis, 256n28
Vigil, Juan Montes, xv, 254n23
Vigil, Juan Montes, II, xv, 7, 13, 15–19, 29, 46, 254n23, 254n28
Vigil, Juan Montes, III, 19–21, 46
Vigil, Julian Josue, 32
Vigil, Lucas Montes de, 15
Vigil, Manuel Montes, 30, 33, 256n28
Vigil, María de la Concepción Montes, 23, 27, 30, 31
Vigil, María de la Luz Rolenes aka Rowland, 58, 194, 199, 238, 259n47
Vigil, María de la Nieves Montes, 23, 27, 31
Vigil, María del Refugio Sánchez, 47, 199, 238, 249
Vigil, María Guadalupe, 248
Vigil, María Ygnes, 37, 51, 199
Vigil, Maurilio E., xiii, 248, 251
Vigil, Melecio, 279n7, 279n9
Vigil, Paula, 37, 51, 199
Vigil, Philip, 36
Vigil, Ray, 251
Vigil, Rodrigo de, 14–15
Vigil, Salbador, 32, 34
Vigil, Salomé, 248
Vigil, Tomás, 248
Vigil, Toribio, 246
Vigil, Virgil, 251
Vigil de Quiñones, Sebastian, 13, 15
Vigil de Santillana, Francisco Montes, II, 33
Vigil de Santillana, Pedro Policarpio Montes, 23, 27, 32, 34
Vigil family: cuaderno, 248–49; history of, 7–8, 12–13; in New Mexico, 31–34
Vigil Index, 137, 215–17; Mathews-Lamb on, 216; Tyler on, 235; Vigil, A. B., on, 215
Vigil y Alarid, Juan Bautista, 37, 45, 115, 158, 177, 199, 265n45
Villanueva, 198
Villasur, Pedro de, 30
Virreinato de Nueva España, 7
Viscarra, José Antonio, 47, 55, 57–58, 76
vocales, 4, 82, 87, 89, 92–94, 107–8, 116, 121, 136, 236

Waldo, Henry L., 128, 144
Ward, John, 179
Washington, George, 78
Washington, John M., 5, 147, 157
water use, 225
Watts, John S., 155, 230
Weber, David, 4, 80, 94–95; on land grants, 180–81
Weightman, Richard H., 150, 156, 165
Westphall, Victor, 176–77, 207, 224; on Indigenous people, 232–33; on Pelham, 224–25
Wharton, Clifton, 57
Wheaton, Theodore, 174
Whig Party, 147, 148
White (Lieutenant), 126
Willock, David, 125
Wilmot Proviso, 160
Wilson (Lieutenant), 127
Wilson, Francis C., 179
Wilson, John, 224, 225
Workman, William, 69
Works Progress Administration Writers Project, 241
writing style, of Donaciano Vigil, 95

Zacatecas, 15, 19–20, 22–23, 25, 26, 27, 30, 31, 32, 46, 59, 64, 66
Zuloaga, José Miguel, 58
Zuloaga, Tomás, 66